Taking Our Place

Aboriginal Education
and the Story of the Koori Centre
at the University of Sydney

John Cleverley & Janet Mooney

SYDNEY UNIVERSITY PRESS

Published 2010 by Sydney University Press

SYDNEY UNIVERSITY PRESS
University of Sydney Library
sydney.edu.au/sup

© John Cleverley and Janet Mooney 2010
© Sydney University Press 2010

Reproduction and Communication for other purposes

Except as permitted under the Act, no part of this edition may be reproduced, stored in a retrieval system, or communicated in any form or by any means without prior written permission. All requests for reproduction or communication should be made to Sydney University Press at the address below:

Sydney University Press
Fisher Library F03
University of Sydney NSW 2006 AUSTRALIA
Email: sup.info@sydney.edu.au

Readers are advised that laws can exist in Indigenous Australian communities against speaking names and displaying images of the deceased. Please check with Indigenous elders before using this publication in their local communities.

National Library of Australia Cataloguing-in-Publication entry

Author:	Cleverley, John.
Title:	Taking our place : Aboriginal education and the story of the Koori Centre at the University of Sydney / by John Cleverley and Janet Mooney.
ISBN:	9781920899387 (pbk.)
Notes:	Includes bibliographical references and index.
Subjects:	University of Sydney. Koori Centre.
	Aboriginal Australians--Education (Higher)--New South Wales--Sydney.
	Adult education--New South Wales--Sydney--History.
Other Authors/Contributors:	
	Mooney, Janet.
Dewey Number:	378.1982

Cover image: 'Sea of Hands 2008', photograph by Curtis Flood, the Koori Centre
Cover design by Jorge Vega, the University Publishing Service

Contents

Foreword v
Preface viii
1. Setting the Scene 1
2. Generational Change 27
3. Aboriginal Education and the Department of Adult Education 49
4. ATA Training Underway 67
5. Aboriginal Engagement 91
6. In Partnership with Education 111
7. Management Restructure and Reform 131
8. Creating a Centre 147
9. Aboriginal Education Centre – Early Years 161
10. Independence 183
11. The Koori Centre 197
12. Aboriginal Education into the New Millennium 221
Notes 245
Abbreviations 271
Selected Bibliography 273
Index 277

Foreword

We are all indebted to John Cleverley and Janet Mooney for this first history of the interaction between the Aboriginal community and the University of Sydney. Indeed, this fascinating account appears to be the first scholarly record of the many and varied relationships between an Indigenous learning community and a tertiary education institution.

That is a formidable task because there are so many themes which can be pursued. For example, a university is necessarily a part of its society and should contribute actively to that society. That includes critical analysis of existing mores and advocacy of change. How closely have this University's interactions with Indigenous peoples mirrored evolving attitudes over the years and to what extent has the University anticipated and helped foster beneficial change?

Wisely, the authors have tackled such issues by giving a factual account and allowing the reader to make the value judgements. I am sure that everyone will find examples (different from individual to individual) where some action may seem too brave or idealistic, inhibiting cooperative support from external agencies and other cases where timidity or slowness seems to have condoned practice which should have been challenged.

For me this is an account of painfully slow incremental progress, but of real progress in an atmosphere of consistent and increasing respect.

The authors also needed to prioritise and focus. They have done this by describing the development, consolidation and success of the Aboriginal Teachers Aides Training Program and then the creation and development of the Koori Centre. This latter is distinguished by its autonomy and Aboriginal direction, by its own research and teaching capability as well as its support role for students more generally. It is crucial to increasing the numbers of Indigenous students undertaking mainstream degrees throughout the University. The increase in these numbers has been encouraging – but encouraging also of much greater effort to boost them further.

The focus to which I have just referred inevitably brings some drawbacks and another encouraging phenomenon has been given less emphasis. In the last few years, I have been heartened by individual scholarship support and research program support coming from friends and alumni of the University. Moreover, the residential colleges have been highly supportive of facilitating Indigenous access.

Let me return to the main theme by posing some further issues. To what extent are the social obligations of a public university determined by the funding it receives? How does a university best assist an economically and socially disadvantaged group where the problems ideally need to be tackled in early schooling? What, if any, should be the role of a research intensive university in providing sub-degree programs?

A recommendation pertinent to the last question came from the Martin Report in 1964 when it proposed that Adult Education should not be a university discipline but that the CAE and TAFE sectors should discharge the responsibility at lower cost. There are two interesting aspects of this timing. The first is that in 1963 the first identified Aboriginal students entered Sydney University, Charles Perkins and Peter Williams, both in mainstream BA programs. While Perkins completed successfully within the minimum time and Williams did not complete but put his studies to good use in later life, both had to work exceptionally hard to overcome earlier educational gaps. (Although there may have been earlier students of Aboriginal descent, undeclared as such, it took more than a century of the University's existence for a recognised Indigenous matriculant to arrive.) The other timing issue is that, 11 years after the Martin Report, the discipline of Adult Education at the University of Sydney was the chosen location for the training program for Aboriginal Teachers Aides.

That program and its successors took some 690 Indigenous people on a significant educational journey and they, in turn, contributed importantly to their schools and regions. The last graduation ceremony was in 1998 when the program had been absorbed in TAFE. Improbably, therefore, we see that the University began a doomed sub-degree program in a doomed discipline (it was closed in 1984 and the program transferred to Education) and it was a success. This is a great tribute to those who worked within it and for it. The detailed story set out by Cleverley and Mooney is enthralling and, of course, these developments were seminal for the Koori Centre about which we shall soon speak. Meanwhile, let me quote Linda Burney, the first Aboriginal to be elected to the NSW Parliament, speaking of the Aboriginal Teachers Aides (ATA) Program:

> The important point about the Koori Centre's genesis was that it was the first Aboriginal Program to be run at an Australian university. The AEAs [Aboriginal Education Assistants] came to the university setting to gain formal training, the fact that the qualifications didn't mean much in the wider world was not important. To many Aboriginal people who didn't have any formal education, the fact that the course had the University of Sydney blessing meant the world to them. It was a groundbreaking program, and it opened up universities for Aboriginal people.[1]

At least by the mid-1980s, the University understood that it needed a focal Aboriginal centre but there was insufficient will for self-help to make this a reality. Paradoxically, the Dawkins amalgamations provided the mechanism and the opportunity. The strength of our ATA history had its potential negatives (with an evolution through Adult Education and Education) for a freestanding centre with university-wide responsibility and further evolution is still under way.

My last general question is, "Should the academic and research activities of a Koori Centre be distributed to disciplines, with the centre providing a general student support role?" My answer is a firm "No!" – but the trouble with a history is that analysis of the present is never objective. Let me simply congratulate the authors on their book and their work over the years for Aboriginal Education.

Emeritus Professor Gavin Brown, AO FAA Corr FRSE
Inaugural Director of the Royal Institution of Australia

Preface

The story of the Koori Centre celebrates the achievements of Indigenous people in the creation of an enlightened learning community at the University of Sydney. Australians are more likely to hold higher educational qualifications today than previously and Indigenous people have matched this trend with an increase in post-school awards. That able Indigenous students perform at the highest levels is evident in the excellent results gained by Indigenous students across university courses. The outstanding results of these men and women testify to their preparation, study and research skills, and their full involvement in University activities.

Western education, as distinct from Indigenous learning in Australia, is a product of European settlement, persuasion and coercion. The University's Camperdown, Darlington and Mallet Street campuses are built on the territory of the Cadigal people of the Eora nation whose ancestral land included the University of Sydney's site and beyond. Its boundaries extend to the Parramatta River, across to the Balmain Peninsula, up to Sydney Cove and out to Botany Bay. When the site for the University of Sydney was alienated, the government recognised no prior Aboriginal occupancy. No written records addressed the rights of the Indigenous people of the time, although some things are remembered.

In the 19th century, the University largely ignored the existence of Indigenous communities except insofar as they were specimens of curiosity driven study or charitable good works. The relationship between University and people was exemplified by white staff and seniors who researched "archaic man" and collected artefacts and remains. Professorial perceptions of Indigenous people were of a race frozen in time and rapidly diminishing in number: any possibility that an Indigenous person would enrol at their own teaching institution appeared a fancy.

The arduous journey of Aboriginal children through the white school system was frequently at odds with their culture and needs. However, as specific grants targeted school attendance and secondary school opportunities increased, educational talent was identified and an occasional individual reached the upper grades. The passing of the Great Depression, and enthusiasm for postwar reconstruction, brought more positive attitudes; furthermore, the overwhelming result of the National Referendum of 1967, which enabled the counting of Aboriginal people in the Census, encouraged the inclusion of Aboriginal students in tertiary education.

The day dawned in 1963 when two young men, Charles Nelson Perkins and Peter Gary Williams, the first students to identify themselves as Aborigines, walked through the

University gates. It is possible, indeed likely, that Aboriginal people had attended earlier but they did not identify for reasons not known. The first group of Aboriginal people arrived on campus in 1975, during the Vice-Chancellorship of Sir Bruce Rodda Williams, when 25 men and women enrolled as non-degree students in the Department of Adult Education in a training course for Aboriginal Teachers Aides. In 1980–81, two Aboriginal staff members were appointed to this program, the first a secretary, the other a lecturer. Despite this achievement, progress was painfully slow: by 1988, the University had six Indigenous students enrolled for a degree qualification and about the same number employed as general staff. The founding of the Aboriginal Education Centre (AEC) in 1989–90 was an important step forward. It coincided with the University's amalgamation with several Colleges of Advanced Education, some of which had their own Aboriginal education units. With the arrival of substantial Commonwealth funding and, following the appointment of an Aboriginal acting director, Veronica Arbon, in 1992, the AEC was renamed the Koori Centre. Two years later, the Koori Centre became an autonomous grouping in the University in association with the Aboriginal Education Unit in the Faculty of Health Sciences on the Cumberland Campus known as Yooroang Garang.

Although the focus of this book is on the Koori Centre and its antecedents, other landmarks in Aboriginal education in New South Wales are recorded where they are precursors for university enrolment. Chapters 1 and 2 offer a snapshot of Aboriginal contacts over an extended time frame pointing to people, events and issues: it should be noted though that these recognitions are not a substitute for a full history of Indigenous education at the University of Sydney. Chapters 3 to 5 locate Aboriginal education in the Department of Adult Education with its leadership courses, cultural programs, and vocational skills training including counselling. In particular, it traces the Aboriginal Teachers Aides Training Program, the longest running single program mounted by the University, the appointment of the first Aboriginal member of staff, and the establishment of an Advisory Committee with Aboriginal membership. Chapters 6 to 10 trace major changes under the Faculty of Education through to the establishment of the Koori Centre, the arrival of substantial Commonwealth funding, and the appointment of an Aboriginal director. The last two chapters, 11 and 12, provide a narration for the new millennium.

So far as the authors are aware, this is the first account of the diverse interactions between an Indigenous learning community and a tertiary education institution. Given that the University shares in the strengths and vices of the nation at large, more of the former than the latter hopefully, it does not surprise that contention between black and white occurred along the way. The objectives of the University of Sydney were satisfied initially by teaching about Indigenous people and researching their cultures, especially traditional mores, although many individual academics and students did engage with Indigenous people directly. With the establishment of the Koori Centre things changed: now learning and research and support in Indigenous education are led by Indigenous people in partnership.

Sources for this book are diverse and include oral, written and photographic materials from the University and outside, including documentation held in Koori Centre files.

Background information has been drawn from the University of Sydney history, *Australia's First*, and other published and unpublished sources as listed. We have put to use interviews collected for the Koori Centre by Julie Janson, including her own reminiscences; also others assembled by Jane Kirton and other accounts passed on by Laurie Craddock, Dennis Foley and Ray King. We are grateful for their statements and wish to acknowledge them. Lynette Riley and Noeleen Smith read through a draft making useful suggestions. Sections were also circulated to Koori Centre staff and we thank Diana Day, Curtis Flood, Sharon Galleguillos, John Hobson, Arthur Smith, and Katrina Thorpe, for their input. The authors wish to thank other staff who have contributed including Deborah Kirby-Parsons; staff from Archives, Records Management Services, including Timothy J. Robinson, Manager, and Julia Mant, Reference Archivist; and help from Julia Horne, the University Historian, and Denise Donlon, Curator, at the J.L. Shellshear Museum of Physical Anthropology and Comparative Anatomy. Photographic records have been drawn from various University sources as indicated.

The authors would also like to thank Emeritus Professor Gavin Brown for his generous foreword; the University of Sydney for a Sesquicentary Award; Professor Derrick Armstrong, Deputy Vice-Chancellor (Education) for his encouragement; and John Shipp, the University Librarian, Ross Coleman, Director, Sydney eScholarship, Susan Murray-Smith, Business Manager of Sydney University Press, and Agata Mrva-Montoya, Publications Coordinator, for their hard work on our behalf. Most of all we thank our wonderful Indigenous students.

> John Cleverley
> Janet Mooney
> Koori Centre, University of Sydney

1

Setting the Scene

> To look at the development of the Koori Centre is to look at the reflection of the broader development in Aboriginal education.
>
> Linda Burney, Interview, 2000[1]

The teaching rooms of the Koori Centre surround the "Naked Lady" courtyard with its fine bronze statue, "Spring", in the solid, red-brick Old Teachers College building (OTC). Here, students, staff and visitors can meet and mingle amid palms, running water and jacaranda trees. Before relocating to the OTC in 1994, the centre was housed across Parramatta Road in the wedge-shaped, brick-fronted Mackie Building with its internal fibro partitions, odd triangular-shaped spaces, and linoleum-covered floors. Classes for Aboriginal Teachers Aides (ATAs) operated here for just on 20 years. Linda Burney, of the Wiradjuri Aboriginal Nation, and the first Indigenous person to be elected to the New South Wales Parliament in its 180-year history, taught Aboriginal history in its all-purpose lecture room, bringing her baby Binni to class where he was shared around the Koori mums. As she tells it:

> The atmosphere at the AEA Program was nurturing and full of joy. The AEAs didn't get the recognition they deserved in terms of financial rewards, but their communities valued them highly. The important thing about the AEA Program was how unifying it was: it empowered the Aboriginal community. The AEAs were often in Sydney for the first time, they supported each other and also had a barrel of laughs.

Born black and illegitimate in Whitton in 1957, a small Riverina farming town, Burney was reared by elderly white relatives not knowing her Aboriginal father. When they met after 28 years, his half ashamed words were, "I hope I don't disappoint you."[2] Burney went on to contact her ten brothers and sisters – they had lived separate lives though only 40 minutes journey away. Burney seemed destined to leave school early however personal encouragement from the headmaster and a careers' counsellor telling her she had the ability to be a barrister changed her thinking. "I didn't even know what barrister was but it sounded important, so I stayed at school to become a teacher."[3] She completed Years 11 and 12 at Penrith High before earning her Diploma of Teaching degree from Mitchell College of Advanced Education (now the Bathurst Campus of Charles Sturt University), its

Figure 1. Glen Campbell receiving his certificate from Linda Burney, with Veronica Arbon at the podium. Image courtesy of the Koori Centre.

first Aboriginal graduate. Her initial school appointment was to Lethbridge Park Primary in 1979. Asked how she had made it to Parliament in 2003, she replied, "I was fortunate enough to be literate and that is such a determinant for anyone, no matter what their background."[4]

The ATA training program was important for Aboriginal people in New South Wales as it represented one of few career options in the 1970s and 1980s for men and women who had at least finished primary school. Burney puts it well:

> The important points about the Koori Centre's genesis was that it was the first Aboriginal Program to be run at an Australian University. The AEAs came to the university setting to gain formal training, the fact that the qualifications didn't mean much in the wider world was not important. To many Aboriginal people who didn't have any formal education, the fact that the course had the University of Sydney blessing meant the world to them. It was a groundbreaking program, and it opened up universities for Aboriginal people.[5]

Place and Purpose

Little is known of the early association between Aboriginal people and the University of Sydney. Where the University stands was once the preserve of the Cadigal (Grass Tree) clan of the Eora Nation whose community fished the waters of the harbour and hunted its wooded slopes along the south side of Port Jackson where rock carvings and middens pay tribute to their occupancy. Tragically, these same Cadigal people bore the brunt of the first

European contact. By the end of 1791, most of the community was dead from smallpox, respiratory diseases or scurvy, a toll so high that the remaining Cadigal had no time to complete their burial rituals, their bodies found floating in the harbour or huddled in rock shelters. The handful of survivors would lose access to their land and its resources – clean water, food, medicine and sacred sites,[6] and to the Elders whose duty it was to pass down the clan's learning. Aboriginal people were truly "the dispossessed",[7] declared John Woolley, the University's first Professor of Classics.

The University of Sydney was established on 1 October 1850 operating out of buildings in the city before moving to the Grose Farm site. What remains of times past on this campus at Camperdown has been collected by Dennis Foley, lecturer at the Koori Centre in 2005, as oral history told by his grandmother, Clarice Lougher (nee Morris), her half-sister Eunice Watson, and their cousin Willie De Serve, an initiated man of the Hawkesbury who was over 70 when he disappeared in 1959.[8] Foley records:

> To the east of the great court, down the hill (near the current swimming pool) there was a marsh area where a spring was located, this was an important site for the women folk as two Koori Roads joined just down the hill near where City and Parramatta Roads meet. This was a sit-down spot where the southern clans would come and sit and do business with the Cadigal.
>
> Where the east wing of the great court stands was a paint up spot, perhaps a circle as this adjoined an open forest of mature trees that went to the north, over the Parramatta Road cutting, past Arundel and Ross Streets, along the ridge. This was a sorry site as after cremation, wrapped bones were placed in some of the trees, not all of the trees as this was also a possum area and was important to the Cadigal. It is said the Great Hall and the Macleay Museum stands on what is a part of the Cadigal cemetery, perhaps this is why it is so cold there?
>
> Another fresh water site was located approximately where the tennis courts are off Physics Road which also fed a small marsh. This water was also very important as there were two more sit down sites, one on the western side of St Johns oval, which was where the western clans would trade and meet with the Cadigal. The ridge that Missenden Road follows is roughly the divide between Cadigal and Wongal land and has a story that is based on the spine of a giant monitor who once lay there. The other important site was on the hill top, at the highest point near St Andrews College, this was purportedly a men's sit down site as it was a high point and the hill top was kept cleared as it gave a view of the surrounding country. I do not know if it was an initiation site, highly unlikely in view of the two major sit down sites close by.
>
> There used to be two scar trees on the University. My father's mother, Ruby Foley worked at the Uni for approximately 20 years often spoke of them. I looked for them in the 1970s but they are long gone.

Figure 2. View of the grounds in 1887. Image courtesy of University of Sydney Archives.

Figure 3. University of Sydney Common Seal, c. 1852. Image courtesy of University of Sydney Archives.

Land and Building

The 30 acres of the original site of the University was leased to Major Francis Grose in 1792, under the authority of Governor Arthur Phillip, when clearing and fencing began. By then the alienation of Sydney's Aboriginal clans from their traditional lands had started in earnest despite growing black resistance around Parramatta and the Hawkesbury. When Grose left the colony, his lease was applied for the benefit of the Female Orphan School with the stream running through the site known as Orphan School Creek. By the time the University resumed Grose Farm in 1855, its 126 acres of cattle pasture was the largest parcel close to town.

Construction of the Great Hall and East Wing of the Quadrangle built on a knoll with extensive views of Sydney soon took recognisable shape. Understandably, its architecture and stonework were demonstrably British, although a small number of Australian carvings

Figure 4. Bill Ellwood plants the Aboriginal flag on the front lawn, officially opening the SRC's Aboriginal Week, 1990. Image courtesy of University of Sydney Archives.

were cut over time – a kangaroo, a bush baby, and a boomerang. The original symbol of the early University, the Common Seal of c. 1852, included the Southern Cross and a blackboy plant, "a touch of local colour",[9] however the plant was excluded when the Seal of 1857 was adopted. Beneath the University's coat of arms was the motto, *Sidere Mens Eadem Mutato* – "Though the constellation has changed, the spirit remains the same." More than a hundred years later, during the student radicalism of the 1960s, the motto was described by campus activists as a colonial remnant that denied the validity of Aboriginal knowledge.

Recognition of Aboriginal custodianship of the University site has received occasional attention. In a gesture of ownership during the Student Representative Council's Aboriginal Week in 1990, the Indigenous student in Anthropology and SRC member, Bill Ellwood, planted the Aboriginal flag on the lawn in front of the Quadrangle. It was, he declared, "Aboriginal land".[10] Two years later the University adopted the name Cadigal for its special admissions and support scheme for Indigenous Australians, and the first Aboriginal Director of the Koori Centre, Veronica Arbon, would dedicate her graduation address on 6 April 1993 to the Cadigal people. Seven years on, the Aboriginal Embassy, "in occupation of Victoria Park", part of the University's original grant, asserted Aboriginal sovereignty over the land by ancient right passed down by the creation ancestors.[11] Affirmation of past Aboriginal occupancy is heard today in the "Welcome to Country" address that acknowledges the traditional owners of the University's campuses.

Setting the Scene 5

> The Gadigal peoples of the Eora Nation; Deerubbin peoples; Tharawal peoples; Ngunnawal peoples; Wiradjuri peoples; Gamilaroi peoples; Bundjulung peoples; Wiljali peoples and the Gureng Gureng peoples.

So far as naming buildings or roads goes, the blind alley leading to the underground carpark off Western Avenue is called Cadigal Lane; and when the Sydney University Village was built on the Carillon Avenue site in 2003, one hall of residence took the Aboriginal name, Wanamatta.

Western Education Arrives with the First Fleet

As to education in the new colony, the first schools were for whites. Arthur Phillip, who supported the first classroom in 1789, and other governors who followed him, held the optimistic philosophy that schools would tame "the rising generation"[12] – the children of convicts. Post-elementary classes took learning beyond the elementary level in the 1800s, and small private colleges were offering a foundation for university education by the 1850s. The elite who patronised them were seeking a good education for their sons and grandsons in Sydney town rather than risk dispatching them to the home country, fearing shipwreck en route and delinquency after arrival. Locals also hoped that a university would impress the mother country and hasten the colony's transition to self-government. The University of Sydney's first teaching began with a Faculty of Arts degree, which demanded three years of Greek, Latin, Mathematics and Science.

William Charles Wentworth (1790–1872) is considered a prime founder of the University, and his statue stands in the Great Hall. Son of a surgeon father and convict mother, he was a passionate advocate of the Select Committee of 1849 and influential in the drafting of the University's establishment bill in the Legislative Council, joining the first Senate in 1850. He shared the prejudices of his day: "The aborigines of this country occupy the lowest place in the gradatory scale of the human species."[13] Even 30 years of intercourse with Europeans, as he put it, "has not effected the slightest change in their habits." They were a "confused and barbarous" people with only a rude knowledge of God or place. And Tasmania's Aboriginal people were still more uncivilised, "if possible".[14] He did though concede that the hatred and revenge they displayed towards many colonists was understandable because of the bloodthirsty butchery taken out on them. While his 1850 *Act to Incorporate and Endow the University of Sydney* promised "a regular liberal course of education" for "all classes and denominations of Her Majesty's subjects ... without any distinction whatsoever", it was designed for the white inhabitants, the 'true natives' of Australia, who would build this "new Britannia in another world".[15]

The University's first Vice-Provost (1851–53), Charles Nicholson, had come to Australia, he explained to an English friend, to minister to "the wants of the miners and aborigines." However, at the Inauguration Ceremony in 1852, Nicholson told the gathering, "Australia has no past, but she has a future."[16] Whether he thought the Aboriginal people would be part of it is unknown. The country was, as Robert Dallen told readers of his University history later, "an empty continent".[17]

The Building Blocks for University Education

Any account of Aboriginal people and the University of Sydney cannot be adequately appreciated without prior understanding of the short history of Aboriginal education. Significant questions demand attention. How was such schooling conceived? Who was eligible and over what period? What educational resources, human and material, were provided? What were the outcomes of the educational process? And what impact did these factors have on the entry of Aboriginal students to the University of Sydney?

Prominent colonists in the late 18th century adopted Aboriginal "orphans", attempting to teach them the rudiments of reading, Christian prayers and good manners. The next stage in colonial education was the classroom. Aboriginal students first entered a school door in 1815 when Governor Lachlan Macquarie and Rev. William Shelley inveigled boys and girls inside their Black Native Institute, training males as farmers and females as servants. Those who survived were married out and settled on plots of land nearby with a one-off gift of tools, seed, a barrow and a cow.[18] Macquarie and Shelley's social program was based on the Lockean belief that men, Aboriginal people included, were not doomed sinners but could raise themselves to grace and usefulness through religious knowledge and the three Rs. Their hopefulness cut against the grain of some local luminaries like the Rev. Samuel Marsden who doubted that Indigenous Australians were educable other than through physical labour.

Evidence contrary to the Marsden line surfaced in 1819, when 20 Aboriginal children competed in the Anniversary School Examination at Parramatta against some 100 Europeans. The *Sydney Gazette* of 17 April reported the outcome: "a black girl of 14 years of age, between three and four years in the school, bore away the chief prize." It seems that the young woman was Maria Lock, daughter of the Richmond Elder, Yarramundi, who would be married out of the Native Institution in 1824 to the assigned convict, Robert Lock, a carpenter.[19] When Maria died in 1878, having borne ten children, her family were small landowners in the district. Some 130 years later, a descendant of the same Lock family, Richard Green (Ricky Webb), a Darug Nation man and recognised Yellamundi storyteller, was enrolled for the BEd (Secondary: Aboriginal Studies) at the Koori Centre.

By the mid-19th century, a few classes for Aboriginal children were supported by philanthropic station proprietors and missionaries in the bush though the whole amounted to little. In the 1860s, the lady of the lamp, Florence Nightingale, asked the New South Wales government for details of the sickness and mortality rates of "native children" who had attended school over the last five years. The Board of National Education, which managed public education at the time, replied that there were no Aboriginal students in its classes because the "wild habits of the Native Tribes"[20] made their schooling impracticable.

No Aboriginal children were found in Anglican, Roman Catholic or Wesleyan schools in Sydney either, although the Anglican Bishop of Newcastle did count two or three enrolled over the last 13 years, and the Catholic Vicar-General recalled "a few half-caste children in the distant country".[21]

i) Indigenous Australians Enter Elementary Schools

It is thought that the first Aboriginal people entered public schools in the period of the Council of Education in the early 1870s, with some 200 enrolled in elementary classes by 1880.[22] The passage of the *Public Instruction Act* that year committed the government to the provision of universal primary schooling, and some secondary places, and a number of Aboriginal students were among the beneficiaries attending either an Aboriginal school on a reserve or station, or a regular primary school. When these reserves were first opened by the Aboriginal Protection Board (APB) in 1883, they usually maintained small schools taught by masters approved and supervised by the Department of Public Instruction.[23] The teachers were frequently the wives of the reserve or mission managers, being minimally qualified or unqualified, and many of their Aboriginal children left after a year or two.

Initially, the Board had been happy to see Aboriginal children, especially those "on the white side",[24] attend public schools provided they were "clean, clad and courteous".[25] From 1907, however, they became subject to "expulsion on demand", white parents finding exclusion orders relatively easy to obtain from sympathetic school principals and departmental office staff. With labour short during World War I, some Aboriginal families moved to country towns, however the Great Depression forced many back to the reserves increasing the total number of segregated schools. Reliable figures are hard to come by as the number of Aboriginal children in the state school system was considered a confidential statistic.

After the Conference of Commonwealth and State Aboriginal Authorities in 1937, assimilation was adopted as a general policy. This was applied in education with the reformed Aboriginal Welfare Board (AWB) transferring responsibility for its reserve schools to the New South Wales Department of Education (NSW DoE). About 40 Aboriginal schools were affected in 1940. Most of these places provided a three-year equivalent primary school syllabus emphasising manual training and sewing, later extended to a fourth year. Another step towards assimilation was taken in 1943, when the New South Wales government determined that children of Aboriginal people deemed "non-Aborigines" could attend public schools irrespective of whether an Aboriginal school was available or not; and, immediately after the war, Aboriginal parents could enrol their children in integrated classes provided they supplied a medical certificate of good health.

Aboriginal people attending the integrated public schools of the day had an uncertain reception. Certainly, there were good teachers who taught Aboriginal students with perception and skill opening up employment and other opportunities. Other pupils experienced the opposite. Lester Bostock, who left school at 13, remembered his schooldays in the 1940s: "My experience at school was pretty horrific."[26] Sent out of the classroom by the day, and by the week, "because the teacher would not or did not want to have anything to do with Aboriginal children", Bostock learned little. "By the time I left school," he admitted, "I was just able to write my own name." When Indigenous people did enrol in a white school, said Bostock, "teachers refused to teach them. They were sent into the garden to do the gardening when things such as sums and English were being taught." Such personal memories weighed with the parents of later generations themselves unwilling to enforce compulsory attendance. "Many Aboriginal parents were treated so badly at school that today they shiver when relating their experiences."[27]

Unfortunately, the abilities of Aboriginal children who excelled in school work or in sports, dramatics and music were seldom listed in official reports or were trivialised. When the Chairman of the Joint Committee upon Aboriginal Welfare asked a primary school principal in 1966 about the special abilities of Aboriginal children, swimming, athletics, singing and dramatics were mentioned, but the principal could not stop himself going further: "One of their greatest aptitudes is picking up marbles between their bare toes. They are most adept at that. Drop anything in the playground and if you were not fast it was gone too."[28]

ii) Education and Integration

Backed by the view that Aboriginal and white children ought to have similar educational opportunities, the closure of reserve schools gained momentum. Research showed that children in non-segregated environments in townships performed better in class than those on reserves and it was accepted that integrated schools promoted racial harmony. Still, things moved slowly. In 1955, the English born Governor-General of Australia, Sir William Slim, passed through Gulargambone where he was astounded to see children from the Aboriginal school waving at him from one side of the street and white children from the Central School from the other.[29] A concerned Slim raised the issue of black-white separation and it was taken up by Head Office. The town itself had a history of segregation, a number of Aboriginal children having been excluded from its public school despite the fact that they were "full and properly clothed".[30] This particular issue was resolved to the residents' satisfaction when the department accepted their offer to build a separate Aboriginal school.

In 1966, the NSW DoE admitted to having "soft-pedalled"[31] integration down the years. "We have tried to create the atmosphere which will permit this change to take place with the least possible repercussions in the community." However, some progress towards the closure of Aboriginal schools was evident. In 1956, there were 22 separate Aboriginal schools in New South Wales, ten years later the number was down to 12, with an enrolment of 630 pupils.[32]

Access for Aboriginal children to classes in white schools begged the question of continued Aboriginal support for black schools. From the 1950s, growing cooperation between white and Aboriginal communities was apparent with students from both groups mixing together in sporting activities, scouts and guides, and in religious and community programs. In some places, Aboriginal parents preferred this kind of cooperation above integration, vigorously opposing the shut down of their own schools. For instance, at Mehi Crescent near Moree, parents at the Aboriginal school slated for integration in the early 1970s believed their children would suffer educationally in white dominated classes.

> In our Aboriginal schools our children were the leaders and were trained to be leaders by their teachers. It made us very proud to see and hear our children who were the school captains, give their speech on special occasions – to visit their school and see their beautiful handicraft work as well as drawings and their school work.[33]

Their opposition went unheeded and the school at Mehi Crescent was closed.

iii) Change over Time

While the integration movement was unstoppable, the NSW DoE did recognise Aboriginal opposition to an extent, agreeing that segregated schools not be closed without consultation. Additionally, compromises were arrived at sometimes allowing a preschool or infants division to remain open for a period. In 1961, Doug Swan, later Director-General of Education, became Principal of the newly integrated Gulargambone Central School, whose practices had so disturbed Slim. A firm friend of Aboriginal people, Swan's successful management of the situation, one of the first of the major integrations, brought him to the attention of his superiors, a stepping stone in his eventual appointment as departmental head. Swan is on record for stating that he would have welcomed an ATA or Aboriginal teacher on staff at the time.[34] A backer of the training of ATAs at Sydney, Swan provided constructive advice and moral and financial support from Head Office. This account relates to one of the ATA graduations he attended:

> Seated among the students was Mrs Milgate, the mother of children I had taught in 1959–1961 at Gulargambone. I knew her living conditions and realised the immense sacrifice she and her family had made for her to do the ATA Course. The fact that I recognised her and her children seemed to overcome her but teachers do not forget their pupils. The dignity, poise and bearing of Mrs Milgate on that occasion reinforces my view that programs such as this one would do much to bring about reconciliation.

By the 1960s, more positive experiences of schooling were recorded, an outcome of improved teaching and social attitudes. The ATA, Auntie Emily Walker, who studied and taught the Gumbaynggirr language for Nambucca communities, recalls her own schooling.

> When I started school, this was a frightening time for me, a different community all white faces (the teacher had to teach from first class to sixth class in one room). My older sister (who Granny was rearing), was sitting up the back of the room with me, when the teacher wanted all the new kids down the front. I was petrified. The teacher said if you don't move he'd get two sixth class boys to carry me out, which they did. The acceptance of us in this school community, being the only Aboriginal family, didn't make us feel any different from them. I went

to this school until I was 11. I can't finish this section of my life without saying what a wonderful teacher I had in Mr Billy O'Neil. I ended up going to Nambucca Primary and then to Macksville Primary, and one year at Macksville High – the first year it opened. During these school years I never had anyone call me black or harassment. Once a girlfriend was called "a black gin" by a boy, so I slapped his face. His friend stuck up for him, and we had a fist fight – after we shook hands and walked home friends.[35]

In August 1972, the NSW DoE dropped the stipulation from the *Teachers' Handbook* that an Aboriginal child could be removed from school given health reasons and substantial objection.

iv) Removing Children from their Families

Through the *Aborigines Protection Act of 1909* and its amendments, the Board had gained the right to assume full custody and control over any Aboriginal child if it determined the action in the interest of the child, the onus being on the parents to demonstrate that the child was not at risk. Some officials pursued their mission with zeal: for instance, the one-time politician, Robert Donaldson, who advocated that children "with white blood"[36] be removed from Aboriginal camping sites, was known as the "kids' collector". Other politicians though stood against Donaldson's dogma, arguing that Aboriginal children educated in their own communities were "a valuable resource in the country".

The APB indentured many of these separated children, the majority of them female, having "some Aboriginal blood".[37] Sent to welfare homes, Bombaderry for infants, Kinchela for boys, Cootamundra for girls, they were listed as "neglected", "delinquent", "uncontrollable" or "committed at parents' request".[38] Many died after entering care.[39] Others sent to foster homes had some schooling, which would have been little consolation for removal under duress. The report, *Bringing Them Home*, estimates the number of children taken as between one in three and one in ten of the child population in the period 1910–70,[40] the uncertain figures telling their own story. In 1969, a new *Aboriginal Act (NSW)* replaced the legislation of 1909, the Minister for Child Welfare and Social Welfare now taking responsibility.

The first case of court-awarded compensation to one of the Stolen Generation, $775,000 in damages and interest, was awarded to Bruce Trevorrow in South Australia in 2007–08. After complaining of stomach ache, the 13-month-old boy was taken to hospital on Christmas Day 1957. He never returned home and was given to a white family by the Aboriginal Protection Board. The Trevorrow family was lied to about his whereabouts: Bruce Trevorrow never saw his father again and it was a decade before he met other family members. Growing up in his white family would prove a disorienting experience. "I kept asking my parents why I was different to the other kids. They said I had dark relatives."[41] School life was miserable. "Being the only black person, I was bullied at school. That was very traumatic. I got called names like nigger and black." The Supreme Court ruled that his illegal separation from his family was a material cause of his chronic depression. In making Trevorrow's case, his solicitor revealed that his three siblings who had stayed with their parents were all high achievers. The SA government declared its intention to appeal Trevorrow's award but the man died prematurely in 2008.

v) Post-primary Schooling

It seems the first Aboriginal student enrolled in a post-secondary school in New South Wales was John Bungaree, son of Chief Bungaree. Adopted by a white farmer on his father's death in 1830, John was boarded at the Normal Institution, a college founded to train the colony's teachers, where the 12-year-old excelled in arithmetic and drawing maps from memory and won prizes in writing and geography.[42] Alas, he found himself caught between two worlds on graduation, and not fully accepted in either. He eventually moved to Queensland where he took work on the McIntyre River as a Sergeant in the Native Police.

Of course, the University itself had a direct interest in the quality and growth of secondary education. Enrolment at the University of Sydney was through the institution's own matriculation examination in classics and mathematics, the preparatory subjects taught in a post-secondary college or by a tutor. In 1867, Junior and Senior Examinations were organised, the latter for University entrance, however the small number of the schools and colleges in town, and their high fees, remained a serious impediment to any numerical expansion. In 1881, 51 matriculants (males) presented themselves. After several state high schools were founded under the *Public Instruction Act,* and "superior public schools" began to offer secondary classes, a healthy 171 matriculants presented a decade later. Among this number were women who had been admitted to University privileges by Senate in 1881. The growth in enrolments also benefited from the establishment of evening lectures, additional state funding and bequests, and from the growing attractiveness of university education itself, especially after a shift from a classical to a modern curriculum in Arts. Furthermore, the state's growing demand for professionals, especially in medicine, engineering, mining and teaching, boosted numbers. Between 1880 and 1890, total enrolments increased from 76 students to 409 and, by 1940, to 4078, one quarter female.

In the post-World War II years, individual Aboriginal children began transferring from primary classes into the lower secondary classes including junior or domestic high schools. By 1951, 30 Aboriginal students were counted in government secondary classes.[43] The same year, Victor Chapman, a state bursar, became the first Aboriginal graduate from a New South Wales Teachers College. The one time "dusky captain"[44] of Dubbo High School, as he put it, eventually rose to principal of a state primary school. As yet, the University had no identified Indigenous Australians in its student body.

Influences from Mental Testing

Given prevailing mindsets, little attention was paid to the quality of Aboriginal education. In evidence given before the Legislative Council and Legislative Assembly in 1966, Sydney's Professor of Anthropology, William Robert Geddes, blamed the psychologist, Professor Stanley D. Porteus, a graduate of Melbourne University, for perpetuating the fallacy that

Aboriginal intelligence was below average[45] and that Indigenous Australians were "extremely primitive people".[46] Perhaps their offspring could hold their own with whites up to nine or ten years of age, Porteus surmised, but beyond that their intellectual development slowed, most likely ceasing by pubescence, a fact he attributed to a smaller cranium size.[47] Geddes dismissed such suppositions out of hand: "there is no innate difference between racial groups."[48] Still, the concept of Aboriginal intellectual inferiority was slow to disappear as was evident in this quote from the AWB Report for 1961: "Aboriginal children, as a whole, do not possess an intelligent quotient comparable to that of their white counterparts."[49]

By the mid-1960s, social theories were changing and it was widely accepted that major barriers to achievement for Aboriginal children were absenteeism, poor health, malnutrition, uninterested parents, and an inadequate grounding in the basics. Research in public schools in 1964 revealed that Aboriginal children were approximately a year older than white children by Grade 4 and the longer they remained at school the greater this retardation.[50] Given that the cause was nurture not nature, educators began to consider whether unsuitable teaching methods and inappropriate curricula were to blame. The NSW DoE had previously held the position that its common curriculum was suitable for all children in the state except for those who were physically afflicted and, if Aboriginal children failed, the fault lay with them not the department. It was an educational strength, the department insisted, that "we have never regarded them [Aboriginal people] as a special group."[51] It is not surprising then that the overwhelming number of ATAs who trained at Sydney in the late 1970s and 1980s possessed an incomplete secondary education with one or two years of high school an achievement.

Virtually no Aboriginal adults worked in schools as role models for young people. Appearing before the Joint Committee on Aboriginal Welfare on 6 April 1966, Vernon Truskett, Assistant Director-General of Education, said he knew of only one Aboriginal teacher, a woman at La Perouse, and none in training. The department's record was described by the Chairman of the Select Committee on Aboriginal Welfare, Maurice Keane, as "a sorry one", the attack bringing a defensive retort that the department ought not to be singled out as the government as a whole determined the state's social priorities.[52] By the late 1970s, departmental attitudes had changed dramatically with the need for special educational services now readily accepted. There were, however, few research studies in Aboriginal pedagogy beyond general comments that Aboriginal children frequently rejected peer competition, and put mutual support and cooperation above personal achievement.

Contact with the University Community

i) The Collectors

The ethnographical collections of the Scottish immigrant and member of Senate, William John Macleay, and his relatives, brought together in the name of 19th-century scientific curiosity,[53] exemplified one kind of relationship between University and Aboriginal community during the late 19th century. Macleay had succeeded in obtaining government funds to build a fine museum on campus, (its display area now reduced largely to a loft), and he and staff assiduously collected Aboriginal paintings, cultural items and human remains, purchased or gifted. The University also acquired Aboriginal art and artefacts for its own art collection and for the Power Gallery and sponsored exhibitions at the Tin Sheds Gallery and the War Memorial Gallery. In one particular initiative in 1990, two administrative staff and one postgraduate student, Juanita Gabriel, Jennifer Harrison, and Patricia Rovik, dismayed at what they considered an absence of Aboriginal art on campus, launched a Koori Art on Campus Fund promising to have their acquisitions prominently displayed. The Koori Centre itself holds a small collection of art and artefacts passed down from Sydney Teachers College, and there are also human remains in the J.L. Shellshear Museum of Physical Anthropology and Comparative Anatomy.

In 1994, the University adopted a policy in regard to Aboriginal and Torres Strait Islander ancestral remains and culturally significant objects to operate through the Macleay Museum. Its aims were:

- to consult with Aboriginal and Torres Strait Islander communities or nominated organisations regarding the future management of human skeletal remains and secret and sacred objects held by the University,
- to ensure that the human skeletal remains and secret and sacred objects held by the University are stored in a sensitive manner, and will not be displayed to the public except with the specific permission of the relevant Aboriginal and Torres Strait Islander communities or organisations,
- to determine, as far as possible, the community origins of all items held within these specific collections, and report to the relevant parties on the cultural and scientific significance of items,
- to work closely with identified Aboriginal and Torres Strait Islander communities or organisations to facilitate the return of such items in a proper and dignified manner.[54]

A University Advisory Committee was established to execute the policy which included University personnel and external Aboriginal membership from the NSW Aboriginal Land Council and Aboriginal staff of the Australian Museum. Its advisory work is assisted by Rosemary Stack, one-time Acting Director of the Koori Centre, who became the University's first Indigenous Heritage Officer in 1996 based at the Macleay, and Denise Donlon, Curator of the Shellshear Museum in the Anderson Stuart Building.

ii) The Settlement

Most likely the main contact between University men and women and Aboriginal people in the second half of the 19th century was through social welfare clubs and societies. Both men's and women's projects were inspired by Oxford University's Toynbee Hall experiment which saw a community to promote popular education and civic leadership set up in

Whitechapel's socially devastated Jack-the-Ripper territory. Sydney projects included the University Boys' Club in Darlington, the Toynbee Guild for University Men of 1886, and The University of Sydney Settlement from 1891, when the SU Women's Society began its charitable activities in the inner city.[55] Though the University of Sydney and the Settlement were united by name, the institution was never officially part of the University, being reliant on public and government donations and volunteer labour like Jim Young's contribution from University Accounts. Numbers 17 and 19 Edward Street, Chippendale, were purchased in 1925 as a base for its youth projects, scouts and guides, and hobby groups. It was also home to a well-organised Mothers' Club whose duties included the distribution of woollen comforts and small packages of food at the Newington State Hospital and Asylum.

As Aboriginal families moved into Redfern and Darlington in significant numbers, with an estimated 3000–3500 people living in the Redfern and Newtown area by the 1960s,[56] the Settlement directed its activities towards their needs linking up with organisations like the Foundation for Aboriginal Affairs. The Edward Street organisation was reconstituted as The Settlement Neighbourhood Centre in 1973, with significant Aboriginal membership, and a representative from the University joined the Board to assist with the placement of Social Work students. Additional funding in the 1980s from the New South Wales Family and Community Services Department and the City of Sydney and other agencies extended the range of Settlement services, which included drug and alcohol workshops, tenancy issues and assistance for children in court. Recent progress has not been without controversy

Figure 5. Two girls in the Settlement craft room. Image courtesy of University of Sydney Archives.

Figure 6. Kitchen in the Settlement c. 1978: Volunteers with children. Image courtesy of University of Sydney Archives.

as local whites have differed over the Aboriginal presence, with the possible sale of the property and its relocation mooted.

iii) Evolution, Race and Beyond

The Darwinian theory of evolution had encouraged studies of the physical characteristics of "the Aboriginal race", viewing Indigenous people as representing an early stage of humankind. Professor T.W. Edgeworth David, Sydney's renowned geologist, Antarctic explorer, soldier, and teacher, had a strong scientific interest in so-called archaic man, spurred by the fear that they faced extinction inside one generation. At the Jubilee Celebration of the University in 1902, he declared "the ethnological study of our Aborigines a matter of great urgency".[57] Here Edgeworth David was influenced by Walter Baldwin Spencer, the Melbourne Professor of Biology and the Chief Protector of Aborigines for the Commonwealth, who accepted that the Aboriginal race presented a unique cameo of the life of man before the dawn of history.[58] While valuable collections of artefacts and photographic recordings were made by these early observers, they measured the worth of Aboriginal people against Western civilisation and found them wanting. In 1970, Reubin Kelley described such theorising from his people's perspective – Aboriginal men and women were portrayed as human antiques.[59]

Figure 7. Professor T.W. Edgeworth David, 1924. Image courtesy of University of Sydney Archives.

By the end of the 19th century, Edgeworth David's notebooks were filled with references to Indigenous Australians to which he referred in geology lectures. However, it was the Talgai Skull debate which brought his research to public attention.[60] Discovered in 1886 on the Darling Downs, "Australia's first fossil human skull"[61] was identified in 1914 by Edgeworth David and Sydney's Professor of Anatomy, J. (Jummy) T. Wilson, as belonging to the Pleistocene period of the Great Ice Age. Nonetheless its dating remained the subject of acrimonious disagreement, some claiming it was the skull of an Aboriginal man murdered in the mid-1880s. Furthermore, another researcher, who testified to its antiquity, discerned "the traces of the common ancestral or ape-like character".[62]

The dating issue was finally put to rest by the Challis Professor of Anatomy, N.W.G. (Mac) Mackintosh, Head of the Department of Anatomy, a noted physical anthropologist and expert on "early Aboriginal man".[63] After meticulous research and a re-examination of the skull in the 1960s, the professor placed it in the period 9000–10,000 BP (before

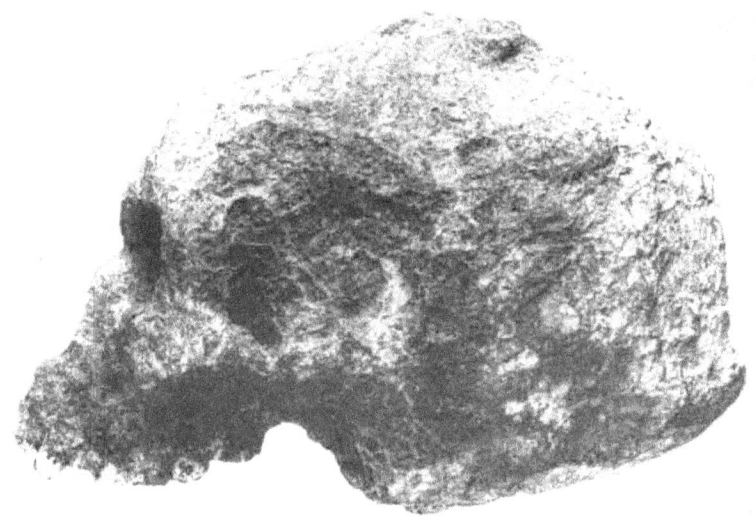

Figure 8. Talgai skull. Courtesy of Shellshear Museum of Physical Anthropology and Comparative Anatomy.

present), and he declared Edgeworth David's earlier efforts surprisingly accurate given his limited access to technology. This dating of the remains of a youth who lived in the Warwick district, apparently killed by a blow to the head, provided the earliest substantial evidence of the existence of Aboriginal people on the Australian continent millennia back. Mackintosh's own scientific interest covered Aboriginal art and artefacts and extended to a genetic breeding program for dingos on campus, caging some animals in the Old Medical School. Mac and his wife, Ann, could occasionally be spotted exercising them on leashes in the University grounds.

The human cranium was originally sent to Edgeworth David for valuation, the finder being aware of its pecuniary value. Given that Aboriginal people were expected to become extinct, there was a brisk trade in bones at the time. As one observer of the practice wrote: "A 'racially pure' Aboriginal skull complete with jaw was worth seven shillings and sixpence."[64] After Edgeworth's and Wilson's 1914 assessment, the cranium was purchased for the University by Joynton Smith, then Sydney's Lord Mayor, reputedly for £150. Today, both the "Talgai skull", along with the substantial Mackintosh papers, which include his studies on fossil skulls, and Aboriginal art and stone implements, are held in the University's Shellshear Museum of Physical Anthropology and Comparative Anatomy. The museum also cares for the remains originally found on the East Talgai station with the agreement of the traditional custodians.

Edgeworth David's willingness to engage in controversy may well have influenced the style of his brilliant student and demonstrator, Thomas Griffith (Griff) Taylor, a graduate in science and engineering, whom the Professor backed as Head of the Department of

Figure 9. Exercising dingoes. Courtesy of Ann MacIntosh.

Geography in 1920. Taylor, who had initially studied geology, extended his career to include meteorology, palaeontology, ethnography and geography, would join Captain Robert Scott's ill-fated expedition to Antarctica in 1910. Like his mentor, Edgeworth David, and good friend, Baldwin Spencer, he was an early researcher in the field of archaic man and a convert to Spencer's philosophy that Indigenous Australians represented primitive man preserved in time. Their view fitted Taylor's theory that human evolution related principally to geographical conditions and represented migration from central Asia over thousands of years.

Armed with cephalic callipers, camera and hair clippers,[65] Taylor undertook fieldwork among Aboriginal people in inland New South Wales and Queensland in the 1920s, collecting data on local languages, customs and artefacts. Bashford and Strange have said of him:

> He claimed, rightly, that he was the first professor at the University of Sydney to offer anthropology, since he taught anthropometric and ethnographic theory to his geography students five years before Radcliffe Brown founded the anthropology department, Australia's first.

Taylor was also a fearless and imaginative writer on "the colour question", prophesying that the marriage of Europeans, Sino-Japanese, and Aboriginal people (largely bred out) would create a dominant race in Australasia. His "mixing of good *stocks* – till the world's one nation"[66] clearly undermined the national government's White Australia policy. Another of his controversial stands was his conservationist viewpoint that the nation was not "Australia Unlimited".[67] Australia's maximum population, he said, was 20 million and its state governments deserved criticism for misrepresenting desert land as arable. Although Edgeworth David spoke of Taylor's determination to bring "light to dark places",[68] Dr Dismal's (Taylor) unconventional theorising was declared unpatriotic. Such public controversies set back his prospects for a full Chair at Sydney and "sighs of relief"[69] were

Setting the Scene 19

heard from academics, politicians and business boosters when Taylor left the University in 1928 for a more appreciative Chicago, his students left to lament the loss of their thought provoking, multi-talented teacher. Down the track, the Geography Department Building was re-named the Griffith Taylor Building, its unappealing architectural style fittingly described as "Postwar International".

Commonwealth Government Involvement

Participants in the Pan-Pacific Science Congress of 1923, including Baldwin Spencer up from Melbourne, Edgeworth David, then Chair of the Professorial Board at Sydney, and the influential expatriate, Grafton Elliot Smith, one-time Demonstrator in Medicine at Sydney and Professor of Anatomy at London's University College, argued strongly in support of a Chair in Anthropology funded by the Commonwealth. Canberra's sudden appreciation of the discipline sprang not so much from any concern for Indigenous Australians but rather from the need to train patrol officers and officials following the capture of German New Guinea.[70] During World War I, the northern part of this island had become an Australian Mandated Territory under the League of Nations and the new Australian administration had to report annually on the progress of its "sacred trust".[71] Similarly, the Papuan administration in the south wanted the Commonwealth to establish anthropological training for its officers. In 1924–25, Commonwealth and state government funds, and Rockefeller Foundation money were put together to establish a chair and academic discipline at Sydney.

The Department of Anthropology under its first professor, the British theorist, Alfred R. Radcliffe-Brown (1926–31), offered a Diploma in Anthropology and, over time, introduced individual subjects in the discipline in Arts and short courses in "practical Anthropology"[72] for government officials, AWB welfare officers and missionaries.

The urbane Radcliffe-Brown thought the study of Aboriginal people a research priority though not one having practical utility. "If not doomed to extinction as a race," Radcliffe-Brown reflected, they were "at any rate doomed to have their cultures destroyed."[73] This was the inevitable result of the coming of Europeans and the expropriation of Aboriginal land. Among Radcliffe-Brown's major studies was *The Social Organization of Australian Tribes*, with its emphasis on kinship. He also edited the quarterly journal, *Oceania*, whose focus was "the study of the native peoples of Australia, New Guinea and the Islands of the Pacific." The journal was founded with money from the Australian National Research Council (ANRC), which became the main source of funding for anthropological research before World War II. His successor at Sydney, Raymond W. Firth (1931–32), a New Zealander, was no less alert to the "native question".[74] Firth thought Australia's Aboriginal affairs was characterised by "exploitation, ignorance, apathy, and colour prejudice", and he proposed an educational program for "civilised natives" who would be taught technical and agricultural skills and absorbed into society. However, the professor was not optimistic that his proposal would gain official support and his scepticism was confirmed.

Figure 10. Photograph of A.P. Elkin, c. 1933. Image courtesy of University of Sydney Archives.

In the Depression years, the Commonwealth came to the view that anthropology was not making a practical contribution to "native affairs",[75] hence it no longer warranted a subsidy. This uncertainty over funding contributed to the decision of Sydney's first two professors to return to London though they were not cut off from the Antipodes altogether as local students travelled abroad to earn their PhDs. Fortunately, the University and friends, in particular Elliot Smith, undertook a rescue mission in 1933, and anthropology was sufficiently entrenched to survive a second threat to scuttle it in the 1940s before Canberra accepted a role for the study in postwar reconstruction. In 2008, the Macleay Museum mounted an exhibition, "People, Power and Politics: The First Generation of Anthropologists at the University of Sydney", which looked at the achievements of its early staff and students, including Charles Hart, William Stanner, and A.P. Elkin, supported by Radcliffe-Brown, as well as Marie Reay and Ronald and Catherine Berndt backed by Elkin. The exhibition's opening address was given by Janet Mooney, Director of the Koori Centre.

Sydney's School of Public Health and Tropical Medicine, which had responsibilities for Aboriginal health in Central and Northern Australia, was also reliant on Commonwealth funding. The University had been involved in the north since 1909 through the Institute of Tropical Medicine at Townsville, when public interest was focused on the capacity of whites to adapt to life in the high tropics. As with Anthropology, the School of Public Health had

Figure 11. Arnhem Land Expedition, 1949. From left: A. Capell, F.D. McCarthy, J. Buffem, N.W.G. McIntosh and A.P. Elkin. Image courtesy of University of Sydney Archives.

links with PNG. In 1933, its director, Professor Harvey Sutton, instituted a short course at Sydney for Papuan Medical Assistants, 12 students coming to Sydney. On arrival, they were housed at the Quarantine Station at North Head, a location sufficiently isolated to prevent "frequent and too close contact with the general public".[76] The program was a successful one from Sutton's viewpoint and there was time for a cricket match. However, settler interests in PNG were against sending young New Guineans to study in Australia citing the expense and fearing they would adopt Australian work attitudes.

Elkin's Days

The University's best-known authority on Aboriginal people, who bestrode the pre- and postwar eras, was Adolphus Peter Elkin (1933–56), appointed Professor of Anthropology on 1 January 1934.[77] A one-time bank officer in Quirindi and an ordained Church of England clergyman, Elkin had entered St Paul's College in 1912, taking out a BA (Honours I), and an MA under the renowned Professor Francis Anderson, his thesis topic, "The Religion of the Australian Aborigines". Graduating with a PhD in Anthropology from University College, London, Elkin returned to undertake fieldwork in the Kimberley in 1927. His two books, *The Australian Aborigines: How to Understand Them* (1938), and *Aboriginal Men of High Degree* (1946), mapped the social and cultural structure of Aboriginal communities, and became bestsellers at home and abroad. Elkin would also encourage Phyllis Kaberry to publish her work, *Aboriginal Woman: Sacred and Profane* (1939), which extended knowledge of women's ceremonies in the Kimberley.

Elkin had an excellent self-opinion and great energy, traits which attracted both converts and conflict among colleagues, officialdom and the public at large. His enormous influence in Aboriginal affairs was strengthened by his immense academic authority and an unrivalled network of friends including Edgeworth David, Elliot Smith, and Neil Mackintosh who had studied under Elkin for a Diploma in Anthropology. As to policy, Elkin wanted the Commonwealth government to take full responsibility for Aboriginal affairs; he thought "citizenship" should be based on the social advancement of groups of Aboriginal people; and he regarded "assimilation" as a "practical thing",[78] not requiring the sacrifice of Aboriginal identity or community.

Taking appointments where he thought he could make a difference, the professor served as President of the Association for the Protection of Native Races, President of the SU League of Nations Union on campus, and Vice-Chairman of the Aboriginal Welfare Board, having suggested the name change from the Aboriginal Protection Board. On his advice, the AWB found places on its board for an expert in sociology and/or anthropology, and one in agriculture, a position filled by Professor John McMillan, Sydney's progressive Dean of Agriculture. The task of his new AWB, Elkin declared, was a simple one: "to get rid of itself". His last long-term commitment was as a member of Senate from 1959 until 1969.

Elkin cited educational opportunity as an important way forward for Aboriginal people. He had backed the board's policy of replacing untrained teachers with full-time departmental teachers in the 1940s and condemned the existing cut-back primary school curriculum for Aboriginal students. Elkin thought students should be moved out of the segregated schools on reserves and the places shut down. He also wanted the introduction of more preschools for Aboriginal children, additional Grants-in-Aid paid to parents to keep their children at school, and improved employment opportunities for young Aboriginal people providing incentives for study. It was not easy being a voice for education on the AWB as seen in comments by a board member of 18 years, Michael Sawtell, a grassroots activist. "I have had a lot to do with University people. They are the biggest dunces I know. I worked once for a millionaire who could hardly read or write. Too much is made of so-called education."[79] Progress in Aboriginal education demanded a perspective, Elkin argued, along with workable policies backed by ongoing research and a capacity not to be put off by short-term failure.

From his office in Mackie, "a tiny room on the wrong side of campus",[80] Elkin continued to work for the AWB after retirement in 1956, using his influence to secure a staff tutor position in Aboriginal Adult Education for the Department of Adult Education designed to encourage Aboriginal parents to understand the importance of regular school attendance. Elkin also found time to encourage the participants of the ATA Training Program at Mackie, chatting with them when an opportunity arose. Avis Ivanoff, a graduate from 1975, recalls that Elkin remembered meeting her grandfather.[81] In its Annual Report for 1969, the Department of Adult Education took space to thank the man "so far as the whole of our work with Aborigines is concerned". Elkin was also a friend of the Department of Education and of its forward-looking Professor, Alexander Mackie, commending the latter on his "fine Teachers College",[82] completed in 1924. He also valued John Mackie's philosophy of teaching secondary trainees the latest educational theory not just instructional techniques for the classroom.

Growing Aboriginal activism led to various attacks from black critics who resented Elkin's undue influence and rejected his paternalism. Attacks on white authoritarianism came as Aboriginal people strengthened their public voice. The "Day of Mourning and Protest", held on 26 January 1938, was followed by a national conference which denounced "theft and genocide" and argued for full citizenship rights including "the right to a full education for our children".[83] Perhaps Elkin's most controversial public remarks were in the answer given at the 1966 Joint Committee on Aboriginal Welfare on 20 March 1967. Queried about the state of Aboriginal culture, he replied

> All that has gone in this state today. If they want to know anything about it they come to me. There was some resurgence up on the North Coast in the early 'thirties. It was interesting but it was only a passing phase. Here and there you get a few of these customs but the old grandmothers have gone and so everything is passing.[84]

The Islander leader, Faith Bandler, named Elkin "a very wicked man".[85] He stood accused of revealing secret male ceremonies in his books; of not consulting with Aboriginal people; and of having backed harsh policies in New South Wales and other states, including the forced removal of children.[86] Some non-Aboriginal depicted him as cold and manipulative, a person whose devotees were mainly women because he thought them "easier to dominate".[87] Yet it was admitted that under his headship, Anthropology boasted more distinguished female academics than any other Arts department.

Elkin has frequently been judged from outside his historical period, with little recognition given to his capacity to shift his own position on big issues over time or of his deep respect for Aboriginal people. On learning of the admission of 14 medicine men into the Medical Health Service in the Northern Territory in 1978, he was profoundly moved.

> The world has changed for them, but it seems to be recognised at least in the Central area, that they have a place in it. For I have seen a miracle. Aboriginal culture is not lost, merely changing.[88]

Among the many tributes to Elkin was an obituary written for the Newsletter of the Aboriginal Education Council (NSW) by the secretary-administrator in the ATA Training Program, Deirdre Koller:

> He thought of the Aboriginal culture as having its own dignity at a time when most Europeans denigrated it as worthless. He helped educate a generation of ordinary people in having an understanding of and empathy with the First Australians.[89]

The University would establish the A.P. Elkin Fund for students of Aboriginal descent in tertiary studies with grants of up to $500 awarded on the recommendation of the Head of the Department of Anthropology.

The University Takes a Stand

There is no published record of Aboriginal students enrolling at Sydney before 1963, though it is likely that some students of Aboriginal descent would have joined. What kind of reception would such identification have received in the University community? Perhaps an event in 1941, when the issue of displaced students from the Netherlands East Indies was debated at Senate, can throw light. After considering the United Kingdom High Commissioner's request for possible fee remission and scholarships on behalf of students of European-Dutch origin deprived of university facilities in Holland by the German occupation, Senate was sympathetic.[90] Subject to the Dutch students meeting its matriculation requirements, it saw no problems with fee remission and possibly scholarships though the latter must be referred higher up.

However further communication passed on by the UK High Commission raised a related question – the acceptability of "coloured or partly coloured students" – a prospect not alluded to earlier.[91] Senate was told that the Commissioner had received instructions on the matter from the Dutch government which was concerned about any social consequences.

> The Dutch authorities had expressed the opinion that unless unqualified official and social acceptance could be guaranteed, it would be better not to raise the question of the provision of resources in Australian universities at all.

Obviously the Dutch were concerned over their students being processed under the White Australia immigration policy and of the Australian public's reaction to the entry of non-whites. Senate deliberations led to the minutes' entry of the 5th of May.

> With regard to the coloured or partly coloured students, it was resolved that, provided the question of social acceptance referred to the University only, the High Commissioner be informed that these students will be accepted on the same terms and conditions as the European-Dutch students.

While the University stood on the side of the angels in this matter, it recognised it was in no position to speak for government policy or for Sydneysiders. No students were sent.

After World War II, the University began to accept numbers of non-white students under the Colombo Plan. Otherwise the University let in very few Asians, its policy discouraging rather than seeking foreign enrolments. The perceived generosity by the Commonwealth government towards Asians, Indians and Africans, who received living allowances and free tuition, drew fire from Aboriginal leaders. Noting that there were 5000 Colombo Plan students in Australian universities in 1970, they contrasted the advantaged Asians and Africans with their own situation:

> At home the general welfare, social, medical and educational needs of Aborigines are deliberately neglected. We are getting Australia's dirtiest deal.[92]

2

Generational Change

> I belong to a past epoch … The situation has changed tremendously and the mind of the aborigines – those of 40 and the younger ones – has changed. They are the ones that will count so you want your research going on all the time.
>
> A.P. Elkin, Joint Committee of the Legislative Council and Legislative Assembly upon Aborigines Welfare, 1967[1]

The national referendum of 1967, passed by a majority of ten to one, overturned Section 127 of the Constitution, that "in recognising the numbers of people of the Commonwealth, or of a state or other part of the Commonwealth, Aboriginal natives shall not be counted". It also amended Section 51 enabling the Commonwealth government to pass laws directly benefiting Aboriginal people. Discriminatory definitions of Aboriginal people were removed and they now had less need to hide their Aboriginality. No longer "the statistically invisible",[2] 40,000 Indigenous Australians were counted in NSW, 47 percent of them under 15.[3] Commonwealth funding would increase five times between 1970 and 1975,[4] its expenditure guided by Indigenous-led bodies, as a new sense of purpose gripped the national scene.

Expanding Secondary Enrolments

"Secondary education for all", the postwar educational call, was the key to opening up the tertiary sector for Aboriginal people. Appearing before the Joint Committee on Aboriginal Welfare in 1967, Elkin anticipated that Aboriginal secondary school students would be among the beneficiaries. "We are getting a few now who get through high school. If we can get a few more to the university, somehow the gospel might be spread."[5] The Aboriginal Welfare Board (AWB) increased the number of its secondary bursars in support, 13 of them passing the Leaving Certificate in the period 1946–65. In 1967, the AWB summed up its efforts in tertiary education.

> Two former bursars entered Teachers College and were subsequently appointed to schools. One girl successfully completed a university course in physical

education and proceeded overseas for further study and one boy unsuccessfully attempted an Arts course at Sydney University.

A girl bursar is at present undertaking an Arts course. One of the board's bursars – a blind boy – after matriculation was enrolled at the Institute for the Blind in London to undertake a three-year course in physiotherapy. He is at present in his final year and cost of tuition (£1487) while undergoing training has been met by the board.[6]

The girl who completed the university course was Margaret Williams. She had attended Casino High on an AWB scholarship of £50, including time as a prefect, before completing her Leaving Certificate in 1956. The 17-year-old then moved to Brisbane to rejoin her family, enrolling at the University of Queensland in 1957. After taking up an Abschol award[7] at the University of Melbourne for 1958–59, she graduated with a Diploma in Physical Education. Williams went on to teach at the Presbyterian Ladies College at Ballarat before winning an overseas scholarship in 1961 sponsored by the English Speaking Union. Travelling in Europe, Williams taught American children in Germany before settling for a period in Canada where she became an officer in the Canadian navy. She would eventually return to Australia and complete a PhD at the University of New England.[8]

It was the introduction of the Commonwealth's Aboriginal Secondary Grants Scheme (ABSEG) from 1970 that substantially increased secondary student numbers. Initially for children 15 years or above, it was extended to all Aboriginal secondary school students from 1973, and additional money was released for individual tutorial assistance and homework centres. Progress followed. That same year, 2716 students received ABSEG in New South Wales of whom 43 were in Year 12.[9] However, about half of the Aboriginal students enrolled in secondary classes were categorised as slow learners.[10] By 1979, ABSEG enrolments reached 4972, with 77 in the final year.

There was an increase in other post-secondary opportunities too. In 1967 the Department of Technical Education had observed that just "a few aborigines enrol for one course or other".[11] Here and there a handful of courses in motor maintenance had proved attractive to men and courses in domestic science and craft training to women. Though Technical Education kept no statistics of the proportion of Aboriginal people in its colleges, its director, H.C.M. King, accepted that Aboriginal children were not accessing technical education in proportion to their achievements. "There must be many aboriginal boys in secondary schools," King observed, "whose educational standards are as good or better than many white boys at present entering trades." Similarly, there were girls who could succeed in typing and office operations. In 1973, three or four male Aboriginal apprentices were listed.[12] By 1980, enrolments had reached 135.[13]

Perkins and Generational Change

The first two students to enrol at Sydney who identified as Aboriginal people were Charles Nelson Perrurie Perkins and Peter Gary Williams. Perkins, a 27-year-old Arrente and

Kalkadoon man from Alice Springs, and Williams, a 17-year-old Gumbaynggirr and Mullumbimby man from Bellwood Aboriginal Reserve, entered Arts in 1963. Williams had attended a reserve school for a short time, then Macksville Convent School and St John's College, Woodlawn, on reduced fees and helped by the AWB and the Waterview Group of Seaforth. Though Williams did not complete at Sydney, he continued an active engagement in national and community activities on the north coast of New South Wales teaching the Gumbaynggirr language and commentating for Goori Radio in Nambucca.

School for Perkins began in Alice Springs in a one-room building. As he recalls:

> All I could remember is that the teacher being chased around the room by some of the bigger boys and people throwing things around the room, and some people scribbling things on the board, and me just walking in and out, as other people did. So schooling was non-existent and we just learnt nothing there.[14]

With his mother's support, the nine-year-old Perkins began a memorable journey in January 1945, leaving the tin huts of Alice Springs for the "grand old hall" – the Church of England's St Francis Boys' Home in Adelaide.[15] A group of six schoolboys reached Adelaide on the evening of the third day, starting at a local primary school shortly afterwards. The exercise in group education was an experiment by the Church whose pastor, Fr Percy Smith, created a home atmosphere close to that of a middle-class family, along with its rules and regimes. "At school," said Perkins, "we were 'the abos' and they (the other pupils and teachers) were 'the whites'. Many things reinforced this – our clothing, no pocket money, no bikes like other kids, and horrible lunches."[16] Enrolled first at Woodville High, he was moved to the less academically demanding Le Fevre Boys' Technical School for secondary education. Here the St Francis boys attended as a group. "Everyone knew when the darkies were coming."[17] Perkins' own school record was well below average, the boy assessed as having "no future".[18]

> I was not interested in school. Nobody encouraged me in any way. It meant nothing to me. Nobody ever gave me a reason why I should study hard. I failed miserably and was booted out. The only thing I passed was woodwork, which I hated. I even failed in sheet metal. My drawing was atrocious, my mathematics, my English (I still don't know the difference between a noun and a verb) were below standard. I did not care for learning. The only thing that they told us was that we were trouble makers and that we were eating too much at the home.[19]

On leaving Le Fevre, Perkins completed trade training as a fitter and turner at British Tube Mills, Adelaide, before sailing for England for work experience and a chance to play soccer with Bishop-Auckland. While playing the game against Oxford, Perkins was inspired to attend university, saying it was here that he determined to go further.[20] Returning to Adelaide, where he married, he and Eileen moved to Sydney in 1962. Supported by earnings from his soccer with Pan-Hellenic and income from Eileen, he enrolled in the matriculation class at the Metropolitan Business College. He was encouraged too by his friend, the Rev. Ted Noffs, who had just completed his MA. It was an excited Noffs who sent news of a successful result to Alice Springs in November and more congratulations followed, including a letter from Paul Hasluck. Perkins was one of only two in his class to matriculate being accepted as a mature age student. When Perkins and Williams walked through the University gates in February 1963, they were welcomed at the Matriculation Ceremony by the Vice-Chancellor, Professor Stephen Henry Roberts (1947–67): the two men had won Abschol awards and Williams a place at St John's College. Perkins conceded he was well pleased – one of two Aboriginal students among 4,500 others. Sydney, he mused, was "the oldest, the most beautiful, the loveliest"[21] of places.

> I couldn't wait for the first lecture and when I got in there I was ready to do my degree in five minutes … I sat alone and determined. Anyone that tried to talk with me I'd've flattened them.

Though Perkins studied prodigiously, the teaching absorbed like "water on a dry sponge", he faced setbacks. The first, his ill-conceived decision to leave the Anthropology exam early: "God, I must be brilliant nobody's finished only me."[22] Alas, his name was missing from the results board two weeks later. "It took me a month to get over that, but the next

Figure 12. Charles Perkins attending lecture at Sydney University c.1963.
Photograph by Robert McFarlane.
Courtesy of the Josef Lebovic Gallery.

day I was back there and I was working twice as hard." His BA degree in the social science disciplines – anthropology, government, psychology and social theory – was completed inside the minimum period.

Perkins also continued with his soccer throughout his three years at Sydney.

> Football served a 3-fold purpose. The first was to provide me with finance for my studying. Secondly, it enabled me to keep fit because I needed to study for such long hours. Thirdly, it was a means whereby I could mix socially and enjoy myself comfortably.[23]

"Sheer determination",[24] Eileen said, was responsible for getting her husband through the degree. Perkins worked during vacations, among his jobs cleaning the City of Sydney toilets, and Eileen worked too, boosting their income. On graduation in May 1966, Perkins was roundly applauded receiving a personal commendation from the Vice-Chancellor. He confessed to being quite emotional: "Right, now the fight's on." Then he stopped to correct himself, "Now the hard work really begins."[25]

Looking back on his Sydney years, Perkins thought them seminal.

> At the University, I think that was one of the very first times that I felt completely accepted, and I had no need to feel uncomfortable in the presence of anybody else. You were there to do a job for yourself. You reached certain levels in certain subjects. That was the battle. You did not worry whether you were an Indian, Aborigine or Chinese. People accepted you on this basis alone. The university has a completely different atmosphere. But this is only a temporary thing and you have to come back to the general community.[26]

Appearing as a witness before the 1966 Joint Committee upon Aborigines Welfare, Perkins talked again of the influence of his Sydney days.

> I was bitter prior to going to the University and hated most white people very much, but since going to the University and having had a trip overseas, and so on, I have come to learn that this should not be so. Having gone to university, I now have more confidence in myself, and having had a reasonable degree of success in certain ventures, I now hold no bitterness to anyone at all.

He was aware too of the friendships it brought.

> Most important of all were the friends I made – Jimmy Spigelman, James Kirby, Peter Willenski and John Hewson – who are still friends today. We learnt that we didn't have to accept the status quo and that's how the student action began to combat racism. That led to opposing other issues like the Vietnam War.[27]

Injustice Exposed

Sydney students had formed a branch of Abschol begun by a small Christian group in Melbourne in 1951, and linked with the National Union of Australian University Students in 1953. Abschol aimed "to stimulate the desire of Aborigines for higher education by informing them that Australian university students are anxious that they enter Australian universities."[28] Essentially a fundraising group in which young Christians and the political left were prominent, the charity was selected for the Annual Commemoration Day Collection on the Sydney campus in 1961.[29] Perkins joined the activists helping found Students for Action for Aboriginal Affairs in 1964, becoming its chairman, with Jim Spigelman, later Chief Justice of NSW, and Beth Hansen as co-secretaries.[30] In the summer of the following year, Perkins led a group of 29 young people and supporters all under 30 on the Student Action for Aborigines (SAFA) bus tour or "freedom ride" named after its American progenitor. The young people, including Williams who joined later, drew public attention to social issues such as segregated public facilities and the lack of job opportunities for Indigenous people in rural New South Wales. Funding for the bus hire was collected by Chicka Dixon and Noffs of the Wayside Chapel, SAFA's Sydney base. The same clergyman would send off the party with a traveller's prayer.

Laurie Craddock, who was Principal of Walgett Primary School at the time, recalls the bus entering town: "They staged a demo outside Walgett P.S. against one of the teachers and it was broken up by a literal 'reading of the riot act' by a solicitor. Only time I know of it actually being done."[31] An attempt by locals to force the SAFA bus off the road led to the driver being replaced, the first considering he could no longer guarantee the students' safety; then efforts to lift restrictions on Aboriginal children's use of the council baths at Moree raised a riot with Spigelman punched to the ground and the students escorted out of town by police. Intelligence of Perkins' tour reached the sensationalist Sydney press almost instantaneously which reported the face of rural discrimination – "a crowd crazed with race hate".[32] By contrast, the country press accused the students of "creating an impression that racial discrimination is on a much larger scale than it really is".[33] In addition, the local member for Walgett contributed his assessment: "It is tragic that the university students should stir up trouble on the Aboriginal question."

Contacts made with Aboriginal organisations and survey material collected along the route were welcomed insofar as they publicised the need for better housing, health and education. However, some Aboriginal people complained that the arrivals stirred up local hostilities and it was Elkin's laconic assessment that the freedom riders had come home "but the Aborigines are still in the towns".[34] One indignant country resident wrote to the Premier, Jack Renshaw, telling him to put them in their place. "After all – a student is only a glorified schoolboy – although most of them dawdle through University till they have grey whiskers and where the general public is concerned are of no importance."[35] "We gained much more than we lost"[36] was Perkins' later assessment.

In 2005 the Freedom Ride was retraced in a documentary commemorating its 40th anniversary organised by the youth network, "ReconciliACTION – young people passionate about Reconciliation and Indigenous Rights", backed by the New South Wales Anti-Discrimination Council.[37] This time the bus was sent off with acclamation by the Koori Centre. As with the original Freedom Ride, both Indigenous and non-Indigenous people participated, meeting with Aboriginal communities to see the extent to which original hopes had been realised. The event was followed in the *Sydney Morning Herald* through diary entries as the journey progressed, and a documentary charting the course of the journey and its history was released as part of ReconciliACTION's education toolkit.

Perkins – Beyond University

Perkins argued that his people needed better education to extricate themselves from poverty. "A crash program",[38] he told the 1966 Joint Committee, substantially funded and covering adult and social education was essential for large-scale outcomes. He thought existing educational programs concentrated too much on literacy and failed to provide substantial skills training. Perhaps existing Aboriginal reserves staffed by young, trained people sympathetic to Aboriginal needs could be turned into educational centres. When Perkins stood down, he was thanked by the Committee Chairman for his "wonderful help" in nearly six hours of testimony.

On leaving University Perkins worked first as manager of the Foundation for Aboriginal Affairs for three years alongside an Aboriginal welfare officer for a weekly wage of £30. Sponsored by Elkin and H.C. Coombs, he left for Canberra joining the Office of Aboriginal Affairs, first as a senior research officer. Initially, Perkins had been turned down for a government liaison position on the grounds that he was overqualified: "But we'll offer you another one which will be a research officer because you've got a Bachelor of Arts from the University of Sydney so take that job."[39] A failed kidney brought dialysis treatment and a transplant; and he came back to Sydney in 1988 to head a consultancy after he lost his post as Secretary of the Department. In this later period, Perkins returned to Alice Springs to fulfil his cultural obligations under the law of the Eastern Arrente.

Perkins' unquenched combativeness manifested itself in various Indigenous causes and flourished inside and outside the public service. As might be expected, not all his efforts "to stir up Aboriginal people" were successful. During an airing of the TV show, *A Current Affair*, hosted by Ray Martin on Channel 9 in July 1996, Perkins passed some unflattering remarks on the achievements of Cathy Freeman. The comments brought a rejoinder from 13 Aboriginal Education Assistants on course at Sydney. "We were outraged by the comments, directed at Cathy Freeman made on your program last evening by Mr Charles Perkins."[40] "We wish," the AEAs wrote to Martin, "that in the future, Mr Perkins would realise that he should be praising people like Cathy Freeman not putting them down." Martin, himself an Arts graduate of Sydney, and a member of the Council for Aboriginal Reconciliation, added a short note to his formal reply. "Thanks again. I think Mr Perkins realised that he had been a bit foolish."[41]

Unquestionably, Perkins carried the palm for education for Aboriginal people. His friend, Gordon Briscoe, recalls how he wanted to foster an Aboriginal intelligentsia. "Education is crucial," he remembers Perkins telling him: "It's a liberating exercise, if Aboriginal people don't get there they will wallow in their own ignorance."[42] Certainly Perkins stood up for University education.

> Studying in an academic field will increase your self-esteem and self-worth; ensure self-satisfaction by completing a course; increase employment prospects and enhance your standard of living. Education will empower you to achieve your aspirations.[43]

The Perkins family, including his nephew Neville Perkins, who entered Newington College winning both Abschol and Consultative Committee on Education awards, was encouraged to study further. Neville read Arts at Sydney in 1970–73, and went on to complete a year of Law. "Without Charlie's advice and guidance," he testified, "I would never have got through the University." In 1977, Neville was elected a Member of the Legislative Council (MLC) for the Northern Territory and later awarded the Order of Australia Medal. Charles' educational enthusiasm also extended to friends: one was the Koori Centre student, Larry Hoskins, who had finished Year 10 at Newtown Boys High School.

> I was influenced in my early childhood by Charles Perkins, he would come to tutor me at home before there were homework centres. I maintained a close relationship with him until he died last week.[44]

After Perkins' state funeral in October 2000, Aden Ridgeway, of the Gumbaynggirr people, the second Aboriginal person to enter federal parliament in 1999, recorded a moving tribute.[45]

> I regard him as the champion of champions. None of the Indigenous leaders would be in the position we are today without him having paved the way for the rest of us to follow. Charlie was a man who used the fire in his belly to dedicate his life to fighting for his beliefs and for getting recognition of the rights of Indigenous people.

Ridgeway himself had a remarkable story to tell having moved from the treadmill of poverty on an Aboriginal reserve to public service as Deputy Leader of the Australian Democrats.

Perkins had a great affection for the University of Sydney and the institution for him. Always generous with his time and advice, Perkins joined a substantial review of the Koori Centre in 1998–99, and the institution reciprocated awarding him an honorary Doctor of Letters and establishing the Dr Charles Perkins AO Memorial Oration and Prize. Its recipient was to demonstrate "continuing commitment to fostering excellence in education and leadership among Indigenous staff and graduates". Among the groups supporting the Oration in 2008 was the Charlie Perkins Trust for Children and Students which has established a scholarship for Indigenous students at Oxford University, the first two postgraduates awarded in 2010, were Paul Gray from the University of Sydney and Christian Thompson from RMIT.

Geddes and the Foundation of Aboriginal Affairs

When Perkins was reading anthropology at Sydney, Professor William Geddes, a social anthropologist and New Zealander by birth, headed the department. While Anthropology at Sydney had lost its monopoly influence over national events with the development of institutions like the Australian National University, the Australian School of Pacific Affairs, and the Australian Institute of Aboriginal and Torres Strait Islander Studies, it maintained significant research in the fields of Aboriginal prehistory, culture, language and social life under academics like Jeremy Beckett, Arthur Capell, Lester Hiatt, Mervyn Meggitt and Richard White.

Geddes' own view on black-white relations was succinct: "The Europeans made Australia a multiracial society when they landed here. We cannot avoid the situation. We must make it work."[46] With his interest in Aboriginal urban communities, Geddes became a driving force behind the Foundation for Aboriginal Affairs, the social and welfare institution opening in 1963. The foundation raised £80,000 in a Christmas doorknock appeal and £10,000 from the New South Wales government in 1964, applying the money to purchase the old Wood Coffill Funeral Parlour near Central Station. In effect, it was a one-stop shop for young Aboriginal people moving from country New South Wales to the inner city seeking cheap accommodation and work on the railways.[47]

From its George Street headquarters, the foundation team organised accommodation and employment, and legal and medical assistance. It also became a focus for Aboriginal social life through its busy calendar – dances, film nights, concerts, plays, and a record club. By 1966, foundation membership had reached 700, including about 300 whites. "A lot of young European people came along including many university students who came down to the foundation regularly." Among those who supported its welfare mission was Elkin who thought its activities had the potential to replace the AWB's own social program. Alan Duncan from the Department of Adult Education headed its Education sub-committee managing the secondary school scholarship program and adult education classes in typing and coaching. The Sydney academic, Professor Robert H. Black of the School of Public Health and Tropical Medicine, was chairman of the foundation's Medical Panel.

Some radical Aboriginal people saw the foundation as essentially a white middle-class enterprise and "Aboriginals hated white people telling them what to do".[48] Serious internal divisions developed over welfare policy, said to represent a handout mentality, and there were claims of undue influence by whites and blacks. Lacking a regular income, the foundation found itself running at a loss and, in 1970, an audit critical of its services was released and another DAA report disclosed gross irregularities. Geddes himself resigned after an all black management committee was formed in 1972 and the foundation's doors closed three years later.

Geddes on Education

Drawing on his first-hand knowledge of Maori achievement in New Zealand, Geddes predicted that Aboriginal professionals would emerge in quantity. Queried as to whether his views were "wishful thinking", Geddes replied, "I do not think so. It would take a little time, of course … once it starts, it duplicates and reduplicates itself. Once you get a nucleus among them, many others will follow."[49] Geddes opposed the common educational assessment that Aboriginal children were best directed to work with their hands in labouring or trade training insisting they should go where their talents led them. He also wanted the foundation to help teachers work more effectively in schools and provide tertiary scholarships for Aboriginal students in medicine, dentistry and economics.

Not all anthropological research was well executed or well received in Aboriginal communities. Geddes himself reported a serious delay in a major survey underway in Sydney because urban Aboriginal people objected to anthropologists treating them as "objects of study, or specimens".[50] University researchers were accused of putting their own academic promotion above the interests and wellbeing of Aboriginal people with claims made that they never consulted Indigenous Australians on the content of teaching programs or employed them as lecturers or consultants. In 1992, the Koori Centre would issue a set of ethical guidelines on Aboriginal research in the social sciences.

Networking

Aboriginal contacts expanded across the University from the 1960s on. The Department of Adult Education appointed a staff tutor in Aboriginal Adult Education in 1963 to teach and manage its training classes, conferences and public speaking nights. Occasional arrangements were made for Aboriginal school students to tour the campus; and in 1964, Oodgeroo Noonuccal (Kath Walker), of the Minjerriba people, launched her book, *We Are Going*, at Sydney, reputedly the first book of poems published by an Aboriginal writer. The Faculty of Architecture collaborated with the Aboriginal Housing Cooperative in Bourke in 1971 over culturally appropriate housing and Colin James helped redesign the Block at Redfern in 1973. Diploma of Education students shot film of activities at the La Perouse Study Centre in 1976, the project supported by the Aboriginal Education Council (NSW); and Professor John Eggleston and John Synott from English promoted a high-school debating competition between Aboriginal students in 1977, with Tom Williams and Terry Bostock the judges. Three teams from Matraville, Marrickville and Randwick North Boys Highs competed for a set of Aboriginal artefacts, the winners, Randwick, receiving their prize from the Aboriginal politician, Senator Neville Bonner. Prominent Aboriginal men and women addressed student groups on campus; staff and students tutored in the Aboriginal homework and study centres; and senior University academics held community posts that brought them into regular contact with Aboriginal people, for example, Professor Tom Stapleton from Medicine served on the Child Welfare Advisory Council.

Figure 13. Aboriginal Education Assistants and wellwishers at the opening of Pemulwuy High School in Newtown, 27 February 1991. Image courtesy of the Koori Centre.

Aboriginal services in the University's immediate environs were extended. Tranby, the Cooperative for Aborigines Ltd (1956), continued with skills training in Glebe in collaboration with the University; and in Redfern, the Aboriginal Legal Centre (1970) and the Aboriginal Medical Service (1971) made regular use of Sydney staff and students. Murawina (Black Woman), the Aborigine-run preschool, operated a breakfast project in an old warehouse in Redfern in 1973, sending several staff to Sydney for training; and the Eora Centre, a TAFE college for Aboriginal students, opened in 1984 opposite the University's Services Building in Abercrombie St. Several Sydney staff were on the Board of the National Aboriginal and Islander Skills Development Association (NAISDA) formed in 1988, and others joined in programs of the Aboriginal and Islander Dance Theatre in Glebe. Lastly, there were the inner city primary and high schools with substantial Aboriginal populations located around the University's perimeter in Darlington, Redfern, Glebe and Surry Hills, which were accessed for practice teaching by the Faculty of Education's teacher trainees.

Pemulwuy College

Sydney College of Advanced Education's Aboriginal staff and graduates, Margret Campbell, Vilma Ryan, Pauline Button and Mary-Lou Buck, were active in the inner city project, Pemulwuy College, named after the formidable black resistance leader shot dead in 1802, his head dispatched to Sir Joseph Banks in London. Momentum for the venture came from the Aboriginal community's unease over the poor quality of local secondary schooling that had seen Aboriginal students stage a walkout from Cleveland Street High. The college opened its gates in 1991 in the old St Joseph's School premises leased from the Catholic Church in Newtown, the celebration bringing together fiery speakers and cheering supporters, many University people among them. Koori and non-Aboriginal students could now access a dedicated coeducational school from Year 7, one able to take boarders if need be.

> Pemulwuy College is a vision which has come from listening to Koori people who are totally dissatisfied with the present process of education for Koori people. They say their young Koori people are being failed by the present school system because Koori values and systems are not taught in a positive manner.[51]

The college's school work promised to draw on the multiculturalism of Australian society, as well as the Aboriginal cultures of its student body, blending them in a vibrant exciting whole.

Although widely supported by Aboriginal and community organisations – among them Murawina, the Aboriginal Education Council (NSW), the NSW AECG, and the Australian Council of Churches – the college's promise was not fulfilled. The school closed within a few years. Reasons for its failure are not yet documented, however there were enrolment problems, bureaucratic departmental issues and internal disputes. In addition, some Aboriginal opponents claimed the project took Aboriginal children back to reserve days through a substandard curriculum.

Attack and Counterattack

In 1976, the University was engaged in public controversy when Professor Harry Messel, Head of the School of Physics, warned readers of *The University of Sydney News* of the "impending massacre of wildlife in Arnhem Land by Aboriginal huntsmen"[52] under the guiding hand of the white people, prophesying that this slaughter could lead to the "extermination of essentially all wildlife". His article's extensive claims provoked a follow-up letter from Les R. Hiatt, Reader in Anthropology, under the by-line, "Melodramatic and Unsubstantiated Assertions".[53] A member of the Aboriginal Education Council (NSW) and an informed supporter of Aboriginal causes on campus, Hiatt declared his own belief that less wildlife was being killed today than 50 years back. Messel's assertions served as "a smokescreen for an attack on Aboriginal interests, which must not be allowed to stand in the way of a multi-million dollar research project" – by inference, the Northern Territory and University of Sydney run facility at Maningrida researching the ecology and biology of saltwater crocodiles.

Further tension arose over the content of occasional articles for the *Sydney Morning Herald* written by the manager of the facility, Graham Gifford. On the 14 March 1977, his story, "No Way for a Nice Girl to Behave", told in racy language the treatment meted out to a young Arnhem Land "teacher" married off to a man from a neighbouring tribe as wife "Number Six".[54] Some three months later, Gifford allegedly wrote another provocative piece for the *National Times* (6–11 June 1977) under the pseudonym, Michael Davenport, which attacked the outstations' movement that cited "two cases of alleged rape".[55] Davenport described the life of the tribal Aborigine as "one of dirt, squalor, brutality and drunkenness".[56] He went on: "What may have, perforce, been acceptable to a mob of half-starved vagrant hunters cannot be permitted when it is provided at enormous expense to the taxpayer."

On 27 June 1977, Hiatt took up the cudgels again in his article, "The Outstations Controversy",[57] with the Gifford/Davenport writing singled out. Hiatt's response was direct: "For my part, I believe that, although the stories may contain elements of truth, they are in important respects concoctions of ignorance and inflamed imagination." Hiatt feared that picturesque writing by the *Sydney Morning Herald's* correspondent and Messel could lead to a breakdown in relations between Arnhem Land people and the University and harm valuable scientific work underway. Hiatt made it clear he particularly admired the work of the Sydney biologists on site.

Duran-Duran, journal of the AEC (NSW), picked up the Davenport story, its editor concerned that Gifford's argument denied the right of Aboriginal children to be educated wherever they lived.[58] After complaints to the Press Council by Marcia Langton, General-Secretary of FCAATSI, and others, the newspaper company told Gifford it would no longer publish him.[59] Some time after Gifford's death, in May 2006, his writing was raised again, this time in the context of violence and child abuse in remote Aboriginal settlements with the *Sydney Morning Herald* columnist, Michael Duffy, describing him as "brave, thoughtful and independent". Two years on, an Aboriginal perspective on the dysfunctions of these communities by one of Sydney's well-known Aboriginal graduates, Noel Pearson, was argued in *The Australian*, "Homes Built on Despair".[60]

Overcoming Barriers to Entry

From its earliest years, the University had recognised the importance of public scholarships for students of merit allowing fee exemption and small stipends and, later, bursaries for the financially indigent. The state government also offered a few university bursaries in the 19th century. Such assistance reached a peak during the Great Depression when nearly half the student body held a benefit of one kind or another. Help also came from the Student Representative Council which managed a loan fund for those about to abandon their studies "for lack of a few odd pounds".[61] From the start of 1945, ex-servicemen and women received fee remission and living allowances under the Commonwealth Reconstruction Training Scheme, later the Commonwealth Scholarship Scheme.

In 1969, the Commonwealth introduced the Aboriginal Study Grants Scheme (ABSTUDY) which paid a living allowance, compulsory fees, some travel costs, and book and equipment allowances for tertiary education. Funding was also allowed for various bridging and special courses as part of students' educational preparation. On campus, five individual scholarships were designated for Aboriginal students: the Duncan Bursary, the Alice Mary Wingrove Bursary, the Australian Aboriginal Scholarships, the Konstantin Gawrilow Scholarship (including the study of Russian), and the Bridgitte Oppen Fund. As well, supplementary funding could be tapped through regular student services and from the Chancellor's Committee. Given that most scholarships and bursaries were competitive, or were accessible only after students had matriculated, they did not fit the diverse needs of Indigenous students.

Matriculation requirements based on results from a five-year Leaving Certificate continued to be a high hurdle for Aboriginal people. During World War II, the University had relaxed its matriculation demands for servicemen and women and provided study facilities for German Jewish internees at Hay; and, at the war's end, it had introduced adult matriculation for Australian applicants over 25, subject to academic safeguards. So far as Aboriginal students went, the University was loath to admit them as a separate category outside its admission quota. "In the University view it did not take into account other socially underprivileged groups who, like Aborigines, did not enter university in big numbers."[62] In February 1973, *New Dawn* contrasted Sydney's reluctance with the University of New South Wales' policy that admitted Aboriginal students outside the normal quota. Ten years on, Sydney would set aside 130 places for mature age and disadvantaged students able to demonstrate that their educational progress had been affected by circumstances beyond their control over a substantial period and who scored well in external tests. Again, the program took no account of Aboriginal students' special needs and was not accessed.

A Radical Perspective and Redress

At its inauguration in the 19th century, the University of Sydney had described itself as "the first colonial University in the British Empire".[63] However, a century on, the University stood accused of practising "internal colonialism",[64] its once proud claim appearing as an indictment in the rhetoric of the late 1960s. Accusations of institutional racism at Sydney were part of an ongoing critique of Western universities over the claims of the counter culture, black rights and feminist ideas. Whereas Sydney students prewar concerned themselves with debating their big issues – unemployment, communism, the League of Nations and Andersonian free thought, the language of the postwar years favoured individual liberation, social transformation and action. Radicals claimed that Sydney had never shed its colonial heritage of monocultural teaching and learning.

In 1976, when the young David Patch stood for election as a Student Fellow of Senate, his platform argued for a significant number of places for "oppressed minority groups",[65] Indigenous Australians among them. Despite individual effort, the Commonwealth would chart a decline in the participation level of disadvantaged young people in higher education in the early 1980s, and it identified Aboriginal people as a significant group at risk. Ken Jones, former Secretary of the Department of Education, put the point frankly to the Australian Vice-Chancellors Committee (AVCC) in 1983.

> On a population basis Aboriginals are very much under represented at the higher education level when compared with other groups in Australian society. This is particularly so in respect to universities. This imbalance is apparent not only in terms of general access to higher education, but also in the range of courses being studied, retention rates and success experienced in studies.[66]

Jones also observed a disproportionately low representation of Aboriginal people among Australian university staff.

The Commonwealth offered additional funding in December 1983, and the Australian Vice-Chancellors Committee pledged support for improved special entry arrangements and more teacher education places.[67] Progress was slow. In 1985, the Chairman of the Commonwealth Tertiary Education Commission (CTEC), Hugh Hudson, in a talk on "Equity and Higher Education", observed Aboriginal enrolment and employment rates with dismay questioning how discouraged students of Aboriginal background would ever enter institutions applying high entry standards. Recognising itself in Hudson's sights, the Vice-Chancellor and Principal, Professor John Ward (1981–90), responded in *University News*.

> The University of Sydney, for example, now has entry standards so high that some people think them unachievable and discouraging. Mr Hudson would point to disadvantaged areas and to the Aboriginal population as likely to contain many such disadvantaged people.[68]

Ward defended the University's practices. It had, he said, "no need and no right to compromise our standards and no case for inflicting disappointment on ill-selected students." However, he did note that Senate had asked the newly created Joint Senate Academic Board Committee on Admissions Policy to review Sydney's policies and that the committee had acknowledged the existence of "certain groups, such as Aborigines, to whom the community had a special obligation and to whom the University should grant special entry provisions".[69]

Two of Sydney's faculties, Medicine and Dentistry, eased entry for Aboriginal students in 1987, and the Faculty of Arts commenced detailed discussions, though a suggestion that it widen any concessions to encompass the New Zealand Maori was not adopted.[70] The Arts subcommittee eventually adopted an "outside quota" scheme for ten places from 1988, subject to the provision of support facilities for such students. Education was also easing its entry requirements offering places to AEAs who had earned Stage III or good Stage II passes; and six faculties were operating special admissions – Medicine, Dentistry, Education, Arts, Veterinary Science and Economics by 1990.

There was an assumption around the campus that any relaxation of entry standards would release a pent-up demand for places, perhaps an overwhelming one. However its holders were disabused: in the first year of the operation of special admissions only the Faculty of Arts secured an Aboriginal enrolment.[71]

Looking in from Outside

Sydney was slow to recognise that word-of-mouth recommendation was a superior mode of recruitment. Although University staff and local Aboriginal people worked together on individual and group projects, community linkage failed to flourish. Indeed, local Aboriginal assessments of the University could be harsh as these comments taken from the report, "Recommendations for Educational Equity for Aboriginal People at the University of Sydney", indicate.[72]

> The main and original Broadway Campus of Sydney University has coexisted in close proximity to Aboriginal communities for generations. Interaction has been mainly marginal and limited, although valuable individual or small group contacts have existed; this is despite the fact that thousands of staff and students almost daily travel through, or nearby Aboriginal communities surrounding the University ... Whereas other universities have begun to gain a "reputation" for positive achievement, Sydney University has suffered by contrast ... Where they [local Aboriginal communities] hold any opinion at all, it is of a negative stereotype of a rigid elitist institution, immune or even hostile to the needs and aspirations of Aboriginal people.

Similar feelings were expressed by Maureen Williams, a representative of the Metropolitan Local Aboriginal Land Council, in comments published by the *Daily Telegraph* on 26 July 1990.

> Aborigines are made to feel they're not good enough to come here. It doesn't seem to be encouraging Aboriginal students as much as the other universities, even though it's just a hop, skip and jump from Redfern.

The Aboriginal perception of Sydney above was not ill-founded. Its outcomes were evident in a survey on Aboriginal student housing conducted in 1991,[73] which recorded no full-time students living in Darlington, Redfern, Botany and La Perouse, and one part-timer in Darlington. South Sydney residents also expressed concern that the University failed to employ unemployed Aboriginal workers when vacancies occurred, and Aboriginal staff complained that their children were hassled by security staff dare they walk through the University grounds. A largely negative perception about Sydney saw its name raise hackles in some Aboriginal quarters overshadowing the good work undertaken by individuals and University departments.

Action against Disadvantage

Professor Sam Ball from the Faculty of Education was an advocate of affirmative action as a counter to disadvantage, a position spurred by his own experience coming to University through a state bursary, the first in his family to do so. Assisted by Associate Professor Ken Cable from History,[74] Ball persuaded the University to back his SUCCEED project in 1985, bringing together 24 disadvantaged students from Year 11 for extra tutoring in mathematics, science and English. He anticipated a "ripple effect"[75] on participants' home schools creating positive values and strengthening academic outcomes. The Commonwealth government invested $30,000 as a start and the University another $15,000,[76] with additional help from Val Street, Principal of the Women's College, and 30 or so volunteer staff and students supporting tutoring, recreational activities and counselling. However, SUCCEED did not attract more than one or two Aboriginal students in its early years.

Three years later, Ball promoted a more ambitious scheme, Broadway. His three-year pilot project targeted youngsters with non-competitive entry marks suffering from long-term educational disadvantage offering them 200 places across nine faculties from 1988.[77] Medicine, for example, which normally demanded an entry of mark of 445, would accept Broadway students with a minimum of 400; and Architecture, which required 371, would accept 350 or above. This so-called tampering with Sydney's standards brought an immediate, largely negative public response from politicians, *Sydney Morning Herald* letter writers, disgruntled parents, and the 2UE radio personality, Alan Jones, who criticised the idea on air on 15 June 1987.

> To think that someone is excluded from Sydney University next year who in fact has secured a higher mark than someone who is going to be admitted makes an absolute mess of the quota system, the marking system, the admission system and the education system.[78]

Broadway faced similar discontent on campus. A "long and bitter fight"[79] between some Sydney Deans and the Senate was reported by the *Sydney Morning Herald*, the newspaper itself regarding the scheme as "a modest attempt to redress the geographical imbalance in enrolment".[80] Among opponents was the Dean of Medicine, Professor Richard Gye, who argued that the new Broadway quotas could push up the high entry marks in his Faculty.[81] He already operated special admission for some ten nurses, five refugees and at least one Aborigine, he said, and foreshadowed that the Broadway scheme could force him to restrict or eliminate them. In the event, Senate approved the scheme and Medicine would establish its own arrangements for special admissions through the Graduate Medical Program in 1996.

Broadway did not prove as attractive among disadvantaged students as anticipated. Only 50 of the 200 places were taken up in 1988, 71 in 1989, and 44 in 1990. Despite Aboriginality being defined as a category of disadvantage from 1990, just one application was received from an Aboriginal person that year among 404 enquiries.[82] A Broadway Review Committee reported on the scheme the same year.

> All members agreed that, on the basis of individual student performance, the scheme appears to have been successful. It was noted however, that the numbers involved were too few to assess, with any high degree of reliability, the benefits of the scheme.[83]

Figure 14. Liesa Clague (left) is the first Aboriginal graduate of the Bachelor of Nursing for registered nurses, with her aunt Christine Mumbler, Aboriginal Employment and Liaison Officer of the EEO Unit at the University of Sydney, 11 June, no year given. Image courtesy of University of Sydney Archives.

Enrollees as surveyed did achieve creditable examination results at least up to the University average, and Broadway outlasted its doubters.[84]

Institutional Initiatives and Equal Opportunity

In 1983, Senate adopted the policy of Equal Employment Opportunity (EEO) bringing the University in line with the requirements of the NSW *Anti-Discrimination Act*. It also introduced an internal management plan designed to assist women, the physically impaired and minorities. In 1989, Suzanne Jobson, the EEO coordinator, whose previous experience with the NSW Anti-Discrimination Board had included organising programs for Aboriginal people, appointed an Aboriginal clerical officer, Christine Mumbler, on secondment from the Department of Industrial Relations and Employment. Mumbler's duties were threefold: to encourage the employment of Indigenous Australians on campus; to support Aboriginal students and staff; and to liaise with the Aboriginal community. Shortly after she joined Sydney, Mumbler told *University News*:

> The people here know what questions to ask; they have read and they know the problems of Aboriginal people, unlike the Public Service where I found I was always having to educate non-Aboriginal people.[85]

At the time of Mumbler's engagement there were perhaps five Aboriginal employees on campus; the figure would increase to 25 by 2003.[86]

In 1988, a Working Party of the Deputy Vice-Chancellor's Committee, under Associate Professor Margaret B. Clunies Ross, a Nordic and Icelandic scholar from the Department

Figure 15. Noel Pearson, Arts and Law graduate c. 1993. Image courtesy of University of Sydney Archives.

of English, prepared an Equal Opportunity in Education (EOE) report. Two submissions took up Aboriginal concerns.[87] The first statement, which came from the EEO Office under Catherine Glass,[88] contained a list of strategies to improve the participation rates of disadvantaged students. So far as Aboriginal students were concerned, she recommended a support base on campus through an Aboriginal Education Resource Centre or Aboriginal Liaison Office; the provision of personal tutors as well as academic tutors; assistance for schools in identifying individual students likely to succeed at University; and improved special admissions arrangements. Aboriginal studies should be promoted in professional courses; greater assistance given staff in identifying and combating racial bias; and occasional childcare places made available.

The second submission came from Associate Professor Raymond King, Director of the Aboriginal Education Assistants Training Program. He highlighted the results of a survey at Mitchell College, Bathurst, which emphasised the importance of enclave support for young male and female Aboriginal students.[89] Sydney should open its own support centre, he argued, which could also publicise the good work underway in Aboriginal studies and develop a database for research and teaching. He wanted Aboriginal people appointed to significant decision-making committees on campus noting that his own submission had been prepared with assistance from Aboriginal staff members.

When the EOE Working Party circulated its report, the findings on Aboriginal education were placed under the heading: "Priority goal or research area for urgent attention".[90] The report noted the incomplete and inadequate special entry provisions of faculties; the absence of outreach programs in schools; and the lack of publicity about the University generally among Aboriginal people. It declared that "Aboriginal Education (attraction, support and retention)" was the Committee's number one priority admitting at the same time

Figure 16. David Malangi and Margaret Gindjimirri, visiting artists to the University's Art Workshop from the Northern Territory, 1993. Image courtesy of University of Sydney Archives.

that much remained to do. For example, the special admissions schemes of Sydney's faculties had proven paper exercises and planning for a support centre had barely commenced.

Activities of the 1980s

Aboriginal graduates appeared irregularly in the graduation ceremonies in the 1980s. Among them was Denis McDonald, BArch (1986) and BSc (Arch.) in 1990, who worked with the Aboriginal Housing Commission in Redfern. McDonald, who was raised in an Aboriginal community on Stradbroke Island (Minjerriba), was the son of a white mother and black father. "Our elders really drove home the fact that we were black. Among their generation, having white skin had been a way for some people to denounce their Aboriginality. Our elders didn't want to lose their families so they kept reminding us – don't forget your roots."[91]

Another graduate was Noel Pearson, the activist for the economic and social development for the Wik people, whose father was from the Bagaarrmugu and mother from the Guggu Yalanji people. From his Hope Vale Mission home in North Queensland, and a Lutheran secondary school in Brisbane, Pearson would graduate with Honours in History in 1987, having his thesis published by the University's Department of History, and earning an LLB from Sydney in 1993. Another kind of publishing in which Pearson engaged led to the

Figure 17. The University of Sydney *Gazette* 1993.

publication of a children's book, Caden Walaa! (*Caden, Watch Out!*), written and illustrated by Karin Calley which Pearson translated into Guugu Yimithirr, his father's language. The University's first Aboriginal master's graduate, Ian Perdrisat, whose mother's family was Wangkumarra from Bourke, was awarded an MEd in 1990. Pedrisat and his partner would establish and manage a small NGO, Madjulla Inc., which enabled them to assist Indigenous community development "without government or community politics hijacking the agenda".[92] They became project managers of a cultural centre near Derby and supported a Nyikina culture and language program which included an electronic dictionary and plant database.

Inside the Faculty of Arts, staff in Anthropology, Archaeology and Prehistory, and in Linguistics, engaged in significant Aboriginal projects. Terry Smith in Fine Arts led *The Dictionary of Art* to revalue the significance of Aboriginal art; Christian Alexander of Social Work produced a report on the rate and causes of recidivism by Aboriginal prisoners; Deborah Rose and Tony Swain assessed Christian mission activity; and Robert Eagleson undertook a major research project on Aboriginal English in the inner city where he was taken to meet Redfern people by local Meals on Wheels volunteers including Joyce Black.

Outside Arts, coursework was available on Aboriginal topics in Architecture and Town and Country Planning, Economics, Medicine, Public Health, Social Work and the Centre for Cross-Cultural Studies in Health. The Faculty of Education taught a compulsory core of

Aboriginal studies in its Bachelor of Education (Primary) degree from 1989, and it offered a Diploma in Aboriginal Assistants Education from 1990. Three years later, the faculty was teaching three master's courses in Aboriginal education. In architecture in the 1980s, five non-Aboriginal undergraduates won a UNESCO UIA award for work on Aboriginal housing on the Murray River; Radio Skid Row played the music of Aboriginal artists out of the Wentworth Building; and the Union-supported organisation, Contact, relayed information about coaching, recreational classes and counselling for Indigenous students.

University-based media continued its occasional comment on Aboriginal issues and topics through *Oceania* and its monograph series, the publications of Sydney University Press, and *Honi Soit*, *Hermes*, *University News*, and *The Union Recorder*. In 1993, the University of Sydney *Gazette* was dedicated to the 1993 Year of the World's Indigenous People, initiated and edited by Susanne Ainger of *University News*, a doughty advocate for Aboriginal people on campus. Non-Aboriginal Sydney graduates also contributed extensively, for instance, Tom Roper, an Honours graduate in Arts, edited the book, *Aboriginal Education: The Teacher's Role*, drawing on papers from the Abschol Summer School of 1968. Roper himself was appointed Minister for Aboriginal Affairs in Victoria in 1991.

The University had demonstrated its credentials in a substantial way in teaching and research. For instance, at least 12 University departments and schools were engaged in research on Aboriginal issues in 1989.[93] However, on the debit side, the University had very few Aboriginal students across its mainstream degrees. Well aware of the deficiency, the Vice-Chancellor, John Ward, put a suggestion to Senate in 1987 that he chair a working party investigating all aspects of Aboriginal education within the University. "This will provide me and the Joint Committee with a firm basis upon which to formulate policies and plans for submission to the Senate."[94] Senate adopted the Ward resolution aiming for a 1988 start.

3

Aboriginal Education and the Department of Adult Education

> People who make decisions and do things <u>for</u> Aborigines are in fact taking away pride, dignity and self respect … Aborigines are no longer looking for "handouts" and paternalism, what they want are opportunities and a "fair go".
>
> Alan Duncan's Talk to the Aboriginal Education Council (NSW), August, 1969[1]

The Department of Adult Education was the first to offer regular classes for non-degree Indigenous students in 1975. Teaching adult learners at Sydney had begun in 1886, the task eventually organised by the University Extension Board and extended into coursework by the Joint Committee for Tutorial Classes before World War I. Adult education would consolidate itself as a field of study during the Great War when soldiers at the Australasian Corps Central School at Rue, France, studied for university matriculation, civil service examinations and subjects like accounting. The army school was led by Robert Strachan Wallace, an Arts graduate from Melbourne, and Sydney's popular Vice-Chancellor from 1928 to 1947. Wallace also served as chair of the Education Advisory Council of the Army Department of Education during World War II.

Elkin was among those happy to teach adults outside Sydney. In addition to his priestly duties in the Hunter region in the 1920s, he tutored in cultural anthropology, charging five shillings for 24 sessions. As he remembered it: "The first courses in Anthropology given under the auspices of our University were, I think, given by me in Cessnock and Newcastle for the Tutorial Class Department in 1923–25."[2] Indeed, Elkin was still taking extension classes after his retirement in the 1960s. Another academic, Hermann David Black in Economics, toured regularly and gave radio broadcasts during World War II and talks at military camps in New South Wales. Educated at Fort Street Boys High School, Black had graduated from Sydney with BEcon and MEcon, both with Honours I, joining staff at Sydney Teachers College under Alexander Mackie. In 1933 he was appointed assistant lecturer in Economics in the Faculty of Economics. The academic engaged himself in public life as Economic Advisor to the New South Wales Treasury throughout the war and was a regular visitor to the United States afterwards. Chancellor 1970–90, and Knight Bachelor and Companion of the

Order of Australia, Black, and his wife, Lady Joyce Black, were constant and active friends of Aboriginal students and Koori Centre staff. Among their projects was the Chancellor's Committee, which raised money for Aboriginal and Torres Strait Islander scholarships.

High hopes by enthusiasts for a Chair in Adult Education in 1945 failed to materialise though the field was well served by the appointment of J.L.J. (Lascelles) Wilson, an ex-Lieutenant Colonel in the Army Education Service, as Director of the Department of Tutorial Classes in 1952. As the Aboriginal Welfare Board (AWB) began to remove its managers from the reserves, a premium was put on leadership training for Aboriginal people covering organisational arrangements, the duties of office bearers and the chairing of meetings. Wilson responded by mounting a residential summer school on community advancement and cooperative activity for 22 Indigenous Australians from urban and rural New South Wales.[3] Held at Moore Theological College in January 1963, with running costs met by the University, the Australian Board of Missions and the AWB, the fortnight comprised lectures, discussions, film shows and visits. The activities were thought "the first of their kind arranged in Australia", and it was supplemented by residential summer schools for Aboriginal students in collaboration with Tranby. On a personal note, the director found time to assist individuals like Charles French, a Sydney matriculant, who took up a UNESCO travel grant to North America in 1964 and later enrolled in the Faculty of Arts.

A Staff Tutorship

The filling of a tutorship in Aboriginal Adult Education in 1963 was the result of behind the scenes moves by Elkin wearing both his University and AWB hats. Quizzed at the Joint Committee upon Aborigines Welfare in 1967 as to whether he was the one responsible for Aboriginal adult education at Sydney, Elkin's reply was unequivocal.

> Yes, it was in the mind of the Board that you had to have adult education so that the parents can understand why you wanted the children to go to school. We learned that in Mexico forty years ago.[4]

The tutor was directed to help parents learn the value of education for themselves and their children.

Elkin had insisted that the project be attached to a university to give it "some status"[5] and ensure its long-term viability, and he cajoled the NSW DoE hierarchy into a firm commitment, the only way he could access a trained teacher.

> At present the University has not any money to use in this way, and that is the reason why the Board is of value. It can come in and help where help is wanted, and the Premier of the day is sympathetic, whereas the whole matter could be lost in the University or the Department of Education. The department can recommend a special project and the Board can then say, "Go ahead, we have the funds".

Figure 18. Alan Duncan 1983. Image courtesy of the Koori Centre.

The scheme was funded under a two-year arrangement, with an option for a third.[6] Under the deed of arrangement, the AWB met course costs and expenses, the NSW DoE the salary of a tutor, and the Department of Adult Education (founded in 1964), travel expenses and office accommodation. Wilson was happy to chair a tripartite project committee regarding the tutorship as a valuable extension of his department's community arm and one available at little cost. In June 1963, Alan Towers Duncan, a graduate of Sydney in Arts with Honours in history and diplomas in anthropology and education, was appointed tutor on secondment from the NSW DoE. He was warmly welcomed by Wilson who told him, "Do what ever you need to do".[7] The young teacher's interest in Aboriginal issues had been sparked during his undergraduate days. Confronted by an essay task, "Half-castes inherit the vices of both races and the virtues of neither. Discuss",[8] Duncan read more and took field trips to Bourke and Brewarrina to check things at first hand.

Duncan's first teaching appointment in 1952 was teacher-supervisor of a one-teacher school on Moonahcullah Aboriginal Station where he taught and managed the reserve's affairs. By coincidence, Moonahcullah had its own place in New South Wales educational history as John Lewis, its teacher in 1911, was the first Aboriginal to lead a public school in the state.[9] Lewis, who was described unflatteringly by his Department of Public Instruction Inspector, J. Dunlop, as "a hunchbacked coloured man who has a certain amount of superficial education",[10] held his classes in a small, galvanised iron structure belonging to the Aboriginal Protection Board (APB).

Prior to Duncan's time, Moonahcullah's teacher, the mission manager, was assisted by his wife. Neither of them, it seems, was trained as no courses had been offered to managers of reserves since 1940. The school itself was shut for 18 months before Duncan's arrival and open only two or three days a week before then. Facing children as old as 12–15 who were "quite illiterate",[11] Duncan, with the support of an "advanced" inspector of schools, tossed out the old Aboriginal syllabus and his pupils were entering Deniliquin High in proportion to enrolments from other places inside three years.

Duncan's next appointment was Acting Principal of the two-teacher Woodenbong Aboriginal School. Racial prejudice in the town had prevented Aboriginal pupils entering Woodenbong Central and it took lengthy discussion over several years before Duncan overcame the problem enabling several Woodenbong children to get through to the Intermediate Certificate class. Duncan also joined the Australian-Aboriginal Fellowship (AAF), an organisation that would merge with the Federated Council for the Advancement of Aboriginal and Torres Strait Islanders (FCAATSI), whose educational platform demanded improved facilities and opportunities for Aboriginal children. After Woodenbong, he was promoted Principal of Hillston Central, a school with 10–12 percent Aboriginal population.[12] One of his Hillston students, (Patricia) Ann Flood, would become the first Aboriginal to graduate with a BEd (Primary) degree from Sydney's Faculty of Education in 1993. Flood took up a lecturing position in the Koori Centre and become the Director of Goolanguillia Aboriginal Centre at the University of Western Sydney. Duncan sought to return to Sydney after Hillston and had thought of applying for a counsellor's job at the University. Instead, at Elkin's suggestion, he put his name down for the adult education position.

Expanding Aboriginal Adult Education

With Duncan on board, the Department of Adult Education operated remedial study and leadership classes for Aboriginal students at Tranby, typing at the Foundation for Aboriginal Affairs, and motor maintenance, knitting and dress-making at Nowra and Kempsey Technical Colleges. There were also discussion groups on Aboriginal issues in city and country in collaboration with the Workers Education Association, Adult Education's ally. Duncan was helped by Catherine Guiness, a professional social worker who managed a project for Aboriginal women at Nowra and Wreck Bay, and by cadets training at the Australian School of Pacific Affairs. In 1965, the Department of Adult Education and the Consultative Committee on Aboriginal Education organised a conference on Aboriginal education. Here Duncan presented the paper, "Looking to the Future", which expounded his philosophy of encouraging Aboriginal people to examine their own problems and suggest means of solving them.[13] Another conference on the education of underprivileged minority children was organised the following year when Adult Education assisted with a large gathering in the Town Hall on National Aborigines Day in 1967 when 2000 senior secondary and 200 tertiary students expanded their knowledge of Aboriginal society and culture.[14]

Helped by the renowned Maori politician, Matiu Rata, Duncan toured New Zealand with an Adelaide group in 1966, which included two Aboriginal representatives funded by the Aboriginal Education Council (NSW), the party inspecting trade training programs and the play centre movement. A preschool project for Maori children and parents was trialled in New South Wales under the title Aboriginal Family Education Centres (AFECs), the first opening at Coraki. Also in 1966, Duncan won a Churchill Fellowship for a six-month study program overseas, presented a paper at Monash University, "Training Aborigines for Employment in NSW", and campaigned in support of the "Vote Yes" in the national referendum campaign. The man's energy and productivity persuaded the tripartite committee to extend his tutorship into a third year and it petitioned the University to have the position made permanent, the AWB offering an annual payment as an inducement. Senate agreed.

Duncan was re-appointed as tutor following advertisement, and secured sufficient funding for a secretary/research assistant, Gwen Watt, and an area counsellor, Steven Guth. Elkin was well pleased with Senate's action and hopeful for the future of Aboriginal adult education despite some disappointment with its limited take up.[15] NSW DoE was also delighted that the University had taken over the tutorship as it resolved worries that the department would get caught up in the funding of adult education. In March 1966, the assistant director, Vernon Truskett, was representing the Sydney program as a "slight development",[16] something his department would have to make up its mind about.

Duncan exercised his Churchill Fellowship in 1968, re-visiting New Zealand and touring Hopi, Navajo, Pueblo and Apache communities in the US, Mexico and Canada. Among the social projects inspected was the War on Poverty and Chicago's Job Opportunities through Better Skills (JOBS) program which linked pre-employment skills training for unemployed youngsters with techniques of positive reinforcement and personal counselling. Duncan was quick to recognise the importance of improving rural work opportunities as a motivating factor in retaining Aboriginal children in class, the point being brought home to him when he asked an Aboriginal father why the man hadn't kept his son at school. "Does that mean a sharper pick or a brighter shovel?"[17] the parent replied.

The Department of Adult Education persuaded the Commonwealth to release $17,250 to fund a JOBS pilot in New South Wales launching it in 1970.[18] Initially, 42 students aged 16–21 were enrolled for 16 weeks pre-vocational training, 36 completing and all but six finding suitable employment. Although the program was assessed as "sufficiently successful to warrant repetition",[19] the Commonwealth determined not to take JOBS further. Of course the essential problem remained: the NSW Anti-Discrimination Report of 1978, for instance, estimated Aboriginal unemployment as close to 60 percent with young people significantly over represented.

A View from a Joint Committee

The appalling living conditions in Aboriginal communities came under the microscope in late 1965 when the Joint Committee of the Legislative Council and Legislative Assembly upon Aborigines Welfare began its investigation. Duncan and John J. Skelton, a retired Lieutenant Colonel and trained psychologist, presented a submission on behalf of the Consultative Committee on Aboriginal Education: this statement supported more preschools, an improved curriculum, extended remedial teaching, and a comprehensive survey of Aboriginal numbers and achievements in primary and secondary schools. They wanted adult Aboriginal people working full-time as teachers of Aboriginal culture in schools and community organisations.[20] Duncan cited his employment of the poet and writer, Oodgeroo Noonuccal (Kath Walker), and Pastor Doug Nicholls of the Yorta Yorta people, Governor of South Australia in 1976, in a leadership training course at Evans Head. Both had proved highly effective teachers: "They definitely have an empathy with them [Aboriginal people] which no European can attain."[21] As well, the council submission wanted non-Aboriginal teacher trainees better prepared to teach Aboriginal students and in-service training available for public school teachers on Aboriginal culture and pedagogy.

Encouraging more Indigenous Australians to take up teaching as a career was not an initiative favoured by the Joint Committee when it presented its report in September 1967. Nor were its members impressed by arguments for special courses in Aboriginal education for teacher trainees given that NSW Aboriginal people were not in a tribal situation. "Provided teachers are sympathetic and have had adequate teaching experience, they can more than cope with the problem."[22] Indeed, the very idea of such training seemed to exasperate. When Gwendoline Phelan, the Research Officer of the NSW Teachers Federation took the stand, she found herself the object of a sharp lecture. "Why this particular class of people with a little different pigmentation of skin should require special attention," declared one committee member, "I cannot fathom."[23] Testiness was also displayed towards arguments that members thought not practically grounded, one witness being reminded that the committee must make its findings without the benefit of a professor of sociology or social work, and that its members did not have ten years to spare for social experimentation.[24]

However, Joint Committee members did attribute the low IQ scores of Aboriginal children and poor academic results to deprivation rather than innate difference, and they recommended an increased number of preschools, improved employment opportunities for school leavers, and more Grants-in-Aid and Commonwealth subsidies to keep children at high school. Extra places should be funded in technical education and classes for parents introduced to improve children's classroom behaviour and social conduct. Recognising that problems connected with housing, education, employment and welfare were interrelated, the Joint Committee welcomed the forthcoming abolition of the AWB and the integration of welfare services under a Director of Aboriginal Affairs. The report concluded on a party political note commending existing government policy on assimilation and opposing anti-discrimination legislation and land rights.

A Work of Many Hands

The Joint Committee of 1966 had praised the activities of the Consultative Committee on Aboriginal Education founded in 1963–64. Known as the Aboriginal Education Council (NSW) after 1968, the group was conceived originally to back the Department of Adult Education's programs. "Where possible," its draft constitution declared, "the Committee will assist in the work carried out by the tutor in Aboriginal Education, Department of Tutorial Classes, University of Sydney."[25] A substantial agency, the AEC (NSW) brought together Aboriginal leaders like Ken Brindle, Bert Groves and Clive Williams, and major Aboriginal organisations and education and school groups. Duncan was appointed the council's convener at its first meeting in April 1964 and continued in the chief role through to the end of 1975. Lee Gaynor was the Council's first Executive Secretary, later succeeded by the impressive Shirley Berg, previously President of the New South Wales Federation of Infants' School Clubs. Council funding relied on government assistance, business donations, and sums from individuals including the Nobel Laureate, Patrick White.

From a small office in Glebe paid for by a $10,000 donation from Victa Mowers, the AEC (NSW) organised tutoring, coaching and study centres. It also arranged an annual conference in collaboration with Adult Education and administered the substantial funds of the Norman Catts Trust and Abschol money. The council's Incentive Scholarship Scheme, which had begun with a pilot of six recipients, raised $10,000 in the period 1966–67,[26] funding 62 secondary and adult students. The scheme itself was based on personal links with scholarship holders and it demanded reasonable performance so as to eliminate any "hand-out" mentality. Many Aboriginal leaders in education benefited including Robert Morgan, Kay Mundine, Phil Nean, and Neville Perkins who took over its Ex-Scholars Association a year after he gained his HSC in 1970.

Another valued AEC (NSW) project, the Compensatory Assistance Scheme, supplied classroom materials for public schools with high Aboriginal enrolments at Weilmoringle, Wilcannia Central, Baryulgil, and Cabbage Tree Island public schools, and for the convent school at Wilcannia, St Theresa's. Compensatory assistance aimed to arrest the regression in the IQ of Aboriginal children as they progressed through the grades: "In the case of 150 children, he [Duncan] found their performance fell by one-third between the ages of 5 and 12."[27] Among those who assisted the assessment was Sue Pauling, the NSW DoE counsellor, a member of the AEC (NSW), and several Sydney staff members. It is estimated that the scheme assisted over 2000 students in primary and 500 in secondary by 2003, across 85 schools.[28] For all its good works, the council was not immune from controversy with members called "communists" during the Vietnam War.[29]

Two More Initiatives from Adult Education

In 1967–68, two new projects were launched, the first led by Ken Brindle, an Aboriginal Liaison Officer from Redfern, who organised regional conferences on Aboriginal self-engagement. Brindle's life story is remarkable. Taken from his parents aged ten months and made a Ward of the State, he progressed to Kinchela Boys Home, working on its farm and dairy before and after school. Shirley Berg was told "tales of the children having to go out to round up the cows bare foot and several of them ending up with very serious cases of frostbite".[30] At 15, Brindle was placed as a rouseabout on a sheep station before joining the army and fighting in Korea where he reached the rank of sergeant. Brindle advised

Geddes and Perkins in the management of the Foundation for Aboriginal Affairs, though sharply critical of its practices, and he was Vice-President of the AEC (NSW) and State Secretary of FCAATSI. His lasting achievement was the compilation of an index for 45,000 dusty files of children separated from their families held by the New South Wales State Records Office Archives.[31] After his death in 1987, the AEC (NSW) established the Ken Brindle Memorial Scholarships for Aboriginal students, providing $2000 for tertiary study for Indigenous Australians over 20. The first awards were presented in the Aboriginal Education Assistants lecture room in the Mackie Building in 1990. Ann Flood was the first ex-ATA to receive a Brindle Scholarship in 1991, when she was in the second year of her BEd (Primary).

Adult Education's second initiative, the Aboriginal Family Education Centres (AFECs), was led by the staffer, Alexander (Lex) Grey, a preschool extension officer with the Maori Educational Trust who had attended the Evans Head leadership course at Duncan's invitation in 1966.

> I took heart at the way in which the aboriginal people entered into the spirit of the course. I was not amazed; it was the reporters who visited the course who were surprised at how these people could concentrate.[32]

In 1967, Grey settled in New South Wales becoming staff tutor in psychology at Newcastle before taking charge of the new five-year AFEC scheme in 1969, assisted by his wife. Based on the Maori play centre concept, the project developed community networks through which Aboriginal families established their own preschool centres, running them themselves with help from Maori women as preschool supervisors and on-site trainers.[33] Most AFEC centres were in rural New South Wales but others opened in Chippendale, Redfern and Seven Hills. Centre work made good use of self activity materials, the learning occurring in a family setting with no formal class work. Certificates were awarded from Level I to VI (equivalent to a regular preschool qualification) to parents or grandparents who volunteered as teachers. The certificate ceremony at Mackie was hosted by Adult Education, the Chancellor presenting the awards during a program of Aboriginal language, poetry reading and music. Later, Aboriginal and non-Aboriginal individuals joined the training teams.

Despite a substantial grant from the Dutch-based Bernard Van Leer Foundation, supplemented by funding from the Commonwealth and state governments, and the Aboriginal participants holding the project manager, Lex Grey, in "very high regard",[34] the centre's results were mixed. In 1970, only eight or ten of the 100 families involved were displaying real commitment.[35] Other serious difficulties emerged, "mainly in the attitudes of whites",[36] some politicians and bureaucrats greeting the AFECs with patronage and condescension.[37] One federal minister suggested the Van Leer money would be better spent on creating sports trophies for athletics. As Grey reports:

> It was not uncommon to learn that we were regarded as city slickers, and therefore to be taken down a peg or two, and also because we belonged to the University to be regarded as, therefore, by hypothesis, communists.[38]

A number of non-Aboriginal people would take advantage of the scheme – buildings that should have taken ten weeks took ten months, and a rumour circulated that the AFEC was an Aboriginal women's movement.

While there was progress with Aboriginal efforts, "more than commensurate with their skills and circumstances", and "feelings of success",[39] Adult Education was told, "their priorities and emphases are not ours". Of the 13 centres established, six had lapsed by 1972. Other participants voted against accepting further government funding, it seeming not worth the effort to apply, and the trained preschools teams were disbanded, individuals joining groups like Save the Children Fund or the unemployed. However, Grey's informed study of the AFEC movement in 1975 made it clear that valuable lessons were learned.[40] Although a failure systemically, the AFECs did benefit individual children and their families, many parents becoming literate through them. Among the visitors in its later stage was Paulo Freire who told the workers: "You are building a people".[41] Grey himself moved on to other projects in Adult Education including working with disadvantaged children before joining the Aboriginal Affairs Advisory Team in the premier's department.

Introducing Aboriginal Teachers Aides (ATAs)

Aboriginal adult education progressed project by project at Sydney until the training of ATAs commenced at Sydney in 1975, a commitment that would last over 20 years. On the national scene, ATAs had served in Northern Territory government schools as helpers and substitute teachers from the early 1960s and in mission schools before then. By the 1970s, they were carrying substantial responsibilities across the Northern Territory as the Minister for Aboriginal Affairs, Les Johnson, noted: "Some are teaching on their own in schools (often no more than bush shelters) in decentralised communities, however, they are assisted by frequent visits from qualified inspectors."[42] Over time, many had become qualified teachers. New South Wales was the last of the mainland states and territories to appoint ATAs citing lack of funds, and the Commonwealth exerted pressure on the state to establish such a program, "since it was the last state to do so".[43] By the early 1970s, the failure of the New South Wales government to appoint Aboriginal aides had become an embarrassment.

Vera Byno is regarded as the first Aboriginal Teachers Aide in New South Wales. The young woman had enrolled in correspondence lessons in English and mathematics at Form 2 level at Weilmoringle Public School in 1969 relying on an Abschol payment. The following year, the school's Principal, Peter Dargin, announced: "Vera Byno has now finished her formal studies but is staying on at school to work with the younger children until she can start nurse training."[44] For this to have happened she required financial assistance. Here the AEC (NSW) came to the rescue paying her a double "Adult Incentive Scholarship", funded by Arunta Investments, a company established by the philanthropist, Gary Richardson, a Sydney graduate in Psychology. Dargin employed the 15-year-old five hours a week to assist three staff and around 50 children, principally in the Lower Division.[45] Byno has recalled these early days: "They wanted me to help with the children. I was nervous when I first started, but all the kids knew me and within a fortnight I got over it. I had no real problems."[46]

The Byno family, her mother, three sisters and a brother lived on the Weilmoringle Reserve on the banks of the Culgoa River about 110 kilometres north of Brewarrina and south of the Queensland border, home of the Aboriginal rainmakers. The township of 100 to 200 people comprised little more than a store, an Aboriginal settlement and a school. Most of the Aboriginal families were housed

> in tin humpies, basically 10' x 10' with branch shelters attached. Cooking is mainly done on open fires but some families have a special outdoor cooking gallery and two have wood burning stoves. Diet is limited, tea and damper being the staple food, with tinned food and fresh meat when available. Fish, yabbies, rabbit, kangaroo, pig, emu and porcupine are all additions to the diet. The campfire is still the social and domestic centre. Chairs and tables are few.[47]

Up to 1961, white children at Weilmoringle relied on correspondence lessons and there was no schooling for blacks. In 1962, a new public school replaced a temporary structure built the year before by the local Parents and Citizens Association, the complex also serving as an occasional preschool, local cinema and church.

The start of the Weilmoringle school year was typically unsettled with several weeks taken up determining just who was coming back after seasonal absences for cotton and fruit picking. Severe flooding in 1971 saw enrolments drop to 18 or so, and then to 11, after the local store ran out of food for school lunches. But by mid-year, numbers had built up again with 33 Aboriginal and 22 non-Aboriginal children enrolled across the school's three divisions, the Lower, the Upper and the Activity Group. Towards the end of 1971, Regional Office decided to cut the number of Weilmoringle's teachers from three to two.

Under guidance from Pat Dargin, Byno worked mainly with the Lower Division, helping with literacy groups and assisting in drill lessons, correcting papers and preparing craft work materials. From a desk in the First Aid Room, she handled the school banking and mail, helped prepare pupils' report cards, and operated the school duplicator; and, with Dargin or his wife occasionally absent, "Vera has been available to effectively supervise the Lower Division Groups which is of great importance as relief staff is unavailable." Dargin described her responsibilities "as more in line with those of an assistant teacher rather than the list of menial duties of a teacher's aide as set out by the Education Department."[48] All in all, the young ATA especially enjoyed the teaching side of her work: "I think the kids like it because they can get on better with an Aboriginal teacher."[49]

Dargin had film shot of Byno's work, especially her skill in assisting with the school's teaching kits, which boosted her case for continued employment. Weilmoringle had received its first grant of materials under the AEC's Compensatory Assistance Scheme in 1969, including additional sets of reading and maths boxes, a film projector and sewing materials, delivered by Duncan and Brindle in a "station wagon packed to the gunwales with goodies",[50] much to the excitement of all. This backing by the AEC (NSW) encouraged the Dargins to extend their time at Weilmoringle to six years in all.

With Byno employed close to full-time, the AEC (NSW) reimbursed the NSW DoE a teacher's aide salary of around $2500 from first term in 1973.[51] At last, Byno could support herself in her own community rather than having to subsist, as Dargin put it, "on the soul destroying acceptance of Social Service Assistance."[52] Her growing maturity was evident among her own people where she served as Deputy Chairman of the housing company, negotiating with the Lands Trust to build new homes on 16 acres of the Weilmoringle Station leasehold. She also went further academically, joining the first cohort of ATAs in training in 1975, and two others in her family, Josie and Rosie Byno, had connections with Sydney. It was this educational door that Byno opened for young adults that saw another ATA, Chris Tyson, who had trained as a teacher at Armidale College of Advanced Education, become Weilmoringle's first Aboriginal principal. When Dargin wrote to the AEC (NSW) in 1975, thanking members for their support of Byno and the school, he quoted a Chinese maxim: "If your plan is for one year plant rice; for ten years, plant trees; for a hundred years, educate men."[53]

Weilmoringle school had a reputation as a progressive institution in the Walgett district having introduced "open plan schooling", the children moving readily in and out of age groups according to their academic level, and from chair to floor. Byno's skills matched the progressive philosophy and her confidence encouraged local Aboriginal people to speak up at Parents & Citizens Association meetings and attend school occasions like sports days.[54] By the time Dargin took a promotion to Dubbo in 1976, he could report, "Children of our ex-pupils are now coming to preschool at three and four breaking the old habit of enrolment at six or seven years and indifference to school."[55] The school's best ever academic results were achieved in 1975, when Robyn Willis passed her school certificate. Weilmoringle's achievements overall were well received back in the Department of Adult Education whose Annual Report for 1971 singled out Byno's helpfulness as "very beneficial". Still, big problems continued especially for older children. Bussing them to Goodooga for secondary education created difficulties as did housing the students in hostels, with many of the Weilmoringle class ending up back on the river bank.

The Walgett Setting

It was no accident that the ATA movement was a product of the North West Education Region which contained one of the largest concentrations of Aboriginal students in the state. Seven hundred kilometres from Sydney, it supported a pastoral industry of mainly wool and wheat with Walgett at its centre. About 16 percent of the population of around 7000 was Aboriginal and, if the nearby reserves were counted, 45 percent altogether. The same town had a history of child removal and segregated schooling. Most of the Aboriginal people in the district were unemployed making for a dispirited school climate, an estimated 35 percent of Year 6 students being functionally illiterate, the bulk of them Aboriginal.[56] That

Figure 19. Laurie Craddock, Principal at Walgett Public School 1972. Image courtesy of Laurie Craddock.

this was not due to any natural deficiency was demonstrated by Laurie Craddock, Principal at Walgett Public, and his wife Peg, the school's librarian. "Aboriginal children will learn as well as their white counterparts," observed Craddock, "as long as the relationship between teachers and students is empathic, the pedagogy is right, and the curriculum relevant." In 1971, Craddock would report the greatest experience of his career when he took "twenty-four non-readers from third class and by the end of the year, they could all read".[57] Results under the Craddocks were validated when a specialist examiner sent to the town by the Director-General, Jack Buggie, reported literacy levels "on a par with the better schools in the state".

Among the Walgett educators who worked cooperatively to raise educational standards were the Dargins of Weilmoringle, Ed Gaskell from Walgett High School, Tom Allport, the District Inspector, and William (Bill) Rose, Assistant Director of Special Services. Duncan continued his role too, urging local principals to employ Aboriginal adults on scholarships to help with school work. "I had been impressed with the use of Indian teacher aides in schools on Reservations in Arizona and New Mexico, and made submissions for the appointment of Aboriginal Teacher Aides in schools in Australia."[58] As public racism diminished, the town was more supportive of Aboriginal education with attention paid to health issues through nurse appointments to schools and greater effort directed towards raising literacy. In the early 1970s, the Walgett people initiated a series of conferences, the Walgett Aboriginal Education Conferences, whose first Aboriginal contributor, Pastor Abel Morgan, gave a memorable talk on the theme of maintaining Aboriginal culture through the school system. Morgan's initiative led to the introduction of Aboriginal studies in schools in the region well before other places.[59]

The acceptance of ATAs moved a step forward in 1973, when the Walgett Aboriginal Conference executive sent a submission to state government arguing that "Aboriginal Teachers Aides be appointed to all schools with significant numbers of Aboriginal students."[60] Rose, playing his part, sent a separate memo to head office backing the idea. "The time is opportune," he wrote, "for this Department to seek the involvement of responsible Aboriginal adults of post-school age in the educational process."[61] Were ATAs appointed, he said, children would be better motivated to learn and stay longer. Attached to his memo was a draft set of guidelines for the ATA position put together by Rose and members of the Walgett Executive.

Allen at Walhallow

It was a legitimate boast of the AEC (NSW) that it had "pioneered"[62] the state's ATA movement. In 1972, the council took a step further by funding a second ATA, Heather Allen, at Walhallow Public, awarding her an Adult Scholarship followed by a salary the following year. As Walhallow's Principal, Eric Draper, told Duncan in 1973, "The Aboriginal Education Council is to be congratulated on the initiative shown in making the Aboriginal Teachers Aide Project possible."[63] Allen had left school in second year aged 14 and was in her 20s when she rejoined its three staff and 60 or so students.

Allen's people had long camped on the banks of the Mooki River at Walhallow Station where a 240-acre reserve was established in the late 19th century. In 1908 a school known as the Caroona Aboriginal School opened and a trained teacher-supervisor was appointed in 1962. Already well known in the Tamworth and Quirindi region for its sporting prowess, the Aboriginal school was renamed the Walhallow Public School five years later. However, shortly after Allen's appointment, news came that Walhallow would close in three years, its pupils to move to Caroona township. Vigorous objection from Aboriginal parents and local support by the AEC (NSW) followed and staff from Armidale Teachers College joined them arguing that Walhallow offered their trainees unique opportunities for practice teaching in a sympathetic Aboriginal community. Luckily Walhallow's case coincided with a shift in NSW DoE policy away from enforced closures and a stay of execution was allowed. The decision was also well received by parents from the nearby Caroona School who opposed the merger for other reasons.[64]

Aboriginal Education **61**

Allen proved her value in class and out. On a typical morning she taught infants and primary classes pre-reading, and the three Rs, making good use of the school's SRA Reading Laboratory and Triad and other kits. For three afternoons a week, she organised the library, filling out lesson plans, and familiarising herself with the teaching materials and school equipment and, on the other two, she worked at her own English assignments through the College of External Studies. Like Byno, Allen received full backing from her principal.

> Miss Allen has been able to establish her position with the children and at all times she has been treated with respect shown to the other members of staff. I feel this is indicative of her personality and impact on the children because she has to overcome the fact that she lives in the reserve and has close contact with the children on a vastly different atmosphere than that of school.[65]

After Draper moved to Kemblawarra Public School in 1974, his replacement, Reg Sams, made good use of Allen whose teaching skills were affirmed by departmental inspectors. In 1975, the NSW DoE finally took over payment of both Byno's and Allen's ATA salaries relieving the AEC (NSW) of what had become a significant financial drain. In December 1978, Allen became the first ATA to qualify as a fully trained teacher graduating from Guild Teachers College.

Further Recognition

In June 1974, Jack Buggie, Director-General of Education, took up the suggestion put by Rose at Walgett applying to the NSW Public Service Board for permission to seek Commonwealth funds for 20 ATAs who were to assist teachers through one-on-one activities in the classroom, small-group teaching and liaison with the local community. Buggie pointed out that this move would open up career opportunities for "responsible Aborigines of post-school age".[66] In 1975, a further 27 aides were appointed, and 13 more up to 1976, bringing the total number of Commonwealth-funded positions to 60. Non-government schools employed another ten.[67] Their success was immediate and the New South Wales government was soon protesting that numbers were too low: one count in 1979 recorded 122 state schools with at least 25 Aboriginal children enrolled, however the Commonwealth refused to fund more than 60 places.

ATA positions were advertised by individual schools with applicants selected by school based committees usually with Aboriginal representation and confirmed by Regional Office after consultation with the District Inspector. Listed as temporary ancillary staff members, they worked on average 31.25 hours a week for an annual wage from $3718 to $6320.[68] While ATAs were not paid during school vacations or entitled to superannuation, and their positions were reviewed annually, they did receive four weeks annual holiday pay and study time in the home school if on course.

Up to 1987, ATAs were known variously as Teacher's Aides (Special), Teacher's Aides (Special and Ethnic), and Teacher's Aides (Aboriginal). However, those ATAs who underwent training at Sydney called themselves Aboriginal Teaching Assistants, the title better reflecting their duties, an opinion the University shared as it named its training program the Aboriginal Teaching Assistants Training Program (ATATP). However, use of the title, Aboriginal Teaching Assistant, was opposed by the NSW DoE on grounds that it confused ATAs with regular teachers who were designated Assistant Teachers. Another matter of contention was whether priority should be given to the "teaching" component of their work or the "aides" component. Finally, in 1986, all parties agreed to adopt a new title, Aboriginal Education Assistant (AEA), and their training course was renamed the Aboriginal Education Assistants Training Program (AEATP).

When the first duty statement for ATAs was issued in 1975, there was no direct reference to any teaching function in the classroom.

> Aides' Duty Statement
>
> 1. Under direction of the class teacher (the aide) assists children in practising general social skills in personal hygiene and domestic tasks, including table setting, washing up, floor sweeping, hand washing, teeth cleaning, cleaning and changing soiled children.
> 2. As required, accompanies teachers on class outings and excursions.
> 3. Cares for and issues some equipment required in classroom activities, labels towel racks and case lockers, unpacks and fits special sports uniforms.
> 4. Assists in preparation of food for children.
> 5. As required, launders and irons such items as tea towels, lunch mats and oversights children who assist in these tasks.
> 6. As required, prepares teaching materials, particularly for art and handwork activities, also physical education and rhythm.
> 7. As required, assists at arrival and departure of children.
> 8. Assists in care of sick children, and where in receipt of a first aid allowance, administers minor first aid.
> 9. Any other related duties as required by the Principal from time to time.[69]

This omission of the teaching function encouraged the view of some principals that ATAs were no different from general clerical aides, a misconception that led to confusion and occasional acrimony.

Tales out of School

In her book, *Over My Tracks*, the respected Auntie Ev Crawford of Brewarrina wrote about her experiences teaching Aboriginal children that started with her engagement as an unpaid "reading mum at Brewarrina".[70] Crawford and her close friend Olive Brown were later talked into applying for one of the new ATA jobs by Rose and to move to Sydney for training.

> Olive was like me. We were both sort of hungry for knowledge because it was from Bill Rose that we both got a taste of how important education is. We know that if we wanted to be in that education system, and get other people to come forward and do the same thing after us, we'd have to work bloody hard to get in, and to be accepted, because we started from scratch. The challenge was there for me, an old woman almost fifty, and I never, ever walked away from a challenge in my life and I'm sure Olive and Yvonne [Bolton] never did either. So we hung in there.

Returning to her home school in 1977, Crawford found the white teachers assumed that ATAs were there to wash cups and tea towels and, when children made a mess, to clean it up.

> We tried our level best to become friends with all the teachers on a professional basis, as colleagues. One of the white teachers said, "Where do you get all the confidence from, anyway?" Blanche said, "Well, me and Aunty Ev got ours from Sydney University. We trained there …" Lots of teachers just assumed that we were picked up out of the gutter, dusted off and put in the classroom. They had no idea that we were trained people, and they never asked.

However, it was not long before these redoubtable women educated their schools of their value for their own people and for white children.

> If there was a kid who could not, or would not, learn to read and write, he'd be handed over to us and in no time at all we'd have that kid out of his shell, startin' to read and write, talkin' up, mixin' at sports with the rest of the kids. When other teachers seen what we were doin' on a one-to-one or small group basis – there were two more aides then – they'd send us more kids and we'd send 'em back to the classroom confident kids.

Schools that employed ATAs like Auntie Ev and Olive Brown were indeed fortunate. They became the mother to all the kids of the school, increasing the status of the ATAs and benefiting their communities. As numbers increased, more children took ATAs as their role models. Grace Coe, the ATA at Condoblin, explains:

> Many of the Aboriginal kids at the school are my nieces or nephews and the white children might say "That is your auntie." And they say "Yes." They use me as the ideal. The white children than realize that the black kids won't all grow up to be alcoholics or no-hopers or gaol birds, perhaps they will become teachers' aide or nurses or whatever.[71]

For many Aboriginal women and some men, an ATA position was a genuine career option. By the end of the 70s, the NSW DoE bureaucracy had become the largest employer of Aboriginal people of any NSW government department, with 60 ATAs on staff and another 20 Indigenous Australians employed in various other positions.[72]

Rose, who had persuaded several uncommitted headmasters to accept ATAs, spoke with confidence of the success of the Walgett initiative and the skills of his recently recruited men and women. Aboriginal children could now look up and say, "There is one of my people in my school."[73] Rose also drew attention to the small number of Aboriginal teachers employed in state schools in 1975, four in all, and another 18 in training – still they were a start. "Admittedly they are not at the decision making level, and I would have to agree that that is so. It will take time in education, and in law, medicine, local government, and in industry and commerce to reach top management positions." The departmental head observed that Aboriginal people were now working effectively in the education sector, a clear Aboriginal voice in a partnership of black and white. Education had shown itself "the most important strategy for achieving realistic self-determination for the Aboriginal people of Australia".

Further Initiatives from Adult Education

Duncan's activities in Aboriginal adult education were increasingly valued inside the University. He was promoted to senior staff tutor in 1968, then lecturer and, following his MEd thesis on the history of Aboriginal education in New South Wales, senior lecturer. In 1974, Duncan organised a second visit to New Zealand for staff from the Department of Technical Education investigating trade training for Aboriginal people, the experience leading to pre-vocational training in NSW; and, around that time, Duncan took up cudgels for another major project – the introduction of an Associate Diploma in Aboriginal Rural Education.

> I put up the idea of a rural studies program for a Diploma of Education; the University of Sydney was horrified. The Macarthur Institute of Higher Education introduced the Aboriginal Rural Education Program which was very successful. John Lester assessed it and helped introduce it.[74]

Down the track, Duncan's good relations with Macarthur would prove a valuable lever in the institution's acceptance of Sydney's training certificate.

In 1976, increasing recognition of ATAs' classroom teaching role saw the time available for home liaison fall off. That year a decision was taken to trial an Aboriginal Home-School Coordinators Scheme (AHSCS) focusing on external community involvement, an initiative led by Duncan and Kay Mundine from the AEC (NSW), and backed by Associate Professor Arthur J. More, from the University of British Columbia and architect of a similar plan in Canada's Western Provinces, who was visiting the Department of Adult Education. AHSCS received a Commonwealth Schools Commission grant and Avis Ivanoff, an ATA from Marrickville Girls High, Mary Button from Kempsey South, and Ev Crawford of Brewarrina Central were appointed coordinators. While they did an exceptional job, the project failed to attract long-term Commonwealth or state money,[75] folding in September 1980 despite a highly favourable evaluation. A few years later, the New South Wales Department of Education did recognise two Home-School Coordinators in Penrith and Dubbo and Regional Aboriginal Community Liaison Officers (RACLOs) were introduced in 1989 with somewhat similar duties.

Taking six months study leave in 1979, Duncan was back in Canada and Scandinavia researching teacher education among indigenous minorities. He also found time to hold office in the AEC (NSW), advise the Labor Party and the NSW Teachers Federation on Aboriginal education, and serve as part-time State Commissioner for Multicultural and Ethnic Affairs. His contribution to national life was recognised by an OAM in 1982.

Not everything went smoothly on the administrative side though. Originally Duncan had money for research and secretarial assistance from the AWB and Commonwealth, but the winding up of the AWB and changes in Commonwealth funding led to the loss of the research position in 1973, and his secretarial assistance and travel payments were threatened. Help from the YWCA and the AEC (NSW) rescued him at least until 1975, but when the council could no longer continue payment, Duncan was restricted to the secretarial resources of the ATA training program.

As Aboriginal adult education established itself in the University, the openness and evident good will towards Aboriginal people by staff in the Department of Adult Education made Mackie a reference point for those seeking career materials and educational advice. Altogether, the department's Aboriginal Adult Education program covered leadership training, organisation seminars, ATA training, cultural, trade and vocational education, and counselling. Here, director Des Crowley speaks for its philosophy:

> Work in the area of Aboriginal adult education is always, to some extent, experimental; it is, in effect, a program of action research in which University expertise and standards need constantly to be applied. It is complex work, carried on within a section of society undergoing constant and rapid social and political change. It profits from being carried on in a University, with its strong traditions of objectivity and independence and with a high level of acceptance in the Aboriginal community.[76]

4

ATA Training Underway

> The importance of the New South Wales scheme is in the proposed training program which will be carried out through the University of Sydney's Adult Education Department.
>
> Eric Willmot, *Walgett Papers*, 1971–75[1]

When the Commonwealth government indicated that it would fund the training of ATAs as well as their salaries, the Department of Adult Education, a formidable candidate given its expertise in non-degree teaching, was the successful bidder. No consensus existed nationally as to the best training model for teacher's aides: some states and territories utilised school-based and in-service training; others preferred short departmental courses or TAFE qualifications; and one state, South Australia, operated a superior program through Torrens College of Advanced Education. By 1974, a determination as to what kind of training should be undertaken at the University was urgent as the first ATAs were close to appointment.

As early as 1972, Duncan had started to think about training, having discussions with Byno and the Walgett educators as to content.[2] As his draft took shape, Duncan made use of the Walhallow ATA, Heather Allen, as "guinea pig",[3] the young woman visiting Sydney periodically, her travel paid for by the AEC (NSW). Their draft training outline was well received when passed to a joint committee comprising Adult Education and the NSW DoE, members anticipating that the program would attract candidates from other government and voluntary agencies.[4] Adult Education was represented on the panel by its new director, the New Zealander, Desmond (Des) W. Crowley, with a doctorate from the London School of Economics. Prior to his Sydney appointment, Crowley had been Assistant Director of Adult Education at the University of Adelaide. An active supporter of programs for Aboriginal people, he accepted that the training program now engrossing Duncan was a legitimate expansion of his duties and time well spent. Alas, his own period at Sydney was bedevilled by financial stringency and schemes to shut down the department.

Early in 1975, the NSW DoE told newly appointed ATAs they must enrol in a "substantial course of training at Sydney University, under the direction of Mr A.T. Duncan",[5] in their first year. While the language of the departmental memo inferred that the training was a condition of employment, this requirement was not enforced although a willingness to travel to Sydney was raised in the selection process. To enable the better acceptance of training time spent away from home, Buggie directed that all students receive full salary while on course.

"Pioneers of 1975"

New Dawn sent a reporter to the opening of the Aboriginal Teaching Assistants Training Program (ATATP) in March 1975, when 20 women and two men, aged from 16 to 47 years, started the first session of 12 weeks training in the Mackie Building. Most class members were married women in their 30s with families at school.

> The areas from which the trainees come (such as Narrandera, Menindee, Brewarrina, Foster, and Bomaderry) are as varied as their ages and education. They range in Education standard from "just left in primary" to Higher School Certificate level.[6]

Later in the session, a Commonwealth-funded ATA would join the group from St Ignatius Convent School, Bourke.

Kerry McLeod was appointed the ATATP's "teacher-educator"[7] and given the duty of escorting the arrivals on an orientation tour around town. The places of interest included Parliament House, where the Minister of Education provided morning tea. One of the newly enrolled ATAs, Avis Ivanoff, has recorded her fears and feelings at the time:

> When I first went to Sydney to do the training course for the "Teachers Assistant", I had a lot of doubts about a lot of things. What would the others be like, was I only having myself on? Would I be able to keep up with the others, did any of the other women smoke? I always feel uncomfortable if I am the only one that smokes. Did any of the others drink in excess or I might end up with a bible basher?

> Then at "Kirinari", as we waited for the people from the department, were they genuine in what they were doing? What did they care about us "blacks"; just a lot of do-gooders, who will take these little blackfellas and mould them into what they want. But as always the more one worries about things the worse they appear to be, and as it happens everything turned out very good. The group of teachers' assistants turned out to be a great lot of people, and the people from the department were absolutely marvellous.

> I feel that having "Teachers Assistants" of Aboriginal descent is a big step up the ladder and that all Aboriginal children will benefit by it, even though most Aboriginal people don't see it now?[8]

To round off the year, the students of '75 attended the AEC (NSW) conference, Education Without Discrimination, hearing papers from the Minister for Aboriginal Affairs, Les

Figure 20. Six graduates of the Aboriginal Teaching Aides Training Course, 1975. Image courtesy of the Woodbury family.

Johnson, and the state department's Bill Rose, and mixing with established Aboriginal educators like Eric Willmot and the Queenslander, Margaret Valadian. It was the latter who urged the students to take their learning further – the ATA position, she said, must not become "a dead end road".

> Somehow we must begin to think as to how these members of the community can be given the support they need and the assistance they need to become fully fledged teachers in the community, if they so desire.[9]

Comments from Students on Course

Students soon made themselves comfortable in the classroom as Norma Hayman, the lecturer in communication, told the AEC (NSW) newsletter, *Duran-Duran*.

> Pluses are impressive. Some of these students arrived in Sydney a while back as frightened "bushies", terrified of the noise, the pace, the task they had taken on by accepting their job in the local school as an Aboriginal Teaching Assistant. Most had left school early and many told stories that revealed how cursory most of their education had been. Even the lucky ones had not seen their schooling as relevant to them. Now they sit in class with an idea of their own worth, an eager acceptance of the strain of new ideas on old concepts. We are working on methods to cope with this strain when it arrives.[10]

Hayman recognised the need to extend ATAs ability to express their ideas, setting a class exercise one lazy Friday afternoon: "All right you tell me. What on earth makes you an Aborigine?"

THE UNIVERSITY OF SYDNEY

DEPARTMENT OF ADULT EDUCATION

ABORIGINAL TEACHER'S AIDE CERTIFICATE
1975

This is to certify that

Joyce Woodberry

has completed at a satisfactory standard
the study assignments, seminar discussions and written exercises
in conjunction with practical classroom experience
in the Aboriginal Teaching Assistants' Training Course
conducted by this Department at

FIRST (ELEMENTARY) LEVEL

Senior Lecturer   Director
Aboriginal Adult Education   Department of Adult Education

Figure 21. Aboriginal Teachers Aide Certificate, 1975.
Image courtesy Woodberry family 2009.

One response to Hayman's question was from Denise Kelly, an ATA at Nanima Public.

> Well, I think that it's because my parents and aunts and uncles and cousins and all the rest of the clan are Aboriginal. If people look at me they can see that I am an Aboriginal by the colour of my skin. I am very proud to be an Aboriginal. I know other nationalities are better off than the Aboriginal or at least they think that they are. If it was possible for me to learn how to speak my own language I would use it almost all the time. I would love to teach the younger Aboriginal children how to speak their own language and I'm sure that when they are older that they would be very grateful to me for teaching them. I know a bit about some of the Aboriginal rituals but I cannot tell anybody else about them. If I do I was told that something will happen to me.

This second extract was written by Vickie Stanley of Wellington Public.

> What makes me an Aboriginal? Well, the thing I love most is the colour of my skin. I have been told that I am a lovely chocolate colour, and I am so different

Figure 22. Aboriginal Teaching Assistant Course and Koori Centre lecturer, Julie Janson. Image courtesy of the Koori Centre.

to my close white friend. I have so many jokes about it, like in the summer time I have to sit in the shade because I peel first. Strange, isn't it? I really laugh about this, because the white girls sit in the sun for so long just trying to turn brown, but we're lucky, we've got it all year round. The thing I treasure most of all are my parents. They are both proud Aboriginals and so am I.

This third example comes from George Day, the ATA at Deniliquin, which tackled some of the differences between Aboriginal and non-Aboriginal people.

> We do not seek fortune, we are content with what we have. We live every day as it comes, not as it should be. We are very spiritual. We believe in the supernatural and believe that they can communicate with us in different ways. I never had to be told that I am Aboriginal, it came from within. The way I eat, the way I think, the way I feel, it is all Aboriginal. If a person you're with claims to be Aboriginal you can soon pick up if he is or not, just by studying and observing his actions and his reactions to different situations. An Aboriginal can share thoughts and secrets with another Aboriginal in depth. Can a European do this?

With some students fearing that formal education would make them more white and less Aboriginal, Hayman created a two-way perspective on issues in class.

Julie Janson joined the ATATP in 1979 as lecturer in creative and expressive arts, holding a BVis Arts, and DipEd, and, later, an MA in Theatre Arts. A woman of Aboriginal descent, Janson was a gifted teacher, playwright and painter, and her lively accounts of ATA life speak for themselves.

> There was a small courtyard where student ATAs could have a smoke or glimpse the sun. We would take our cups of tea out there and have a laugh. It was like a

family, some of the students and occasionally lecturers, would bring their babies in to look after them in class, I remember breast feeding my baby with Veronica Davison feeding hers too.[11]

As to teaching activities, Janson wrote:

> We improvised and performed plays about Koori lives in country town, about Debutante Balls and football knockouts and love and alcoholic uncles and great Koori matriarchs. We went on Aboriginal site visits to [an] ancient petroglyph rock engraving in the Sydney sand stone country with Koori site officers. We recorded the large rock engravings on plastic sheets and brought them back to the classroom to create huge murals. We visited the storage rooms of the Australian Museum and drew the ancient artefacts from individual NSW Koori nations.

The Curriculum

When the ATA curriculum received the stamp of approval from its Joint Committee, five fields of study and one optional subject were listed:

1. Educational Psychology which covered genetics, and the nature nurture debate, and prenatal development. Language, personality, emotional and social development, and perception, were also included.

2. Educational Methodology dealt with the role of the ATA, teaching methods in Aboriginal schools, the teacher-child relationship, and child study and experiential applications. The Educational Psychology and Education Methodology courses ran parallel to each other and were related in the timing of content.

3. English/Communication/Expressive Arts promoted written and oral communication skills, understanding communication, Aboriginality, appreciating others and self confidence, arguing and debating, appreciation of literature, expressive art classes and relaxation exercises.

4. Elementary Anthropology and Sociology was in two parts: a) Anthropology, the comparative study of traditional and contemporary cultures and societies including Aboriginal, and the impact of Europeans on Aboriginal society. As well, Aboriginal and Western values, Aboriginal education past and present, and Aborigines in contemporary Australian society were studied; and b) Social Sciences, the comparative study of multicultural societies, rural and urban society, environmental issues, prejudice and discrimination, disadvantaged and pressure groups. An important aspect of this subject was the development of a critical awareness of the media in its various forms.

5. Government and Current Affairs outlined the establishment of government in Australia including NSW, functions of local, state and

federal governments, and government attitudes and action on Aboriginal affairs. Current national and international issues were discussed in class.

6. Optional: the St John's First Aid Certificate course.[12]

As Janson explains, not all content was available in acceptable form as much information about Aboriginal culture found in textbooks and school libraries was distorted and outdated.

> We rewrote the history of NSW from an Aboriginal point of view on the board, before the historians such as Peter Read and Henry Reynolds had their books published to guide us. We investigated family histories and Aboriginal language; we recorded interviews with elders to preserve the heritage for our children.[13]

Revised materials were typed on roneo sheets for classroom use and copied laboriously into exercise books.

Training Operations

The ATATP certificate comprised three levels: Level I (Basic) was equivalent to the School Certificate, Level II (Upgrading) to Form V, and Level III (Intensive) to the HSC. It was intended that the certificate be awarded only after completion of the full course but demands for recognition of lower level attainments, including attendance, saw statements of achievement issued along the way. Normally, the Basic course ran for 12 weeks over four sessions under the "block release" mode whereby full-time study was interspersed with school employment and vacations. This delivery mode enabled adult students to attend the program in Sydney, with minimal time away from families and community. Initially, the NSW DoE wanted ATAs in Sydney for eight-week sessions but the trainees thought the maximum time they could spare was two to three weeks at a time, a point the department conceded. Students who were performing well in the Basic and Upgrading were invited to join the Intensive course held over five weeks in November, which demanded examinations. Furthermore, second-year students who held the Basic and wanted to try for the Intensive could join the five-week Upgrading and enter the Intensive later that year. Two Sydney CAEs, Guild and Milperra, recognised a pass in the Intensive for entry to their teacher education qualification from the beginning.

Course assessment was flexible. Those who failed assignments were given the opportunity to re-submit and students could bank subjects for later recognition should they not complete the full year. It was ATATP's strength, said Duncan, "That no-one ever failed – the course was designed to meet the students' own needs."[14] Workloads were heavy, every week on course requiring about 25–30 hours face-to-face teaching, and further study was demanded back in their schools on one or two afternoons a week helped by local tutoring if available. In 1976, lecturer numbers were increased to three to cover the ATATP's work demands, including an in-service program, with new staff briefed on how to overcome residual negativity from students' past educational experiences.

The program's first Aboriginal lecturer, Barry Thorne, reported that progressive teaching arrangements were the cornerstone of the ATATP's success.

> With the flexibility attached to the Program you could really let your head go whilst remaining within the structure of the course outline. I think that's good for teachers because it allows them to be a little more creative, and exposes, through their creativeness, an opportunity for the students to capitalise upon whatever teachers want to offer them or expose them to.[15]

Staff meetings were held regularly to assess individuals' progress and the teaching program was evaluated in open session with students present.

While a few of the older ATAs had no more than primary schooling, most students had one or two years of secondary, and the youngsters could often boast three or more. The fact that course results were frequently outstanding can be attributed to the students' high motivation. "Very often students with very little formal secondary education," Duncan revealed, "are the ones who are subsequently invited to undertake the highest level Intensive Course and do so with distinction."[16]

Country students commuted to Sydney by bus, train and plane, their travel and accommodation arranged by office staff. Various venues were tried out – among them the YWCA and the People's Palace in the city, International House at the University, Kirinari Aboriginal Students Hostel established by the Aboriginal Children's Advancement Society at Sylvania, and the Whitehall Motor Inn at Rushcutters Bay. No location proved ideal given noise, house rules, high cost, and distance from the University.

When funding allowed, program staff visited ATAs in their schools. In 1975, Duncan toured several schools in north and northwest New South Wales and John Skelton and staff visited other regions a year later. A set of guidelines was prepared for the visits reminding lecturers of the significance of good relations. Their calls were "a public relations exercise made primarily in the interests of the ATAs",[17] and outcomes should aim at mutual cooperation and respect. "Should any Principal show evidence of negative attitudes or prejudice against Aboriginals, there is no mileage whatsoever in confrontation." For their part, students were asked to complete a survey about their home schools including their own duties, and assessments of class tone and discipline, a task calling for tact and diplomacy. Returns indicated that principals interpreted ATAs' duty statements quite differently: some ATAs were fully engaged in teaching and community work while others spent up to 80 percent of their time on administration chores such as covering books, checking rolls or duplicating.[18]

Graduation

The academic year for ATAs ended with a Graduation Week celebration, family and friends coming up from the country for the big day. Their graduation ceremony captured the essence of the University occasion. On the day, the Chancellor, Sir Hermann Black, presided in panoply of gold and black embroidered silk as the students, in their black gowns, and called by name, came forward to receive their awards and prizes. As Duncan saw it:

> The Chancellor of the University of Sydney considered the ATA Graduation Ceremony to be of equal importance to any graduation ceremony at the University. He would don his Chancellor's robes and there would be an academic procession and there would be all the "la-di-da" of an academic occasion. It was tremendously impressive. I've never forgotten it to see those first students – heads held high, walk down to receive their certificate. That was one of the greatest impressions I had of the Program.[19]

In fact the trappings of the day had their own part to play. Inside the NSW DoE, there were powerful doubters of the worth of the University's ATA Certificate, however the fact that Black presented the awards, preceded by the mace bearer symbolising the authority of Senate, was considered proof positive that the award was bona fide.

in 1975, 19 ATAs, including two men, graduated at the Manning House ceremony, seven with Level I Certificates, seven at Level II, and five at Level III.[20] Four ATAs did not complete for various reasons, one taking alternative employment, the others unable to attend all sessions; the latter three were expected to return in 1976. Eric Willmot, Senior Education Officer with the Commonwealth, one-time horse-breaker, graduate in science from the University of Newcastle, and teacher, gave the address. The ATA training program, the audience was told, was "just a beginning in providing for Aborigines a more equal op-

Figure 23. Aboriginal Teacher Assistants relaxing in the Mackie Building Courtyard: Emily Walker, Raymond Donovan, and Helen Archibald. Image courtesy of the Koori Centre.

portunity in education".[21] The Manning ceremony concluded with Jackie Field replying on behalf of the students and Joyce Black, who presented the posies and buttonholes, accepting a sheaf from David Green.

It was evident that ATA training added an essential element of academic preparation for full-time teaching. As one trainee told Duncan, "It was easy after what you gave us."[22] Four of the five Level III graduates, Heather Allen (Walhallow), Rita Bostock (Redfern), Jackie Field (Lethbridge Park), and David Green (Moree), entered the teacher education course at the Guild Teachers College, however the fifth, Carol Wilson (Baryugil), was unable to join them having a young family to care for. One of the group, Rita Bostock, transferred from Guild to Kedron Park Teachers College in Queensland. On graduation from Kedron Park, she taught at Bendool Primary in Brisbane before taking up an identified curriculum consultant's job with the Queensland Education Department. "The fact is that she is the only person in Brisbane with the proper qualifications to take this job – Aboriginality and teacher training."[23] The significance of these ATA pioneers entering teaching can be appreciated as just four Aboriginal teachers were employed in New South Wales in 1976, where an estimated 10,000 Aboriginal children were in class.[24]

Kerry McLeod was succeeded as lead teacher in 1976 by Chris Adams, well qualified with a DipTeach, BA, and MA in Education (Human Development), with previous teaching experience in Australia and the US. She was responsible for the lectures in educational psychology and educational methodology. Other members of her full-time team were Norma Hayman in communication, and Geoffrey Hunt, who taught introductory anthropology and sociology, current affairs and government. On Hunt's death in August 1977, Wayne Hooper from Adult Education saw the year out. Deirdre Koller was Graduate Clerk in the ATATP, Leslee Curraey, Secretary, and John Skelton and A. Madge Dawson from Adult Education, part-time counsellors. Skelton also served as deputy director when Duncan was out of town.

Course enrolments increased to 38 in 1976, the extra numbers enabling students to split into "north" and "south" groups in Level I. Eventually, 35 students graduated, six in Level I, 20 in Level II and nine in Level III, including four who had upgraded from the Level II course.[25] Another 36 ATAs had joined the in-service training program where Oodgeroo Noonuccal (Kath Walker) was among the teachers. Wilmot gave the address to the gathering of 200 relatives and friends. Of the Level III graduates, three would enrol in CAEs and another, Barbara Kennedy, was admitted to the BEd (Primary) at Sydney, though forced to withdraw for home reasons. Kennedy's recognition by the Department of Education was the first at the University. "We now feel we can venture into anything and succeed",[26] one graduating student told an AEC (NSW) representative.

Although the Commonwealth had frozen the number of ATA positions at 60, course numbers were maintained by the turnover in appointments and additional enrolments from non-government schools and preschools. At the end of 1977, 28 trainees graduated, eight in Level I, and ten each in Levels II and III. This third graduation was chaired by Joss Davies, Acting Director of Adult Education, with Yvonne Bolton, the ex-ATA and Aboriginal

Figure 24. Aboriginal Teachers Aides: Hilda Duncan (Moree Primary), Kevin Williams (Brewarrina Central), and Rhonda Gray (Research Liaison Officer, from "Murawina" Redfern) talk with Program Lecturer, Chris Adams, 1979. Image courtesy of University of Sydney Archives.

Liaison Teacher, on the dais.[27] Sheilagh Williams replied for the students. "We are role models for both black and white children", she told the gathering. Williams went on to pay Duncan a special tribute: he was their "Big Daddy" who is "really one of us".[28] Eight students were accepted for tertiary education that year, the highest number yet.

Funding Arrangements

The big challenge of the late 1970s was how to balance income and expenditure. The initial Commonwealth allocation of $26,000, paid via the NSW DoE, was deemed sufficient for the initial intake in 1975 and the grant was increased to $85,450 for 1976, when numbers were expected to double.[29] Although this sum was adequate for teaching and secretarial help, the Commonwealth would not fund travel or accommodation costs. Duncan explains:

> Each year I had to write submissions for funding to DAA. Their staff, always white people, would come and "inspect" the place. They were critical and most unsympathetic and always demanding of their "pound of flesh". They never ever could see what the Program was about. I was always going cap in hand asking for

cheaper rates for books, materials, accommodation etc. I could never get St John's Ambulance to cut their fee or official rates for the First Aid course they ran for the Program. We had to drop it in the end because funds were so limited … It really was a disgrace the lack of funds – I just had to scratch around all the time.[30]

The AEC (NSW) helped the budget by picking up travel and accommodation costs in 1975 but was in no position to underwrite the program longer term, as its president noted:

> The drop in public donations this year reflects a situation which is facing all voluntary organisations working in the field of Aboriginal advancement. The tremendous increase in government expenditure on Aboriginals has been taken to mean that voluntary organisations no longer require the level of public support they previously received.[31]

Indeed the AEC (NSW) was the meat in a sandwich. While there was a public perception that Aboriginal people were receiving more than their fair share of government assistance, Aboriginal opinion was that this money went to white administrators. Nor could Commonwealth largesse be relied upon. In 1970, it brought the AEC (NSW) $20,500, in 1972, $10,850, and, in 1974, nil. A significant drop in donors had followed Commonwealth intervention, contributions falling from $42,419 in 1972 to $13,753 in 1974.[32] This led the council to consider biding for government project work and for donations for primary student scholarships outside the Commonwealth's remit. Nevertheless, it did find the money for small payments for the ATATP like conference expenses and graduation extras and for reference and textbooks from the Margaret Kent Hughes Memorial Trust Fund. Individual ATAs from remote townships facing family emergencies at home could also draw on council money.

> For example, there was the case of the Aboriginal trainee who had left her children in a remote country town in the care of a relative. News arrived that the relative had taken ill. The mother needed to return to her home to see her children and to make other arrangements for their welfare. But she had no money for the return fare.[33]

In such instances the AEC (NSW) provided an airfare, rescuing them from two or three days of bus and train travel. The inability of the AEC (NSW) to assist further meant that the NSW DoE was forced to apply one or other of its Commonwealth accounts for travel and accommodation in 1976.

A spotlight was put on ATAs' miserable pay and conditions in 1980 when a group of ATAs aired grievances at the Anti-Discrimination Board, the Commissioner assessing them as grossly underpaid at $4.85–$5.44 an hour. Economic hardship was exacerbated for those on course as many had young children but no childcare money and no per diem allowance in Sydney. Their shabby treatment aside, the Anti-Discrimination Commissioner pronounced the ATA positions as "one of the more important avenues of educational advancement for Aboriginal people."[34] It seems some notice was taken of the complaints with ATAs receiving a salary boost to the level of Teacher's Aides (Special and Ethnic).

Gaining a Reputation

Knowledge of the University's unique ATA training scheme spread beyond Sydney. At the National Conference on Aboriginal Education held at Mt Lawley College of Advanced Education in August 1977, an interested audience heard Duncan explain the workings of the ATATP.[35] Duncan's talk was followed by a paper from Davina Tyrrell, an ex-ATA and student at the Guild Teachers College, who claimed that ATA students received a more comprehensive training at Sydney than was the case elsewhere, no other training program being comparable. These talks, and a third by Craddock of Walgett fame, encouraged lively discussion at an institution itself renowned for having opened one of the nation's first enclaves in 1975.

Testimony to the worth of the ATATP also came from state and Commonwealth politicians. ATAs had met the Minister for Education at Parliament House in 1975 and local politicians spoke at Mackie and during graduation ceremonies. Two supportive Commonwealth Ministers for Aboriginal Affairs were Les Johnson and Robert Ian Viner, the latter informing the AEC (NSW) by letter on 30 July 1976 that the ATATP set an example for other states to follow. "The training of Aboriginal teaching assistants," he wrote, "has high priority in the programmes administered by my department."[36]

ATAs were making an impact inside the University as well. Those working in inner city schools helped Associate Professor Robert Eagleson in 1983 with a study of Aboriginal English; Delma Davison acted as Professor Sam Ball's research associate in 1985 in the ATATP Evaluation; and Barbara Kennedy, an ATA from Wee Waa Central and a member of the National Aboriginal Education Committee (NAEC), was the Research Associate for Associate Professor Arthur More in his ATATP assessment, *A Solid Link in the Chain*. When Kennedy submitted her application to work for More, she attached a statement reflecting favourably on her Sydney training.

> Because the education system is directed at the middle-class European child, the Aboriginal child comes to think that he and his family are not "normal". This sometimes causes him to deeply resent his parents. They soon discover that their pattern of life is not socially acceptable. They are made to feel inferior. So I attacked this problem and with the training we do at the Sydney University in self-development, academic improvement and communication lectures, I can truthfully say that Aboriginal parents and children are beginning to want to understand each other again.[37]

Funding for the More evaluation proved tight. A request for $1800 to cover Kennedy's travel and accommodation costs was turned down by the NSW DoE before DAA's research division came to the rescue. Only $1600 was available at the end point, the University deducting $200 from the Commonwealth cheque for payroll tax, workers compensation and annual leave.

Joining the Debate on Aboriginal Education

ATAs were soon contributing to the public debate. In 1977, *Duran-Duran* published a thoughtful paper by Laurie Crawford, an ATA at Walgett High School, who had not proceeded beyond Level III training, the journal said, for family obligations and because he had chosen "to stop within the school and work for his own people".[38] Crawford made telling points on the situation of the Aboriginal child in the New South Wales school system.

> For white children early home experiences and perceptions were deepened by school. For Aboriginal children though, their home experiences and perceptions were abruptly discontinued unless the teacher understood Aboriginal values. In short, they were ill-understood or denigrated.

Crawford asked his readers, "Is it really the Aboriginal child failing to cope with the education system? Or is it the education system failing to cope with the Aboriginal student?" Crawford would train as a primary school teacher at Mitchell CAE, graduating in 1982, and eventually taking a lectureship at the Bathurst Campus of Charles Sturt University. A story is told that when Crawford's first school appointment was known, local parents sent an unsuccessful petition to the NSW DoE to block it, but when the man was marked for transfer, a petition was forwarded to retain him.

At the end of the 1980s, ATAs collaborated with the director and coordinator of the program in writing accounts of their communities including memories of their own schooldays. One underlying issue was how an Aboriginal world view could be retained in a white classroom.

> The difficulty is that Aboriginal culture is not strong in some Aboriginal communities utilising the white schools for their children, and the assimilationist culture of the school is difficult for the pupil to resist.

New South Wales teachers were urged to accept that Aboriginal culture had distinctive characteristics not shared by other community groups and that black and white should recognise each others' strengths.

> The need [is] to recognise each Aboriginal child as an individual, to recognise that Aboriginal children are individual within a group. Recognise that some traditional concepts still maintain a very strong influence on contemporary life. Recognise that Aboriginal children from other parts of Australia have different cultures. Recognise that two hundred years of oppression by the dominant white society still determines that economic domination has resulted in hardships for most Koori people in the areas of health, housing, employment and education. At the same time Kooris themselves need to feel that they can trust the schooling system. They need to understand that a main way they can improve their standards of living is by using education. Students can feel more comfortable at school by parents and well known community members being in close proximity by actually working inside the school classes.[39]

Figure 25. Aboriginal Teachers Aides: Millie Ingram, Wayne Cook, Delma Davidson and Debbie Walford, 1977. Image courtesy of University of Sydney Archives.

A number of these accounts identified positives in local schooling.

> We were superior at school in many ways – we were the better sports people, competing in the classroom for top position, and some of our Aboriginal parents had control over P&C meetings. My primary school days were fun. We used to walk to school along the beach – any number of us. On the way we would pick neulies, and any berry that was in season before we would head for the "rocks" to look for octopus. We would also pull out the vines that grew on the sand hills for skipping ropes. Everyone would play skippy and any other game that was decided.[40]

Several ATAs used their training experience at Sydney to forward their own social interests. Lillian Mosely, for example, recognised that her year at Sydney had broadened her horizons in literature, art and culture. "The era I grew up in had prejudice and racism. I went to a segregated school."[41] During and after her Sydney experience, Mosely would investigate her clan's heritage and wrote corporate plans making a case for better housing, electricity and water in the "third world conditions" of her Dhungutti community.

Problems and Outcomes

Of course problems existed on course, some barely surmountable. A number of school principals put too much emphasis on their ATA's capacity to relate to children in the appointment interview, an insufficient base for educational demands to come. It followed that inadequate attainments on entry saw several ATAs drop out or barely meet minimum Level I demands. Some ATA graduates were known to avoid home-school liaison duties or felt uncomfortable working with higher grades; and the partners of a few women were unhappy about their wives' achievements thinking they interfered with their own personal and community standing.

Nonetheless, after eight years of operation, over 160 ATAs had successfully completed the Level I course, 20 percent of them from non-government schools.[42] This result was achieved despite many having been "written off as failures by the school system".[43] A 1984 report listed 57 ATAs with a Level III Certificate of whom 29, including four Level IIs, had enrolled in tertiary institutions. Another 13 ATAs had already gained full teaching qualifications.[44] "Almost all who have completed their Diploma in Teaching have done so in the minimum time and there is not one ex-ATA student who has left because of academic failure."

ATAs Appear at a Select Committee

Among those who spoke up for ATAs at the Select Committee of the Legislative Assembly upon Aborigines 1979–81 was Lynette June Riley, a qualified remediation teacher appointed to Moree High on account of her Aboriginality, she believed. "They had a lot of trouble with the Aboriginals in Moree."[45] Trained at Armidale CAE in 1975–77, Riley was one of three Aborigines among 500 college students studying infants and primary teaching; in 1980, she would become academic coordinator at the Koori Centre. Giving evidence in support of ATAs at the Select Committee, Riley represented the case of Sheilagh Williams, an ATA who had crossed the ill-defined boundary between teacher and aide by helping a young boy to read.

> One of the masters blew sky high – ran into her – and said, "Who do you think you are? You are a clerk, you have no right trying to teach any child to read." That put her off. Every time she tried to help she was knocked back.

After completing her ATA training at Sydney in 1977, Williams found herself the only trained aide among five in Moree and called on to mentor the others by working across three schools.

On 7 March 1979, Williams appeared before the committee herself speaking with pride of her Sydney certificate.

> I am a teacher assistant. I was an aide and went to Sydney University for a year and sat for examinations and when I passed them I became qualified as a teacher's assistant. Where my role differs from that of the aide is that I do counselling with the kids and work in classrooms. I also help with the sports.[46]

Members of the Select Committee heard several instances of petty racism and discrimination from ATA witnesses. Were a child hurt in the playground, ATAs were forbidden to attend; they were not given jobs where money was handled; and they were not permitted to share space with white aides and instead were put in with the school secretary. There were complaints too that older teachers passed on one-sided information about Aboriginal people, putting them down in the eyes of young staff.

After returning to Sydney for an update, Williams quizzed her colleagues and discovered that over a quarter were not doing the work they were trained for. Many were still expected to undertake menial duties like photocopying, stencilling, and paperwork almost exclusively, and a few complained of not being invited to staff meetings or of being discouraged from visiting Aboriginal communities. ATAs were the school's dogsbodies, Duncan was told. It should be added that these inappropriate duties occurred most frequently in the early days and that many schools did integrate their ATAs successfully as testified by letters on file in the Koori Centre.

All ATAs who appeared before the Select Committee backed the Sydney training program. Asked whether the course at Sydney was relevant, Olive Brown of Bidwell Primary replied: "Yes, it is very useful and helpful to understand the teacher and what we are teaching the children. It makes us more qualified to teach the child."[47] Similarly, Pam Koeneman from Bombaderry Infants declared it "very helpful".[48] Koeneman would eventually move on to a NSW Teachers Federation post.

The Select Committee was given evidence of their good work by the NSW DoE which had undertaken a pilot evaluation in 1980 of their contribution in the North Coast Region. "All schools," it reported, "welcomed the services performed by the ATAs, which involved interactive duties in the classroom with Aboriginal as well as non-Aboriginal children."[49] John Lester, one of those who helped with the project's evaluation, stated that "the results were fantastic".[50] Another departmental survey at Wreck Bay found "a surprising number of Aboriginal children aspiring to be teachers"[51] – it attributed their new horizons to an ATA role model.

The submission from the Catholic Commission for Justice and Peace documented ATAs' contribution from a different perspective, observing that advances in Aboriginal education were few and rudimentary. Unfortunately, the Commonwealth and other grants designed to keep Aboriginal children at school were widely resented in the white community and the Commissioners queried whether using Aboriginal people as aides would prove counterproductive by giving the role low social status. "They [Aboriginals] are frequently the subject of hostility from whites in the general community and particularly in the educational system."[52] The nub of the problem remained how best to help Aboriginal children in the current environment.

> The real situation is that our education system has failed. The schooling to which most Aboriginal children have been subjected has been designed to fit them into the dominant white Australian society. The content of many courses is at best

irrelevant to them and at worst hostile. They are presented with values and views which damage their self-esteem and reinforce the prejudices of white society.

When NSW Teachers Federation representatives took the stand, they argued for more ATA appointments. "In the absence of sufficient Aboriginal teachers, Aboriginal teachers aides provide the major positive role model for Aboriginal children in New South Wales schools where they are employed."[53] Select Committee members heard several requests for additional ATAs even where Aboriginal numbers were as low as seven in a school; and some witnesses wanted ATAs trained more conveniently through regional CAEs. When the Second Report of the Select Committee appeared, it recommended more ATA and Home-School Coordinator positions, a revised set of duty statements, and the employment of aides on a permanent basis.

Money Matters

The ATATP was funded under a complicated arrangement involving Commonwealth, state and University. Under the 1975 Commonwealth–New South Wales Agreement, the federal government accepted responsibility for financing programs for Aboriginal people, pledging at the same time not to derogate the authority of the New South Wales government, a recipe for shuffling responsibility between them. The Commonwealth interpreted the agreement as requiring that its projects be handed back to the New South Wales government after three years, thus releasing its funds for other worthy activities. If the New South Wales government thought the ATA project important enough to continue, then it should fund the program itself. The state returned fire insisting that the Commonwealth's commitment was long term and could only be severed by mutual consent. Indeed, the state government viewed its stand as a matter of principle losing sight of the educational need. However, Craddock from the NSW DoE believed that the federal government did deal with New South Wales harshly. "There was a belief in Canberra that there were no real Aborigines in the east coast."[54] In the Northern Territory, the Commonwealth funded 100 percent of Aboriginal projects, in Victoria, 95 percent, in Western Australia, 80 percent, and in New South Wales, 40 percent. New South Wales also claimed that interstate Aborigines failed to press its case around the grants table.

When the Commonwealth government entered a regime of cost cutting in the mid-1970s, Aboriginal funding was not spared. No money was allocated for ATA salaries or training in the Commonwealth's Forward Estimates for 1976–77, the whole program being left "to wither on the vine".[55] Serious and intensive lobbying followed. A visit to Canberra on E (Education) Day, 29 April 1976, saw Kay Mundine, President of the AEC (NSW), corner Minister Viner,[56] and other delegates sought out John Carrick, the Minister for Education, Gough Whitlam from the Opposition, and Senator Neville Bonner who had expressed regrets that his own lack of schooling had made his entry to Parliament difficult.[57]

In August 1976, the Commonwealth blinked. It would continue funding up to 60 ATA salaries in New South Wales, however money for the ATA training program would end. In future, Commonwealth money would be reserved for self-determined and self-managed projects. Protests continued and Canberra finally agreed to provide training money up to the end of 1977, $100,000 in all, however New South Wales must draw down its own general revenue after that.[58] The hard line meant that ATATP staff left for their Christmas vacation unsure about whether the program would re-start in 1978.

Mundine wrote again to Viner early in the new year pleading to have the ATATP grant restored, her letter making an excellent educational point.

> We consider the teaching program to be an essential element of the overall scheme; without it, the Aboriginal Teaching Assistants Scheme becomes little more than another employment program for the small number of Aboriginal people, rather than an educational development program which is of major significance to the future of Aboriginal education in New South Wales and a model for similar developments in other states.[59]

Viner responded by releasing $20,000 for one training session for six months but indicated this payment was final. The effects of the Commonwealth's intransigence were publicised on 17 October 1978 when the *Sydney Morning Herald* printed Chris Adams' article, "Teaching Course in Jeopardy". Adams declared that the ATATP staff had been cut from three lecturers to two and its intake reduced despite the program having trained 70 ATAs over four years and placing 16 ex-students in teacher training. She added:

> It seems so sad that what has proved to be the most successful of all schemes to help Aborigines to benefit fully from their education looks like sinking into oblivion because Governments can't get together in the interests of the people they are elected to help.

Duncan too fought to maintain the program, writing to Stephen Albert, Chair of the NAEC, on 9 May 1978, telling him ATATP reserves were seriously depleted with just two persons on staff. He continued:

> Despite the undoubted success of the Teaching Program (14 students are now enrolled in teachers college and C.A.E.s) no funds have been provided this year and it looks as if the training program will have to fold. I would be very grateful if the NAEC would continue to press for further funds for this program in the interests of all Aboriginal children in this state.

The ATATP was kept alive in the second half of 1978 by deploying unexpended funds from the previous year and delaying appointments – a lectureship and a graduate clerk. Regular staffing was now down to one full-time teacher, Chris Adams, and the secretary, Leslee Curraey. By good fortune, the war chest was boosted by $20,000 drummed up from the New South Wales State Development Committee for in-service work and other groups chipped in: the Aboriginal Study Groups of the North Shore gave money; the YWCA through the Wood Trust donated nearly $5000 in 1977–79;[60] and the AEC (NSW) covered some conference and graduation costs.

In 1978, 15 students were enrolled in the Basic course, and five in the other two levels, with 17 women and two men graduating at the Manning House ceremony on the 22 November.[61] Willmot and Duncan spoke at the gathering, the latter reporting the success of the Level IIIs, his words given meaning when Heather Allen, recently appointed to Bellbrook Public School, told guests of her own experiences. Beverley Manton replied on behalf of the ATAs and David Green presented a bouquet to Joyce Black. Help from the AEC (NSW), and from the Phyllis Hollings Cohen, Edith McCarthy and Grace Beardsley memorial funds, was gratefully acknowledged.

A Victory of Sorts

As negotiations over funding continued, Canberra suggested that the state take over payments for ATA employment and training progressively and provide a career structure in teaching. Macquarie Street ignored the advice holding out for full reimbursement, the Minister for Education, Eric Bedford, insisting, "It would be constitutionally illegal for the Commonwealth to hand over the responsibility to the state."[62] Eventually a compromise was negotiated: ATATP funding was restored for 1979–80, with $86,000 made available, however ATAs' travel and accommodation must be paid from grant money. Furthermore, the money drawn from reserves in 1978, $23,000 in all, must be repaid in full. Duncan's

Figure 26. Aboriginal Teachers Aides graduation, Senator Fred Chaney, 1979.
Image courtesy of University of Sydney Archives.

own estimate was that the program required $30,000–$35,000 above the Commonwealth allocation were it to function.⁶³ Financial problems continued into 1979 which saw course lengths suffer: study time in the Basic was reduced by three weeks; the Upgrading and Intensive were cut by two weeks apiece; and the in-service experience was reduced from two weeks to one.

When news of the Commonwealth funding arrangement reached the ATATP in January 1979, two extra full-time staff were appointed. Adams was joined by Debbie Robinson, BA, DipTeach (Adelaide), with teaching experience in Wilcannia and South Australia, as communication lecturer; and Ranald Allan, BA, DipTeach, with three years experience on Elcho Island, was appointed to lecture in Aboriginal and cultural studies, and government. That year the versatile secretary, Curraey, left the program and was replaced by Moira Tierney as secretary-organiser. A number of external lecturers were also drawn on for special topics, some supplying their services without charge; others, including some from within the University, charged a fee. Duncan paid up but complained.

> These were full-time lecturers and we had to pay them on top of their salaries – that always intrigued me. I always wondered how they could not only do that professionally, but also do it morally – but they seemed to be able to work around it!⁶⁴

On 5 December 1979, 16 ATAs graduated, five each at Levels I and II, and six at Level III of whom three accepted teacher training offers.⁶⁵ The good results owed much to Adams' dedication and hard work. Absent from late March to early October 1979 in Canada, the UK and Scandinavia, Duncan made his debt public.

> I feel that it is Chris who should really be taking my place this year because it has been proved conclusively that I am quite superfluous. It was rather a shock when I returned early in October for Chris to say "Have you been away for a few days, Alan?"⁶⁶

Duncan also used his 1979 address to reveal remarks heard from one student who had failed to gain Level III entry. "I guess it is my own fault. I didn't work hard enough." The director had another slant: "I didn't say at the time, as I perhaps should have said, that the reason was the cutback in the length of the training sessions due to lack of finance." He went on: "I make no apology for taking this opportunity this afternoon to make a plea to both the federal and state governments. Forget about the money problem and concentrate on people's needs." Of the 20,000 teachers in New South Wales, Duncan said, 17 were of Aboriginal background. "Instead of making a concerted effort to rectify the situation our federal and state governments spend precious time and energy arguing over which government will provide the money."

The keynote address was given by Pat O'Shane, a graduate from Queensland Teachers College and law graduate from the University of New South Wales. Born in Queensland in 1941, the eldest of five children, O'Shane recalled a tent with dirt floor, poverty at home and discrimination at school. In 1986 she was appointed as the first Aboriginal magistrate in Australia under the New South Wales Local Courts Administration. Among the speakers on the day was the Minister for Aboriginal Affairs, Senator Fred Chaney, who announced that the Commonwealth would continue funding the ATATP in 1980. Jackie Field responded on behalf of the ATAs.

Falling Enrolments

Graduation numbers continued to be low in 1980. There were five at Level I, four at Level II, and ten at Level III, three of them destined for teacher training.[67] Certificates that year were presented in the Wool Room at International House by the Deputy Chancellor, Mr Justice David Selby, and the flowers by Barbara Selby. This was the first of the graduations Black had missed, on account of illness. The keynote speaker, John Lester, a Wonnarua man from the Upper Hunter Valley and an Aboriginal Liaison Teacher, "spoke from the heart".[68] In 1986, Lester would be appointed Principal of Grafton TAFE, the first Aborigine to hold the position, and he became Director of Aboriginal Education and Training for the NSW DoET in 2007. The ATA, Olive Brown, an experienced aide in the Mount Druitt region where 3000 Aboriginal school children were in class, responded. At the close of the ceremony, after the group photograph was taken, students were told: "You can get rid of your Batman gear at this point."[69]

Between 1976 and 1980, NSW DoE students in training fell from 38 to 13, due mainly to the limited number of ATA positions.[70] Total enrolments were maintained on course only by enrolling preschool trainees funded under schemes such as the Commonwealth's National Educational Strategy for Aborigines (NESA). The ATATP budget of $90,000 was retained for 1981,[71] the Commonwealth thinking the payment fair enough given its view that the program's raison d'être was the Basic training of government students. Despite the need for more Aboriginal teachers, the Commonwealth did not consider Level II and III enrolments especially important or those undertaking in-service. An attempt by the Department of Adult Education to build up course numbers by enrolling Aboriginal students seeking Adult Matriculation, estimating that as many as 20 externals would join the course annually, was denied by its Commonwealth minders.

The More Report

In 1977 the Department of Adult Education instituted an evaluation of the ATATP, commissioning Arthur J. More, Associate Professor and Supervisor of the Native Indian Teacher Education Program at the University of British Columbia. Assisted by Barbara Kennedy, his final report, *A Solid Link in the Chain*, provided a comprehensive statement on achievements and problems in the ATATP.

More suggested a number of practical ways to improve the program: ATA job descriptions needed tightening with fixed hours set aside for connecting directly with children and parents; there should be regular regional workshops for ATAs and teachers; and closer links should be forged with teacher training institutions, though he noted that every request to a College of Advanced Education to admit a Level III graduate had been successful. Aides' salaries remained wholly inadequate, said More, some ATAs finding it impossible to support themselves in Sydney. He also identified serious deficiencies in the University's accounting that left bills unpaid by the University for six months or more with the ATATP still adjusting its budget up to a year later. It was, he said, impossible to calculate the financial state of the ATATP at any given time.

As to the overall state of Aboriginal education in Australia, More noted:

> A great deal of improvement has occurred over the past ten years – possibly more than in the previous 100 years. But one can dwell too long on that improvement. The growth of the past few years is infinitesimal in comparison to the growth that is required before Aborigines take their rightful place in society.

The Canadian went on to praise Adult Education for its "very effective job"[72] both in the Basic and Advanced programs, and he identified ATAs themselves as deserving the greatest credit.

More's thorough and balanced analysis was a vindication of the efforts of the Department of Adult Education and of the ATATP staff and students and it was accepted as such by the state and Commonwealth governments. However, the gloss was taken off by the financial crisis of 1978–79. With stringent economies in place, Duncan was reduced to carrying the More Report in bundles to DAA in Sydney asking that its office post them to interested parties. "Our funds are so low that postage is quite a prohibitive expense."[73] Among those applying for a copy was H.C. ("Nugget") Coombs, the architect of Commonwealth Aboriginal policy and Visiting Fellow at the Australian National University.[74] The sole dissenting voice on the More evaluation came from those who dismissed the ATATP as "an exercise in assimilation".[75]

5

Aboriginal Engagement

> Sweeping staff changes are being made in 1981 in accordance with a policy decision to "Aboriginalise" the program.
>
> Department of Adult Education: Report
to the Board of Adult Education, 6 March 1981[1]

When the Canadian evaluator, Arthur More, gave his blessing to the ATATP, he expressed two caveats: he was surprised that Duncan aside, no staff member had qualifications or experience in teaching Aboriginal children and, secondly, that no policy existed to ensure Aboriginal appointments, academic or general. He did, however, accept that there were "very few Aborigines at present with appropriate qualifications and experience. And those who are qualified are needed for even more important jobs."[2] The first Aboriginal employee to join the ATATP was Roslyn Blair, who was appointed in October 1980 as a trainee under the NESA scheme hopefully to replace Moira Tierney as secretary-organiser, however she did not continue beyond 1981. Securing other qualified Aboriginal staff proved no less difficult as Duncan notes.

> I approached Eric Willmot to be a lecturer at the Aboriginal Teaching Assistants Program, but the University was not supportive. I also signed up Pat O'Shane to be a lecturer, but she was involved in the Royal Commission into Black Deaths in Custody and couldn't take up the position.[3]

Admittedly, there was just a small pool of Aboriginal Australians with the necessary qualifications but individuals were discouraged from applying because of Sydney's elitism and non-competitive career opportunities.

Good news arrived in 1981 when the first Aboriginal lecturer, Barry Thorne, DipTeach (New England), was seconded from Condobolin High to lecture in English and communication. One of the first Aborigines to complete secondary education at Walgett in 1973, Thorne described his school experiences in *New Dawn*. "There used to be a lot of prejudice from kids at school. The teachers didn't really know about it and so didn't do anything. But the Aboriginal students stuck together and fought it. Now it's no longer a problem."[4] School vice-captain and "sportsman of the year" in 1972, Thorne toured the University in

August that year under a careers day arrangement. His decision to teach was influenced by the staff at Condobolin High and his family including his mother, Thelma, who herself came to Sydney for ATA training in the mid-1980s. Also, Thorne declared, "the job itself appealed". The significance of Thorne's appointment went well beyond his contribution to the ATATP classroom as it sent a message to government funding bodies and the schools of the program's intention of becoming Aborigine led.

Staff Changes

Lecturer positions in the ATATP were extremely testing, their incumbents expected to teach across traditional subject lines and work in intensive bursts with students in session. Dedication was taken for granted. After five years of outstanding service, including time as deputy director, Chris Adams resigned in August 1980, replaced as lead teacher by Denise Mondini who lectured in Aboriginal and cultural studies, and government and current affairs. After Duncan was appointed Acting Director of the Department of Adult Education in mid-1982, Mondini handled accounts as an extra. On the secretarial side, Moira Tierney, Jane Douglas, and Rhonda Conroy assisted as secretaries, and the Egyptian-born, Nadia Messih, joined in 1982. The time was especially busy given staff changes and reorganisation, and Messih sought an upgrading to administrator claiming she was undertaking senior office work out of a sense of duty in the absence of others.[5] She was unsuccessful. Part-time and casual teachers continued to be employed, Julie Janson, Alan Liddle, John Rivers and Stephen Wale being prominent.

After admitting to knowing nothing of the ATATP before appointment, Thorne identified an urgent need to promote the program:

> My greatest concern at the time was that the teaching staff of schools never really understood the role of the A.T.A., or what the Program was about. They thought "Oh well, the A.T.A.s are racing off to get another two weeks in Sydney."[6]

To counter the prevailing view, he and Mondini spent much time visiting and corresponding with schools and supplying details of course units. The extract below is from a Basic course session in communications prepared by Thorne for circulation to school principals.

> Other than our lecture sessions and notes the students studied a variety of poems, extracts, short stories and their own personal experiences to help illustrate and explain more clearly the topic being discussed, the students also participated in group dynamic exercises and carried out some interesting role play situations. I felt that overall the session was most beneficial and that the group is keen to continue with the remaining topics yet to be covered.[7]

After Mondini left the program at the end of 1982, Thorne was appointed acting coordinator. While it put him above the other lecturers in the organisational structure, it did not carry a salary increment. Course numbers began to fall off and Thorne found himself increasingly engaged in a search for students among other tasks.

> When I actually did the job it wasn't that easy. It was a job which involved a lot of understanding about schools, communities, kids, Aboriginal education and education in general as well as all the negotiation between the institutions. It was difficult to suddenly handle the change in responsibility – not being fully responsible and then being responsible for the whole program. Your attitude and the way you worked had to change.[8]

Thorne led the staff team, advised on curriculum reform, approved students' travel and accommodation, visited schools, and negotiated with the internal and external authorities. He found the University of Sydney bureaucracy among the least easy to deal with, change appearing a suspect activity and success not guaranteed.

> You had to go slowly, because it's a very hard institution to change. It's hard to change any of its courses that are offered – let alone try to get Aboriginal education entrenched in an institution like Sydney. You just had to bite off little bits at a time and be satisfied with the small gains – and have the attitude that you've got to lose some as well as win some.[9]

Snapshot of a Graduation

Thorne attended his first graduation in 1981, which was held in the Wool Room and Cafeteria in International House. By November, staff were well into making students' travel arrangements and booking accommodation. The pre-dinner sherry and the chicken and wine supplies for the picnic were ordered and arrangements made for the "students only" formal dinner at the Holme Building. Certificates were designed and signed, book prizes and flowers chosen, and a guest list of near 90 invitees compiled. Closer to the occasion, the special events itinerary, including the performance of the Aboriginal and Islander Dance Company, was checked out and the graduation gowns ordered.

Duncan gave a preparatory interview to the *University of Sydney News* on Aboriginal education just prior to the big day. He explained that starting school for the Aboriginal child "was a bit like being dumped in a foreign country",[10] telling *News* readers that ATAs bridged the gap between Aboriginal and non-Aboriginal worlds. They were the state's educational "ambassadors".

After the rehearsal at 10.00 am on Wednesday 2 December, Mondini granted the students free time: "A few hours to become even more beautiful (and handsome)."[11] Returning to the Wool Room in the afternoon, the students and the 200 or so family members and friends, including prominent Aboriginal figures, public servants, politicians, school principals, sports identities and people from the press, were welcomed by the Director of Adult Education, Crowley. After apologies from Al Grassby, John Aquilina, and J.R. Buddy of the NAEC were read out, Duncan announced that 11 ATAs would graduate as qualified teachers by the end of the year and he expected several of the present Level IIIs to follow their footsteps.

The Walgett educator, Robert (Bob) V. Morgan, spoke next. Morgan, of the Gumilaroi people, had been inspired to leave his home town by Perkins' Freedom Riders: "I wanted to be like them, I wanted to go and do something."[12] Catching a train to Sydney, he was grateful for the offer of a bed at the Central Police Station for the night. Morgan received a small scholarship and living allowance from the AEC (NSW) while studying at Sydney Technical College in 1969, eventually working for the Foundation of Aboriginal Affairs as a field officer where he contacted new arrivals, some 40 a week, and assisted local residents to find work. Dr Morgan became President of the NSW AECG (1977–87), joined the New South Wales Education Commission, headed the University of Technology Sydney's Jumbunna, Indigenous House of Learning, and established Murri Consultants and Associates.

Morgan's first graduation address lamented the lack of Aboriginal teachers – just 58 in all among 20,000 whites – whereas the national target for New South Wales was 258. In fact, Morgan's figure of Aboriginal teachers in the state appears an exaggeration as an official estimate in 1982 counted only 38 teachers, education officers or consultants in the NSW DoE, and there were few if any in non-government schools.[13]

After Morgan's talk, Jill Wran, wife of the Premier, reiterated the importance of education in the lives of Aboriginal people and the need to advance land rights. Then David Nicholls, the ATA from Brewarrina Central, and a Level III graduate, replied to Morgan and Wran. "Each individual," he told his audience, "is unique and therefore has different needs. Each and every one of us has potential, but if this potential is not exercised through opportunities and experiences we will never come to understand or appreciate our real values."[14] Nicholls went on to thank Duncan and staff for the course: "It has played a very important part in our lives."

Speeches over, the students ascended the stage to accept awards from the Chancellor with Joyce Black presenting the posies and button holes. That year, five ATA certificates were presented at Level I, 14 at Level II, and eight at Level III, nine awards being in the "academic merit" or "most improved" categories. Ages of students, four men among them, ranged from 23 to 54 while 14 of the 27 graduates were employed outside the ATATP scheme funded under the Aboriginal Study Grants Scheme, and seven were employed in private or community preschools. As some of these non-government trainees received no salary on course, the AEC (NSW) established a fund of $5000 to help meet their incidentals and accommodation costs. Also recognised were 11 men and women from the two week in-service experience. The 1981 event was televised for TV news, and, at the close, participants moved on to a "wind down" at the South Sydney Leagues Club.

The following day an article appeared in *The Australian* under the headline, "Premier's Wife Faces Criticism of Government". Whereas Wran had identified education as the most important route for Aboriginal people towards equality, security and satisfaction, the newspaper reported, Morgan had accused the state government of dragging its feet, lacking any sense of urgency when it came to training Aboriginal teachers. Its approach, Morgan said, mirrored public attitudes. "For too long, we have been surrounded with a cloak of myths

– the myths that denigrate Aboriginal people from the day we are born to the day we are laid to rest."

Failure to Train Teachers

Up to the 1980s, the NSW DoE had done little or nothing to encourage Aborigines to become teachers. Although the Commonwealth provided study grants for Aboriginal teacher trainees in CAEs and universities, the department delayed their appointment claiming the students had not been guaranteed employment: in 1976, four teacher graduates from Armidale CAE trained through Commonwealth-funded places went unemployed.[15] In 1981, the situation was remedied when the NSW DoE granted Aboriginal teachers priority appointment.

Aborigines had been discouraged from adopting a teaching career by past racist attitudes. Burnam Burnam (Henry Penrith) had enquired about teaching on leaving school in 1954: "I had great ambitions of becoming a physical education teacher",[16] but had pulled out after an official in the NSW DoE told him: "This is not the life for you. The children will call you black." Reared in Bombaderry Children's Home and at Kinchela Boys Home, Burnam Burnam (Great Warrior of the Wurundjeri Nation), was the one member of his class to enter third year high school. He has described his time at Kinchela: "Being in the home, we had plenty of food, though no love whatsoever, but still and all because of sporting ability we were accepted." Eventually appointed Assistant Registrar at Wagga Agricultural College, Burnam Burnam found that the colour label accompanied him. Asked to report on his request for a salary increment, his superior had written: "Whilst Mr Penrith is keen and conscientious, his limitations are of racial origin."

Author, rugby player, activist and elder, Burnam Burnam left a distinctive mark on Aboriginal Australia, his keen sense of justice never forsaking him. In 1980, he told the Commissioners at the Select Committee on Aboriginal Welfare that the Aboriginal people had "witnessed the greatest theft in the history of mankind. The white people stole our land from us."[17] Then, on Australia Day, 1988, Burnam Burnam got his own back on the white colonisers by famously raising the Aboriginal flag at Dover on the English coast claiming the land and its possessions for Aboriginal Australians.[18]

With a small group of high school graduates from which to select, teaching as a career had to compete with alternative employment for qualified Aboriginal people. In the mid-1980s, the NSW DoE took up the idea of recruiting ATAs as conditionally trained teachers but arrangements had to be negotiated with individual CAEs or universities since the government no longer controlled its own teachers' colleges. Furthermore, there was little enthusiasm for the idea in the bureaucracy, or in the teachers union for that matter, for what was seen as a sub-standard solution. No progress was made on this front. So far as the University of Sydney was concerned, its first BEd (Secondary: Aboriginal Studies) students would not graduate until 2001, three in all.

Revising Course Content

Fresh from the schools, and with personal knowledge of Aboriginal learning styles, Thorne was uniquely placed to reassess and revise the ATATP syllabus. "Some of the stuff was so old you think – it's got no relevance – or cuts no ice with someone who's going back to Gulargambone next week – to hordes of screaming mad kids!"[19]

Not enough content, Thorne thought, was of value in the present-day classroom and school principals were querying its relevance. "What use is Piagetian theory to my ATA?"[20] One reason for the existing mix of subjects was the need to cover the diverse roles of an ATA, as well as the program's reliance on theory taken from regular teacher training degrees. Duncan himself believed that courses like Educational Psychology were "a little too theoretical",[21] an opinion the compulsory question in the Basic Educational Psychology course from 1978 supports:

> Piaget's work on children's intellectual development has generated more interest and research than that of any other person in Psychology in the last fifty years. Summarize and illustrate the major aspects of Piaget's theory of cognitive development.

If some content was too theoretical, other content was thought to lack substance. Gathering responses from staff visits and questionnaires, and through in-house discussions with Level III students, Thorne, helped by Mondini and the part-timers, put together a revised curriculum statement.

> 1. Communication
> To enhance ATAs' interpersonal communication skills and ability to communicate effectively in a variety of situations; to extend students' awareness of their world and their capacity to pass this to others; to promote an interest in literature, film and live theatre; and to encourage an autonomous learning style.
>
> 2. Community Arts
> To develop visual arts skills and the capacity to initiate projects for Aboriginal students and groups; and to provide ATAs with a knowledge and appreciation of traditional and contemporary Aboriginal arts.
>
> 3. Teaching and Learning
> To create a practical understanding of child behaviour and the psychological aspects of the educational process; to teach skills for use in classroom situations; and to develop an understanding of ATA roles and related competencies in the classroom and in liaison activity in the community.
>
> 4. Current Affairs
> To expand the general education of ATAs by familiarising them with government processes in regard to law and administration; and to note and discuss significant current affairs in Australia and the world.

5. Aboriginal and Cultural Studies
To equip students with a tolerant understanding of cultural processes; to explain how cultural differences develop in response to different environments; and to increase ATAs' awareness of the uniqueness of their own Aboriginal cultural heritage.[22]

Curriculum objectives were now better related to ATAs' teaching conditions and course content took some account of the needs of preschoolers entering the ATATP. Efforts were also made to improve the sharing of training material between staff, Thorne and Mondini setting an example by circulating their lesson notes and post-teaching evaluations. In 1982, the NSW DoE published its *Aboriginal Education Policy*, and the booklet, *Strategies for Teaching Aboriginal Children*, which became the anchor for the practical side of class work.

More staff with Aboriginal background experienced in teaching Indigenous children made teaching Aboriginal topics and themes easier, with learning difficulties confronting Aboriginal children better understood. Janson tells how "the Aboriginal world" became the central feature of her Community Arts lessons.

> We hung paintings on the walls and made Koori Emu feathered jewelry, and threaded porkipine pigibilla echidna quills, or carved emu eggs. We wove string dilly bags on the back of chairs and dyed them with ochres. We painted each other with ochres in traditional patterns inspired by Eora paintings and performed Yolngu dances with clapsticks and didjeridoos played by students. One student even gave us the gift of teaching us a Yuin corroboree (South coast) of robbing a honey tree … (we received) … the special wonder of a women's Inma ceremony performed in our lecture room by visiting Pitjantjatjara minima tjuta elders from Central Australia (male students were asked to be occupied elsewhere). We all sat around afterwards while the women taught us the meaning of the ceremonial markings painted on their breasts. They performed with us, the ceremonial story of the seven sisters, and explained the meaning of all the movements.[23]

Operational issues beyond the curriculum, however, remained in contention. One particular problem, Thorne admitted, was the sandwich mode of study which upset continuity in learning as groups moved in and out of class.

> You know you've got them down for three weeks – then a different group comes down for a couple of weeks, then they disappear for four weeks and then an entirely different group comes down.[24]

The program's unique design led to intensive bursts of lecturing, 25 or more hours a week, straining the concentration of students and sapping the energy of teachers who had little time for study or research themselves. The use of external staff and casuals also made it difficult to coordinate planning and undertake evaluation. From the vantage point of the ATAs, the steady flow of course work, staff turnover, communal life in a Sydney motel, and ongoing family responsibilities with no cash in hand kept the pressure on. At the same time, back in their schools, students had to complete assignments relying on the minimal facilities of their country towns.

The ATA Fellowship

For all the difficulties ATAs faced, a remarkable bonding made the ATATP unlike other University programs. Students and staff worked cooperatively from the start.

> I was lucky in the sense of having a number of people who had a history with the Program. They were very good and worked well together as a team. Julie, Alan, Stephen – all had an understanding and knowledge of the program and were able to laugh about some pretty serious problems. We still treated it as a serious matter, but because we could laugh about it, we managed to deal with it a lot better, and I think – got better results.[25]

Then there was a strong internal attachment as Sheilagh Williams, the ATA at Moree High, recognised. "We the members of the Aboriginal Teaching Assistants class are a very close group. As soon as we were brought together for this course, we have come together as one big happy family."[26] Janson has expressed similar feelings.

> The ATA program was a place where Koori, Goori, Murri and Torres Strait Islander ATAs all met and became friends and professional colleagues. Where people from Bourke, Redfern, Kempsey, Walgett, Moree, Orange, Dubbo, Nowra and everywhere in NSW came to study as Aboriginal Education Assistants. There were women and men in their thirties, forties and fifties who had been denied access to education. Koories who had grown up on Missions or in country towns. Some were members of the Stolen Generation, who had been brought up in Children's Homes or by white foster parents. Some had lived in poverty, on rations of tea and sugar and flour and whatever their families could work for. There were ATA grandmothers and grandfathers; there were ATAs who had ten children to look after at home. Some young ATAs had completed high school and were hoping to go on to become teachers. All of the ATAs were important hard working educators in their schools and communities, all of them had a strong desire to learn and teach.[27]

In 1977, Chris Adams collected material for the *ATA Times* in 1982. Its November issue began with an article by Thorne on ATATP happenings, including news that he would return to teaching in the coming year. Other short items related to Duncan's purchase of a house in Camperdown; a skiing accident for Mondini; the retirement of Rhonda Conroy and appointment of Nadia Messih; and Ev Crawford stepping down at Brewarrina Central to allow time for NSW AECG activities. There was a brief statement from Darrell Thorne about the Aboriginal Education Resource Centre recently opened in Chippendale and a report from John Lester on the NSW DoE's Aboriginal Education Unit established under Trevor Cook and Yvonne Bolton in 1979. Student poetry and jokes were interspersed throughout. However, one particular item stood apart. "ATAs will be saddened to hear of

Figure 27. Aboriginal Education Unit of the Directorate of Special Programs, NSW, 1982. Back row: Bill Rose, Bob Morgan (President, NSW AECG), Jack Harrison. Front row: Lynette Riley, John Lester, Lindy Burney, Trevor Cook and Davina Tyrrell. Image courtesy of the Koori Centre.

the untimely passing of Mr Les Toomey." Les, who had attended the ATATP in 1977, had returned to complete a Level III certificate and Guild training before taking a teaching post at Collarenebri Central. The magazine closed with a dozen "hints" for teachers in schools having no ATA appointments but with substantial numbers of Aboriginal pupils.

External Aboriginal Involvement – the Advisory Committee

Aboriginal projects in receipt of Commonwealth and state government funds were expected to establish advisory committees with significant Aboriginal representation. This had not occurred at Sydney and the Director-General, Doug Swan, found it necessary to write to Crowley on 11 May 1981, telling him that both Canberra's Department of Aboriginal Affairs (DAA), and the NSW AECG, had raised the matter with him. DAA had complained over the program's growing reliance on non-government and Intensive course enrolments and the NSW AECG was worried about the ATATP's internal management in particular staffing inadequacies, inappropriate course content and the absence of long-term planning. It was his department's philosophy and that of the Commonwealth, Swan told Crowley, "that wherever possible, Aboriginal people should share in the decisions which affect them." Swan proposed the formation of an Advisory Committee (AC) and Crowley took up the suggestion immediately offering himself as Chairman.[28]

Initially, Swan had wanted five of a nine-member AC drawn from the NSW AECG and the NSW DoE, however Crowley thought a smaller group more manageable and ATA representation essential. His view was persuasive. When the AC (Adult Education) was formed in 1981, its membership comprised Bill Rose as the state department representative with Linda Burney as alternate, and two members from the NSW AECG, Laurel Ralph and Diane Stewart with one alternate, Norma Williams. Duncan was the University staff representative and Thorne the ATATP staff person with Modini the alternate. Pam Kelly represented ATAs and David Nicholls the students.

At the inaugural meeting of the AC at Mackie on 11 November 1981, Duncan defended Adult Education's past policy on Aboriginal representation telling members that "an ad hoc advisory committee" composed entirely of Aboriginal people had met at "infrequent intervals", and that regular meetings were held with the NSW DoE. He did concede though that there was "an urgent need to formalise these previous flexible consultations". Duncan went on to raise the issue of funding inadequacies over the last two years with one full-time lecturer and one administrative assistant lost, while his own timetable for visits to schools was disrupted and reduced. "The course had only survived this year because the University paid the salary of the Program Director who had accepted responsibility for most of the administrative load as well as a full teaching load in one of the subjects." Accommodation costs particularly remained a major impost on the ATATP's budget as reasonably priced accommodation close to the University was difficult to find. When students had been placed at Kirinari Hostel at Sylvania, it was necessary for staff to travel there at least one day a week to keep down the cost of student travel.

Members moved down the agenda items to discuss DAA's worry that the balance between government and non-government students inside the program was shifting – there had been 13 government enrollees in the Basic in 1980 and five non-government but by 1983 there would be nine government and 12 non-government.[29] Duncan defended the enrolment of non-government aides, mostly preschoolers, saying they imposed no burden and that the Commonwealth should fund them irrespective of their place of employment; and he strongly supported the existence of the Upgrading and Intensive courses as routes for teaching. In fact, the University Department of Adult Education wanted to extend the program, having plans to enrol adults seeking university entrance, develop in-service courses for teachers, and train Aborigines as assistant school counsellors and teachers of Aboriginal studies. Other possibilities Adult Education had in mind included the introduction of a Diploma of Aboriginal Adult Education and a University Research Centre for Aboriginal Adult Education.

Though the Commonwealth had allowed the ATATP a budget of $90,000 in 1981,[30] travel and accommodation remained outside the remit and the state government was deducting a five percent administration fee. The result was a likely shortfall of $12,600 in 1982. Here, members of the AC (Adult Education) sympathised with the Department of Adult Education's remark that financing the course was causing it "considerable problems"[31] and, in a supportive move, the Commonwealth signalled a takeover of the program's travel and accommodation payments from 1984.

Strengthening External Advice

A one-off meeting held at Mackie in December 1982 brought together University, state department and the NSW AECG personnel to consider financial issues raised by Mondini and the program's long-term viability. Its recommendations were passed to a working party convened by Thorne drawn from AC membership,[32] which proposed that the AC (Adult Education) be replaced by an expanded Management Committee (MC), with 50 percent Aboriginal membership in line with NAEC policy. There should be representation from DAA and DEET, with Margaret Ramsay and Evan Sutton appointed, the latter having a long association with Aboriginal education putting in "endless hours"[33] on its behalf.

The new MC proved zealous in its oversight with members arguing that their role as representatives of state, Commonwealth and Aboriginal community opinion went beyond merely passing advice to the director. Their assessments, they believed, should be carefully weighed and followed up by the University. Seven main issues caused them concern:

- The curriculum remained under fire despite Thorne's earlier efforts. Some members thought it too academic and too extensive given the educational levels of the ATAs. They also claimed it put insufficient emphasis on teaching English and mathematics. Members also noted that the absence of detailed course outlines left new staff with little idea as to what had been covered by their predecessors or of the academic levels of students; and they wanted more school visits by staff as a means of improving feedback and reform.

- The Intensive course of five weeks was considered far too short. It should be lengthened and strengthened to equate with bridging courses available in other places and Level III students should be taught tertiary academic skills. Members wanted the possibility of weekend teaching during the Basic course explored and in-service activity extended and made available on a regional basis.

- All members wanted a thorough evaluation of the ATATP, professionally delivered, with a completion date no later than April 1984.

- The MC then took the University to task over staffing. Thorne was due to return to the schools and Duncan had recommended that any replacement supervise the ATATP and manage Aboriginal adult education. Members made it clear that their interest was not in Aboriginal adult education but in the ATATP. They were worried too about the lack of definition of staff duties, particularly those applying to the coordinator, and by the continued turn-over of staff.

- The hazy status of ATAs as students of the University was another pressure point. Because the ATATP relied on Commonwealth project funding, ATAs had no right to borrow from Fisher Library, to use the University's sporting facilities, or to graduate in the company of regular students. Furthermore, certificate holders were not guaranteed direct entry into any University degree or diploma suggesting that the University did not recognise its own qualification.

- Members also raised the issue of their own standing in the University. What were the MC's terms of reference and powers and responsibilities? Otherwise, what was the point in their meeting?

- Lastly, the MC called for a commitment from the University on the future of the AEAP, a determination necessary because of its serious financial situation and uncertainty over the future of its host, the Department of Adult Education. Yes, Management Committee members accepted the good will behind Duncan's assurance that the University greatly valued the ATATP, but they wanted more than a gentleman's agreement.[34]

Thorne, whose appointment as coordinator was confirmed, was elected chair of the MC, and he forwarded several submissions to the University taking up members' anxieties.[35] Few responses were received. At the meeting of 21 September 1983, one aggrieved member from the NSW AECG laid down a complaint.

> The Department of Education has given clear mandate to Management Committee to oversee function of program, but Committee still in limbo; has tried to put questions on paper but still no answers – in order to ensure the best program for ATAs, there must be distinct changes. At the moment, Director [is the] only authority, against advice of AECG and Committee. Committee would like to have some say in the suitability of staff, should not only be function of Director, otherwise defeats purpose of Committee. The AECG expressed very much concern: AECG had great role in establishing Committee, did not envisage it to become puppet. Concerned about suitability of University to mount such a programme.

Stimulus and Response

Although Duncan had welcomed the MC, he was upset about the direction it was taking. While recognising that the MC had an important advisory role and a right to monitor progress, he would concede no authority over policy or action. On 29 August, he wrote directly to the Vice-Chancellor.

> It now seems that the committee assumes an authority over the Program that was not intended and which, in my view, would not be acceptable to the University. Whilst it is especially necessary in Aboriginal adult education to maintain close liaison with the students and with the Aboriginal community generally, it is vital,

> I believe, for the Program to remain firmly under the control of the University, if it is to bear its imprimatur.

Attempting to clarify matters further, Duncan drew up a set of Functions for the Management Committee specifically limiting the MC's role, forwarding same to the Vice-Chancellor. The terms had Swan's approval, Duncan said, and he had raised the question of the MC's authority with the Minister for Aboriginal Affairs, Clyde Holding, when they had met in October.[36]

The Vice-Chancellor was equally unhappy about the MC's standpoint raising the issue of its powers with both Holding, and the Minister for Education and Youth Affairs, Senator Susan Ryan. Holding's reply to Ward was received on 6 December, delayed for more than two months by the Canberra mail strike. The Vice-Chancellor was assured that the Commonwealth was not attempting to set academic standards, however it did expect management committees like Sydney's to express opinions on Aboriginal perspectives and student needs freely. In summary, the University should listen to the MC's recommendations but not necessarily follow them. Holding agreed that Duncan's proposed Functions for the MC document was in line with the Commonwealth's position. A year later, the Commonwealth minister would take a stronger position requiring that state governments put effective consultative processes in place empowering Aboriginal people in decision-making through senior appointments.[37]

In a follow-up letter to Swan of the 8 November, Ward reiterated that the University remained committed to the ATATP, however he spoke of various misunderstandings surrounding the program's operations. He also took up the MC's complaint over the status of ATATP students in the University. "They have the rights and responsibilities spelled out in Chapter VIIIA of the University By-Laws as they apply to non-degree students." Furthermore, their certificate was awarded by the Chancellor and Duncan had always been able to negotiate use of any University service like Fisher Library or the Sports Union.

An Evaluation Proposed

All parties agreed that any reform of the ATATP should await a formative evaluation. This was expected to define staff roles, certification standards, and Aboriginalisation policy, and recommend future funding and expansion. A budget for the purpose, $20,000, was allocated from carry-over funds. Thorne had suggested to Swan that this ATATP evaluation be "Aboriginally managed",[38] possibly through the NSW AECG, and the Director-General replied that MC members should consult among themselves over this one. In late December, Swan released Laurie Craddock, who had succeeded Rose in July 1983 as Assistant Director of Special Programs, to chair an Evaluation Committee Working Party. Craddock's committee discussed possible chief evaluators at its meetings in December and January, among them Eric Willmot, Betty Watts, Roberta Sykes, and Victor Forrest, Principal Research Officer with the NAEC.[39] At the time, Craddock agreed that the ATATP courses be shut down from February to April 1984, ensuring that the final report would be available by 7 May.

Duncan was happy about Craddock's deadline, convinced that the sooner the evaluation was over the better. He told Ward that there was no suggestion of any major deficiency in the existing program and that no action would be taken "without the support and concurrence of the University of Sydney".[40] Nor did he doubt that the NSW DoE would discuss the appointment of a chief evaluator with him well in advance. Duncan could afford optimism: he had good relations with the major players and his ATATP staff, and he knew that the critical approach of the MC towards the University in 1983 was not shared by all members. Even so, the Vice-Chancellor was not convinced that the evaluation was a force for good. "I am very uneasy indeed about the proposed evaluation,"[41] Ward told Duncan, and he asked him for more details of the selection of an evaluator and his/her terms of appointment. Given the University's minority representation on the Evaluation Committee, Ward feared that demands unacceptable to the University would be pushed through.

Neither Duncan's optimism nor Ward's reservations were put to the test. First came news of the appointment of at least 25 additional ATAs for 1984, confirmed on 7 December,[42] so the question arose – how could a moratorium proposed for Semester I training remain in place? Secondly, the University signalled its intention to shut down the Department of Adult Education from the end of 1983, sundering the ATATP from its University base.

Life Goes On

Disputes within the MC, and the academic politics around Adult Education's death agonies, did not impact much on the daily activities of the ATATP staff and students. The graduation in 1982 was the usual grand occasion marked by pre-ceremony drinks in the anteroom of the Great Hall attended by the Chancellor and Joyce Black, the Hon. Ron J. Mulock, New South Wales Minister for Education, Davina Tyrrell, Education Officer from the Aboriginal Education Unit, and the Vice-Chancellor.[43] When the apologies were read out, there was a telegram from Charles Perkins, Chairman of the Aboriginal Development Commission: "Regret am unable to attend presentation ceremony on 23 November as I will be overseas on that day. Please convey my congratulations to the successful Aboriginal teaching assistants."[44] Eighteen ATAs, including NESA trainees, graduated in the company of 240 parents, relatives and visitors, four of the students achieving Level I awards, seven Level II, and seven Level III. Just under half the student body received prizes for outstanding work. Another 30 students had attended in-service training. When Mulock spoke to guests, he confirmed the appointment of 30 more ATAs in 1983, with another 40 likely the following year. The new appointments were especially newsworthy as they were the first funded by the state government outside the Commonwealth quota.

Thorne's revised ATATP curriculum was introduced in early 1983, and both he and Duncan visited rural schools in the north and north-west to explain its features and get feedback. Duncan also reported on the Commonwealth's disadvantaged schools program in rural New South Wales which included a visit to Tingha Primary where an ATA was developing a locally based Aboriginal studies program. They would return together to join an ATATP

Figure 28. Aboriginal Teachers Aides Graduation. Back row: Barry Thorne, Lee-Ann Sheridan, Iris Johnson, Janice Dennis, Lexine Skuthorpe and Jenny Wright. Front row: Sandra McGrady, Raylene Saunders, Sir Hermann Black, Coral Wright and Waine Ellis, 1983. Image courtesy of University of Sydney Archives.

organised Aboriginal Education Social Function in Mackie, which brought together trainees and representatives of the major Aboriginal organisations in Sydney.

Nine government students graduated in the Great Hall on 23 November 1983, along with 13 non-government enrolments,[45] and another 20 students passed through the in-service program, four of them ATAs attending in lieu of an Upgrading session. Thorne's graduation address took up the theme that had preoccupied Morgan earlier – the need for more Aborigines in the teaching force. While the NAEC had set a target of 1000 Aboriginal teachers nationally by 1990, Thorne doubted its feasibility as New South Wales boasted only 35 to date, most of them ex-ATAs. There was good news on the ATA front, however, with the NSW DoE signalling its intention of employing 200 ATAs by 1986.

Figure 29. Aboriginal Teachers Aides graduation 1983: staff, including Nadia Messih, Barry Thorne (left), Julie Janson (back, right), and ATAs. Image courtesy of University of Sydney Archives.

Two other speakers addressed the gathering – Peter Schnierer, Senior Education Officer with the North Coast Region of the NSW DoE, and Joyce Woodberry, an ATA from La Perouse Public. Schnierer told of the role ATAs performed in diverse cultural situations and Woodberry of her nine years as an ATA.

> When the first 20 ATAs went through it was a lot different to today. A lot of the ATAs were used to make tea for the teachers and to run messages in those days. I suppose I was lucky because I had two great principals who understood what an ATA was employed for. I was able to work with the children and the Aboriginal parents. Today we are not only ATAs but act a school counsellors, liaison people and health workers. Our job doesn't finish at 3.30 p.m. when school closes. If a parent wants to talk with you, no matter where you are, you need to talk with them. I believe along with the Aboriginal people that our future lies with our children and we want a good education for them. ATAs are providing our

children with positive roles which are also educating teachers and staff about Aboriginal society.[46]

Both Woodberry and Schnierer would serve as ATATP coordinators in the years ahead, as would a third guest, Rosemary Stack, who was representing Windradyne Aboriginal Education Resource Centre.

When the last report to the Board of Adult Education was presented in 1983, 177 ATAs had completed Basic training since 1975, and 65 of them had returned for the Upgrading program. Another 58 had graduated from the Intensive course of whom 31 had already completed tertiary education or were on course.[47] Duncan estimated that 15–20 percent of ATATP students had, or were, studying at tertiary level, and another 30–50 percent had the capacity.[48]

Perhaps Burney has summed up the achievements of these early ATAs and their training truly: "What the AEA Program meant to individual Kooris, it can't be measured. People's lives were changed, they got a formal education and it had a ripple effect throughout their communities. It put Aboriginal education on the map in a sandstone university."[49]

Death of a Department

In his retirement speech in June 1982, Crowley found space to laud the record of the ATAs trained at Sydney and their dramatic impact on schools. Crowley had always backed Duncan's initiatives through time release and material assistance and had involved himself personally in ATA meetings and graduations. He had also done his best to win Commonwealth and state government grants for Aboriginal education. Unfortunately, his later years at Sydney were consumed by struggle inside the University and he stood down a disappointed man. The portents were there as far back as 1964 when the Martin Committee came out against Adult Education as a university discipline recommending that CAE and TAFE sectors take up the slack at lower cost. In 1978, the University began its own review of Adult Education under Vice-Chancellor and Principal, Professor Sir Bruce Williams (1967–81). A follow-up report came from the Registrar, Ken Knight, broadly in line with the findings of the 1982–84 Triennium Report of CTEC that proposed universities concentrate on self-funded continuing and professional education.

Early in the 1980s, the University's deteriorating financial position saw Ward under pressure from influential academics to cut Adult Education out of the budget. Responding, Ward admitted that the operation of the department had not been smooth. "It is painful to record that the department does not appear to be a happy one. I believe that at present it lacks a firm sense of acknowledged common purpose."[50] In November 1981, he signalled the closure of Adult Education and its replacement by a Centre for Continuing and Adult Education.

Duncan's work in Adult Education, especially in Aboriginal education, had been recognised by Ward when he appointed him acting director on Crowley's retirement. The unenviable task of winding up the department came with it. In 1983, Duncan joined a Committee on the Future of the Department of Adult Education led by Associate Professor Ian Jack, Chairman of the Board of Adult Education whose conclusions were similar to those taken by Ward. Indeed the Jack committee went further dropping "Adult" from the title of the new Centre for Continuing Education. The committee did however recommend that Aboriginal adult education activity and the ATATP become part of the responsibilities of the new centre. This was an important concession as there was real concern in Aboriginal circles that the ATATP would close altogether.[51] The report also recommended the appointment of an Aboriginal staff member in Continuing Education.

> In the current social and political climate it has become essential that a suitably qualified Aborigine be included in the teaching staff associated with the Aboriginal Education program and the Committee recommends that the University take account of the financial and other implications of the need to include a suitably qualified Aborigine in the teaching staff of the Aboriginal Adult Education program.[52]

Jack recommended that the University continue to pay Duncan's salary, handle the ATATP budget, and provide office and teaching space.

> The Committee is of the view that the program [ATATP] should be maintained provided the employing authorities wish it and the funds continue to be provided. The Committee feels that it would be desirable for the possibilities for developing additional programs in this area of work to be explored.

The closure of Adult Education and its replacement by a Centre for Continuing Education directly responsible to the Vice-Chancellor was adopted by Senate on 5 March 1984, the new centre opening in April. However, so far as Aboriginal education went, Continuing Education was an unsuitable location, the unit being devoted to professional education and profit. Towards the end of 1983, it was proposed that the ATATP be transferred to the University's Department of Education. After opposing the plan initially, Duncan agreed with the new suggestion. "Both the work in Aboriginal Adult Education and the Discussion Group Scheme could be considered more appropriately the responsibility of the University's Department of Education."[53] He also accepted that the study of Adult education as a teaching methodology pass to the Department of Education.

The move was discussed at a meeting between Duncan and Professor Cliff Turney, Head of the Department of Education, in early January 1984. Duncan had expressed worries about the ATATP's relationship with the Board of Studies in Education which determined Education's professional curriculum and he wanted to delay the transfer until he had returned from study leave among the Native Americans, and the Inuit and Sami people. Another staff member from Adult Education with previous experience of the ATATP, Wayne Hooper, was put forward as the best person to take charge in the interim, there being "no one in the Department of Education who has been involved with the program in any way".[54] But events overtook him. In his memo of 28 February 1984, the University Registrar, Keith Jennings reported:

> In establishing the centre it has been decided that the Aboriginal Training Scheme will be transferred to the Department of Education and this action has already taken place including the secondment to that Department of Mr A.T. Duncan who will continue to have prime responsibility for this scheme.

Senate approved the arrangement on 5 March 1984, and Duncan and the ATATP were relocated in the Department of Education where he remained on staff until his retirement from the faculty in 1988. So the baton for Aboriginal education passed from the Department of Adult Education to the Department of Education. Arthur More, who evaluated the Department of Adult Education's contribution in happier days, deserves the last word.

> In doing the study I became aware of extensive involvement of your (Crowley's) department in innovative projects in Aboriginal education. This involvement appears to go back over twenty years to a time when it was not at all popular to be involved in Aboriginal advancement. Your department should be proud of its record.[55]

6

In Partnership with Education

> It is interesting to note how central the Aboriginal Education Assistance Training Program, (AEATP), is to many Koori members of staff and students at the moment.
>
> Catherine Glass, EEO, acting coordinator, 1988[1]

When the University's Department of Education took over the ATATP in 1984, Duncan and his team had established their training program and outlasted government penny pinching and other crises. However, the ATATP had not embedded itself in the University to the extent hoped as Duncan reveals in this comment to Jane Kirton:

> The lack of recognition by the University – the program was always considered an offshoot, something over the road that had nothing to do with University life. I resented the way the University viewed the program – it was never seen as a "real" program, and it was never made a proper part of the University.[2]

Thorne, the first Aboriginal coordinator, has put forward a similar assessment:

> If you took the Commonwealth funds away, the University certainly wouldn't have coughed up the money to continue the Program. It had been there for a number of years and was still seen as a periphery type of thing. It was not entrenched in the structure of the University or the Department of Education. None of these institutions would take responsibility for the Program despite the fact that it had been running successfully for six or seven years.[3]

The ATATP's new start in the Department of Education was not an auspicious one; indeed, there was doubt whether it would survive the replanting. As the Head of Education, the bluff and forceful Professor Cliff Turney, has recorded: "I was asked by the Vice-Chancellor whether I would agree to Duncan becoming a Senior Lecturer in my department with special responsibility for the AEAP; consequently, after consultation with colleagues, Duncan and his Program were somewhat grudgingly transferred to the department."[4] Taking over the program put an extra load on Education which was facing testing times. It was busy upgrading itself to faculty status in an atmosphere of academic politicking and there were no discretionary funds to ease the ATATP's consolidation.

Although several staff in the Department of Education had taught Aboriginal children, they had little or no knowledge of ATAs or the ATATP. Turney himself knew of conditions in Aboriginal schools in western New South Wales from his Isolated Schools research (1980), which concluded that Aboriginal education had "all but failed",[5] the finding bringing him a rebuke from the NSW DoE. On re-visiting the assessment 20 years later, Turney could only reaffirm his earlier one.

> I doubt whether much has been achieved in the past twenty years. The continued restricted funding for education and the inertia of the Education Department do not encourage a more positive view.[6]

As mentioned by Duncan, prior to the takeover staff in Education knew nothing of the achievements of the ATATP under Adult Education. Neither of the two departments had much contact with the other. A few Education staff including Joyce Wylie and Ray Stroobant, senior lecturers in education, and John Cleverley, took tutorial and discussion classes for Adult Education, and Cleverley was on the editorial panel of its flagship publication, *Current Affairs Bulletin*. From the Adult Education side, two staff, Joan Allsop, a senior lecturer, and the Director, Des Crowley, taught in the Adult Education major in the Master of Education; and several of Crowley's staff like Darryl Douglas had enrolled in Education as postgraduates. So far as the ATATP went, there was no connection between the two, a state of affairs made obvious at the 1983 graduation when one invitation from 175 went to the head of Education for form's sake – it was not taken up.

A Change in Director and Coordinator

Turney asked Cleverley to act as Director of the ATATP in 1984, moving the program away from its Adult Education roots. "It fell on me," Cleverley recorded, "because of my interest in cross-cultural and comparative education."[7] After graduating from Balmain Teachers College in 1953, he had taught in inner city and suburban public schools, including special education classes. Next came a lectureship at Wagga Wagga Teachers College, then a year with the Commonwealth Office of Education in the Colombo Plan section. Cleverley returned to the University as Teaching Fellow in 1963, completing a PhD in education, before moving to Monash University as lecturer. After his return to Sydney in 1972, he was appointed Professor and Head of the School of Social and Policy Studies in Education in 1987, and Pro and Acting Dean of the new Faculty of Education where he worked closely with Turney. He was also chair of the faculty's Users' Committee responsible for the brief for the New Education Building Complex where the Koori Centre would be located eventually. Serving as ATATP director from 1984, he taught the subject, Introduction to Education, in the Basic course "to get a feel for things".[8] After standing down in 1987, he returned to Aboriginal education in 1990, becoming acting director of the new centre prior to the appointment of an Indigenous director. He returned later to assist with specific projects.

After the closure of the Department of Adult Education, Duncan transferred to the Department of Education as senior lecturer, teaching Aboriginal pedagogy and Aboriginal

Figure 30. Head of the Department of Education, Cliff Turney. Image courtesy of Roslyn Turney.

studies in the Bachelor of Education (Primary) and the Diploma of Education. He also continued with his research in Indigenous comparative education benefiting from a grant from the AEC (NSW). Although no longer director, Duncan maintained personal contacts with ATAs in the Mackie Building and taught occasionally in the ATATP. In 1985, he put forward a plan for a Centre for Aboriginal Studies in the University. This "centre of excellence,"[9] he told Vice-Chancellor Ward, would build on Elkin's worldwide renown, the reputation of the ATATP, and the advanced course work and research planned or already underway in Aboriginal Performing Arts, Music, Law, Linguistics and Fine Arts. Duncan also promised to visit government departments and Aboriginal organisations to engage them in sharing basic data. The cost of the project, exclusive of his own time but including travel and secretarial assistance, was put at no more than $20,000. However, the Deputy-Vice-Chancellor (DVC), John Dunston, opposed Duncan's involvement and Turney had reservations as to its likely cost which led the Vice-Chancellor to hold back, "at least for the present, but shall keep in mind".[10]

Duncan's idea had progressed no further when he retired in 1988. In remarks to Jane Kirton the same year, the ex-director looked back at the transfer period.

> Although it seems to be running quite successfully now, I feel there needed to be a more consistent, dedicated, professional approach to the running of the Program. I was really disappointed to see it not being run for periods of six months or more. There were a lot of groups to blame – both Aboriginals and others, like employees of the University and the Department of Education.[11]

Shirley Berg, the Executive Officer of the AEC (NSW), summed up Duncan's qualities as educator in Aboriginal education after he stepped down.

> Perhaps one of the most important gifts that Alan had was his ability to stir interest in people and to inspire them to use their talents in the projects decided on. He always sought to work closely with Aboriginal people so as he could determine what they thought and what they wanted, and needed. He had them take him to the Aboriginal Reserves and to show him what sorts of projects could help most.[12]

A change in coordinator in 1984 saw Joyce Woodberry from La Perouse Public School, a graduate of the first ATA training session, replace Barry Thorne in June. Auntie Joyce Alice Woodberry was a foundation member of the NSW AECG and a devoted member of her school community. At Sydney, she collaborated with Julie McNab, "a really a hard worker",[13] who held the lecturer position, and Nadia Messih, who continued as secretary. Cleverley was committed overseas for seven months so Turney asked a short-term appointee in Education, Audrey Aarons, to assist Woodberry. A talented Melbournian, Aarons held an MA (Educational Planning) from London having practical experience in curriculum development in Papua New Guinea. She would move to London in 1985 where she joined UNICEF as a staff member.

New and Old Issues

One of Education's first changes was to replace the Management Committee with an Advisory Committee (AC) from 1 May 1984, its membership expanding to 11. Among the new faces were Davina Tyrrell, representing the NAEC, Ken Ralph, DAA, and Florence Ramstead and Laurel Williams, NSW DoE. A year later, the AC was cut back to seven, a more manageable size.[14] Fortunately, Thorne agreed to continue to act as Chairman for 12 months providing much needed stability.

The 1984 transfer was not plain sailing. Negotiations between Ward, Duncan and Turney over the relocation of the ATATP had not involved members of the old Management Committee, an omission that bred resentment. Emotion was fuelled when Turney made it clear that he saw the role of the newly appointed AC as a strictly limited one. It was to advise him on organisational matters, and the coordinator on content and implementation, however it had "no executive function"[15] and its recommendations must go through him and not be conveyed as coming from the University.

Thorne was among those who thought that the University was back-tracking on agreements made in Adult Education days especially the need to take Aboriginal advice, and he put his reservations in a letter to Woodberry.

> It would seem to me that this Advisory Committee has been formed to be used as the University of Sydney sees fit. Is it that the University is going to seek Aboriginal advice and recommendations on a whole range of issues and then

Figure 31. Joyce Woodbury, coordinator, Aboriginal Teaching Assistants Training Program 1984. Image courtesy of the Koori Centre.

use those [that] suit and discard those that don't? Does the University intend to call this Aboriginal consultation to support the initiatives they agree with for the development of the Program![16]

On the 30 May 1984, Turney sent Cleverley a further list of arrangements asking that these be closely followed. All ATATP operations should be consistent with the University's "expectations and rules"; external correspondence from the ATATP, including correspondence on funding, administration and students, must go through his office; and all casual teachers needed University approval and, wherever possible, should be drawn from Department of Education staff. By way of consolation, full-time ATATP staff were entitled to membership of the department's staff meeting and the coordinator and lecturer could join the Board of Studies in Education. Were any serious disputes to arise inside the ATATP, Turney should be alerted, and he promised that all members of the program would have access to the Head of Department for consultation, "on any matter at any time".

Worried that the AC and the ATATP would go their own ways making waves for Education, Turney sought control from the beginning. Unfortunately, his list of dos and don'ts raised issues dormant since Adult Education days. Smarting over the unannounced transfer of the ATATP to Education, AC members were concerned that Turney's directives worked against DAA's policy that government-funded projects be managed through consultation and self-determination. As Aboriginal representatives, they had a duty to put forward their views which should be listened to and acted upon, and Turney's requirements were seen as working against the spirit of the ATATP.

In Partnership with Education 115

The issue of the powers of AC members came to a head at the 5 July meeting when Morgan tabled a paper, "Administrative Structure and Procedures", asking that the University accept the ATATP as a "'Special' Program" based on its Aboriginal nature: "it cannot be compared to any other program within the University".[17] The ATATP was not functioning as well as he expected, Morgan argued, and he proposed various improvements including a review of salaries, superannuation for all staff, the upgrading of Messih's position to administrative assistant, and the appointment of a full-time typist. Woodberry and Messih should be given greater authority, especially in internal financial matters, and the ATATP's organisational arrangements should enable "the disappearance of hierarchical positions where hierarchy has no real meaning and where values are different." Morgan called for

> The recognition of the fact that, as an Aboriginal program, the Aboriginal community has the good of the program at heart and is just as much sensitive to the efficient management and development as the University, and that it is only through Aboriginal participation and shared decision-making that the Program will show its true reflection and worth.

The University must exercise the principle of "understanding, good judgement, and humaneness".

Another layer of bureaucratic control occurred when senior responsibility for the ATATP moved from Duncan's occasional chats with the Vice-Chancellor to oversight by a Deputy Vice-Chancellor, in this case, Arthur John Dunston. A graduate of Reading University and St John's College, Cambridge, Dunston had fought with the Eighth Army in North Africa, Italy and France, returning home to teach classics at London University and Reading. In 1953, he accepted the Chair of Latin at Sydney, the only one in the discipline in the southern hemisphere. His arrival coincided with the landing of Queen Elizabeth II on her first Australian visit, a gala day on Sydney harbour. Dunston soon found himself holding senior academic and administrative positions on campus and in town. Appointed Deputy Vice-Chancellor in 1982, he was the senior contact point for the ATATP through to his retirement in mid-1986. So it came to pass that the miniscule ATATP operation found itself under a director, a Head of Department, a Deputy Vice-Chancellor and an Advisory Committee, truly a surfeit of checks and balances.

A Bad Outcome

Joyce Woodberry, the ATA from La Perouse Public, had accepted appointment as coordinator for three months on leave without pay from the NSW DoE, with an extension for 12 possible. While she and McNab were successful in getting the program underway despite the short notice, things went badly. Towards the end of 1984, and following decisions taken in regard to ATATP resources including a car, Dunston directed Turney to end Woodberry's appointment, thinking her insufficiently experienced in administration. "Indeed he commanded me," Turney said, "to give notice of dismissal to the Director."[18] Under the

Deputy Vice-Chancellor's direction, Woodberry was to receive four weeks pay in lieu of notice from 7 January 1985.[19]

Turney called her into his office in Madsen to break the unwelcome news.

> This I did protestingly, since I believed it was really Dunston's responsibility to take such actions. Obediently I met with the director and told her as tactfully as I could of the Deputy-Vice-Chancellor's decision. Her response was angry, abusive and threatening. "You bastard! – Did I want my name cited as a 'racist Dean' in the national press? Did I want the campus invaded by the Aborigines who lived in Redfern." My response was more one of shock than annoyance. I simply reiterated the Deputy-Vice-Chancellor's decision and suggested she might appeal to him.[20]

It seems an Aboriginal protest did follow under the jacaranda tree in the Quadrangle.

Claiming discrimination and lack of support, Woodberry took her case to the University Academic Staff Association of New South Wales, the union arranging that she remain in the job until June 1985. However, the coordinator determined to resign immediately, among her reasons, "lack of a fair go", and an unwillingness to "cop more shit". Woodberry said later she had been given no support from the University and had contacted the Anti-Discrimination Board before finally returning to her ATA position at La Perouse.[21] She was, as one writer remembered her, "A strong person and very much an individual".[22]

Morgan strongly backed Woodberry in remarks published nationally in Helen Trinca's article, "Aborigine 'not Given a Fair Go'", in *The Australian* of 8 February 1985. The Aboriginal educator weighed into the University and called for the ATATP to be taken away from Sydney and relocated at a more suitable campus. "There is an insensitivity to Aboriginal needs at the University and they really have no understanding or desire to become involved." "It has always been our view that the Aboriginal training program should be Aboriginalised," said Morgan, but "there was little Aboriginal involvement in, or control of, the curriculum". When Dunston responded: "He declined to comment on the background to Mrs Woodberry's case but said she had been offered the chance to continue on the grounds that she had not in fact received formal notice and because she said she had not been given a chance to prove herself." The Deputy Vice-Chancellor anticipated that the post would soon be re-advertised with the University looking "especially for an Aborigine to fill it".

Turney was furious when he read Morgan's comments reflecting on his department. An acrimonious phone exchange followed and the Head of School refused to re-start the ATATP without an apology. None was forthcoming. With no coordinator in place and time fast running out for 1985, the Director-General, Doug Swan, called a crisis meeting in May in Bridge Street attended by Cleverley, who had recently returned from overseas leave, and Burney from the NSW AECG, where there was quick agreement to press for an immediate resumption.[23] Turney took the group's advice and the ATATP re-commenced in June. "This unfortunate episode," commented Turney, "damaged relationships between the Aboriginal Centre and the University which took time and hard work to heal."[24]

Woodberry would look back on the unhappy events.

> When I was appointed they said there would be a chap who would be in charge of the Program. He went overseas and that meant there was no-one I could work closely with who knew the Program. I think that if I had someone I could have worked closely with, I probably would have stayed on longer and things would have worked out better. There were no links to the University and I didn't have the support of the administrative staff – I was really left in limbo.[25]

She believed that the University still had much to learn about Aboriginal education, a process that called for help from Aboriginal people too.

> They need to start really listening to Aboriginal people because they've not got a very good record even though the Program has been there for over ten years. I also think that the Program needs a lot of support from Koori people, and from teachers and other people in the Education Department. It needs to keep in touch with what is happening in schools, in Aboriginal education, and in all other areas of education. It shouldn't just be left on its own.[26]

Her commitment to Aboriginal education, including over 20 years as an AEA in the La Perouse community, was recognised in the New South Wales Parliament by the MLA, Michael Daley. Daley described her as "a mentor, auntie, friend, educator and guide".[27] *Pemulwuy* also relates further details of her remarkable career and of her grandmother, Mrs Alice Ralph, a fighter for Aboriginal education who had marched on Bridge Street. In the same newsletter, Bob Morgan described Woodberry as "a warrior for Aboriginal kids in schools". In 2009, her daughter, Narelle Daniels-Woodberry, would enrol at Sydney for the double degree, BEd (Secondary: Humanities)/BA.

Things to Follow Up

The Department of Education, the ATATP's new host, was accommodated in the Madsen Building near City Road, the one-time headquarters of the National Standards Laboratory, a solid brick and stone structure built by the Commonwealth in the 1930s to withstand Japanese bombing. However, the ATATP's teaching rooms were located in the Mackie Building on the boundary of the University, an inconvenient although healthy 10–15 minute walk from Madsen. From the Aboriginal staff's perspective, the Mackie location reflected the adage that they were best out of sight. As Woodberry explained, "I felt they weren't interested and being across the road made us really isolated."[28] Peter Schnierer, coordinator in 1985, made an identical point saying: "It's always been an add-on to the place, physically separated from the faculty that looked after it, that kind of sums it up really, being on the other side of the road, separated by a bridge."[29] Security at Mackie was poor with several break-ins and Cleverley wanted the ATATP moved to Madsen as soon as possible, however it was decided to wait on advice from the evaluation study due to be completed inside six months.[30] When this failed to materialise, he proposed moving the Basic course to Madsen immediately staking a claim for the rest of the program, however nothing eventuated as AC members were unwilling to see the program split.[31]

Inside the ATATP, it was decided to abandon the terms Basic, Upgrading and Intensive, and to replace the descriptor, "Level", with "Stage". Education's plan was to offer Stage I as a 12-week unit and Stages II and III as 14-week units every alternate year. While the new schedule was laid down in the ATATP handbook, in actuality training weeks were cut ruthlessly when exigency demanded, with Stages I and II reduced by two weeks apiece in 1986 to save money. Such reductions affected the quality of the ATATP training by shortening time available for remedial work and training.

Shorter training periods also weakened the program's claims for accreditation. In the early 1980s, the certificate was accepted as the equivalent of the Clerical Entrance Examination by the NSW Public Service Board and Duncan was able to win recognition from CAEs for individual applicants. When the ATATP moved to Education, Turney wanted the program put under the department's Board of Studies in Education but this was not followed through because the certificate was not regarded as a regular academic qualification. Schnierer's view was that "So many of the students put so much into the Program and they came out with such a weak, pathetic kind of accreditation." He thought the existing "fancy Graduation ceremony"[32] built up "a false expectation of what the certificate actually was". He also said that a few students earned it too easily: "Because of this the certificate wasn't worth the paper it was written on." Other coordinators thought similarly, as Williams explains:

> The Program might only be seen as a Mickey Mouse Program by University staff and school staff. It certainly wasn't. It had a valid, professional place within the training of educators. It was not seen as valid by the University, educational institutions or the Dept. of Education because it did not have adequate accreditation.

The breakthrough inside Sydney came in 1987 when Arts and Education admitted Stage III graduates and exceptional Stage II students, however the program was less successful in gaining formal recognition from other tertiary and TAFE institutions given that course lengths were a movable feast and the University offered no reciprocity.

On Moving into the Mainstream

When the ATATP joined Education in 1984, it became more visible on campus and staff and students anticipated that more doors would open. Cleverley explains how this expectation was tempered by reality.

> Individual Vice-Chancellors were personally sympathetic but good will was slow to translate into action – the University was a place where time was seldom of the essence. The Sydney hierarchy valued the ATATP for various reasons. Having an Aboriginal program was useful for the University's self perception if you like, aside from meeting any educational demand. It also appreciated the fact that

the ATATP's operations were self-funded and the program was stable, that is, it attracted little public debate.

Across the University, enthusiastic academic staff members full of energy and ideas were doing things in their own departments and some other staff in the administration were extremely helpful when called on, creative in finding solutions.

Of course there were the self-designated gate-keepers, academic and administrative. I heard the views – "Your Aboriginal program really has no place in a university." "These Aboriginals are well-to-do and have good jobs, why the special treatment?" "That certificate you give out has no standing you know." Ill-disposed because Education was putting the case, or on account of the Aboriginal connection, or whatever?

Once I asked for extra funding from the University's reserve for out-of-pocket expenses for a newly appointed Aboriginal coordinator. I had obviously crossed a boundary. "When the program has proved itself, John" – in other words, no. What of the ATATP having operated for ten years and having 200 graduates? It seemed there were many more worthy causes around.[33]

A View from the Schools

Preoccupation with ATATP affairs on campus diverted attention from the question of the effectiveness of the training. How did principals and teachers think the training program was fairing? Here the work of Professor Sam Ball from Education, who had taken over responsibility for the evaluation in 1984, assisted by Associate Professor Ray King and the ATA, Delma Davison, as research associate, provided crucial evidence. The completion date for the evaluation, set for December 1984, was put back to August 1985, and delayed again by the time demands of Ball's SUCCEED scheme and a Commonwealth Universities' Travelling Fellowship. Ball promised to submit early in 1986, citing "necessity as the mother of closure",[34] but the plan came to naught following the theft of data and documents from his university car. Over the period, the helpful Davison would move to a RACLO position, being replaced by Stephen Wale as researcher. Finally, on 26 October 1986, a partial draft was passed to the director which proved the end of the matter.[35]

Although incomplete, Ball's research did contain valuable findings. Responses from school principals and teachers returned a preference for training away from Sydney and closer to home, thus limiting disruption to the ATAs' family and school life and making travel arrangements easier and less costly. This school staff opinion was also supported by students and ex-students. "In general most students and ex-students had a preference for a tertiary institution closest to their home wherever that might be in the state."[36] Other negatives attached to Sydney were the very small number of regular Aboriginal students, the absence of a support centre, and few local community links. Ball's finding cut across conventional wisdom at Sydney that the University was the best of all locations given its central location and high prestige.

Clearly principals valued the work of their ATAs, especially in teaching individual children and small groups and in liaising with Aboriginal parents and communities. They did want more taught about their own priorities though – the curriculum, the school system, and the requirements of the NSW DoE. In addition, extra time should be found for counselling skills, conflict resolution, community interaction and small group management. ATAs were clearly a positive in their school and communities: "Principals felt strongly that the ATAs were doing the specifics of their jobs well in the circumstances of some racial tension and racist attitudes in some towns."[37]

Teachers also emphasised ATAs' liaison role with parents and the help they gave individual Aboriginal children. Asked what criteria should be applied in their selection, they rated motivation, empathy and communication skills above academic qualities. While some teachers reported a lack of initiative and self-confidence in their ATAs, others took the time to write a personal comment on their particular aide: "very competent", "outstanding", "one in a million". Both principals and teachers recognised and valued the outcomes of the ATATP in personal development, communication skills and relationship building, and agreed that the Sydney program broadened outlooks. Most of them thought that ATAs deserved a career path leading to full-time teaching.

Familiar problems also surfaced. Some principals were still using ATAs as clerical aides ignoring their educational role and others engaged them in relief teaching though this was expressly forbidden. A number of ATAs still had no space where they could talk privately with children and parents, and several principals expressed disappointment that ATAs were not upgrading their skills remaining at the one school for up to ten years without academic extension. Questionnaires revealed a drain of talented ATAs from the classroom as individuals climbed higher up the career ladder. So far as the ATATP went, most principals and many teachers admitted to knowing little of the program having virtually no contact with University staff except when discussing urgent problems by phone or letter.

Ball's findings were largely confirmed by the newly appointed ATATP lecturer, Rick Daly, the replacement for McNab, who undertook a field trip over five days during August 1986 in far west New South Wales visiting Wilcannia, Bourke, Gulargambone, Brewarrina and Dubbo. Daly's report emphasised the need for greater liaison between the ATATP and the schools, and greater recognition and understanding of local diversity. The lack of information about the course continued to be a sore point with many principals and Aboriginal communities. Too few schools were visited by university staff, he wrote, with some not visited for several years.

> The ATATP needs to spend more time in individual communities and needs to stay for longer periods so as Aboriginal communities can see how interested the ATATP is in listening to their ideas and then implementing them within the programme.[38]

Both Ball and Daly indicated that ATAs they interviewed were deeply committed to the training program and proud of it and that a network of ATAs had developed state wide.

Coordinators – Peter Schnierer

The Woodberry saga led Education to realise the importance of the Aboriginal coordinator. For students on course, the coordinator was the most important person: they were the personal face of the University acting as confidants and counsellors as well as teachers and administrators. When ATAs complained about their treatment in schools over release time or classroom issues, they usually took the matter up with the coordinator. Further, it was the coordinator who was called on to present an Aboriginal perspective in the University and outside.

Some five months after Woodberry left, Peter N. Schnierer, a graduate of Mullumbimby High School with a BA DipEd (UNSW), took the post of lecturer/coordinator on secondment from the NSW DoE. In the haste to get things moving, the vacancy was not advertised though the NSW AECG was consulted.[39] More experienced than his predecessor, Schnierer taught at Matraville High before working as a Regional Aboriginal Education Consultant and then coordinator of the Introductory Studies Program at Northern Rivers CAE. His final acceptance followed a sharp wrangle with DVC Dunston over an appropriate salary level,[40] Schnierer finally winning Step I (fixed) on the senior lecturer scale. In mid-June, Thorne announced, with relief, that the ATATP had "finally gotten underway for 1985".[41] Schnierer would replace Thorne as Chairman of the Advisory Committee, the AC thanking its past chairman for his "excellent contribution".[42]

Schnierer was on hand to welcome the new Director-General, Robert Winder, when he visited Mackie on 30 September 1985. Just before Winder's arrival, Cleverley sent him a comprehensive letter on behalf of the program.[43] Could Winder help with:

- study leave of half a day a week for ATA students in schools;
- a regional training trial for Stage I students of 2–3 weeks;
- encouragement for training institutions to accept Sydney's certification;
- the tying of ATA salary increments to the completion of each of the three stages;
- the appointment of regional ATA support staff to assist ATAs in the field and support in-service arrangements;
- payment of living-away-from-home allowance for rural ATAs to cover Sydney expenses;
- the introduction of a "whole-of-school" policy with school based in-service for staff (teachers and general) and community representatives; and
- an appropriate industrial award for ATAs, with the title "aide" replaced by one not suggestive of a clerical function.

Winder was supportive. As an initial move, he agreed to remind school principals of ATAs' unique duties as set out by the Public Service Board; their need for study time while on course; and suitable school accommodation where they could talk privately. Taking the point that some newly appointed principals were not aware of ATAs' duties, the Director-General issued a three point directive: i) principals should understand that ATAs were positive role models for Aboriginal children; ii) that they were interpreters of Aboriginal children's needs to teachers; and iii) that they were the major contact point in the school for the local Aboriginal community.[44]

The NSW DoE, in collaboration with the ATATP, supported an Industrial Award for ATAs in 1986. The department had collected a group of ATAs to substantiate the case and membership of the Public Service Association Union was agreed upon. The recognition brought improved working conditions, opportunities for permanency, and pay increases linked with training levels. The Stage I qualification put a graduate on the third incremental step of the ATA award, and the Stage III qualification, the sixth step. It was also agreed that ATAs be renamed Aboriginal Education Assistants (AEAs), the title better fitting their duties, and that the ATATP acronym be changed to AEATP from 1987.

The NSW DoE then issued a revised set of responsibilities for AEAs, the base document used into the 1990s.

> The Aboriginal Education Assistant is responsible to the Principal in the following areas:
>
> A. Pastoral Care of Students
>
> Assisting the Principal and teachers in:–
>
> 1) monitoring the attendance, behaviour and progress of Aboriginal students;
>
> 2) interviewing and advising Aboriginal students in relation to 1) above;
>
> 3) attending to personal needs of Aboriginal students in relation to hygiene, health and injury;
>
> 4) advising Aboriginal students on matters relating to school, family or personal problems.
>
> B. Community and Parent Liaison:
>
> 1) assisting the Principal to establish and maintain effective relationships with Aboriginal parents and the Aboriginal community;
>
> 2) assisting the Principal and teachers in interviewing parents of Aboriginal students in relation to their school progress;
>
> 3) undertaking approved visits to Aboriginal parents in their homes in relation to their children's school progress or problems;
>
> 4) assisting the Principal and teacher in informing the Aboriginal community of the objectives and organisation of the school;
>
> 5) informing the Principal of activities and attitudes in the Aboriginal community which may affect the Aboriginal students in the school.

C. Teacher Support:

1) assisting teachers with individual or small groups of Aboriginal students in the classroom or excursion situation;

2) assisting teachers with matters affecting the behaviour or progress of Aboriginal students;

3) assisting teachers in the development of programmes for Aboriginal and non-Aboriginal students with particular emphasis on Aboriginal education;

4) assisting teachers in the production of materials with particular reference to Aboriginal education;

5) assisting teaching staff in developing and implementing a curriculum which is appropriate for the Aboriginal students in the school.

D. Other Duties:

1) carrying out other related duties as required by the Principal.[45]

The effects of linking of training skills with salary levels and a clear duty statement stimulated enrolments in the program.

The Curriculum and Other Matters

While Thorne's curriculum revision had served its immediate purpose, pressures demanded a more professional statement. Apart from their internal usefulness, the director wanted up-to-date materials available for faculties to help them determine special entry arrangements; Turney asked for a detailed statement of course content for presentation to the Board of Studies in Education; various tertiary institutions in New South Wales sought information for accreditation; and the Public Service Board and the NSW DoE needed more information on standards given that AEA increments were under determination. A Curriculum Development Committee was formed to prepare an ATATP curriculum for the Board of Studies in Education in 1984,[46] which promised to incorporate new teaching content required by the NSW DoE and the introduction of diagnostic testing skills. However, the turmoil inside the ATATP and doubts that the Board had any authority over the certificate course halted progress.

This Curriculum Advisory Committee was reactivated in 1985 outside the Board, as Schnierer recalls.

> There had to be a fundamental change to what was being taught there. I virtually had to throw the first program out of the window and start again. I wasn't going to be part of a tourist venture that sat on the back of hard fought for resources from D.A.A.[47]

The certificate, he thought, was given to students who had not handed in all assignments or attended lectures regularly, the result of the University not fulfilling its responsibilities.

"The University," said Schnierer, "should have been responsible for the A.E.A.P. staff in terms of staff and curriculum development. They didn't recognise them at all."[48] However, he did accept that: "There weren't many people at the University with expertise in the area of Aboriginal Education or Aboriginal people in NSW."[49] He thought that those who worked with traditionally accented communities in the Northern Territory had a fairly stereotypical view of Indigenous Australians. As to Cleverley's leadership, Schnierer reported: "The Director of the Program had no experience at all with Aboriginal people or Aboriginal Education – but he was generally a nice person and sensitive and responsive to things."[50] Schnierer later supplied a detailed statement of his own thoughts on the curriculum, arguing for greater attention to Aboriginal studies, recognition of cultural factors in teaching and learning, and more action research on Aboriginal learning styles and language.[51] In December 1985, the coordinator told *University News* that Sydney's AEAs took an active interest in curriculum reform and assisted Aboriginal pupils with special difficulties, work that was crucial in removing barriers to learning.[52] Schnierer also advocated more teaching on assessment, claiming that invalid testing in schools was incorrectly labelling Aboriginal children as slow learners.

The Ball evaluation had considered the balance of subjects taught across the AEATP satisfactory, although the curriculum as circulated lacked detail and was of little value to new staff. Considering the length of time the AEATP had operated, Ball thought it surprising and disappointing that no comprehensive set of curriculum materials was extant not just for the AEAs' benefit but for educators generally. "The cupboard," he revealed, "was as bare as the proverbial Mother Hubbard's."[53] An AEATP curriculum of commercial quality should be developed drawing on the experience of past and present AEAs.

Schnierer found the coordinator position limited in terms of a career path. In December 1986, he resigned to take up an education officer position in the Aboriginal Education Unit of the NSW DoE, having charge of the team writing the Aboriginal Studies Syllabus for Years 11 and 12 of the HSC. Though outside the University now, he found time to assist campus projects, advising on the AEATP curriculum, helping introduce Aboriginal studies in the faculties of Arts and Education, and joining a Working Party for an Aboriginal Education Centre. At its meeting of 4 April 1986, the AC passed a motion thanking Schnierer for his contribution to Aboriginal education at Sydney.

The graduation ceremony for Schnierer's year was held on 27 February 1986, when 29 students, 24 of them women, and all bar one from country New South Wales, graduated in the Great Hall. Thorne and Stack were the speakers, along with the Chancellor whose address urged the AEAs to set standards in their future work. "You can't accept the attitude that anything goes."[54] One Stage III student from that year enrolled at Macarthur Institute of Higher Education.

Coordinators – Robyn Williams

The April meeting of the AC in 1986 welcomed Robyn Williams, who held an Associate Diploma in Adult Education from the Institute of Technical and Adult Teacher Education (ITATE), as its new coordinator. She had previously worked for TAFE, where she had managed the Aboriginal New Opportunities for Women Program, and for the Department of Parks and Wildlife. Altogether she would remain with the AEATP from March to December 1986. An unusual series of events brought about her joining the AEATP.

> I'll be honest. I was tricked. I believe there is a need for the Coordinator of that Program to be Aboriginal. I was told about the job and said "Well I'll apply to help make up the numbers." I certainly did make up the numbers – I was the only Aboriginal person to apply. I think that it's important that every time positions like that are advertised, we get lots of Aboriginal people applying. I initially applied to make up the numbers and to let people know there were a lot of good Kooris around – not necessarily to take the position. So I then organised a secondment from National Parks.[55]

Williams was on hand to welcome the AEAs in late May 1986 – ahead of her, "a very interesting year because new things have been tried".[56] Helped by Lorraine Towers, Williams was instrumental in starting the ATATP library and resources centre. She also won greater recognition for the certificate credential, tightened policy on student attendance, and encouraged union representation.

> We started this change by including a section on unions in the curriculum. This started questions about why people join unions and how unions work. It was done as an educational exercise, and out of that the A.T.A.s made a decision to do something about their working conditions – although some people from the department didn't believe that this was the process that took place. I believe that this was a major step forward – for people to take that sort of action.[57]

For all Williams' optimism, there was some regret that AEAs had not joined the NSW Teachers Federation, a viewpoint expressed by Duncan.

> I was also very disappointed that the A.T.A.s never became members of the Teachers Federation. They should have been recognised right from the beginning. Unfortunately, while we were talking to the Teachers Federation about getting membership for the A.T.A.s, one of the staff went to the P.S.A. (Public Service Association). It was all in good faith and with the best of motives, but in fact it exacerbated the problem of the inter-Union demarcation dispute. I always felt responsible, but if I look back now it was the problem of being overworked.[58]

Duncan believed that he failed to communicate the progress underway with the NSW Teachers Federation, hence PSA membership was granted first. "It's meant that the A.T.A.s have never been recognised as professional educators in terms of pay or working conditions."[59]

Under Williams' leadership, the Curriculum Advisory Committee was re-invigorated, (it had only met once in 1985), and a statement on content was in draft form by October 1986.

Figure 32. Graduation of the Aboriginal Teaching Assistants with Nadia Messih (centre) and Peter Schnierer (far right), 1985. Image courtesy of the Koori Centre.

She herself prepared the Draft Working Document for the Aboriginal Studies section.

> The Aboriginal studies component will interlock with other subject strands of the course so that the whole course will be viewed with an Aboriginal perspective and through the experiences of Aboriginal People. Aboriginal studies will be looked at through Regional variants as there were and still are many and not through the shifting perceptions of Anthropological theory. Culture will be looked at and the process of change and how change affects law and culture and land, and how Aboriginal culture still changes within the broad society of Australia today.

As part of increasing local community involvement, Williams advocated strong links with schools close to the University and with local Aboriginal groups like the NSW AECG and Radio Redfern. She was particularly impressed by the Aboriginal counselling arrangements at Cumberland's College of Health Sciences thinking its initiative had lessons for Sydney. She was also determined to help the procession of new teachers and speakers "coming into the Program raw".[60]

At the 1986 graduation on 10 December, the Minister for Education, Rodney M. Cavelier, spoke in the Great Hall, along with Pat O'Shane. The AEA, Grace Crossley, made an "excellent speech"[61] on behalf of the students, four of whom entered Macarthur Institute of Higher Education, and PVC Susan Dorsch signed and presented the certificates.[62] This ceremony was Williams' last as she resigned to become Regional Aboriginal Coordinator for New South Wales TAFE in the Liverpool area.

During her nine months at Sydney, Williams had criticised the ATATP operations, its low budget, minimal staff numbers and material inadequacies. "It's like all Aboriginal Education programmes – under funded, under resourced, under staffed." While the premises were supplied by the University, she found "no resources – no photocopier, no computer or other things which I believe are essential for any educational program". She argued that AEAs should be recognised as the skilled Aboriginal educators they were and given the same resources allocated other University courses. Another weakness she discerned were patronising attitudes. "I think that the University staff could do with a lot of staff development on Aboriginal issues. The staff was very patronising." She also found people outside the AEATP knew next to nothing of its block mode arrangements: "Blacks have got special jobs and they're never here." The situation was interpreted by Williams as the University virtually washing its hands of things. Looking back, she would concede her own needs in regard to management skills. "I needed some staff development. I was so busy at the time I didn't notice it, but looking back I can see I should have had staff development – there was so much that I was expected to do all the time."[63]

Though Williams was a doughty critic, her professional commitment to the AEAs and Aboriginal education was unwavering.

> Eventually, the program will be recognised for the vital part it will play in the struggle for changing the system for Aboriginal students. Because when they understand the system well enough to see that the problem is within this system of education, they will then take the step of doing something about it.[64]

The loss of Williams, and of Schnierer before her, was a blow to the AEATP signifying its uphill battle to secure and retain capable people.

Reviewing the AEAP

At the AC meeting of 5 September 1986, Cleverley put the case for a "full-scale review" of the AEATP, focusing on staff roles and internal operations. As the issue of special admissions for Aboriginal students was under consideration in the University, he thought it "a good time to make changes or improvements to the ATATP which would highlight its value and improve its profile within the University". Associate Professor Raymond King from Education agreed to chair the review assisted by Williams, Daly and Messih from the AEATP office. Robert Lovell, a postgraduate student from Education, who had previously helped Williams prepare her curriculum document, acted as research assistant.

Presented to the Advisory Committee on 12 December 1986, the report recommended that NSW DoE policies receive more space in the curriculum, particularly discipline, pastoral care and community participation.[65] AEAs should be better prepared to promote and critically review Aboriginal studies in schools and should be taught how to introduce Aboriginal perspectives across the curriculum. Greater use should be made of interviews in determining students' progress and individuals helped make realistic assessments of their own academic progress. The Commonwealth's school tutor scheme deserved more use and its tutors should be workshopped; and the small library and resource collection deserved expansion under a part-time librarian assistant. As to staff, duty statements should be expanded, equity in workloads pursued more vigorously, and staff meetings chaired by the director held regularly. The AEATP should not attempt to teach more than two stages annually unless additional resources became available. It was also proposed that this stocktake of the AEATP become an annual event.

At the AC meeting of 5 September 1986, Cleverley reported his intention of taking study leave for six to seven months in 1987 and he recommended that King, from the School of Social and Policy Studies, serve as acting director. King's qualifications, which combined doctoral qualifications in the social sciences with managerial experience in the New Zealand civil service, were strong; and he was highly regarded on campus for his leadership of the Sydney University Community Research Centre. The man relished the challenge of a significant role with a social purpose as he felt his talent was constrained by the school work preoccupation of the Faculty of Education. If the AC members were happy, Cleverley said he would write to the PVC recommending the appointment. AC members had already come to value King's qualities during the internal review and his appointment as acting director was deservedly applauded.

7

Management Restructure and Reform

> You are challenging some of the implicit racism and prejudice which pervades our public institutions. You give an Aboriginal presence to the education system, a presence disturbing by its smallness in number, not by its smallness in spirit.
>
> Alan Ruby, Director Special Programs, AEATP Graduation, 1988[1]

By the mid-1980s, the AEATP was operating as a de facto department drafting its own budget and determining its curriculum and standards, though it was likely the University's smallest teaching entity. When King became program director in mid-1987, he set about formalising its duties and responsibilities. Conflict between the AEATP and the Faculty of Education in the past was unlikely as the director was also Pro-Dean but relations between the program and the faculty could alter if faces changed. To cover the eventuality, King prepared a set of "Authority and Responsibilities",[2] attempting to clarify the PVC/DVC connection, and lessen the direct role of the dean and head of school by delegating considerable powers to himself in academic matters, as well as staffing, accommodation, financial management and external liaison. The parties largely agreed with King's thinking provided he kept the faculty informed of significant developments and submit the annual budget through the head of school. King also retained his associate professor appointment in the School of Social and Policy Studies in Education, taking a reduced load in teaching and research. He was not so successful when he tried for a seat for the director on the Academic Board which was denied.

Change at the Top

AC members had briefly discussed the role of the Deputy Vice-Chancellor position just prior to Dunston's retirement in 1986[3] and before news came that Professor Susan E. Dorsch had been passed the responsibility. Dorsch was experienced in Aboriginal health having served in the School Medical Service in rural New South Wales. After completing a PhD at Sydney, specialising in transplantation immunology, she was appointed to the Chair in Pathology in 1983, the Faculty of Medicine's first female professor. Designated Pro-Vice-Chancellor in August 1986, Dorsch signalled an interest in "dealing with people and solving problems".[4] It was agreed that Linda Burney from the AC would brief her on the AEAs and their training program at a meeting with Williams, the coordinator, and Mike Strokowsky, Regional Director of DAA. There was also an invitation from AC members for Dorsch to lunch with AEATP staff and students early in 1987.

Dorsch took a more active role in Aboriginal education than Dunston, providing a sounding board for the AEATP directors and participating directly in community occasions. On the founding of the Aboriginal Education Centre in 1989, she chaired the committee for the appointment of the first Indigenous director. She was also responsible for compiling the annual Aboriginal and Torres Strait Islander Education Strategic Profile for Canberra and chaired the Fulbright Commission in Sydney which announced an award for a postgraduate Aboriginal student in 1993. Importantly, she would insist that Aboriginal education at Sydney receive the full amount of dedicated Commonwealth funding unlike some universities that absorbed a fixed percentage of Aboriginal money into general administration. Dorsch was also instrumental in devising the new organisational structure for the Koori Centre in the period of the Boston Consulting audit of 2003.

Coordinators – Rosemary Stack

The fourth Aboriginal coordinator, Rosemary Stack, appointed in January 1987, would remain with the program for a decade, serving as acting director for periods. A registered nurse from Western Australia specialising in geriatrics, she had moved east to head the Windradyne Aboriginal Education Resource Centre (named after a famed Aboriginal warrior) established in Chippendale in 1982, where users were famously greeted with a cup of tea. In 1983–84, Stack became secretary of The Settlement in Edward Street before moving to Tranby for three years, taking responsibility for its library. As her career interest moved into administration, Stack applied for the lecturer/coordinator position in the AEATP, learning to keep pace with King's whirlwind style. Six months later, the AC commended her "commitment to the job".[5] As a resident of Chippendale, Stack engaged with the local Aboriginal community assisting the Royal Commission into Aboriginal Deaths in Custody, 1988–91. She also started an MEd degree in the Faculty of Education. In 1991, Stack became the first Aborigine granted academic tenure at Sydney eventually resigning from the Koori Centre five years later.

The 1987 graduation ceremony was fixed for 15 December, after the Chancellor and his wife had accepted their usual roles "with pleasure".[6] Organised by Stack in the Wool Room at International House, 43 students received awards, 18 at Stage 1, and 25 at Stages II and III. Six were admitted to Macarthur Institute of Higher Education. All graduates were presented with a copy of the latest AEATP publication, *Wiimpatjai Bulka Pipinja: Black Fellas' Messages*, a collection of AEAs' writing. The keynote address was given by Morgan and the certificates presented by Dorsch. Speaking on the students' behalf, Neil Mort pledged that the AEAs would pass on their knowledge "to the future proud generation of Aboriginal people". In the evening, the celebratory dinner was held in the Withdrawing Room in the Refectory under the Aboriginal flag where the company enjoyed "The Butcher's Choice" menu "served with Garden Fresh Vegetables, and homemade Sherry Trifle, and Coffee".[7]

The Budget and Related Matters

Education had secured an improved budget for the AEATP of $106,840 in 1984–85, raised to $120,800 in 1985–86, and $127,200 for 1986–87 (though an increase of 21 percent had been requested). This latter sum became the base payment over the next two years.[8] The fact that the budget was not adjusted in line with real costs for three years related to DAA's own need to cover AEA salary increases, which came out of the same pot as training, and perhaps an opinion that the AEATP need no longer pay accommodation costs.[9] Alarmed that the program was heading for a deficit of $37,000 in 1989,[10] the AC asked the University to direct any unattached bequests to the AEATP and King mentioned a private donor in the wings. Nothing materialised.

As had been the case in Adult Education days, the training program was kept alive by applying savings from the turnover of staff, shortening training periods, and assistance in kind and cash from friends including the School of Social and Policy Studies and the AEC (NSW). It was evident that the AEATP could not continue in its present form into 1989, salaries alone being estimated at $135,106, some $8000 above the total budget.[11] The program was saved at the bell by a windfall of $60,000 from the NSW DoE for additional training; and there was another significant benefit when IBM donated eight computers, a printer and software, the University finding $7000 to air-condition a computer lab in one of the Mackie rooms.

However, there was no expectation that the University would bail out the AEATP. Sydney kept its own income well quarantined from that of the program. Ball has explained its standpoint: "Sydney University adopts the understandable policy that when 'soft money' is being used, that staff employed with that money should be employed only for the terms of (and as long as) the money is made available."[12] By soft money, Ball meant short-term funding such as the AEATP project grant. The University, he said, was suffering hard times itself under a cumulative drop in funding from the Commonwealth forcing it to freeze academic positions in the early 1980s. DAA took a similarly parsimonious line arguing that the AEAs were well looked after because they were receiving salaries while on course, a view that took no account of the AEA's low income, continuing home commitments or the extra cost of living in Sydney. DEET's position was equally tight. It assessed AEAs as part-time students not entitled to a full-time allowance and it compounded students' distress by paying their $240 book allowance late. As King has noted:

> Now very obviously not every student suffers hardship but a substantial number do. This has ramifications for the program for it may lend itself to a high attrition rate. From experience, most Aboriginal students drop out of courses because of financial problems.[13]

Bureaucratic procedures arising from the payment of Commonwealth money via the state government introduced other difficulties, including the need to reappoint staff in midterm as government funding followed the financial year. Cleverley has remarked on the arrangements in place.

Figure 33. Aboriginal Education Assistants Training Program: Sitting at the computer is Norma Davison from MacIntyre High School, Inverell, while IBM corporate program manager, Sarah Portway (standing, left) and Rosemary Stack, the AEAP Coordinator, observe, 1988. Image courtesy of University of Sydney Archives.

Pretty well around every Christmas I was told not to confirm any appointments for the new year until the state government's letter approving the AEATP budget for the upcoming financial year crossed the University's desk. Similarly, the state government was waiting on the Commonwealth's approval, so Sydney staff didn't know whether they had jobs for the year and I didn't know whether we had people. Sometimes it was two or more months into the new year before the state government letter arrived so everything was running behind. While the University did carry over full time positions already agreed to, it did so in language full of warnings of dire happenings if the Commonwealth pulled out of the deal. This complex administrative arrangement put me under a lot of pressure as I had to commit to the appointment of essential staff at some point when the University kept reminding me I had no authority to do so. It meant that new staff and good part-time lecturers were kept on tenterhooks or lost altogether. This annual funding charade added to the sense of impermanence surrounding the whole program. Why such a cumbersome process should apply to Aboriginal money when the Faculty of Education managed other Commonwealth funded projects like the Teaching of English as a Foreign Language on a three-year cycle, was a complete mystery to me.[14]

On Course 1987–89

At the close of the 1980s, the AEATP was led by a part-time director, a coordinator, a 1.5 lecturer position, and a secretary, with casual staff helping out if funding allowed. Annually 40 to 50 AEAs were enrolled. Those who completed three stages, usually over two years, could expect 1080 hours face-to-face teaching: King contrasted this figure with the 936 hours expected for a three-year BA degree.[15]

Many individuals assisted the AEATP on an ad hoc basis. In 1987, for instance, over 50 externals helped with teaching in their special fields, among them visitors from Ernabella – the Pitjantjatjara people – who offered a workshop on Aboriginal dance. The engagement of occasional teachers was justified on the grounds of economy, as many went unpaid, and also as a means of widening horizons, and thus overcoming the "effects on the Aboriginal students of the Program's physical isolation off the main campus of the University".[16] The passing parade made programs difficult to coordinate and examine with some students finding exposure to many different people unsettling. Cleverley recalls one situation when "an Aboriginal male student joshed a female lecturer who took umbrage and a nasty stand-off occurred before matters were finally resolved".[17]

When Daly resigned in 1987 to return to the schools, Kay Anderson, DipTeach, PG DipEd Studies, was appointed lecturer. Together with Stack, she visited schools in country New South Wales – Anderson the north coast, Stack the western region. While they were warmly greeted by the AEAs, Stack observed, "The reception from some Principals left a lot to be desired."[18] Stack also presented a paper at the South Pacific Association of Teacher Education, Janson another at the Nepean Conference on Aboriginal Studies, and they attended the "Learning My Way" Aboriginal Adult Education Conference in Perth together in 1988. Stack also joined a Year 12 Aboriginal Students' Seminar at Mitchell CAE, Bathurst, circulating a questionnaire on student destinations, its responses strongly supporting the case for an Aboriginal enclave or centre at Sydney.

In a busy spell in 1989, Anderson visited the University of New England and Armidale CAE discussing the accreditation of a new diploma program for AEAs. She introduced training in supervision techniques and conflict management for AEATP staff; joined the AC as the program's representative; met with regional and metropolitan NSW DoE staff in Sydney; and led the Curriculum Advisory Committee in further curriculum revision. King also took on external activities – he chaired the Aboriginal Higher Education Network, helped the Commonwealth evaluate its Priority Schools Program, and addressed a meeting of RACLOs in Sydney.

In 1988, practice teaching for AEAs was introduced in eight inner-west Sydney schools. Prior to the program's start, a briefing session was held with the schools' principals attended by the Aboriginal Education Consultants for Metropolitan East, Elaine Bennett and Janet Mooney, and two AEAs, Delma Davison and Marie Cohen. Students worked together in pairs during a one-day school orientation followed by three days in the classroom and two days back at Mackie for an evaluation. Special workbooks were printed for the AEAs and course outlines for schools.[19] Although well received by students, and expanded to rural areas, practice teaching was restricted to the diploma students in the 1990s on grounds of cost. As well as the practicum, AEAs undertook tertiary familiarisation visits in their region and there were regular visits to the Australian Institute of Aboriginal and Torres Strait Islander Studies (AIATSIS) in Canberra where Stack won a $3000 grant for community research. And a significant number of AEAs continued to receive in-service training – a three-day conference was held at Gosford in May 1987, another at Ettalong in 1988, and a third at the Elanora Conference Centre was held over five days in April 1989.

Janson has recalled some of the out-of-class activities within the AEATP.

> Students learnt to handle school Principals and parents and how to build bridges with teaching staff and community. We had barbeques in the courtyard and picnics in the bush at Kur-ring-gai National Park where kookaburras swept down and grabbed steaks off our plates and wallabies begged for food. We collected bush tucker and ate wild figs, Lilly Pillys and Geebung. We walked along the beach in the National Park to stand on a great midden and identified ancient stone scrapers amongst the shell and charcoal.[20]

Literacy Issues

At a Conferring Ceremony in the Great Hall on 17 March 1987, Pat O'Shane, the New South Wales magistrate, took an opportunity to attack state governments, (with the exception of Queensland), for failing to equip Aboriginal people with living skills in basic literacy and numeracy. The states, she said, just passed the buck to the Commonwealth in justification for their deplorable inaction.[21] Within the AEATP's own ranks, low literacy and numeracy scores were common at commencement, not surprisingly given the limited schooling of many. In 1988, a survey of 33 AEAs in Stages I and II counted four with primary schooling only, and 19 had not completed Year 10. Just three students held an HSC.[22] Additional classes were run for students with very low scores and an effort made to integrate literacy and numeracy teaching through computer instruction.

These low levels of attainment were a reflection on school processes. In 1987, a research team of Stage III students published a journal article identifying poor attendance at school, deficient health and nutrition, and stereotypical Western learning methodologies as significant causal agents.[23] The team accepted that negative attitudes from Aboriginal parents towards schooling did much harm; if parents were illiterate themselves, there was nothing for their children to build on. Many Aboriginal men, the article reported, viewed education

Figure 34. Shannon Delaney, Janet Mooney and Helen Ware lunching in the Mackie courtyard. Image courtesy of the Koori Centre.

as a woman's domain. AEAs also identified several white teachers coping with large classes who "just could not be bothered to teach Aboriginal children". The children dropped out ashamed of their poor performance. The team's response was to promote a "whole of school approach" involving family, teachers and students working together to raise self-esteem and assertiveness in cooperation with adult education and TAFE outreach. A second article on the topic was published in the *Dubbo Daily Liberal* on the 16 May.

Aboriginal English and its acceptability on course and in schools was a related issue. Here the Aboriginal Education Centre report, "Researching Community: Aboriginal Perspectives", recognised the raw power of Aboriginal English.

> Aboriginal children come to school and find it very hard to understand the spoken standard of English and the English learning process having already a language that is considered the home base language. Aboriginal English is the language of their home family and community and it is through this language that many Aboriginal children will learn about most of the important aspects of life, especially their Aboriginality – who they are and where they come from.[24]

Standard English was insisted on from AEAs, staff arguing that this put students in a position to choose the best form of expression for a given situation. "Students will develop an awareness of the advantages and disadvantages of selecting a particular communication technique in relation to the context and the desired outcome of the communication transaction."[25]

In 1989, literacy teaching was strengthened by the appointment of Helen Bell, BA, MA, and GradDip Adult Education (ITATE), to a half-time lectureship. With experience at Tranby, and as a Research Fellow in Aboriginal Adult Education at ITATE, Bell's philosophy for teaching Aboriginal adults was founded on culturally appropriate learning materials and pedagogy.[26] That a need existed was apparent following an in-house assessment of literacy standards. An average literacy mark for Stage I students of 59.5 percent was recorded, the percentage increasing to 61.3 for Stage IIs, and 67.3 for Stage IIIs.[27] Results were suggestive of on-course improvement. As well, Stage I scores were widely dispersed around the mean but Stage III scores were clustered which pointed to the effects of teaching intervention. Nevertheless, two very low literacy scores in Stages II and III, of 30 percent and 36 percent respectively, were a confronting finding. Less attention was paid to low numeracy levels until Helen Ware joined the program full-time in 1991.

Staff Changes

Not all went well in 1987. Various internal complaints were made over teaching arrangements and "unrest, whispering, innuendo" spread with sides taken.[28] The experienced Messih who had been with the AEATP since Adult Education days became increasingly aggrieved that her position was not upgraded to administrative assistant, a promotion recommended in 1983 by Morgan, who was impressed by her willingness to take on extra duties. Messih left the program in 1987, and Daly left at the end of that year, making a career in the NSW DoE in special education. A year later, Janson would resign, the AEATP Report recognising, "Her vitality and commitment to Aboriginal Arts". In March 1989, John Maskell, a half-time lecturer, replaced John Butt, who had helped with computer learning and literacy teaching; Frances Peters-Little, completing a degree at UTS, joined the program as half-time tutor; and Ian Perdrisat, an MEd student, assisted with the practicum.

On the administration side, Natalie Brown served as administrative assistant, Peter Beck as clerk, and June Coe, a young Aboriginal woman funded by the Department of Employment and Industrial Relations, trained as secretary for part of 1987. Other assistance through to 1990 came from capable secretarial staff – Dorothy Harris, Sharon Brown, Monica Martin, Angela Brand and Penelope Brockman. As past experience had shown, staff did not remain long, the AEATP offering no promotion or long-term career prospects.

A Roof over the Head

Securing reasonable accommodation was a headache. In the mid-1980s, Mackie provided an office for each of its three full-time staff and one large and one small lecture room, a rest room, and a small library collection for students. A corridor connection contained a fridge, water and seats, and there was a storage space and photocopier corner. Access to space in Mackie was reduced after Adult Education shut down, although Steve Rawlings, Head of Careers and Appointments, helped out when and where he could. Cleverley had failed to get the program moved from Mackie and King tried again, this time writing to the Bursar, Stephen Harrison, on 8 April 1987, asking for relocation to Madsen on grounds that it would release space in Mackie and link the AEATP with a possible Centre for Aboriginal Education. King complained that the one large lecture room used for art and craft lessons had no running water and that there was no waiting space for senior visitors; he also grudged the time lost walking back and forth from his office in Madsen across Parramatta Road. He saw the move as countering a word of mouth accusation that Aborigines were "relegated to the periphery".

King's request for Madsen space was modest enough – four staff offices, two small classrooms, three auxiliary rooms, and a rest room and reception area. He suggested taking over the space occupied by the Department of Computer Science or the Centre for Teaching and Learning.[29] His thinking was unrealistic – Computer Science was a University priority project and Teaching and Learning had just taken up tailor-made accommodation. Nor was the Faculty of Education pushing hard for King's plan as it had its eye out for extra Madsen space for its own Curriculum Resources and Micro-Computing centres. Furthermore, Building and Grounds in the University was uncooperative. It was unwilling to swap popular space at Madsen for unpopular space in Mackie on behalf of an Aboriginal unit relying on project funding for survival.

King's case for more room somewhere was strengthened when money from the NSW DoE permitted the appointment of two extra staff in 1989. By then, AEATP student numbers had increased to over 50 and a new diploma was in the pipeline. This time King petitioned the Vice-Chancellor directly suggesting a move to the Transient Building near Madsen as a possibility.[30] Awaiting an outcome, King learned that the journal, *Oceania*, was vacating five rooms in Mackie so he applied for a readjustment of current space. The game of musical chairs ended on 10 March 1989 when the AEATP received permission to occupy five additional spaces in Mackie "on a temporary basis".[31]

Graduations 1988–89

On 13 December 1988, 20 AEAs in Stage I, six in Stage II, and 12 in Stage III graduated in the Great Hall. The keynote speaker, Alan Ruby, Director of Special Programs, told the gathering that the number of Aboriginal teachers in the department had reached 15, plus a high school and a primary school principal.[32] He explained that the department had plans to fast track some 10–20 AEAs as Conditionally Certificated Teachers, a proposal enthusiastically supported by the Minister for Education, Dr Terry Metherell, a strong backer of the AEAs. Sydney was a leading contender for the training base. His department relied heavily on its 161 AEAs for four major school programs: Priority Schools, Aboriginal Early Language Development, Aboriginal Studies and Aboriginal Artists in Residence. "So the work you do," said Ruby, "takes on a great importance because you are the Aboriginal presence in the schools. You present models of success to Aboriginal students in academic and public life." Responding to Ruby, Barbara Keeley explained how her own appointment had proved "a turning point in her life". A Stage I graduate employed at James Meehan High School in Sydney's south west since 1988, Keeley was organiser of the annual Careers Market that attracted Aboriginal students from Liverpool to Campbelltown. The 1988 graduation day ended with a dinner dance.

The following year, 34 AEAs graduated in the Great Hall on 12 December, 20 in Stage I, two in Stage II and 12 in Stage III, the Deputy-Chancellor, Professor Dame Leonie Kramer, Chair of Australian Literature at Sydney, presiding.[33] The ceremony was also attended by the Vice-Chancellor Designate, Don McNicol, a psychologist who had moved to Sydney from the Vice-Chancellorship of the University of New England, and an active supporter of Aboriginal education. His educational priorities, he told *The Gazette*'s reporter, were "access and quality",[34] an opinion his Aboriginal students shared. A video recording was taken of the ceremony by the University Television Service and passed to the Chancellor unhappily too ill to attend.

Students and Publishing

Creative writing, an important part of the AEATP curriculum, was enlivened by the appointment of a black American, Lewis E. Scott, as part-time tutor. The youngest of 15 children, and owner of three Purple Heart decorations for bravery in Vietnam, Scott was in Australia collecting stories for American black movement magazines from Indigenous leaders. Scott, who asserted that "generalising about Aboriginals in a negative way is blatant racism", told the Mackie students that their own literature was a powerful tool for exposing discrimination. "Black Americans have used political writing to convey their protest movement."[35]

In October 1986, the poet began collecting AEAs' stories for his publication, "Saving the Children". However, some photographs and written material had to be removed and replaced and there was a dispute over the size of his fee, $3160, for editorial and other work.[36] The University eventually paid up but was unwilling to guarantee publication, finally agreeing that an amended version be photocopied as resource material. Some of the material collected by Scott found its way into *Wiimpatjai Bulka Pipinja*: *Black Fellas' Messages*, and *Pukuda Multhi Puthala*: *Dreamtime All the Time*, two sets of stories, poems and drawings put together by the AEATP with help from the creative David Wansbrough of Gavemer Publications. AEAs also joined in drama workshops and improvisations, encouraging Janson to write and produce *Gunjies*,[37] (an Aboriginal name for police), at the time of the Royal Commission into Black Deaths in Custody. Another of Janson's plays, *Black Mary*, tells the story of an Aboriginal bushranger.

Janson has written of this story-telling side of the AEA course.

> We wrote Koori plays through drama workshops with some twenty-five students

Figure 35. *Wiimpatjai Bulku Pipinja: Black Fellas' Message*, 1987. Image courtesy of the Koori Centre Library.

in each group. Some of the drama improvisations and interviews lead to plays being written such as Gunjies … This play had the collaboration of students such as Veronica Davison, Emily Walker, Raymond Donovan, Ann Flood and many others. Gungies went on to receive a Human Rights Award of Highly Commended and an Australian Writers Guild AWGIE nomination. The Aboriginal actors such as Lillian Crombie, Justine Saunders, David Kennedy and Jimmy Little were all involved. This play went on to professional production at Belvoir St Theatre with Lydia Miller as director and producer.[38]

AEATP students also collaborated with the Faculty of Education in a photographic project of Aboriginal family histories in 1989, in association with Tranby and the Australian Museum.

Curriculum Revision Continues

In May 1987, the Aboriginal membership on the Curriculum Advisory Committee was expanded to include Milton Mercer, Ali Golding, Pam Koeneman, Marie Cohen, Terese O'Rourke and Marie Robinson. Other members were Kay Anderson from the AEATP, and Carmel Young and Susan Groundwater-Smith from the Faculty of Education. Revision and feedback continued from Sam Altman, Lavina Gray, Pearl Bridger and Joy Williams, with a curriculum draft completed for circulation in October 1987. When the final document was released late in 1989, five years in the making, there were three main strands and additional activities for the new Diploma of Aboriginal Assistants Education (DipAAEd).

Curriculum Strands

1. Foundation Studies – Learning and Teaching, Communication, Counselling, Health Education, Reading/Writing, Mathematics, and Computers in Education;
2. Curriculum Studies – Aboriginal Studies, Aboriginal Arts, Social/Political Studies, Curriculum Development;
3. School and Community Experience – School Visits, Tertiary Visit, Home/School; and
4. Additional Diploma Units – Research Practice, Community Studies, Curriculum Studies and Practicum B.[39]

It's task complete, the Curriculum Advisory Committee was disbanded in 1990.

Two Innovations

Greater Aboriginal involvement in the AEATP led to the introduction of Aboriginal studies and Aboriginal pedagogies in the BEd (Primary) degree. In 1989, the Faculty of Education experimented with a mandatory core course in Aboriginal studies using AEATP staff funded under DEET's Multicultural and Cross Cultural Supplementation Program. Led by Groundwater-Smith, a senior lecturer in the faculty and member of the AC, teacher trainees undertook a three-week training session of 14 hours in their third year. Two themes were covered: i) the construction of Aboriginality and its implications for education and, ii) pedagogical issues and the use of resources in teaching Aboriginal children.[40] An overwhelming majority of trainees welcomed the special course. One respondent observed

> As with any marginalised culture or issue a mandatory response is appropriate else it receives little or negative attention in the curriculum. A mandatory policy on Aboriginality goes a small step towards redressing the huge critical imbalances in the curriculum, especially in topics such as history.[41]

Negative opinion centred mainly on the compulsory aspect which some thought "going overboard"; and there was dissatisfaction with the faculty's chalk and talk approach, students wanting "hands on activity" with Aboriginal children.

The second innovation was the introduction of the Diploma of Aboriginal Assistants Education also under the Faculty of Education. Its beginnings go back to 1986 when the director proposed that the Stage III qualification be recognised by the NSW Higher Education Board as an associate diploma. This initiative was abandoned when it became clear that a diploma award would demand teaching and resources beyond the program's means. However two years later it was apparent that the AEATP was haemorrhaging, losing good students to other institutions already offering undergraduate diplomas.

Inside the University there was both opposition and support for an undergraduate diploma. Some staff, already critical of the academic content of the certificate award, feared the diploma would further dilute standards. Others held the view that Sydney should be reducing the number of diplomas on offer or argued that Sydney had no authority to award an undergraduate diploma. In addition, a few objectors asserted that Canberra would not buy the idea and would deny Effective Full Time Student Unit (EFTSU) funding for what was a sub-degree qualification.

However, King had powerful allies. The AC backed him, and its membership included the influential Commonwealth and state government representatives, Sutton and Craddock. Turney and Cleverley in the Faculty of Education were also supporters as was Dorsch, whose assistance in negotiating the University's internal arrangement proved "invaluable".[42] "It's a long haul," King admitted to a friend, "but I have good backing."[43] Another thing working in King's favour was the amalgamation of the University with several CAEs in 1989–90, which themselves offered undergraduate diplomas. After several drafts, it was finally accepted that the new DipAAEd would require satisfactory completion of all certificate requirements plus additional subjects and a research component. The entry level was set at a good Stage I pass or equivalent followed by two years of study: the Stage II course, plus Diploma 1 (three units), and the Stage III course, plus Diploma 2 (four units).

King asked DEET for a special grant of $78,000 for a lecturer's salary and two part-time clerical staff and maintenance money, declaring the University's own contribution the equivalent of $12,000.[44] However, the Faculty of Education did not wait on the Commonwealth's determination. Predicting that enrolments could reach 40 by 1992, thus enabling the diploma to recoup its costs through EFTSU, the faculty's Standing Committee approved the establishment of the new Board of Studies for the Diploma in Aboriginal Assistants Education in 1989, including two external members, Les Hiatt from Anthropology, and Alan Marett from Music. The diploma went through the Academic Board unchallenged and enrolments were approved for a 1990 start. Seven diploma students graduated in the first year.

The DipAAEd qualification, the University's sole undergraduate diploma and its only qualification limited to a specific group of students, significantly boosted the AEATP's educational armoury. At around this time, Craddock observed that community attitudes towards the University were shifting in its favour. "The survey I carried out found that many AEAs wanted to go on to Diploma and Bachelor programs. Some said they would do so, 'only if it's at the University of Sydney.'"[45] Diploma teaching was further strengthened by the appointment of Peter Beuzeville, a lecturer committed to adult education. It was also suggested by King that the diploma could be offered in a distance education mode in collaboration with Charles Sturt University but this failed to eventuate.[46]

Figure 36. Professor John M. Ward, c. 1950s. Image courtesy of University of Sydney Archives.

Getting Better Known

As the 1980s progressed, the AEATP became better known inside the University. Staff within the AEATP undertook training in the Centre for Teaching and Learning, and in Staff Development, and the University and AEATP celebrated occasions like NAIDOC Week together. By the end of 1987, the Vice-Chancellor could report some progress in Aboriginal education.

> The University has not been inactive in this area. The Faculty of Education in particular has been active. Ms. Sue Jobson, EEO Coordinator, has been undertaking research into schemes in other educational institutions. There have been discussions with Aborigines who have interests and experience in the area. Interest is being shown in the postgraduate area as is evidenced by a small number of enrolments and more numerous enquiries.[47]

Ward was kept up to date by the AEATP's Annual Reports from 1987 on, the Vice-Chancellor writing to King congratulating him on their publication.[48] A year later, the Annual Report announced "the professional preparation of over 300 Aboriginal Assistants, most from rural areas. A number of these AEAs have gone on to teacher training, training in community work and welfare work as well as regional liaison positions."[49] Ward, in turn, kept members of Senate informed of the AEATP's successes.

> The 1988 Report of the Aboriginal Assistants Education Program has many most gratifying features, to which my attention has been drawn specially by the Pro-Vice-Chancellor, Professor Dorsch. She mentions particularly the contribution of Associate Professor King of the Department of Education. The Program has always brought credit to the University and never more so than now.[50]

Senate minutes record that the 1988 AEATP Annual Report was "very well received".

There is a danger though that self-congratulation can bolster institutional complacency. In the late 1980s, scarcely any Aboriginal students were enrolling in regular degree programs and the University still had no support centre for the handful it did attract. Indeed it was doubtful whether the AEATP itself could continue into 1990 given its quite inadequate budget.[51] As the attachment relating to Access and Equity Issues in 1993 revealed: "Prior to the establishment of the Koori Centre in 1990, very little funding was spent on Aboriginal and Torres Strait Islander access and support."[52]

8

Creating a Centre

> Enclave support programs assist Aboriginal students to enrol in standard courses with institutions, and give additional support appropriate to their culture, lifestyles and educational background. Such programs should be regarded as an essential part of tertiary education, rather than an ad hoc short term project.
>
> National Aboriginal Education Committee, Statement of Policy, 1985[1]

There were at least 14 Aboriginal centres in New South Wales higher education institutions by 1988, six in Sydney and eight outside, each having its own mix of services – tutoring, Aboriginal studies, bridging courses and counselling.[2] Among the east coast universities, the Monash Orientation Scheme for Aborigines (MOSA) was the exemplar, its centre offering a five day pre-enrolment session, orientation programs for Arts/Social Science/Sciences, and individual support extending to travel subsidies, child care and occasionally winter clothing. Before 1984, Monash had one Aboriginal student enrolled – two years after the centre and support scheme started, 60 students were on course, all with Year 10 attainments and upwards.[3] In Sydney, the leading university for Aboriginal enrolments was the University of New South Wales, with 112 enrolled up to 1988,[4] its centre able to draw on a bequest of $400,000 from Alice Grange.

That the University of Sydney was left in the wake of others was common knowledge. There was negative comment from the NSW DoE in the mid-1980s on the paucity of its Aboriginal enrolments[5] and its unwillingness to open a centre (the AEATP's brief was to assist its own students not others); and Sydney's inadequacies were noted during an AEATP Workshop in 1987 where it was pointed out "no one was referring people to the University of Sydney".[6] The Equal Opportunity in Education Committee (EOE) also accepted "that Aboriginal students will not attend or succeed at University without the support of an Aboriginal Resource and Education Centre with Aboriginal personnel."[7] Nonetheless, the leadership of the University, with a handful of exceptions, did not believe Aboriginal education deserved urgent action.

The first proposal for a centre with a support function was put forward by Cleverley on 22 July 1986. His "Centre for Aboriginal Education" would provide: a home for students entering through special admissions; a location for postgraduate study, particularly masters and

PROPOSED CENTRE FOR ABORIGINAL EDUCATION

The Faculty of Education wishes to sponsor a Centre for Aboriginal Education to be located primarily in the Department of Social and Policy studies in Education. The Centre would be in a position to draw on the resources of the faculty as a whole. It would have particular functions

1. To provide Masters courses suited to the needs of Aboriginal educators and others with a concern in the area, with particular reference to research and related skills. These courses could be at pass or honours level and for some could be a route to the Ph D. They would be designed in collaboration with the Aboriginal community through the appropriate organisations. Courses would be designed to enable Aboriginal students to enter with appropriate qualifications at Bachelor or Diploma level, and could be completed either full or part time. It is envisaged that enrolments would be up to two or three candidates a year. Commonwealth assistance would be requested in regard to obtaining the services of an Aboriginal coordinator/lecturer, preferably full time with some funds also requested for student and other support facilities. The project would need Aboriginal involvement at the planning stage.

2. To integrate the work of the Aboriginal Teachers Aides Training Programme currently operated at the University of Sydney. This course trains teachers' aides for N.S.W. schools through three courses: Basic, Up-grading, and Intensive. It would provide an input into the development of this course, having regard to the changing roles of ATAs and future accreditation.

3. To provide a support base for increasing numbers of Aboriginal students entering the University of Sydney through special entry provisions.

4. To act as a resource and research base for projects related to problems in Aboriginal education.

It is anticipated that some Commonwealth finance would become available in the 1986-7 financial year. However the main cost would be incurred in the 1988-1990 triennium when the programme would involve some 10 candidates in higher education, with a coordinator/senior lecturer position ($40,000 p.a.), and sundry costs of $10,000 covering part time typing, stationery, phone, marking, etc. This proposal is subject to detailed discussion with the N.S.W. Aboriginal Education Consultative Group.

John Cleverley

22.7.86.

Figure 37. First proposal for the establishment of a centre for Aboriginal education, having academic and support functions, at the University of Sydney, 1986. Koori Centre.

doctorates in education designed for Aboriginal educators; and a base for resources and research directed at Aboriginal priorities. External advice on its structure and operations would be sought from the NSW AECG from the beginning. Cleverley anticipated two or three higher degree candidates would be studying through the centre initially, with numbers building up to ten by 1988–90. Total cost was estimated at $40,000 for an Aboriginal senior lecturer/coordinator position and $10,000 for essential typing, phone charges and maintenance.

Finding the Money

The plan of 1986 was passed to Dorsch by King as a "modest beginning"[8] and a grant sought from DEET for 1987–88.[9] When King's final submission went forward, the original estimate was trimmed to $30,000 for an Aboriginal coordinator and $1000 for consumables.[10] The University's own investment was calculated at $30,000 for King's time and for accounts, office accommodation and facilities, and cleaning. When the Commonwealth queried the number of Aboriginal people on its governing board, Sydney responded: "The Senate which is the governing body of the University has no Aboriginal members." However, it noted that the AEATP had an Aboriginal coordinator. The case to DEET was boosted when the AC agreed to form an Interim Management Committee to get a centre started and there were signals that Canberra was impressed but a cut back in DEET's internal funding ended hopes.

In 1987, King drew up three applications for external funding. The first prompted by Sutton, and supported by Morgan on the NAEC, was for $60,000 from the Commonwealth Tertiary Education Commission for "Special Places" funding.[11] The second, sent by King on 23 December, asked the NSW Minister of Education, Cavalier, for an Aboriginal teacher or an experienced ATA on secondment to the Faculty of Education and a small grant to cover equipment and resources. King reminded Cavalier that Sydney was undertaking a mentoring role for Chifley University and that he expected the initiative would have a flow-on effect. Neither was successful.

The third application, put together at the end of 1987, was a joint request from the Faculty of Education and the Faculty of Arts seeking funds for an Aboriginal Education Centre located in Education and serving students across the University.[12] Arts itself was planning a quota of ten places, subject to the introduction of a University-wide support program, and the proposal called for a coordinating unit for pre-admission, orientation and support activities.[13] Altogether, $39,911 was requested for a half-time director position and a part-time secretary for 1988–89, along with $5000 for an evaluation. The application spoke of raising the participation and retention rates of Aborigines in professional and technical skills, especially rural Aboriginal women. The combined application failed.

In 1988, King asked for $226,000 in support of an Aboriginal education centre proposed by the Vice-Chancellor's Working Party and recently submitted to Senate.[14] This money was to come from the Higher Education Reserve Fund, which held one percent of the University's operating grant for projects of national priority. Its particular significance was that the application came from the University not a faculty. Again it was unsuccessful. In 1989, King returned to a more modest proposal. Referring to the University's forthcoming amalgamation with Sydney College of Advanced Education (SCAE), he appealed to Hugh Preston, the Assistant Secretary, Equity and Programs Branch, for $50,000 for a director at senior lecturer level to manage a Sydney University Aboriginal Education Centre. Preston was told, "The University is enthusiastic about this plan".[15] The application was turned down. Two months later, another application was sent to Canberra for a grant under the Aboriginal Education Equity Program.

Reasons why the faculty was constantly rejected as suitor were several. There were mismatches between the applications and the particular Commonwealth grant guidelines, some of its requests implying a long-term Commonwealth commitment; further, Canberra was re-assessing the funding of Aboriginal education nationally, making it cautious about new commitments under current schemes. The University also had no high profile Aborigine on staff to make its case. The major reason that Sydney failed to win grants, however, was its unwillingness to apply its own resources to prime the pump. Canberra thought the University a wealthy institution, well able to open a centre if it so wanted. This opinion is supported by a comment in the EOE Committee's report of 27 October 1988:

> To date the University of Sydney has failed to attract government funding for such a program and the White Paper (p. 57) indicates that most resources in this area will go to institutions "with a proven record of supporting Aboriginal students".

So the Commonwealth was unwilling to reward the University for its lack of commitment to Aboriginal equity. The setbacks in the name of the faculties of Education and Arts, and of the University as a whole, were not regarded all that seriously on campus. Indeed, attempt after attempt by King encouraged the attitude that things were in hand: Sydney was like Charles Dickens' Mr Micawber who lived in the expectation that something would turn up.

Faculty Working Party

The Faculty of Education, which had included an Aboriginal Education Centre in its Quinquennial Plan for 1988–92, began planning operational details. In 1987, Turney established a Working Party under Schnierer as chairman, with King, Stack, and Carmel Young as internals, and Hiatt from Anthropology, now Convener of the Steering Committee for the Aboriginal Studies Committee in Arts, and Perdrisat, as externals. The Working Party's early discussions centered on the progress of King's applications for Commonwealth funding and on enclave arrangements in other places.[16] Schnierer promised to promote the centre in public schools in Years 10 and above; Hiatt proposed that it publicise the University's considerable achievements in teaching and research; and Young thought the centre should assist school teachers of Aboriginal studies through research and publications. Pedrisat wanted a focus put on study options for Aboriginal students and interviews in the admissions process. At its 4 August 1987 meeting, Working Party members agreed to draft statements on SUAEC's management, operational activities and accommodation needs. The name, Sydney University Aboriginal Education Centre (SUAEC), was agreed upon.

Planning was taken a step further at a workshop held on 26 August to gauge Aboriginal opinion, members including Stack, Burney, Norma Ingram, an ex-ATA from ITATE, Margret Campbell-Buck, an ex-ATA and lecturer at the Institute of Early Childhood Studies, and Lorna O'Shane, a student. Ray Keipert and Sutton from DEET, and Ed Lukaszewski from the Student Counselling Service, joined the party. After a vigorous exchange of ideas, participants approved three main recommendations:

- that the centre should be led by an Aboriginal director assisted by Aboriginal staff and include an Aboriginal studies specialist and counsellor;
- that its Aboriginal staff should be closely involved with special admissions arrangements in the University generally and in the establishment of associate diploma and diploma courses for Aboriginal people; and
- that cultural sessions designed for academic and general staff should be run by Aboriginal lecturers.

Participants raised pertinent questions. Where would SUAEC stand in regard to the University structure? How could Aboriginal people ensure that their viewpoints were listened to? Where would suitable accommodation be found? What was the University's real commitment to Aboriginal education? What power had the faculty's Working Party to get its recommendations adopted and what steps should come next? The workshop thought that SUAEC should represent the University's wider responsibilities; it must not be a place where Aboriginal issues were consigned and buried. King promised to incorporate speakers' concerns in an Interim Faculty Report which was passed to the Vice-Chancellor on 28 August 1987.

The final report of the faculty's Working Party on Aboriginal Education noted "a genuine desire within the University community for the number of Aboriginal students to increase and for the quality of Aboriginal services generally to be improved."[17] It depicted Sydney as a storehouse of knowledge about Indigenous people and culture with a capacity to play a key role in social change provided it eschewed assimilationism. Education thought itself the best faculty to manage SUAEC given its involvement in the AEATP in a culturally appropriate way for over ten years, and its extensive network of Aboriginal contacts, however the report stressed that the centre should be an autonomous, university-wide facility.

On the support side, it was agreed that SUAEC would serve all Aboriginal students entering under special admissions by offering

- a resource and research base for Aboriginal projects;
- an entry point for undergraduate and postgraduate courses;
- a cooperative place for staff and students across the University, assisting with the assessment of academic and other needs of Aboriginal students; and
- liaison activity serving counselling, learning studies and the Aboriginal community.

Only modest accommodation needs were mentioned: two rooms in Madsen, one for the director, the other for peer support.

Members agreed that the next logical step was to found SUAEC, with an Aboriginal name to come later. While funding was a concern, the Working Party wanted the facility underway at once and it suggested that those involved in a projected Vice-Chancellor's Working Party on Aboriginal Education provide a nucleus for its Management Committee and that a separate Academic Liaison Committee be established to handle academic matters. King cautioned that these and other initiatives must support students' Aboriginality. Passed to the Faculty of Education by Schnierer, the report was endorsed on 27 September 1987, a copy going to the Vice-Chancellor's Working Party for reference.

The Vice-Chancellor's Working Party

The Vice-Chancellor, John Ward, was convinced that the University's emphasis on special admissions was short sighted. "The question of admissions," he maintained, "cannot be separated from the degree of assistance which can be given to Aboriginals after admission."[18] On 6 October 1987, with Senate's approval, he agreed to chair a Working Party to pull together the University's disparate admissions activities and lay a base for future policy. His team was set two immediate tasks: to assess the current admissions policy for Aboriginal students; and to evaluate the case for an Aboriginal centre on campus. King, fresh from writing much of the Faculty of Education's report, acted as Ward's Executive Officer, the others in the group being Hiatt; Associate Professor John Mack, from the Department of Pure Mathematics; Ball, Chair of the Academic Board; Clunies Ross, Deputy Chair of the Academic Board; and Pat O'Shane. Two further names, Schnierer and Burney, were added, however neither they nor O'Shane joined and plans to recruit an Aboriginal student were not followed up.

From the start it was decided to adopt the Commonwealth government's definition of Aborigine as applying to special admissions: "A person being of Aboriginal descent, who identifies himself as being an Aboriginal person, and who is accepted by the community in which they live as being an Aboriginal person." Identification agreed upon, the priority was to find ways to attract Indigenous students.[19] Getting down to figures, Ward told the Working Party that 32 Aboriginal students had enrolled in 1988, double the 1987 number, though he thought the large increase perplexing given the University's lack of action. He attributed the leap to changing community attitudes not to anything the University had done.

In fact, the enrolment figures passed to Ward were a significant over-estimation as his Interim Report would disclose. "Internal statistics as reconciled with Commonwealth Department of Education figures suggest that there was a total of only six students enrolled in 1988."[20] It was clear that the special admissions arrangements for Aboriginal people already in place were quite ineffectual: of 13 Aborigines who applied for places in Medicine in 1988, for example, two were offered places and none accepted; and Arts had one applicant and one enrolled. Ward believed that Aborigines thought Sydney set the rung too high and that its entry requirements were too rigid. As a start, he suggested that enrolment be based on interviews, references and work experience.[21] Sydney's small enlistment was contrasted with the University of New South Wales' effort with 35 on course, and the University of Technology Sydney with 40. "Both these institutions have well developed Aboriginal support structures."[22]

The Vice-Chancellor's Working Party passed its Interim Report to the Joint Senate Academic Board Special Admissions Committee on 1 August 1988. "Existing arrangements at the University of Sydney are inadequate," it asserted, "and are failing to attract or admit sufficient applicants." It wanted faculties' special admissions policies revamped to display a degree of uniformity; further, they should be clearly defined, readily understood, and widely promoted. While possibilities for a modified Broadway Scheme and a SUCCEED type program reaching as far back as Year 9 were discussed, Ward's priority was the establishment of a centre which would ensure an identifiable Aboriginal presence, offer support, orientation and outreach, and engage Aboriginal people in its operations. The Joint Admissions Committee endorsed the Working Party's Interim Report on 10 August 1988, encouraging Ward "to proceed with the development of a policy on Aboriginal education for the University".

As an aid to Ward's second phase, King circulated the submission he had prepared for the EOE committee and he tabled other documents including Monash's Orientation Scheme for Aborigines. Members agreed that "the University should move towards establishing a scheme along the same lines". By its 29 September meeting, King had a substantial draft document in hand and the Working Party anticipated the scheme, along with Sydney's strong reputation in teaching and research in Aboriginal studies, would attract Aboriginal enrolments from across Australia.[23] Senate learned from Ward's final report that one Australian institution had established a teaching centre as far back as 1971 and others had special admissions policies and bridging courses of up to two years planned or in place.[24] Several institutions had strategies for the employment of Aboriginal staff: Melbourne University, for example, had set itself a target of one percent of Aboriginal employees and was offering cadetships, apprenticeships and clerical jobs.[25] In contrast, Sydney's endeavour was largely confined to teaching and research.

As the Ward Report put it, Sydney's initiatives were significant but not extensive. There was an EOE Committee with a brief to report on Aboriginal equity; an AEA training program that had existed since 1975, with 40 or so enrolments annually; and an EEO Unit that had appointed an Aboriginal clerk in 1987. To date, four Aboriginal staff members were counted – two in the AEATP, and one each in the EEO Unit and Computer Science. Four faculties, Arts, Education, Dentistry and Medicine, had special admissions each with slightly different requirements – all to little effect. The University's core activity lay in its departmental teaching and research which included an interdepartmental course in Aboriginal studies in Arts and a mandated course of Aboriginal studies in Education. As the report admitted: "The University of Sydney's provisions for Aboriginal students have not been as extensive nor as well developed as those of other tertiary institutions."[26] Of the six Aboriginal students currently enrolled, two were in the Masters program in Education.

Ward supported the formation of SUAEC along the lines proposed by Education. Its three tasks were: to install a support facility; to manage an orientation scheme for new enrolments enabling one year's specific preparation; and to introduce an outreach program serving schools and the Aboriginal communities. Ward proposed a management committee with substantial Aboriginal membership and an Aboriginal academic liaison committee for the academic side. As to location, his Working Party nominated the Mackie Building, despite the Faculty of Education's preference for the Madsen location, arguing that the Mackie accommodation would enable the AEATP and SUAEC to bond prior to a move to the New Education Building Complex in 1993.

Ward envisaged a three-stage operation. Stage I would establish SUAEC and a support scheme for students.

Stage I	$
Director (Senior Lecturer)	48,000
Lecturer	35,000
Secretary	25,000
Maintenance Fund	15,000
Research Funding (seeding only)	20,000
	143,000

Stage II, the Orientation Scheme, would offer a preparatory academic studies program of up to one year, drawing on the University's extensive services and facilities.

Stage II	$
Part-time teaching allocation	15,000
Tutorials	12,000
Secretarial supplementation (0.5)	12,000
Equipment (computers, etc.)	25,000
	64,000

Stage III, the Outreach Activity, would cover school visits, career and study advice, and network support for Aboriginal school students. It would also introduce a SUCCEED type scheme for older school children.

Stage III	$
Tutor (0.5 Attached to the centre)	5,000
Secretary (0.5)	10,000
Maintenance	2,000
	17,000

For maximum effect, Stages I and II should be implemented in 1988–89, and Stage III in 1989.

Ideally funding, or the guarantee of funding, for these first two phases, which include the establishment of the University of Sydney Aboriginal Education Centre and the Orientation Scheme, should be available in 1988 if these activities are to go ahead in 1989 as proposed.[27]

When Ward passed his report to the Joint Senate Academic Board Committee on Admissions Policy on 4 October 1988, he especially thanked King for his role. The Joint Committee's response to the Vice-Chancellor's report was positive.

The Report was welcomed by the Joint Committee although some concern was expressed about the cost of implementing the recommendations. It was agreed however, that it would be important to establish the proposed centre and its associated activities on a sound financial base with appropriately qualified staff if the overall scheme was to achieve its stated aims. It was noted that it was unlikely that any funds could be made available before 1989 as recommended by the Report. The Committee endorsed the Report and its Recommendations in principle subject to the Vice-Chancellor being requested to report further on the financial and accommodation implications with a view to seeking the approval of Senate at its November meeting.[28]

Senate praised the report on 7 November 1988, again subject to a further submission from the Vice-Chancellor on financial and accommodation implications. Here Ward believed Senate's request set him "a difficult task" though he agreed to report back. "Following this, it is hoped that a time table for implementation of the recommendation can be drawn up." Unhappily there was little to show six months later. When Associate Professor Gagen at Special Admissions expressed "deep concern"[29] over the small number of Aboriginal students enrolling at Sydney, he was told that "the implementation of the proposed Aboriginal Education Centre and Outreach Program endorsed by Senate in November 1988 was being delayed because funding had not been secured" and that "the focus of the proposal was being pursued by the Faculty of Education." Despite Ward's best efforts, his plans for an Aboriginal education centre had been sidelined.

A Plethora of Centres

Sydney's hand in Aboriginal education changed due to events beyond its immediate control. Under the Dawkins' proposals, components of five CAEs merged with the University in 1989–90, of which two operated Aboriginal centres: Sydney College of Advanced Education (SCAE) had its Centre for Aboriginal Studies (CAS); and Cumberland College of Health Sciences (CCHS) had its Aboriginal Education Unit (AEU).

CAS, also known as Nââmoro [Place of Learning] Koori Education Centre, was founded in 1987 by the SCAE's Principal, Michael Koder, as part of his plan to encourage more disadvantaged students to enrol. Koder set CAS three tasks:

- to assist institutes with the design, development and implementation of relevant Indigenous course units;

- to enable support service for Aboriginal students enrolled in SCAE; and
- to advise the college on matters relevant to the recruitment of Aboriginal students and liaison with Aboriginal communities.[30]

The SCAE Principal was singularly successful in obtaining Commonwealth funding for CAS with $395,340 shared across his college's institutes in 1989, the money assisting 52 (EFTSU) Aboriginal students in various courses.[31] Koder would become Assistant Vice-Chancellor at Sydney and he played a role in securing the New Education Building Complex where the Koori Centre was located.

The SCAE Centre was led by Margret Campbell-Buck, an ex-ATA from Murawina and qualified teacher in early childhood studies, supported by two academics, David Prosser, an ex-AEA, and holder of an ITATE Associate Diploma, and Vilma Ryan, also an ITATE graduate, and one-time social worker with the Aboriginal Children's Services, Redfern. The three ran bridging programs for Aboriginal adults, taught electives in Aboriginal studies across the institutes, and helped plan new diplomas and training projects in fields like alcohol and drug rehabilitation. CAS's work was supported by its own Aboriginal Advisory Committee.

The University would absorb two of SCAE's Institutes, the Sydney Institute of Education (SIE) located in the Teachers College building on campus, and the Institute of Nursing Studies (INS) at Mallett Street, Camperdown. While CAS staff taught in both of these institutes, none of the academic and clerical staff from CAS had remained on contract following the merger. However, Campbell-Buck was employed part-time by the University joining John Snodgrass and Alex Rivers in teaching Aboriginal studies and Aboriginal pedagogy in SIE, along with Norma Ingram, an ex-AEA graduate with a Diploma of Teaching (Secondary) from SCAE. Ingram, a Wiradjuri woman, was born the youngest of 11 children on Ernambie mission, and later attended Cowra Public School, thus breaking away from the Aboriginal curriculum of sewing, cooking and cleaning, and a life destination of housemaid "for rich whites".[32] In 1975, Ingram enrolled in the ATATP where she "benefited greatly as a result of doing the AEA course which had enabled her to proceed with her education."[33] Ingram graduated with an MA in Education from Harvard University in 1985, then joined UTS as coordinator of its Associate Diploma in Adult Education (Aboriginal), before taking up an executive position in the New South Wales Premier's Department. She currently runs a Redfern employment service for single mothers.[34]

Relations between the educational leadership in the Faculty of Education, the AEATP, and Sydney Institute of Education (SIE) were especially close. Cleverley and King had served on SIE's Board recruited by John Emery, the director; and this cooperation continued under Graham Boardman who headed SIE after Emery's retirement. Campbell-Buck, head of CAS, had also assisted the AEATP's Stage III students, loaning them space on Carillon Avenue in 1989; and SIE staff and King collaborated in planning a survey of Aboriginal student access and support in 1990.

The Aboriginal Education Unit at CCHS

Cumberland College of Health Sciences (CCHS) had its own well-established centre when it joined Sydney, its Aboriginal Education Unit (renamed Yooroang Garang in 1996) opening in 1983. The following year, AEU staff from the School of Community Health in the Faculty of Health Sciences had 15 Aboriginal students enrolled in a three-year block mode program, the Associate Diploma of Health Sciences (Aboriginal Health and Community Development). It also maintained an External Advisory Committee representative of Aboriginal health and community groups. Cumberland's AEU aimed:

- to consult with the Aboriginal community on issues
- to develop curriculum, programs and administration appropriate to Aboriginal needs and aspirations
- to provide adequate and appropriate curriculum support at all stages of their chosen courses, and to further develop the Aboriginal Education Unit.[35]

The AEU boasted its own study space and collection of resource materials and a liaison officer for special recruitment.

Most Aboriginal students at CCHS were enrolled in the associate diploma, which covered Aboriginal studies, management, community skills, counselling, drug and alcohol rehabilitation, and emergency care, with four weeks of field experience mandatory. Those unable to complete the full program could graduate halfway through with a certificate. Between 1984 and 1990, 32 students graduated with the associate diploma and another 40 took the certificate.[36] Individual Aboriginal students were also enrolled across Cumberland's other diplomas and degrees keeping AEU facilities busy.

In 1986, CCHS introduced special entry provisions through its Aboriginal Health Science Support Program (AHSSP), agreeing to set aside up to five percent of Cumberland's places subject to the head of school's satisfaction with the applicants' academic skills, qualifications and experience. Entry was by written application and interview, and participants could complete the first year over two academic years aided by supplementary tutorials. The scheme was regarded as a pacesetter in special admissions and was the model for the Cadigal Special Admissions Scheme at Camperdown.

The Aboriginal Education Centre

As the amalgamation process took shape, the Sydney University risked having little say on the form Aboriginal education would take as it had no focal point for negotiation with the Commonwealth. Sydney grasped the nettle on 1 July 1989, when the establishment of SUAEC was announced.[37] However, the centre had no staff beyond a share of King's time, no separate accommodation beyond that occupied by the AEATP, and no budget. Still, it did have a name, an address, and an account number. Shortly after its arrival, SU was dropped from the title.

Anticipating a financial contribution from Canberra in the second half of 1989, the University decided to advertise for a director – an Aboriginal appointee with a postgraduate qualification, competence in teaching, administration and research, and the ability to liaise with government agencies and Aboriginal communities. The post would be tenurable and available from late 1989. Three other lectureships on three-year contracts were advertised at the same time with Aboriginality an occupational qualification: a lecturer/coordinator for an Aboriginal Studies unit, preferably with experience in early childhood, a lecturer in Aboriginal studies, and a lecturer/coordinator for the AEATP and the DipAAEd. The University set aside $15,000 should the director's appointment come on steam in 1989, and King was allowed $10,000 for extra duties. All offers were subject to the availability of Commonwealth funding.

Sydney Institute of Education's CAS would merge with the Aboriginal Education Centre (AEC) from the first year of the amalgamation, 1990. Barbara Zaremba, the capable Head of the Guild Centre in SCAE, who was in charge of Academic Services and CAS, had encouraged pre-merger talks with the Faculty of Education in 1989, believing that CAS/AEC cooperation would promote strong pre-service teaching and postgraduate study and encourage an international perspective in research. It could also help overcome Anglocentric attitudes among staff and students. In contrast, Cumberland's AEU continued as a separate entity until its management was placed under the AEC director at Camperdown in 1991.

Figure 38. Acting Director of the Aboriginal Education Centre, Ray King, with coordinator Rosemary Stack, of the Aboriginal Education Assistants Program, January 1990. *UN*, vol. 1 no. 22, 20.2.1990.

The Eagle Lands

At an Advisory Committee meeting on 3 March 1989, Sutton informed King that the responsibility for the Aboriginal education programs of DAA would likely pass to DEET from 1 January 1990. This was a consequence of the Hughes Report (1988) recommending a national approach to funding Aboriginal education in higher education with $25 million proposed. For a slice of the funding, participating institutions must present a three-year plan updated annually and detailing current and planned expenditure, Aboriginal enrolments and target figures, and retention and graduation rates. On 21 July 1989, the Commonwealth Profiles Team visited Sydney, its Aboriginal representative, Nerida Blair, Head of the Aboriginal Education Support Unit at the Catholic College of Education. King followed up the Sydney meeting with a financial submission to Canberra in which he consolidated University projections, with the exception of those from Cumberland, estimating that 40 EFTSU would be enrolled in 1990.[38]

In January 1990, the University received news of "a huge funding boost", $767,611 of Commonwealth money for Aboriginal education.[39] The sum was shared in the ratio of 57:43 between Sydney's AEC and Cumberland's AEU and provided on a rolling triennium basis. Of the total, $200,500 was Aboriginal Education Strategic Initiatives Program (AESIP) money, essentially for support services, and $567,111 Aboriginal Participation Initiatives (API) money based on EFTSU and institutional performance. Altogether the AEC's share was $415,646, around King's best-case scenario, the payment including a one-off grant of $20,000 for an AEATP regional training pilot; while CCHS's share, $351,965, was above the sum the institution was currently receiving. With the AEC receiving a further $168,000 from the NSW DoE to cover AEATP training in 1989–90, Sydney had achieved a fantastic result.

9

Aboriginal Education Centre – Early Years

> The University of Sydney should be accessible to all talented Australians and much of the nation's talent is to be found in the Aboriginal Australian community.
>
> Don McNicol, Vice-Chancellor and Principal, 1991[1]

At the official opening of the Aboriginal Education Centre (AEC) on 26 September 1991, some two years after its founding, 200 well-wishers gathered around the jacaranda tree in the Quadrangle. With Ann Flood as master of ceremonies, the morning began with a

Figure 39. Vice-Chancellor Don McNicol, Joshua Stack and Shannon Delaney at the opening of the Aboriginal Education Centre, 26 September 1991. Koori Centre.

Figure 40. Linda Burney at the opening of the Aboriginal Education Centre, 26 September 1991. Image courtesy of the Koori Centre.

Figure 41. Charles Perkins at the opening of the Aboriginal Education Centre, 26 September 1991. Image courtesy of the Koori Centre.

spectacular show of Aboriginal music and dance by Christine Anu, Phillip Langley, Cedric Talbot, and Wayne Wunun Williams,[2] and poetry readings from Jennifer Newman, Aboriginal studies lecturer at Cumberland. During the speeches that followed, Perkins called on Australia's universities to graduate 3000 Aboriginal students annually, a fair target, he said, given 200 years of neglect. Sydney's Aboriginal graduate of 1967 wanted white adults taught Aboriginal studies and their children Aboriginal stories, songs and a corroboree. As to the present, the AEC should be congratulated on its thorough planning and hard work. "It took some pushing," Perkins insisted, "to get this far."[3]

Other speakers agreed that progress at Sydney had been slow, including the Vice-Chancellor, Don McNicol, who referred to Ward's original submission to Senate as far back as 1988. Delays aside, said McNicol, the remarkable growth of the AEC since 1990 was "symbolic of a change" and the task ahead clear – to ensure that talent was nurtured making Sydney students truly representative of Australia's Aboriginal community. By improving admissions policies and increasing graduation rates, the Vice-Chancellor planned to double Aboriginal enrolments in bachelor and higher degrees by 1994. University staff would not be neglected either and would be given opportunities to learn about Aboriginal culture, and the University would strengthen its links with Aboriginal communities around its campuses.

When Veronica Arbon spoke, she reported 140 Aboriginal enrolments at Sydney across various courses and another 500 non-Indigenous students taking Aboriginal studies. The acting director then announced plans to move the AEAP from Mackie to the Old Teachers College Building in the heart of the University, a much appreciated "step up" in recognition. Among those in attendance were the two previous directors, Cleverley, who had stepped down as acting director early in 1991, and King, who had left Sydney for the bush in February 1990, joining Charles Sturt University (Riverina) as a Visiting Fellow. Speak-

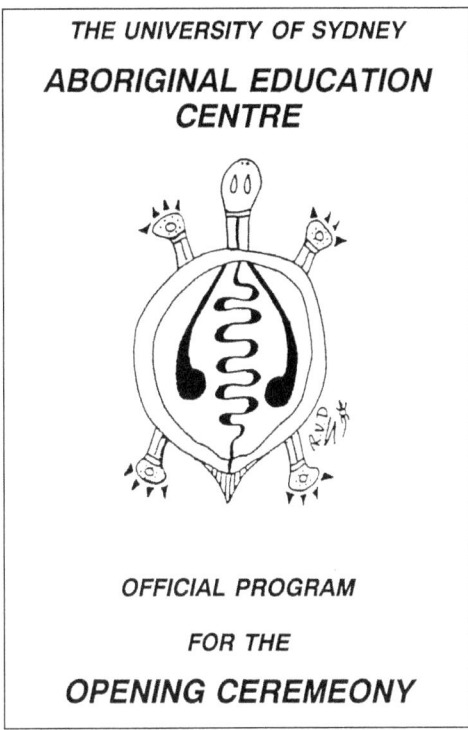

Figure 42. Program of the Aboriginal Education Centre opening ceremony 1991. Image courtesy of the Koori Centre.

ers and celebrants then processed across Parramatta Road to the Mackie Building led by a didgeridoo player and under the Aboriginal flag held aloft by two children of staff, Shannon Delaney and Joshua Stack, (the sons of Raylene Delaney and Rosemary Stack). The ribbon fastened across the door of the AEC was cut by the local community elder, Sylvia Scott, and the party trooped inside to inspect the freshly painted rooms and enjoy tea and cake.

New People, New Structures

Before moving to the Camperdown Campus in 1991, Veronica Arbon had headed the AEU at Cumberland as senior lecturer. Born in Alice Springs, a descendant of the Arabunna people of the central deserts of South Australia, she held an Associate Diploma in Community Development from the South Australian Institute of Technology and a BA degree from the University of Adelaide. As a child, Arbon had grown up on a cattle station. The eldest in a large family, she found herself caring for her people during a measles epidemic – many died including a child in her arms. She also helped others suffering from TB and leprosy calling on the Flying Doctor service and radio advice when necessary. She herself had five children on her appointment to Sydney.[4] Now able to speak for Cumberland as well as Camperdown, Arbon centralised the distribution of funds and the coordination of student recruitment and support across the two campuses. Among office staff who helped were Noeleen Smith, who had joined the Koori Centre in June 1993 as administrative as-

Figure 43. Terry Metherell, NSW Minister for Education, addresses participants in the Aboriginal Education Assistants Program, 1990. (Left to right: Kevin Cook, Susan Dorsch, Terry Metherell, John Cleverley, Sam Ball, Cliff Turney and Davina Tyrrell.) Image courtesy of University of Sydney Archives.

Figure 44. Lecturer Robert Veel with Aboriginal Education Assistants Program students 1991. Image courtesy of University of Sydney Archives.

Figure 45. Aboriginal Education Assistants Program students 1991. Image courtesy of University of Sydney Archives.

sistant for the block course replacing Natalie Brown on leave for 12 months, and Christine Simpson who assisted in the central office. Later appointed Assistant to the Director, Smith took several positions within the Koori Centre over the next 15 years becoming its longest serving non-Indigenous staff member.

Cumberland's AEU was especially strong in Aboriginal education, being responsible for about 45 percent of the University's Indigenous enrolments (54 EFTSU).[5] An upgrade of its Associate Diploma in Aboriginal Health and Community Development to bachelor status was underway making it Sydney's first degree for Aboriginal students. In 1993, seven Aboriginal students enrolled in the Bachelor of Health Sciences (Aboriginal Health and Community Development).[6] The AEU was under Fay Acklin who was appointed lecturer/coordinator in 1992; she was helped by Wayne Fulford, and her staff were active in research as well as teaching. One interesting project led by Acklin, Newman and A. Trindall assessed story-telling as a means of raising awareness of health issues and screening among Aboriginal women.

AEC Operations

The AEC took organisational shape in 1990, consolidating its structures and determining its procedures. Its importance to Aboriginal education in NSW was publicly recognised when the Minister for Education, Dr Terry Metherell, a good friend of Aboriginal education in NSW, visited. He was warmly welcomed and announced recent state initiatives to further assist AEAs in schools.

Figure 46. Aboriginal Education Assistants Program students on South Australian field trip, 1991. Image courtesy of the Koori Centre.

i) AEAP

Four units had been created within the AEC structure reflecting the centre's prime duties: training, student support, Aboriginal studies, and curriculum research and development. The training function was the responsibility of the Aboriginal Education Assistants Program (AEAP). In 1990, its three staff, Stack, coordinator, Beuzeville, the dapper adult educator, and Robert Veel, its lively teacher of English and communication, taught some 60 students across all stages.[7] With the NSW DoSE appointing AEAs to schools with more than 30 Aboriginal students, the future of the program appeared secure, unless, that is, the department determined on another institutional agency to handle it.

In 1990, Janet Mooney, a Yuin woman from the South Coast of New South Wales, joined the teaching team. Mooney's working career had begun in 1972 as a 17-year-old in the Department of Veterans' Affairs. After completing a BA (Visual Arts) in 1982, and a Graduate Diploma in Education (Secondary), she worked as leading hand (carpentry) in the Women's Services Repair Project in 1983–84, before moving to teach art and Aboriginal studies at Cleveland Street High. She then joined the Aboriginal Education Unit in the NSW DoSE, helping develop an Aboriginal perspective in the K–6 Visual Arts Syllabus. Mooney's last position before her AEC appointment was as consultant in Aboriginal education for the Metropolitan East Region. Though originally employed to teach Aboriginal

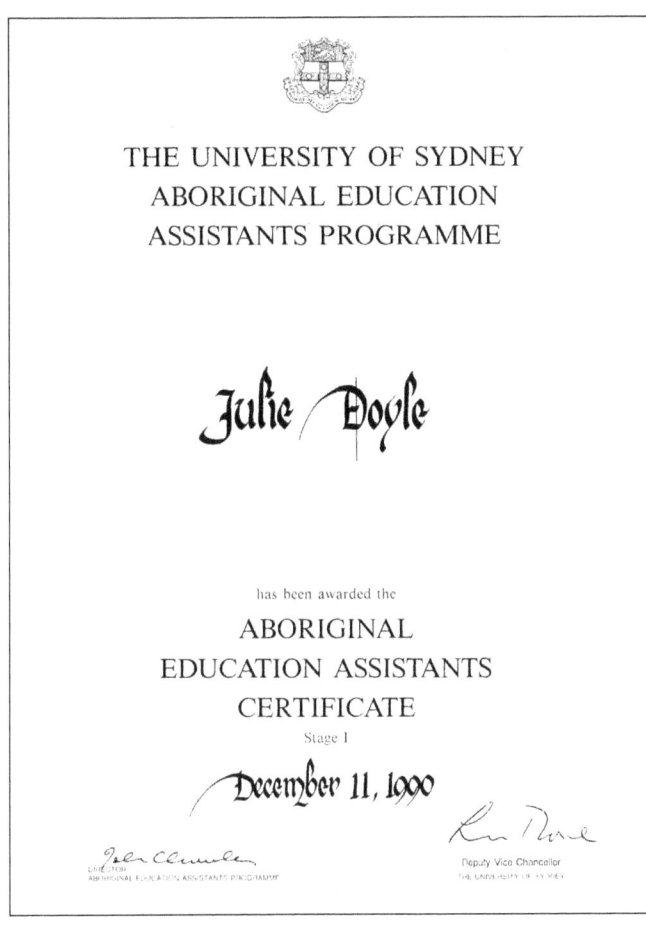

Figure 47. Aboriginal Education Assistants Certificate in 1990. Courtesy of Julie Doyle.

Arts, her AEAP duties were diverse including lecturing in the fields of Aboriginal studies, learning and teaching, and social and political studies. On Arbon's resignation, Stack served as acting director until Mooney was appointed director in 1996.

Stack led a review of curriculum arrangements pressing for a reduction in face-to-face teaching hours for students, more self-initiated learning, and the re-introduction of a Curriculum Advisory Committee under substantial Aboriginal control.[8] However, there was little change on the ground as it was difficult to get agreement within the AEC for major changes likely to benefit one unit above another. Particular AEAP initiatives at the time strengthened the tertiary visits program; extended practice teaching to eight days for second-year DipAAEds; and maintained regular visits to the Australian Institute of Aboriginal and Torres Strait Islander Studies (AIATSIS) by Stage IIIs. A week-long field trip to South Australia in 1991 saw Stage IIIs and Dip 2s tour Aboriginal schools in Point Pierce, Nep-

Figure 48. Administrative assistants at the Koori Centre, Natalie Brown (left), Kelli Collis, 1991. Image courtesy of the Koori Centre.

pabuna and Kaurna Plains and visit the Aboriginal Education Unit in the State Education Department in Adelaide.

In 1991, King and Stack completed a major report, Researching Community: Aboriginal Perspectives, assisted by John Maskell, John Butt, Kay Anderson and Helen Ware. The study stressed the importance of tapping the full spectrum of cultural understandings of Indigenous communities: written accounts, painting, audiotapes, video material, photographs, oral history, maps, and artefacts were all grist to the mill. The report's findings challenged the validity of models of communities applied from non-Aboriginal perspectives.

> If one is working in a different community to which one lives in, it makes a lot of sense to learn about the Aboriginal community from a member of that community. There is little to be gained from consulting a European about this as their understanding and perceptions may not be valid. Their emphasis could be placed on issues that the Aboriginal community may not consider to be of great importance. We need experience in research that is useful in our work. [9]

AEAs were urged to investigate their communities given that Aboriginal culture was formed, sustained and reconstituted through their everyday experiences. "White researchers working within an Anglo-European framework perceive differently from Aboriginal people whose world view is Aboriginal." Diploma 2 students then attended AIATSIS for a full week's intensive training in community research in 1992.

ii) CASU

Formed after a needs' survey by Raylene Delaney and Lorraine Towers in 1991, and headed by Maria Nugent, a lecturer who had come across from Cumberland, the Cultural and Academic Support Unit, (CASU), was primarily responsible for student support. Its aim was to create a sense of place "where local Aboriginals have a right to study and participate, and will wish to do so".[10] The unit's five main responsibilities were the organisation of tutoring arrangements in academic skills and literacy; orientation programs bringing Aboriginal school children on campus; school promotions and expositions; locating cadetships and employment opportunities; and the collection of data and statistics on Indigenous student numbers for the University's strategic plan. It also maintained the library resource collection under Van To, the part-time librarian. CASU recruited several able administrative assistants in the period to 1994, including Cassandra Graham and Kelli Collis; and Vanessa Forrest joined the team as associate lecturer, a specialist in literacy and learning strategies. Other academics and general staff were enlisted as part of a University-wide network.

iii) ASU

Staff in the Aboriginal Studies Unit (ASU) specialised in the teaching of Indigenous culture mainly in the AEAP and Faculty of Education although its members also lectured in the faculties of Nursing, Medicine, Arts, and at the Sydney College of the Arts. The capable Davina Tyrrell, President of the AEC (NSW), headed the ASU until mid-1990 when she left for a position on the South Coast; her teaching duties were taken over by Terry Widders, a lecturer from Macquarie University. Widders found himself overextended and resigned later that year being replaced by Wendy Brady as head in 1991. Brady, of the Wiradjuri Nation, joined the AEC from the ATSI Unit at the Queensland University of Technology. Holding a BA with Honours, she had tutored in Education at Sydney up to 1984, before joining James Cook University. After a period in London with a social policy team in 1988, Brady was appointed coordinator of the Associate Diploma in Aboriginal Health and Community Development at the Northern Rivers Campus of the University of New England. Back in Sydney, she helped produce a curriculum kit in Aboriginal studies and ran a workshop for Indigenous women on management skills in 1991. A year later, she took over the core unit prepared for the BEd (Primary) and the DipEd elective in Education and joined a teaching group in the Faculty of Medicine reviewing the place of Aboriginal health. ASU as a team also prepared an elective course on Aboriginal and Torres Strait Islander health issues in the conversion qualification for registered nurses in the Faculty of Nursing.

iv) CRDU

The Curriculum Research and Development Unit (CRDU) grew out of King's passion for research, an activity he thought essential for informed policymaking and academic respectability. Led by Laurie Craddock as Senior Research Fellow, it opened its doors in

Figure 49. Orana Centre Dubbo, Block One students: Phyllis Orcher, Clare Townsend, Lila Gordon, Robert Smith, Rachel Holten. Front: Julie Doyle, Judith Breckenridge, Denella Olsen, Lee Patterson, Dawn Timbery, and Janet Mooney (lecturer). Image courtesy of the Koori Centre.

June 1991, soon establishing a strong research profile commencing with a project for Metropolitan North Region which focused on the needs of Aboriginal students in minority situations.[11] The unit also met the growing demand for curriculum materials in teaching Aboriginal studies across the K–12 curriculum, work funded by the NSW DoSE. Other CRDU members were Ian Stewart, a Senior Research Fellow, and four research assistants, Jennifer Walton-Smith, Shane Williams, an Aboriginal trainee whose position was funded in part by the Office of Youth Affairs, and Dundi Mitchell who worked for Arbon in 1993.

As well as their university affiliations, AEC staff members were frequently engaged in educational activities with the AEC (NSW), the NSW AECG, The Settlement, Metropolitan East, the NSW DoSE, the AEU, the Aboriginal Higher Education Network, and their own community groups.

The AEAP at Dubbo

Given that most AEAs were uprooted from their country town and replanted in an unfamiliar city environment, it seemed logical that their training would be less traumatic in a "half-way house".[12] King had wanted a rural centre dedicated for the AEAP and managed by a local committee able to organise training itineraries; he thought its total cost unlikely to be greater than Sydney's, indeed it could well be less. King's suggestion was backed by the NSW AECG which asked all the state's universities "to review current course structures and academic regulations to allow maximum flexibility in multi-mode course offerings and delivery, including greater use of off-campus provision."[13] Rural training for the AEAP became a reality when the Commonwealth funded a regional trial at Dubbo's Orana Education Centre in 1990. The town had much in its favour. Dubbo had a substantial and long established Aboriginal community. Indigenous people were employed in a wide range of occupations though not in business ownership and management, and good black-white relations saw a high level of acceptance and integration in schools. Orana was also experienced in planning training and special courses for Aboriginal people. In 1990, three of five-block sessions for Stage I students were taught by volunteer AEC staff, Mooney, Anderson, and Stack, in the Aboriginal Lands Centre building, and the total program was supported by Beuzeville as coordinator, and Terrill Riley-Gibson, as Aboriginal counsellor.

The Dubbo teaching went well, the 20 AEAs comfortable among friendly people. Students enjoyed the walk to classes in a safe environment and, despite occasional flare-ups, group bonding was strong although some sense of belonging to the University of Sydney was missing. Dubbo students printed a collection of writing, *Jungai* (Octopus), and a Directory of Campus Services; and gathered a set of materials on Dubbo's Aboriginal community. The fact that the students were exposed to fewer lecturers than at Sydney helped make learning more palatable. Having AEAP staff on hand to answer students' academic and personal queries was another advantage though staff could not always relax when they wished. Staff and students also missed the library and clerical support available at Mackie.

Survey data and interviews backed the assessment that the Dubbo period raised self-esteem and understanding of the AEA's professional role including an improved ability to deal with unfamiliar situations. While considered a "very positive"[14] experience, participants thought that the training exercise deserved better planning and suggested appointment of a liaison person working with local organisations ahead of the group's arrival. The AEAP decided to extend the program to the northwest, western districts and lower north coast in 1993 but this proved impossible due to lack of funding. Later, the Dubbo scheme was reduced to one block session annually.

Regional Workshops for AEAs

The AEAP had difficulty keeping pace with rising demands. Not only were more AEAs needed for new school posts but vacancies arose when AEAs were promoted out of the classroom to jobs like Aboriginal liaison in the public service or in companies. Others seeking places were AEAs unavailable for training earlier due to family commitments or who worked as relief for AEAs on leave. In 1990, the NSW DoSE instigated a series of two-day regional in-service sessions for untrained AEAs with the Koori Centre invited to manage them. Just under $100,000 was provided for staff salaries and Bob Percival was appointed full time, and Janson and Bennett part time. Run largely by the AEAs themselves, helped by Delaney and Towers, the first of the in-services was at Wesley College in the University grounds from 12–14 December, 1990. The Director-General of School Education, Fenton Sharpe, gave the opening address, "Schools Renewal: Implications for Aboriginal Education and the AEA". A further two regional sessions were held in 1991, the first in the Hunter region in October for 30 participants, and the second in November for 26, the latter a combined metropolitan workshop at Strathfield. Others in 1992 were organised around AEA priorities including student discipline, duties of school councils, school devolution, Aboriginal studies, AEA roles, negotiating with principals, and child sexual assault.

Rachel Carney's paper, "Academic Futures",[15] delivered at the December 1990 conference indicates that presentations were of a good standard. The AEA from Narromine High highlighted problems colleagues faced when University training did not synchronise with school experience. Carney advised AEAs not to simply reproduce Sydney's training recipe; rather they should spend time understanding their own school situation and match their skills against local need. Here it was essential that local community history and culture be explored. The paper cautioned AEAs to stand firm against both white staff intent on shaming them into adopting their own attitudes and Aboriginal communities who labelled them "token blacks". They should seize the initiative by joining committees and regional taskforces, thus establishing their own networks of influence: "Knowledge, self esteem and support are the essential means by which AEAs can achieve their goals." Carney wanted AEA support officers sent to schools where students' results were poor and staff attitudes unimproved, and she thought Sydney should offer additional training for personnel about to enter regional consultant jobs or TAFE coordinator positions.

Janson has written of one workshop session in Tamworth held for 50 AEAs in March 1992.

> When the University of Sydney lecturer brought out some documents on the local language, Kamilaroi, the Aboriginal participants actually struggled with each other to gain access to this valuable information that was not available in their area. The Aboriginal community response was overwhelming because these people had no access to tertiary or adult education of any kind and were desperate for the chance to enter the AEA Program as it offered the only articulation to any form of education beyond school. In these ways the University was facilitating the movement towards a rebirth in Aboriginal access to knowledge and their own history that had been removed from them through generations of denial of education.[16]

Other workshops ran in 1992, but the AEC's estimate of cost escalated to $117,250 in 1993,[17] and the NSW DoSE decided not to continue the project.

The Management Advisory Committee

Under the Commonwealth funding arrangements of 1990, it was necessary that the University constitute a Management Advisory Committee, a duty Cleverley undertook in 1990. Five major objectives were identified:

- to receive reports from the Director in regard to budget and AEC management
- to discuss admission arrangements and the program of Indigenous students

- to consider the effectiveness of support services and students' special needs
- to spread understanding of Aboriginal society and culture
- to develop University and community interaction.[18]

MAC members were also expected to advise on the Aboriginal and Torres Strait Education Strategy Profile required by the Commonwealth as a condition of triennium funding.

The first MAC meeting, held on 19 March 1991, was chaired by Ken Ralph, the Acting State Manager of ATSIC. Familiar faces came together: Adams, Director, Student Services at Sydney; Arbon, Acting Director, AEC; Burney, President, NSW AECG; Cleverley, Head of School, Social and Policy Studies in Education; Dorsch, Deputy Vice-Chancellor; Graham Mooney, Administrator, The University of Sydney Settlement; Phil Nean, Chief Education Officer, Aboriginal Education Unit, NSW DoSE; Stack, Coordinator AEAP; Thorne, Director, Aboriginal Programs, DEET; Sutton (and Roslyn Field), DEET; and Turney, Dean, Faculty of Education. Places were also set aside for student and community representatives and a nominee from Cumberland. The willingness of the high profile Indigenous Australians and other externals to join MAC was testimony of the AEC's standing.

A Visit from the Royal Commission

Outcry at the inhumane treatment of Aboriginal prisoners had forced a Royal Commission into Aboriginal Deaths in Custody in 1987–91. Stack, who was among those assisting in the Redfern/Chippendale area, arranged a discussion group in Mackie drawn from AEAs on course. The visitors, a group of four, were led by Kevin Kitchener from the Commission's Aboriginal Inquiry Unit and the meeting itself was chaired by Louise Casson from the Underlying Issues Unit. Stack, Beuzeville, and 22 AEAs joined the discussion on 8 May 1990 which focused on AEAs' roles and the school as an agent of social causation. Notes were taken on four major issues:

> Racism: – brawling between black and white children – unfair accusations against Koori children for stealing – and the separation of black-white students in religion classes. The concept of the all black school was rejected: "An all black school disadvantages black kids. You have to live as one." It was accepted that little name-calling now occurred in schools however there was concern over racist statements in circulation.

> Weaknesses and strengths of the school system: – poor physical conditions in some schools – a high turn over of school principals who moved to coastal areas to retire – the importance of Aboriginal Studies in schools despite pupils showing a preference for other subjects e.g. cooking – recognition that sport was a valued activity – the need for more Aboriginal teachers and for pre-employment training – the usefulness of homework centres for primary as well as secondary children – improved access to computers under the disadvantaged schools scheme – and the crucial role of AEAs in class and out.

> Lack of interest of Aboriginal parents in schooling: – ways to improve communication between school and parent – children in Year 9 and 10 who "muck up" hiding their lack of skills – and the feeling among some children that they are "ashamed of their mums".
>
> Drug abuse and truancy: – smoking and alcohol in schools and outside – the issue of child abuse – and the need for more truancy and home school liaison officers: "We all have them but we don't know what they look like."[19]

Casson's concluding remarks recognised the indispensable contribution of AEAs and the good relations between AEAs and school staff generally; and Kitchener commended them as "the best group of Koories he had met with, everybody having something to offer". Wirrungah Dungirr (Raymond Donovan), the talented AEA from Bowraville, sketched the four Commission staff around the table presenting the drawing as a memento. When the Commissioner's report was published in 1991, it singled out the importance of Aboriginal education workers in schools and included the corollary that Aboriginal people had a right to expect the same educational opportunities and outcomes as other Australian citizens.

Problems with Arithmetic

More government money brought a flurry of demands for documentation on Aboriginal enrolments and performance. In 1989, the official Commonwealth tally, Aboriginal Enrolments in New South Wales Higher Education Institutions, credited Sydney with 196 Aboriginal students, around one percent of its total enrolment. This gave the University the second largest number of Aboriginal enrolments in the state, exceeded only by Macarthur Institute of Higher Education with 216.[20] The Sydney figures were unsupportable.[21] As yet, none of the amalgamating institutions had merged with Sydney; the AEA Diploma was still in the planning stage; and AEAP students were not counted as EFTSU by the Commonwealth. On the brighter side, the circulation of these inaccurate sums may have raised Sydney's status as a provider of Aboriginal education in Canberra, at least in the short term and, on grounds that two wrongs make a right, similar miscounting took place in other institutions.

Keen to get the enrolment figures right, Cleverley obtained the ID numbers of students who had signified Aboriginal status on their enrolment forms and asked an Aboriginal staff member to ring a sample for checking. Despite students having ticked the box, more than half of those contacted were not Indigenous Australians. The non-Aboriginal signifiers came up with a variety of reasons: some thought that identification meant you were born in Australia; others that there was a cash or other benefit; and a few claimed memory loss or carelessness. In 1990, the Commonwealth government revised its 1989 figure down from 196 Camperdown Campus enrolments to 50.[22]

Two sources of Aboriginal enrolments made Sydney's figures more respectable in 1990: the first, the intake from the DipAAEd; the second, enrolments from amalgamating institutions, in particular Cumberland. In 1989, the AEC had estimated 20 enrolments in the DipAAEd for the following year, 15 of them full-time; and another 20 students were expected to join under the Sydney College of Advanced Education (SCAE) merger, 15 from its Sydney Institute of Education, and five from the Institute of Nursing.[23] After discussions with the Commonwealth's profile group, the University's Aboriginal EFTSU for 1990 was set at 32 continuing and eight new places for the AEC, and 31 and eight for Cumberland's AEU.[24]

Estimates of Aboriginal enrolments at Sydney proved difficult to calculate reliably. The figure proposed for 1992, for example, was 122.5,[25] the actual 93.6.[26] A letter to Arbon from Planning Support Services raised the University's concern. "It was not expected that targets would be achieved every year, however 25% error, as has seemingly been reported by the University was significant."[27] Similarly, the EFTSU estimate for 1995 of 249.4[28] appeared excessive, the University thinking DEET unlikely to accept it. Sydney feared that its overestimation of enrolments would lead the Commonwealth to demand a refund and that legitimate load increases would be viewed sceptically. Of course Arbon had to rely on information given her and there was no past experience of numbers as a guide. It is understandable too that Sydney, having appointed an Aboriginal director and established a centre, would anticipate a rapid increase in numbers.

The University defended its over-calculations in correspondence with Canberra claiming that 80 students had identified themselves as Aborigines in 1992, yet 111 Sydney students were in receipt of Abstudy. Furthermore, another 4.6 Aboriginal EFTSU had joined Sydney in second semester too late to be officially counted. As Aboriginal enrolments were spread over 31 courses with differing EFTSU loads, projections were hard to calculate, and student confidentiality must be negotiated in any checking. Sydney claimed it had not been warned in advance that the Commonwealth intended to invoke refund arrangements for over payment and that any reduction in income would see the AEC lose Aboriginal staff. It also reminded Canberra that the University was experiencing additional cost pressures because the AEC and AEU were on different campuses leading to unavoidable duplication in infrastructure, a problem not of its making, and that the University was putting in significant funding of its own. In addition, it pointed to pioneer work in teaching Aboriginal studies in teacher education, a program of national significance.

Canberra was swayed by Sydney's pleading. It accepted that the University would improve the accuracy of its counting which the University did by amending its enrolment forms (as did the University Admissions Centre at the Koori Centre's suggestion). In 1993, Sydney slipped in an addendum in its Commonwealth profile documentation: "We do not consider our data prior to 1991 to be reliable."[29] It also cut its projection for 1995 from 249.4 Aboriginal EFTSU to 202.8.[30] Eventually Canberra laid down a formula for Australian universities including a participation rate which compared the number of Indigenous students with the number of domestic students as a percentage. Sydney had a participation rate of 0.8[31] in 2004.

In 1990, with figures approximating actual enrolments, Dorsch and Cleverley attended a meeting of deans to discuss implications for strategic planning purposes. Some faculties had no idea whether they had Aboriginal students or not, let alone providing any services. The poor retention and graduation rates of Aboriginal students also needed discussion. In 1991, of 18 bachelor degree students enrolled at the Camperdown Campus, five would discontinue in first year and there were no bachelor graduates that year.[32] Cleverley recalls that particular deans' meeting.

> I felt the atmosphere was more about finding arithmetical errors in the figures I'd produced than where we should go next. I usually found individual Deans constructive face to face, but you could say putting them together in the company of outsiders including a Deputy Vice-Chancellor brought out another side. I remember being given a rough time by several. Then again, after the meeting, I was rung up by two or three in a courteous follow up.[33]

One dean who made a personal effort to recruit Aboriginal students was Professor Stephen Salisbury of the Faculty of Economics, an American by birth and education, and a supporter of First Nations Rights. After the deans' meeting he invited Cleverley, Stack and the AEAP students to the Merewether Building for morning tea, about 20 attending. Salisbury spoke at length of his American experience and willingness to help Aborigines in economics, business and commerce, urging that AEAs study his discipline and contact its undergraduate studies coordinator (introduced at the meeting) who would provide a mentor for each of them and free tutoring. Students were heartened by his generous initiative and, on the walk back to Mackie, they discussed taking up his offer. One jesting remark from a senior administrator queried where Salisbury would find the extra money given his perpetual complaint that the administration short changed him.

Staff Developments

Academic staff took advantage of their location within the University to start higher degrees. Three of the four senior Aboriginal academics on the Broadway Campus, Arbon, Stack and Mooney, were enrolled in Masters in 1992, although Arbon and Stack had deferred study.[34] The fourth, Brady, was finishing a PhD. Recognising the difficulties that Aborigines faced completing their postgraduate qualifications while in full-time employment, Dorsch initiated a Special Studies Program, applying conditions similar to those governing staff from the amalgamating colleges. The DVC argued her case on equity grounds and the urgent need for Aborigines to improve their academic standing, claiming they deserved specific assistance and lower workloads. Over the next five years, Indigenous staff were permitted study leave towards a formal academic qualification, a concession not granted other academics. The first beneficiary, Stack, took Special Studies Leave from March to November 1993.

Figure 50. Terrill Riley-Gibson (Indigenous counsellor), second from right, with students in the Mackie Building common room, Aboriginal Education Centre. From left: Bill Toomey (Wee Waa), Lyn Roberts (Lismore) and Steven McIntosh (Boggabilla), 1990. Image courtesy of University of Sydney Archives.

Appointment of a Counsellor

A demand for counselling was there from the beginning. As far back as 1975, individual students had testified that it was John Skelton's counselling that kept them on course.[35] However, maintaining a counsellor in the program was an expensive option and the ATATP came to rely on individual counsellors from the University Counselling Service (UCS) and on staff members, black or white, who related well to students. In 1987, King raised the possibility of an Aboriginal trainee counsellor to further students' adjustment to city life and better manage unruly pupils and aggressive parents. After discussions with John Chapman from the UCS in 1989, he wrote to Dorsch on the 23 November, proposing the appointment of an Aboriginal counsellor (intern), paid at tutor rate, the cost shared between UCS and the AEC.

Terrill Riley-Gibson, the first identified Aborigine to complete social work at Sydney, was appointed to the UCS in January 1990. Having left school at 15 to work as an enrolled nurse, Riley-Gibson had a breadth of life experience travelling in Europe and Africa for three years before returning to the University of Tasmania and Sydney. Riley-Gibson believed she should be sensitive to people's actual needs and keep her counselling informal and indirect, and that she must attempt to dispel myths surrounding Aboriginal people held by non-Aborigines. "Being Aboriginal isn't just about physical appearance," she told *The Gazette*, "it involves a very broad cultural framework and a sense of identification in being a member of an Aboriginal community."[36]

On the 12 June 1990, the *University News* reported the acting director delighted with the appointment. "Terrill has provided valuable information and suggestions which will enable us to more adequately provide for students." Similarly, the Director of Student Services, Bill Adams, declared her engagement a significant contribution to the University's counselling service. Riley-Gibson founded the SU Aboriginal Education Social Club and introduced regular Tuesday lunchtime get-togethers, however she would not continue beyond the end of the year for reasons unrelated to the AEC. In 1996, the UCS established a dedicated Indigenous Counselling Unit (ICU) under Lisa Jackson,[37] staffed on a half-time basis, whose members visited hospitals and joined doctors' appointments in addition to other duties. Jackson, later Jackson-Pulver, was a Wiradjuri woman. In 2004, she was awarded a PhD in Medicine for the thesis, "An Argument on Cultural Safety in Health Service Delivery: Towards Better Health Outcomes for Aboriginal People", and joined the University of New South Wales.

A Spat over Accommodation

Benefiting from substantial triennium funding, AEC staff numbers built up rapidly with nine full-time and two part-time staff employed by the end of 1990.[38] At the close of the following year, staff numbers including part-timers were double the 1990 complement.[39] While some in the University queried whether such a large increase was justified, suggesting that outreach work could be shared with other New South Wales universities, the staff were on the ground and there was severe pressure on space with no relief in sight until the New Education Building Complex came on line. The Faculty of Education had begun planning its building complex in the mid-1980s, destined for the tennis and basketball courts close to the Teachers College; and Cleverley, who was in charge of faculty planning, wrote to King asking for an estimate of his accommodation needs. King replied that he would be happy to take up space in the refurbished Teachers College Building.

The AEC was awarded some extra Mackie rooms in 1990 as a stop gap measure[40] and, in return, it promised to surrender the CAS office and lecture space on the site across Carillon Avenue inherited from the amalgamation. The extra Mackie space was given it "on condition the centre would not expand its activities beyond the space available in the Mackie Building". Ignoring the constraint on the expansion of the centre's activities, which Cleverley thought a case of the tail wagging the dog, he rashly agreed that there would be no claim on the CAS space.[41]

For a while the AEC staved off the effects of overcrowding in Mackie by borrowing rooms from Careers and Appointments but the situation became dire when these had to be returned. Offices designed for a single staff member now contained up to three administrative staff and one temporary person and there was no space for Aboriginal mainstream students. Like David Copperfield, the AEC asked for more.[42] Building and Grounds replied that it had no spare accommodation and the centre should approach the Dean of Education for assistance from his space envelope.[43] At this point, Arbon asked Cleverley, then University Liaison with the AEC, to take up the AEC's case with Turney.[44] Given that Turney had no vacant accommodation, the best solution appeared the reoccupation of part of the old CAS space on Carillon Avenue utilising three offices and a teaching room. The Carillon space had been empty for about two years though it remained fully serviced.

The dean agreed with the AEC's request as the space had previously belonged to the Sydney Institute of Education over which he had delegated authority[45] and the AEC moved staff to the Carillon Avenue space immediately. The next day, Turney received a blunt warning from Building and Grounds telling him he had no jurisdiction over the Carillon Avenue grounds whose rooms had been kept vacant deliberately "to be used for decanting space for building projects which have been delayed".[46] The AEC must move out. Much heat was generated with Cleverley accused of going back on his word and of squatting; in response, he cautioned of consequences if the Aborigines were evicted from space empty for two years and which had been the Centre for Aboriginal Studies prior to the amalgamation. He also pointed out that the Management Advisory Committee, with its thoughtful and constructive interest in the centre, would likely take a dim view of the dispute which would certainly widen and worsen. Cleverley notes what happened next.

> Education's initiative was reported to the Registrar and Jennings brought the parties together for a tense meeting, the group comprising myself, Turney, and two Building and Grounds staff. Turney put the case for occupation with his customary vigour taking the opportunity to raise other issues for good measure complaining of bias against his Faculty by Building and Grounds. Various accusations flew back and forth and the senior Building and Grounds person appeared ready to walk out but common sense prevailed and Jennings suggested the AEC occupy the Carillon space until the New Education Building came on steam.[47]

Afterwards, Turney objected to Dorsch that he had not been delegated authority over space for the AEC and that the faculty had its own shortages and priorities. Should the AEC make further appointments, he said, he did not consider himself responsible for housing them.[48] The situation was relieved in 1994 when the Koori Centre finally occupied dedicated space on the ground floor of the Old Teachers College around the two courtyards which accommodated its contingent of smokers.

Outside the University's gates the growing cost of rental accommodation under the march of inner city gentrification was working against the attendance of Aboriginal students. In 1991, the AEC commissioned a report from Michele Willsher, a recently graduated teacher with experience at Lamarou in the Northern Territory, who interviewed 25 of the 28 AEAs, and 24 of the 30 Aboriginal mainstream enrolments, full and part time, on the Camperdown Campus.[49] The students opposed hostel accommodation thinking it too restrictive, preferring bed-sitters or two- to three-bedroom flats. Willsher's report

Figure 51. The first graduates of the Diploma in Aboriginal Assistants Education pictured with Lady Black (centre back), the Chancellor Sir James Rowland (Chancellor 1990–91)(centre front) , and Professor John Cleverley (back right). From left to right (back): Gwen Hickling (Casino), Helen Archibald (Kempsey), Neville Naden (Dubbo). Front: Barbara Keeley (Lumeah), Veronica Davison (Taree), Iris Johnson (Lake Cargelligo) and Ann Flood (Seven Hills). Image courtesy of University of Sydney Archives.

recommended that the University seek government and Aboriginal agency funds for a mix of the two types, and that an Aboriginal representative be appointed to the Student Accommodation Steering Committee to move things along. Nothing further was done and the issue of Aboriginal accommodation was never tackled as a priority.

Death of Hermann Black and John Ward

The death of the Chancellor, Sir Hermann Black, on 28 February 1990, a true supporter of Aborigines on campus, was sad news for staff, AEAs and their families. His patronage had put a stamp on the validity of Aboriginal education at Sydney in 1975 and it was his and Lady Joyce Black's personal warmth and the time shared at ceremonies and afterwards that remained with all. Stack, the senior Aboriginal staff member, spoke for the program in her letter of condolence to Joyce Black.

> On behalf of the Aboriginal Education Centre, I would like to express our sympathy on the death of Sir Hermann. Staff of the Centre, myself, Davina, Peter, Angela, Kay, Janet and John have valued your husband's deep attachment and feeling for the Aboriginal people which he expressed in his own personal and unique style. His attendance at our Graduation Ceremony will be missed by us all. We value your own involvement with the Aboriginal Education Centre and trust that you will remain in contact with us."[50]

Joyce Black continued a firm backer of the Aboriginal people up to her death in 2009. Cleverley recalls her talking with him after a Chancellor's Committee meeting around the year 2000 which had just discussed expenditure on Aboriginal scholarships. "I'd rather spend money on people," she told him, "than bricks and mortar."[51]

On 6 May 1990, the AEC lost other strong advocates when the recently retired Vice-Chancellor, John Ward, together with his wife, Patricia, and daughter, Jennifer, were killed in a train catastrophe, along with Moira Jennings, the wife of the Registrar. Keith Jennings, a fine administrator and good friend of Turney's, who understood the needs of the Koori Centre, was among those seriously injured. It was Ward who had taken the original proposal for the AEC to Senate and he had been delighted to find the centre substantially funded in January that year, as King remembers:

> John Ward was an ardent supporter of Aboriginal education and I had several earnest talks with him about the direction things were taking. He was very supportive of me. It was a great blow to the cause and a shock to me when he was killed.[52]

Black and Ward together made a formidable team at Sydney, with Black's open graciousness and rhetorical capacity complimenting Ward's scholarliness, quiet courtesy and thoughtfulness. Patricia Ward was one of those who worked selflessly with the Sydney University Women's Group.

The tradition of the Chancellor presenting the certificates and diplomas continued under Black's successor, the affable and straightforward Air Marshal Sir James Rowland, a Sydney Engineering graduate, who had served with Bomber Commander in the famed Pathfinder Force. Rowland was also Governor of New South Wales from 1988–89. On 11 December 1990, 20 AEAs with Stage I, and ten with Stages II and III received their certificates from Rowland, as well as six DipAAEd students in an inaugural graduation.[53] "It has taken two generations to achieve results in Aboriginal Education," said John Lester, Principal of Grafton TAFE. "Your kids will see the reality of an education that is culturally relevant and sensitive to our needs." In 1991, after Rowland's death, the Chancellor, Emeritus Professor Dame Leonie Kramer, presented 37 certificates in the Wool Room at International House. Margaret Vincent, a community member from Redfern, gave the address. In another significant milestone on 28 May 1992, seven of the DipAAEd students, in their new and distinctive gowns of black, orange and red, processed in the Great Hall on equal terms with the University's other graduands for the first time. Among the diploma graduates that year was Julie Doyle, of the Dharawal people, who would return in 2009 to complete a BEd (Secondary: Aboriginal Studies).

10

Independence

> It is appropriate that the Centre have an Aboriginal name in line with other Aboriginal Education Units in other universities, and the name change [to Koori Centre] is supported by the staff of the Centre.
>
> Don McNicol, Vice-Chancellor, 1992[1]

The search for an Aboriginal director for the AEC was a lengthy one. Over three years in the making, it reflected on the job's daunting description: proven educational leadership, administrative skills, and tertiary experience including a postgraduate qualification.[2] Charles Perkins was among those interested; and one offer of appointment was made in 1990 and turned down. Following re-advertisement, two candidates were interviewed, both meeting with staff in the second half of 1992, with Veronica Arbon successful. Arbon had served as acting director for over 18 months already, spending about three days a week at Camperdown and two at Cumberland, and her standing in education and health was considerable.

Figure 52. First Aboriginal Director Aboriginal Education Centre/Koori Centre: Veronica Arbon. Image courtesy of the Koori Centre.

Reflecting on new challenges, she observed how education had appeared a "weapon of assimilation" but today that attitude was changing, "and in its place Aboriginal people are realising how they can use education for the greater benefit of their communities."[3] Arbon was appointed to the Academic Board, ex officio, and to the Sub-Committee of the Special Admissions Committee. A few years earlier, King had suggested that two Aborigines be appointed to Senate, one representing Aboriginal staff, the other, Aboriginal students given that Indigenous viewpoints "have been excluded in the development of the University".[4] He also wanted a permanent sub-committee on Aboriginal education to strengthen negotiations with the Commonwealth, however neither proposal was taken up.

Arbon moved quickly following up a suggestion of the Faculty of Education Working Party that the name Aboriginal Education Centre be replaced by an Aboriginal title. This would bring Sydney in line with the University of New England's Oorala, Newcastle University's Wollotuka, and the University of Technology, Sydney's, Jumbunna. Writing to McNicol in September 1992, Arbon informed him that "after much debate and discussion, staff have elected to change the name of the centre from Aboriginal Education to Koori Centre."[5] While Arbon was reminded gently that such a decision was the University's, McNicol accepted the recommendation taking the change to Senate which approved the re-naming on 2 November 1992.

Establishing a Research Presence

Curriculum Research and Development Unit (CRDU) staff mounted various research projects, consultancies, in-house and published reports, articles and educational materials. By 1993, significant research projects were completed or underway at the Camperdown Campus applying $90,000 in external funding.[6] They were:

- Education Needs of Aboriginal Students in 25 Schools in the Metropolitan North Region (L. Craddock, S. Williams, J. Walton-Smith)
- Evaluation of Koori Youth Programs for the NSW Office of Youth Affairs (W. Brady, I. Stewart, S. Williams, J. Walton-Smith)
- Local Area Studies Guide for Teachers of Aboriginal Studies (W. Brady, staff)
- Aboriginal and Torres Strait Islander Women in Management (W. Brady)
- Recommendation for Educational Equity for Aboriginal People at the University of Sydney (R. King, R. Stack)
- Researching Community – Aboriginal Perspectives (R. King, R. Stack, staff)
- Shoalhaven Aboriginal Education Research Report (I. Stewart, S. Williams)
- Study of Aboriginal Education Needs in New South Wales Handbook (L. Craddock, S. Williams, J. Walton-Smith)
- Local Area Studies Guide for Teachers of Aboriginal Studies (W. Brady, staff)

- Directory of Aboriginal Education and Training New South Wales (J. Cleverley, A. Perkins)
- Basic Skills Testing and the Practicum (L. Dawe, staff).[7]

Curriculum resources were also prepared for the HSC Aboriginal Studies Syllabus (1992) and for the Modern History Syllabus Years 7 to 10, much of it written by staff in-house, with some assistance from Jack Harrison, the ex-Director of Special Services. In addition, CRDU ran training workshops for communities including one on the South Coast and another at La Perouse.

Other projects were underway at Cumberland with CRDU staff involved. These included:

- Evaluation of Special Health Services for Aboriginal Women Living in the Blacktown Local Government Area (V. Arbon and M. Nugent, staff /AEU)
- Cervical Cancer and Human Papilloma Virus in Aboriginal and Asian Women in the Western Sydney Region (V. Arbon, staff /AEU).

Arbon and Nugent also reported on the effectiveness of Cumberland's Aboriginal Health Science Support Program (AHSSP). Based on interviews with past and present students from 1989–92, they found Indigenous students valued the role of Cumberland's Aboriginal Education Unit. "I think if you take away the meeting place environment," one student told them, "all you have is another academic corridor."[8] Contact with each other, students said, along with their own achievements helped them debunk lack of confidence in their own intelligence, the result of past academic failure, and they recognised assistance given them by caring staff, avoiding the occasional staffer who belittled them. A renewed sense of confidence was carried back to their homes and communities. However, one particular objection related to frustration over racist graffiti in toilets. "There's been so much horrible anti-Aboriginal graffiti that it just made me sick. It's the colleges responsibility when there's that sort of racist graffiti to have it removed. And I mean it has been up here ever since I've been here." All agreed on the importance of quality teaching on course, "not some bullshit sort of program that satisfies the rest of the world but doesn't get anywhere." Hard work, and well-designed, relevant courses, "that's what it's about!!".

The Koori Centre made some seed funding available for research projects thought likely to gain external agency take-up but follow-up money proved difficult to source. When Stewart visited Canberra to check on funding for an extension of his Shoalhaven project results were "very poor";[9] and a new project that Stewart co-sponsored with Wendy Brady, a national research journal to critique theories of Indigenous self-determination and cultural diversity, also went unfunded. Turning for help within the University, the Koori Centre invited Professor Bruce Thom, Chair of the University's Research Committee, to suggest ways the University could lend a hand. The talk started well, Thom praising the centre's research for its good beginning.

> The AEC has conducted self-initiated research focusing on education and has related external work to those in a good position to translate that research into

action. This approach can lead to substantially raising AEC's profile quickly, through the production of research.[10]

Then came the bad news – nothing could be considered by his office without "runs on the board".

From the Other Three Units

The AEAP continued with the teaching practicum in inner-city and rural schools and there were visits to Menindee Cultural Centre, home of the famed Auntie Beryl Carmichael, and to AIATSIS in 1993. That year Phillip Veness was appointed to a lectureship and Helene Orr, a senior secretary from the Faculty of Education, came over to organise the main office. Stack was active in industrial issues again, making a case for an upgrading of the status of DipAAEd graduate to that of education officer in the NSW DoSE. Despite senior support within the NSW DoSE, the recommendation was literally lost in head office.

The ASU benefited from a stepped up demand for Aboriginal cultural studies from non-Indigenous students in fields like history, education, medicine, and nursing, and at the Sydney College of the Arts. Late in 1993, Ann Flood, who had graduated with a BEd (Primary), was appointed to teach in the Aboriginal Health Elective in the BNursing (Conversion), teaching the 12 students enrolled for first semester 1994. Brady, ASU's head, continued to teach Aboriginal studies in the Faculty of Education where she also joined a team preparing a curriculum for children with special needs.

In CASU, top priority went to a new special admissions arrangement initially trialled by Arbon and further developed by Nugent in 1992. The Cadigal Special Admissions' Scheme, along the lines of Cumberland's AHSSP model, was approved by Senate on the 7 September 1992, subject to review in 1994. Entry criteria for Aborigines would count life experience, personal goals and readiness, as well as academic achievement, and students were directed to two academic skills courses covering study techniques, essay writing and referencing. Regular study loads were reduced to make this supplementary training possible, assisted by the Commonwealth's decision to allow students on course full eligibility for Abstudy. The University also played its part by releasing additional space in Mackie for a small common room and learning station. For 1993, 110 applications were received for the Camperdown Campus, with 43 offers made and 25 enrolled. Another eight were enrolled at Cumberland.[11] For the first time, the Faculty of Arts had more applications than Education or Health Sciences, a break in the dominance of the two big social sciences.

Of the 25 continuing special entry students in 1994, three failed, two withdrew with personal problems, and the rest achieved grades from pass to high distinction.[12] The scheme saw some unforeseen consequences. "It was reported that there was a feeling among some whites that ATSI students 'got all the handouts'";[13] and that Aboriginal students were advantaged in competitive study given their lighter academic load in first year. Conversely, some centre staff complained that Aborigines were resistant to taking the academic skills component, including its lighter load provisions, as the requirement lengthened the time span for their degree. The University had anticipated that up to five percent of total places would be available under Cadigal, potentially 1500 students, however numbers never exceeded two figures.[14]

CASU's two administrative assistant positions were re-graded as assistant lecturers to ensure quality in academic skills teaching and tutorial assistance under the Aboriginal Tutorial Assistance Scheme (ATAS). Unit staff also helped with an oral history project at Moriah College and with other curriculum projects. The University assisted too. Mary Edwards, Director of Student Services, ran a counselling skills workshop for Aboriginal women employed in the local community. In other CASU events, a manual covering specific administrative procedures was printed for new staff and a student newsletter published and circulated.

A Matter of Ethics

At Thom's October meeting, the point was made that inappropriate and unnecessary research had been inflicted on Aboriginal communities by scholars unaware of Indigenous values and protocols. He was told that research should be "<u>for</u> Aborigines not <u>on</u> them". This caution represented a growing demand inside the Koori Centre for a set of agreed ethical principles for projects involving Aboriginal communities. In 1992, a major statement on ethics, "Principles and Procedures for the Conduct of Research", was prepared by Brady, Stewart and others. For too long, the paper argued, Aboriginal research had been the domain of non-Aboriginal people running things their way.

> The majority of research carried out in the past, and much of present research is based on definitions, by non-Aboriginals, of what is perceived to be Aboriginal problems. Coupled with this are non-Aboriginal defined solutions. Thus Aboriginal and Torres Strait Islander people become objects of research where problems and solutions are defined outside of Aboriginal and Torres Strait Islander frames of reference. In order to negate pre-defined positions, or an acquisitive desire for knowledge it is essential that researchers choose areas of interest acceptable to all parties, Aboriginal and non-Aboriginal.

"Empowerment and self-determination", the document declared, were at the heart of the Koori Centre's stand. In future, Koori Centre research would address the big issues of culture and law in language understood by the Aboriginal community. Indigenous communities would sight budget details and be paid at award or market rates; and they would be reimbursed for extra costs and royalties. They would also be granted a decision-making role in structuring the research along with the authority to review content thought to be culturally or personally sensitive.

Arbon presented her "Principles and Procedures" document to the Policy Advisory Committee (PAC) of the Academic Board in late April, 1993, in a forthright manner.

> This statement represents the Koori Centre's policy in relation to research that is being conducted under the auspices of the Centre. It has evolved through the

processes of consultation and negotiation with Aboriginal and non-Aboriginal researchers, organisations and community representatives. As such it is part of a national program of reform being implemented by Aboriginal organisations and their communities. It therefore represents the demand by Aboriginal and Torres Strait Islander people for research to be conducted in ways which meet our needs and aspirations.

A New Direction for Research

In an internal move designed to win greater Aboriginal staff involvement in CRDU, responsibility for research projects was taken from the unit in mid-1992 and passed to a Research Committee. When Arbon took the chair at the new Research Committee, its priority agenda item was the endorsement of the "Principles and Procedures" document. As explained at the time: "Its [CRDU's] decision-making has necessarily been ad hoc in the absence of a rationale and set of priorities for research and curriculum development."[15] In future, the unit would operate "under a more rationally based set of guidelines and procedures which are related to a code of ethics".

In April 1993, Arbon asked that the University adopt the Koori Centre's "Principles and Procedures" for Indigenous research on campus.[16] The University's Policy Advisory Committee, she thought, should recognise her Research Committee as the equivalent of a Faculty Research Committee, and the University Research Committee and the Koori Centre Research Committee should exchange members.[17] In 1996, Neil Bechervaise, a senior lecturer from the Faculty of Education, joined the committee which now included Angela Brew from the Centre for Teaching and Learning and Peter Cook, Director of the University's Research and Scholarships Office. Bechervaise also assisted with other training and projects.

History suggests that the laying down of principles, however well intentioned, can lead to problems over interpretation. Would the adoption of the "Principles and Procedures" paper imply that its prescriptions should apply to ongoing research? If so, would consent for the re-working of projects thought ethically deficient require approval from the granting authorities? Would major external funding agencies adopt the ethical standards in their own project briefs? Was there evidence that other Aboriginal centres in New South Wales would apply similar ethical criteria to their research? If not would the Koori Centre's competitiveness in bidding for projects be weakened? Finally, how did the Koori Centre's principles sit with the University's own sub-committee, Principles in the Conduct and Evaluation of Research?

While some staff pushed the ethics paper hard, CRDU personnel were less enthusiastic, regarding its content as idealistic. The document's effects on current operations became apparent as detailed scrutiny of projects under the guidelines delayed the assessment of new research and the Koori Centre's own submissions were held up. When the AEC identified "an ethical problem"[18] in the brief for a NSW DoSE literacy and numeracy project for

Figure 53. Senior Research Assistant: Jennifer Walton-Smith. Image courtesy of the Koori Centre.

example, the Koori Centre eventually declined to bid, which both disappointed the state department's Evaluation Unit and reduced the centre's research income. Ripple effects of the guidelines, good and bad, were experienced.

Eventually, the Research Committee produced its own Indigenous Australian Research Management Plan establishing an Ethics Liaison sub-committee to assess and endorse University research projects utilising Aboriginal content. Despite a favourable reception from a number of Sydney academics, especially those anxious about protocols in Aboriginal research, its principles were not uniformly applied across the Koori Centre and Yooroang Garang. A time consuming business, and one lacking uniformity, it lost its point and was discontinued.

There was an irregularity in AEU accounting and, in 1992, the Koori Centre showed a large deficit. Its research activity was singled out for pre-emptive savings, because its work was not considered essential for teaching or support and its appointees were short term. It was thought its functions could be safely passed to the much lauded new Research Committee, this "much needed step forward for the centre and research generally".[19] Hearing news of the CRDU's likely disbandment in March, Craddock, Stewart, Williams and Walton-Smith wrote to Arbon expressing their dismay and asking for open discussion on consequences by the Executive, MAC and the staff meeting.[20] The unit had a high reputation in the University as was recorded in the 1993–95 University profile. "One of the strengths of the University is its background in research. This focus is also a strength of the AEC through the Curriculum Development and Research Unit." This was now at risk, with CRDU staff described as "shell-shocked".[21]

CRDU staff pointed out that the Research Committee underestimated the effort needed to undertake sustained research. "The effort to achieve the outcomes has not been easy or

Independence **189**

straightforward. It has required skill and determination, and a vision based on realistic and achievable goals."[22] The axe fell irrespective. Research projects requiring funds from the Koori Centre were significantly reduced or terminated and research staff like Craddock, Stewart and Walton-Smith released at the end of their contracts. The precipitate action broke up a research team five years in the making.

Responsibility for the unit's curriculum development side was passed to the re-established Curriculum Development Committee whose external members included Roslyn Arnold and Carmel Young of the Faculty of Education, Deirdre Dragovich from the Department of Geography, and Jan Kociumbas from the Department of History. Ray King and Laurie Craddock joined the team as consultants.

Strained Relations

Two major research projects were discontinued almost immediately. The first, the Shoalhaven Aboriginal Education Research project, was modelling an integrated educational platform in a local community and it was dependent on Koori Centre money beyond a small ARC grant of $4000. The second, the Aboriginal Education Needs in New South Wales Handbook, had built on an earlier externally funded project for the Metropolitan North Region designed to assist schools with small numbers of Aboriginal pupils. The handbook proposal had been carefully considered by the NSW DoSE prior to receiving their enthusiastic endorsement.

> There were numerous principals (the key people) and others in the schools who were really concerned about doing the best for their Aboriginal students. What they wanted to know was how best do you do it? Classroom teachers need to know before it happens how to handle the situation where an enraged Aboriginal kid picks up a chair and threatens to strike the teacher, or another student. If the principal knows how to handle these crisis circumstances he/she can arrange appropriate in-servicing of the staff, and new appointees when they arrive.[23]

Prepared for statewide use, the expanded handbook was a visible contribution of the commitment of the Koori Centre to Aboriginal education. Initially funded from AEC money carried over from 1990, the NSW DoSE offered the Koori Centre a backup grant of $29,157,[24] with additional funding foreshadowed from the Catholic Education Office at Parramatta and the Board of Senior School Studies. Bridge Street especially valued the fact that the research was led by the experienced Craddock. The project stood to meet an identified need which would make the centre known across the state "and be the springboard for further externally funded research in a very neglected area".[25] It would also have returned royalties to the centre. Nonetheless, the Koori Centre indicated it would only continue the project if a much larger sum was committed for a research fellow and one or two research assistants estimated at $92,940. "It appeared to DSE that the centre was trying to get the goose to lay another golden egg." In August 1992, the state department replied that it was unable to find such an amount.[26]

The collapse of the Education Needs Handbook was a blow to the credibility of the Koori Centre inside the NSW DoSE. Traditionally, the Koori Centre's relations with the department had been close. The Director-General, Ken Boston, the first Director-General to visit the Koori Centre since Winder, told Cleverley that the AEAP continued to be "a valued program and significant in the professional development of AEAs".[27] His department had put a substantial sum into the AEAP in 1989, providing $99,500 for its Regional Workshop Program ensuring its viability at a critical time. The department continued to sponsor the AEAP to the tune of around $177,000 annually under Arbon; and it had rebuffed "intense pressure"[28] to have the AEAP monopoly removed from the University and shared around other institutions. From the NSW DoSE's perspective, its handbook had received short shrift. Attempts by the state department to have the handbook declared a Project of National Significance failed, as the approving officer, not having a teaching or education background, "couldn't grasp the concept".[29]

Wrangling over the handbook provided ammunition for those who thought the Koori Centre's management was moving away from education in favour of health. It was also said that the demands of administering Cumberland as well put too big a burden on Arbon, and that an instance of funding misappropriation in the AEU meant less money for the Koori Centre. The NSW AECG, it was claimed, also had concerns over the centre's directions. There was a loss of momentum in plans for a conditional Aboriginal teaching qualification run by Sydney and doubts about whether the Koori Centre would collaborate with the NSW DoSE in other educational projects. At that time, the state department was seeking cooperation in planning the on-site training for AEAs, the fast tracking of Aborigines as school principals, a short course for graduate teachers in HSC Aboriginal Studies, a program to improve mathematics and science outcomes in Years 9–12, and a task force which aimed to lift the attainment levels of Aboriginal children in schools clustered around the University. None of these projects would eventuate through Sydney.

Expanding Student Numbers

Increasing numbers of Aboriginal students on campus were a valuable boost to campus life. In 1992, CASU supported an Aboriginal students' association and helped with a news bulletin. The following year, the Aboriginal student, Heidi Norman, was elected President of the Student Representative Council (SRC). She was joined on Council by Sue Green, who would work for the Koori Centre as part-time librarian and counsellor, and six students became Aboriginal Affairs Officers (including Green). The SRC and Koori Centre sponsored two Aborigines to attend the seminar, "A Just and Proper Settlement", nine other students were nominated for the "Our Way" conference on the issue of Aboriginal mental health; and an Aboriginal student attended the International Year of Indigenous People's Conference in Wollongong. Keith Richards, a second-year associate diploma student on course at CCHS, joined the Koori Centre's Management Advisory Committee and the Aboriginal association produced its own newsletter, Wakool Kungarah (One Blood). In a campus ceremony during the International Year of the World's Indigenous People in 1993, Ken Brown,

Figure 54. Raising of the Aboriginal flag for Aboriginal Week. Ken Brown with Liam Ridgeway playing the didgeridoo and his brother, Jay, playing the clapsticks, 1993. Image courtesy of University of Sydney Archives.

the Health Science graduate from Cumberland, raised the Aboriginal flag in a small garden near the Nicholson Museum.[30]

The Aboriginal Flag

Black is for the people.

Red is for the earth and the blood that has been shed in the past.

Yellow is for the sun, the giver of life.

So long as the sun shines the people and the earth will be one.[31]

"It's a wonderful symbol that the first flag to be raised in this restored area is the Aboriginal flag," declared Professor Paul Crittenden, Dean of Arts, at the commemorative ceremony.[32] Anna Davies, President of the SRC, was among the speakers telling the small gathering that there were 60 Aboriginal students enrolled at the main campus and another 60 at Cumberland out of 30,000 in all. Victoria Robinson, a DipAAEd student, spoke of Aboriginal culture becoming part of the University's culture and Marlene Kong, one of a pair of twins in third year medicine, related the inspirational achievement of the South Australian

Aborigine, David Unaipon, who lectured at Oxford. The occasion ended with music from didgeridoo and clap sticks played by Liam and Jay Ridgeway, pupils of nearby Forest Lodge Public School.

McNicol continued to demonstrate his support for Aboriginal education approving three objectives for Aboriginal education under the Aboriginal and Torres Strait Islander Strategic Plan 1994–96.

- To improve access, participation and outcomes for Aboriginal and Torres Strait Islanders in all sectors of the University of Sydney
- to promote a better understanding of Aboriginal and Torres Strait Islander knowledge, epistemology and frames of reference
- to respond in a timely and appropriate manner to the training needs of Aboriginal and Torres Strait Islander communities in New South Wales through the provision of formal and non-formal courses.

The Vice-Chancellor proposed a short-term goal of 0.5 percent Aborigines employed in each of three staff divisions, academic, administrative and general by 1996. By then, he anticipated, 200 Aboriginal students would be enrolled, lifting the participation rate from 0.3 to 0.7 percent. Arbon also announced an ambitious plan to raise the Aboriginal participation rate to at least two percent of enrolments by 2000.[33]

Restructuring the Koori Centre

When a Program Effectiveness Review was undertaken in 1993, the Koori Centre had firmly established itself. It was a recipient of just on $1.38 million from the Commonwealth.[34] Its Aboriginal staff members now had qualifications from a wider range of disciplines, with more students enrolling in degrees outside Education and Health. However, its graduation numbers remained low, just five in 1993.[35] Given the growing diversity in studies, questions as to the appropriateness of the centre's links with the Faculty of Education surfaced, coming at the time when the University's government was under audit by the Boston Consulting Group. To whom should the Director of the Koori Centre be responsible? What academic structure would best serve the DipAAEd and any new academic programs? Should Cumberland's AEU continue to be led by the Koori Centre? Was the Koori Centre principally an academic unit or an administrative support centre in the University structure? What independence should the Koori Centre exercise as an Aborigine-led institution?

About two thirds of staff in the Koori Centre wanted maximum autonomy inside the University and a break from Education. There was also a strong view that the Aboriginalisation of Koori Centre staffing should be more strictly enforced and the role of the current Executive was questioned – was there a need for an Executive at all? It was argued that staff as a whole should exercise greater authority in governance through the staff meeting and, following a majority vote by staff, the University liaison position held by Cleverley was dropped. Majority opinion was that the centre should initiate and control its own academic qualifications, in particular postgraduate awards. Some advocated the introduction of a timetable for moving to full faculty status.

A minority of centre staff took a more cautious line. Though they supported the Koori Centre obtaining greater independence so far as internal staffing and budget expenditure went,[36] they wanted Aboriginalisation pursued in a measured way. Given the centre's small size, and the limited qualifications and experience of staff, they feared the centre would overreach its grasp, especially in attempts to introduce new degrees. Priority should go towards improving teaching in centre courses including those accessed by non-Aboriginal students. Some members believed that a close association with the Faculty of Education and its resources had demonstrated past usefulness and should continue in some form – they were worried that if the Koori Centre isolated itself from the faculty, it could be cut off from the academic mainstream. They were concerned too that the authority of the University's general administration would limit internal autonomy.

However, most Koori Centre staff wanted quick, radical change towards an independent status. This was not resisted by the Faculty of Education. King had already retired and Cleverley went in mid-1993, the Annual Report recording "a special thanks to John Cleverley as he played a major role in the establishment of the Koori Centre and the constitution of the present Management Advisory Committee". Turney was also close to retirement and his successor as Dean, Professor Ken Eltis, welcomed an independent Koori Centre. While relations between Education and the Koori Centre remained cordial, there was no push from within the faculty to continue with the close association of the past two decades.

Following discussions with Koori Centre and AEU staff, and others, Dorsch forwarded a set of recommendations on restructuring to Deputy Vice-Chancellor Professor Derek John Anderson on 11 June 1993. She proposed:

- That the centre become a devolved management unit within Academic Group D (Faculty of Arts, Sydney College of the Arts, the Conservatorium of Music, and the Faculty of Education) for the purpose of management/financial accountability; and that the director report to the head of that Academic Group

- that a Board of Studies with appropriate representation from Education, the other relevant main campus faculties, and the Unit at Health Sciences, be made responsible for academic matters

- that the Management Advisory Committee continue to provide the links with the Aboriginal community external to the University and provide advice on both academic and management issues

- that the director continue to have access to the Vice-Chancellor through a Deputy Vice-Chancellor, the position providing a measure of overall superintendence.

In supporting a continued role for the DVC in the reformed Koori Centre, Dorsch displayed some caution. "'This will pass," she wrote, "but at the moment I think it is important to retain this bit of overall oversight."

Dorsch's proposal served the purpose of the immediate separation from Education. After further discussion and amendment by Associate Professor Paul Crittenden, Head of Academic Group D, a plan was forwarded to Professor John Mack, Chair of the Academic Board, in December 1993.[37] It was agreed that the previous executive of the centre would be renamed the Koori Centre Management Advisory Committee and comprise the director as chair, heads of the centre's units, and an additional Aboriginal staff member. It would meet fortnightly. It was also agreed that the present Management Advisory Committee would be re-named the Koori Centre Policy Advisory Committee (PAC). In its closing consideration, the Standing Committee of the Academic Board asked that the Koori Centre "enhance further liaison arrangements between the centre and the faculties and Colleges and further appropriate academic programs."[38]

On the academic side, a new Board of Aboriginal and Indigenous Studies would be established within Group D chaired from outside the Koori Centre; and it would include representatives of six faculties, the teaching and research staff of the centre, a NSW AECG representative, and two Indigenous students. This Board would supervise the DipAAEd, introduce new qualifications, and report directly to the Academic Board. No mention was made of the role of the PVC/DVC position.

Uncharted Waters

The ATA training program survived its first ten years from 1975 supported by the Department of Adult Education until its closure. Following its transfer to the Department of Education (Faculty of Education from 1986), a diploma qualification was introduced and recognised by the Commonwealth, and the Koori Centre was founded. What the University had to boast about was the product of these two departments. When Arbon joined the AEC, she inherited a structure largely the creation of the Faculty of Education as was evident in its focus on training, curriculum development and educational research. Likewise, the Faculty of Education's services and facilities, academic and general, were called upon by the centre when needed. At this time, the new centre's institutional and individual relations were predominantly with its educational friends: DEETYA, NSW DoSE, NSW AECG, AEC (NSW), and Aboriginal and non-Aboriginal educators. Under Arbon's leadership, there was a greater interest in Aboriginal health and a move away from education. New alliances must now be forged to meld its academic interests and administration functions into an autonomous entity which would serve the University as a whole. This meant entering unchartered waters. Nonetheless, hesitations were not of the moment: independence had arrived and the future was in Aboriginal hands.

11

The Koori Centre

> Given the length of time I have now worked in the field, at the Koori Centre and elsewhere, I think it is safe to say that I am deeply committed to "the cause" and that my Koori Centre experience clearly influenced that sense of commitment in many positive ways. Although I haven't mentioned students or staff, it is because I can't think of any remotely adequate way to describe how deadly a time I have had with both.[1]
>
> Michael Chin, ex-staff member, 2008

The Koori Centre gained autonomous status in 1994 with high expectations as Aboriginal staff and students brought their unique insights to bear. At this time, there were 12 academic and six administrative staff members led by Veronica Arbon as director, the majority Indigenous. Within the centre, there were 41 enrolments in the Aboriginal Education Assistants Program (AEAP), 19 joining Stage I that year, and there were another 16 in the DipAAEd. In addition, the Aboriginal Studies Unit expanded its teaching to non-Indigenous students in primary and secondary courses in education, in the Aboriginal Studies major in conjunction with the Department of Anthropology, and in the Aboriginal Health option in the Faculty of Nursing.[2] This was the third year of the Cadigal program with 32 students admitted to a range of degree programs, bringing the total Indigenous enrolment to 175.[3] By 1995, EFTSU exceeded 200 for the first time with 207 Indigenous students enrolled,[4] a participation rate of 0.6 percent.

At first, the Koori Centre's operations were not greatly different from those applying under the Faculty of Education. The three unit structure of Aboriginal Education Assistants Program (AEAP), Aboriginal Studies Unit (ASU), and Student Academic Support Unit (SASU) continued to operate. So far as internal governance went, centre authority resided in the director and in an executive, the latter including the heads of units. Staff meetings also contributed and there was external advice through the Policy Advisory Committee and the new Board of Studies in Indigenous Studies. Arbon's own load had been lightened when Yooroang Garang, the Centre for Indigenous Health Studies, appointed Bruno Gelonesi as Acting Head in 1993.

One immediate change came with the relocation of the Koori Centre to the Old Teachers College (OTC) in the heart of the Camperdown Campus. Now staff and students were no longer fringe dwellers on the periphery of the campus. The move allowed more room for SASU's activities, particularly through access to its own tutorial room adjacent to the unit's office with a small computer facility alongside; and the Koori Centre gained considerable dedicated space including a stack area for a growing library and resource collection. As part of the occupation, a "smoking ceremony" was performed. Green eucalyptus leaves were held over a fire and participants immersed themselves in the smoke purifying the site and driving away evil spirits. The ceremony enabled staff to leave troubles from the old Mackie behind them and enter a new beginning.

Pride in the achievements of the centre's Indigenous students was evident to all at the annual graduation. The first in the new facilities in the OTC was held in 1994, when 22 AEAs, and five diploma students graduated, among them Stella Reddy, a first year AEAP student who took centre stage singing in a strong resonant voice a traditional melody set to her own words, "Our special day, We are strong, We are free."[5]

On Governance

i) Board of Studies in Indigenous Studies

While the new arrangements had given the Koori Centre a long rein in managing its own affairs, the Dorsch-Crittenden restructuring posed its own challenges. It removed the centre from a direct connection with the Faculty of Education, replacing it with a Board of Studies in Indigenous Studies with diverse University membership. Some feared that its non-faculty status could insulate it from the main drivers of University change and reform. Financial arrangements also altered significantly. As Crittenden had explained to Arbon: "Primary responsibility for all financial matters involving the centre rests with you, of course, as Director. My position as head of Group involves a general supervisory role."[6] While well-intentioned, the decision had the effect of disassociating the centre from the financial administration of the University, which proved disabling in complex matters such as budget control. This latter activity was becoming a substantial responsibility: in 1996, for example, $845,000 was allocated for the Koori Centre and $807,000 for Yooroang Garang, and another $145,039 was provided by the NSW DoET for the AEAP.[7]

The first meeting of the new Board of Studies in Indigenous Studies was held on 5 October 1995, convened by acting director Rose Stack, comprising internal and external members.[8] At this time, the new Board did not include the Pro-Vice-Chancellor (PVC) position held by Professor Richard Johnstone (Academic Support), who had succeeded Dorsch in the Indigenous Education portfolio. However in 1996 Johnstone, whose special expertise was in teaching and learning at tertiary level, was invited to join. The new PVC was very supportive of Mooney when she became director, assisting her in learning the intricacies of the University system and giving advice and support when trouble arose. In

2005, Johnstone was appointed Executive Director of the Carrick Institute for Teaching and Learning in Higher Education. Another person especially helpful was Helen Ross from Planning and Support whose responsibilities included the reporting and distribution of Indigenous funding grants from the Department of Education, Training and Youth Affairs (DETYA), later renamed the Department of Education, Employment, Training and Youth Affairs (DEETYA). Ross played a major role in advising on the Koori Centre budget prior to her leaving the University in early 2000.

Crittenden had wanted the Board of Studies chair position independent of the Koori Centre and not necessarily an Indigenous person. However, it was decided at the first meeting that: "The Chair must be an Aboriginal or Torres Strait Islander person".[9] Stack was voted in as Chair. This decision made sense as the director of the Koori Centre was best able to determine the agenda and her office was available to make necessary arrangements. A set of Terms of Reference affirmed that the new Board was responsible for the supervision of the teaching and examining of all subjects provided by the Koori Centre such as Academic Skills I and II in Cadigal, and the DipAAEd I and II. In addition, the centre was to report to the Board annually on its other responsibilities including Aboriginal Studies in the Faculty of Arts, Indigenous Health in the Faculty of Nursing, and the Indigenous Australia in the BEd (Primary). The Board had the authority to convene as an Examinations Committee and to report to the Academic Board on all matters relating to its degrees, diplomas and other programs. At the close of the first meeting, Van Holst expressed pleasure at the convening of the Board, a milestone in Aboriginal and Torres Strait Islander education, and Bettina Cass affirmed Van Holst's commendation, passing on "best regards" from members of the Faculty of Arts.

ii) The Policy Advisory Committee

The Management Advisory Committee, the external arm of Indigenous advice established by the Aboriginal Education Centre in 1991, was renamed the Policy Advisory Committee (PAC). Membership remained essentially the same under the Koori Centre although there were some new faces: Professor Ken Eltis, Dean of Education, and D. Rose from Health. PAC's duties were:

- to receive proposals on Aboriginal and Torres Strait Islander educational issues
- to advise on all Aboriginal and Torres Strait Islander educational matters
- to monitor the performance of the Aboriginal and Torres Strait Islander education policy
- to initiate and/or comment on reports on all issues relating to Aboriginal and Torres Strait Islander education within the University.

Given the autonomy granted the Koori Centre, and an increasing number of Indigenous staff, the usefulness of PAC diminished. In 1998, Mooney instigated a working party whose members were Mooney as Chair, Lyn Stewart, AECG Representative, and Margaret Edmonds, Director, Student Services to discuss its future and a new constitution was drafted. However, the committee was convened less frequently over time.[10] After the Review of Aboriginal Education at the University of Sydney reported in 2001, it was renamed the Policy Advisory Group for Indigenous Education and put under Professor Paul Ramsden's chairmanship, with the inaugural meeting held in September 2002.[11] But if anything this group met even less frequently.

iii) The Management Advisory Committee and the Staff Meeting

There were two other structural changes. The first saw the renaming of the Koori Centre Executive, the Management Advisory Committee (MAC); and it was augmented by an additional Indigenous staff member. While MAC met fortnightly to discuss budget and internal policy, it did not work well. Heads of units were too easily caught up with special pleading. The second operational feature of this period was the growing influence of staff meetings where major centre issues were debated and voted on. Although this provided for a wide expression of interests and was a valuable sounding board, some decisions were at odds with those of the Board of Studies, MAC, and the director. It was also used by some staff in attempts to overturn earlier decisions. The governmental arrangements for the Koori Centre were too bureaucratic for such a small entity, with too much overlapping responsibility and too much time wasted in meetings.

Staff Changes – Director and Administration

After Arbon took Special Study Leave in 1994, Stack served as acting director. Arbon, who had completed her MEd in 1996, subsequently resigned from the University for family reasons returning to Alice Springs where her first employment was at a school in Humpty Doo as an Aboriginal education worker. She would tell Mooney later that she wished she had known the full extent of the work of the AEAs during her time as director. Had she her time over, Arbon acknowledged, she would have taken more account of their special needs.[12] Eventually, Arbon took on a major responsibility as the Director of Batchelor Institute of Indigenous Tertiary Education established in the Northern Territory in 1999.

On Stack's resignation in 1996, Mooney took over as acting director, and Deirdre Dorbis, a descendant of the Kamilaroi people, who joined the centre in 1995 as a lecturer, coordinated the AEAP. They were assisted and supported by new people on the administration side including Indigenous staff, Belinda Perry, Christine Porter, and Curtis Flood, a descendant of the Wiradjuri Nation, and Pat Davison, a descendant of the Ngarigo people from the Monaro Plains and the Alps of Kosciuszko.

Mooney's appointment to acting director proved contentious as some centre academics and students thought the position should go to Wendy Brady as she had completed a PhD in education. PVC Johnstone proposed the appointment of Dr Kathleen Clapham, a descendant of the Murrarri people from western NSW, and Head of Yooroang Garang with a PhD in anthropology, however the suggestion was unpopular and contested. Some staff thought that Clapham's experience in Indigenous health research was not pertinent to the direction the Koori Centre wished to take. Eventually, conflict over who should lead the Koori Centre saw sides taken with Johnstone called in to mediate. In 1997, after advertisement, Mooney was appointed director and would serve into the new millennium. Afterwards, relations between the Koori Centre and Yooroang Garang cooled given their different priorities and personalities and it was to take several years before bridges were rebuilt.

Unit Development and Staffing

i) The Aboriginal Education Assistants Program

In 1994, the Stage 3 Certificate and Diploma students participated in field trips with visits to local communities, tours of significant sites, opportunities to observe teaching strategies for Aboriginal children, and examples of Aboriginal policy and programs in schools. The Koori Centre continued to fund Stage I AEAP students taking their first block in Dubbo, receiving enthusiastic support from NSW DoSE Western Region, and staff at the Orana Centre. School visits and the practicum in the certificate and the diploma courses continued in the early 1990s with students undertaking a four-day school visit. In 1994, 21 students were placed in the surrounding inner city schools and preschools;[13] and Diploma 2s continued with their practice teaching sessions over eight days in schools.

At this time, the AEAP had four academic staff: Rosemary Stack, the coordinator, and three lecturers, Janet Mooney, Phil Veness and Elaine Bennett, assisted by two administrative staff, Natalie Brown, a Kamilaroi person, who would graduate with a BA in 1996, and Belinda Perry. Julie Smith, a descendant of the Kalkadoon people, replaced Mooney when she went on maternity leave in 1994, and Kevin Butler also started at this time. In 1996, Dorbis replaced Smith becoming acting coordinator. Debbie Wray, a South Coast Koori woman of the Yuin Nation, joined the team in 1996, completing a MEd (Hons) at the University of Western Sydney in 2007. After Dorbis resigned in 1998, Christine Smith headed up the AEAP for a year from February 1999.[14]

Under Christine Smith it was decided to change the name of the AEAP to better reflect the role of the unit and it was renamed the Indigenous Education Unit (IEU). Cleverley then filled the position as head for three months in 2000, followed by Wray who acted in the position until Arthur Smith took charge in 2001. Another lecturer in the AEAP, Kevin Lowe, from the Gubbi Gubbi Language Nation in South East Queensland, served from January 1999 to December that year. Lowe was responsible for writing the history strand of the BEd (Secondary: Aboriginal studies) along with Jan Kociumbas from the Department of History. He left to take up a position as the Chief Education Officer with the Aboriginal Curriculum Unit at the NSW Board of Studies. On 13 August 1999, Julie Janson, the playwright with a long association with the ATATP, returned on contract. The same year, Sharon Galleguillos, a descendant of the Warumungu of Tennant Creek, joined the centre after working for many years in the Aboriginal Programs Unit at the NSW DoET. In 2005,

Figure 55. Dr Arthur Smith with Year 4, Bachelor of Education (Secondary: Aboriginal Studies) students: Ursula Brown, Ashlee Miller, Melinda Legge, Jenni Tillett and Cynthia Ahmat. Courtesy of the Koori Centre.

she was awarded the Teaching Excellence Award from the Faculty of Education and Social Work for her teaching of "Indigenous Australian Education" and was honoured by the Queensland University of Technology receiving an Outstanding Alumni Award.

A Publication from AEAP

In 1995, 16 students, mostly in Stage 2s, with one Stage 3, helped by their teacher, Nitin Indurkhya, published a set of poems and prose, *Mitigar*, drawn from a computer studies course. "I really enjoyed working with this group of students. They were extremely resourceful, had a great sense of humour, and their eagerness to learn new things made my job as a teacher very satisfying."[15] The extracts below from *Mitigar* contain personal reminiscences. The first is a poem from a Tasmanian Aborigine.

Aboriginality

A Lesson in History – The child sits at his desk
Twiddling a pencil,
Idly staring out of the window, the teacher announces,
today we will learn
about the Tasmanian Aborigines.

> Mind snaps back to the present, attention eagerly given.
>
> The last Tasmanian Aborigine
>
> died in 1876.
>
> Hand goes up,
>
> But, teacher, I'm Aboriginal. How can you be?
>
> Blond haired and blue eyed you are, so white you must be. But teacher, I am, I am,
>
> Mum and dad told me so. No you are not, that's the end of it.
>
> Mouth turns down, eyes glisten and slowly fill;
>
> Yes teacher.
>
> Another lesson learnt, of historical inaccuracies,
>
> closed minds and white impassivity.[16]

The next excerpt, about growing up in Grafton, expresses the havoc and excitement experienced during the floods of 1974.

> **Growing up:**
>
> In 1974 the big floods came to Grafton and my eldest sister was going to have a baby. I was about ten and had to row my dad's little wooden boat to the railway station so we could get her to hospital. Us kids loved it when it would flood because we didn't have to go to school. When the flood waters would recede we would hose and sweep out all the mud, broken glass and any rubbish. The worse thing was the smell of the mud on the ground – it stunk.[17]

Another reminiscence involves the experience of going to school at La Perouse.

> **At school:**
>
> All the kids in the surrounding suburbs attended to La Perouse Public School. I enjoyed my time at school meeting and making lots of new friends, playing football for the school, and the milk that was delivered at the school each day was the best milk I have tasted in my life, the funniest thing was that we had to bring our own mugs or cups to drink out of.[18]

A further description of schooling describes the impact of the AEA program.

> **At Our Lady of Mount Carmel School:**
>
> The teacher couldn't understand why Jake had a behavioural problem. Young Jake suffers from Otitis Media. (A build-up of fluid in the ear that shuts out sound and causes extreme pain. Cheryl Sant, in collaboration with the school, was able to help the boy have a hearing test and specialist attention.) Trudy (the mother) has difficulties also accepting Jake's disabilities but is more happy now knowing that Jake is getting help support from school and home and I am feeling stronger in myself as doing the A.E.A. Program. It has helped me also understand how we as an A.E.A. can help our young Aboriginal children and how to support them in their special needs.[19]

This final reminiscence is part of a poem describing the author's relief and anticipation.

The weekend ahead:

By Friday arvo, we're looking for a break, with no Uni or lectures, the weekends are real hard to take.
The footy, the pictures or just lazing around, there's no shortage of things to do in this great town.
With the weekend over, and our batteries recharged, we start the process again, with our keenness enlarged.
The last week goes slow, we can't wait to go home, as most of us have families, and our minds start to roam.[20]

ii) Aboriginal Studies Unit

The ASU underwent a name change to Indigenous Studies Unit (ISU) in 1995. It continued to be headed by Brady who was appointed senior lecturer a year earlier. She gave papers at both the World Congress in Comparative Education Conference in Sydney and at the Albuquerque World Indigenous Peoples Conference in 1996; and she helped in a collaborative program through the Department of Public Health which established the Graduate Diploma in Indigenous Health Promotion, the first of its kind in Australia. In 1997, Brady took leave without pay, working as a research academic in Newcastle University's Wollotuka Aboriginal and Torres Strait Islander Education Centre and, the following year, she resigned from Sydney to take the position of Head of the Aboriginal Research and Resource Centre at the University of New South Wales. Brady returned to the Koori Centre as the academic coordinator in 2005. Ann Flood, a descendant of the Wiradjuri people, was appointed as a full-time lecturer in 1993. In 1996, Katrina Thorpe, a descendant of the Worimi people of Port Stephens, joined ISU as an associate lecturer responsible for teaching the Aboriginal Education Core Unit in the BEd (Primary). Thorpe was promoted to a full-time lectureship in the ISU and was acting head in 1998. The following year she left the centre to take a position in the Aboriginal Research and Resource Centre with Wendy Brady, but returned in July 2002.

Among other staff who contributed to the ISU was Tjanara Goreng-Goreng who worked as an associate lecturer for six months in 1996 teaching Aboriginal Health and Community Development and in the Aboriginal Studies major. In addition, two undergraduate students, Sue Green, and Ken Watson, a Wurundjeri man from South Victoria, gained experience in University teaching and course development as tutors in the Nursing Conversion Aboriginal Health program. Green accepted the counsellor position at the centre replacing Lisa Jackson. Green is currently an associate professor, and Director of Nura Gili Aboriginal Research and Resource Centre at UNSW. Watson would move to the post of education officer at the New South Wales Art Gallery, then to Jirrawun Arts Centre at Kunnanurra in Western Australia. Other courses taught by ISU staff were Aboriginal Health and Wellbeing for the Faculty of Nursing at Mallet Street and Aboriginal Health and Community in the

Figure 56. Staff of the Koori Centre: Katrina Thorpe and Michelle Blanchard. Image courtesy of the Koori Centre.

Faculty of Arts. Juanita Sherwood, a descendant of the Wiradjuri people, was employed in second semester 1998 to teach in the health units returning in 2000 for a further two years. In Sherwood's absence, Marylyn Pittman, a registered nurse, taught the health program.

In 1998, Michelle Blanchard and Leah Lui (known as Lui-Chivizhe, from 2001) joined the Koori Centre. Blanchard, a descendant of the Nugi/Nunnuccal clans from North Stradbroke Island, was appointed a lecturer in ISU and, later, senior lecturer, heading the ISU for a period in 1999. Blanchard, who holds a BA and MA in creative writing and performance studies from the University of Western Sydney, is an accomplished writer of short stories, and material for stage, radio and film. She was appointed deputy director of the centre under the Change Management Plan reorganisation of 2001. Lui, a Torres Strait Islander, was first employed in a part-time teaching and research position in the ISU before taking up a full-time lectureship in 2000; she also acted for a short time in the academic coordinator's role in 2006 prior to Lynette Riley's appointment. Lui-Chivizhe holds a BA in geography and linguistics, and a Graduate Diploma in material anthropology. In 2008, she graduated with an MSc (Geography) from Sydney.

A Major Responsibility

Of the most significant events in the 1990s, achieved in the spirit of "reconciliation", was the decision to transfer the responsibility for the coordination and teaching of the core Aboriginal Studies Unit in the Faculty of Arts major from the Department of Anthropology to the Koori Centre. Previously, the subject had been offered by the Department of Anthropology and was one of its longest standing, internationally recognised courses. This historic change was achieved with the active cooperation of Diana Austin-Broos, Head of the Department of Anthropology, Bettina Cass, Dean of the Faculty of Arts, Richard Johnstone, PVC (Academic Support), and the new PVC (Humanities and Social Science), Professor David Weisbrot, previously Dean of Law. Diana Austin-Broos was a strong supporter of the transfer, leading the lengthy negotiations up to the handover in late 1997.[21] Worthy of special mention in the process of the handover are the people on the ground including Gillian Cowlishaw and, in particular, Franca Tamisari who worked tirelessly with Katrina Thorpe throughout 1998, ensuring that there was a smooth transition from Anthropology to the Koori Centre. From 1999 onwards, the Aboriginal Studies major was available to Arts and other students in a unit of study planned and taught by Indigenous academics and utilising senior Indigenous guest speakers.

By 1999, ISU staff members were teaching four new or revised subjects in the Aboriginal Studies major:[22]

i) Indigenous Australia

The unit focused on Australian life since colonisation. It addressed issues of the construction of race, the impact of colonisation, and Aboriginal resistance including the effects of legislation, government policies and social movements. The relationship to land, spirituality and systems of belief was at its core. It also examined the structure of Aboriginal societies, cultural practices and maintenance along with issues of ownership of knowledge as well as consideration of the lived experience of Indigenous Australians in the political context.

ii) Indigenous Australia: Land and Culture

This unit focused on issues pertaining to Indigenous cultural maintenance in a contemporary context. It explored themes of land and attachment to place and kin, Indigenous empowerment, intellectual property and manifestations of Aboriginal culture and society, the role of education in Aboriginal nations, and the connection between history and health, healing and restoration of Aboriginal life. It examined the diversity of Aboriginal cultures Australia wide, with a special focus on urban communities.

iii) Indigenous Australians: Policy and Power

In this unit, policy development in Aboriginal and Torres Strait Islander affairs was examined from a historical and contemporary perspective. The unit focused on issues that impacted on policy development for Indigenous people within Australian society, including self-determination, effective communication and consultation processes, mediation, conflict resolution and change, Indigenous leadership and community power bases, intercultural and cross-cultural working in Indigenous Australian communities, and organisations and the workplace. The issues were examined in the context of a continuing cycle of learning for both Indigenous and non-Indigenous Australians.

iv) Health and Community in Aboriginal Australia

The unit discussed the historical and contemporary influences on Aboriginal and Torres Strait Islander health status. It concentrated on the nature of Indigenous health issues raised by Aboriginal people and how this can often be in contrast to development and delivery of health programs by non-Indigenous cultures. The relationship between Aboriginal and Torres Strait Islander communities and the health and wellbeing of community members was covered, which included discussion on aging, ethical practice in Indigenous health research, Aboriginal child-rearing, Aboriginal mental health, and traditional medicines.

Aboriginal studies units were also available from other departments of the University at this time:

- Aboriginal Peoples and Australian Legal Systems (Law School)
- Australian Aboriginal Religions (Religious Studies)
- Contemporary Aboriginal Art: Race and Representation (History and Theory)
- Cultures after Colonisation – Indigenous Australia (Anthropology)
- Human Rights and Australian Politics (Government)
- Indigenous Rights and Political Theory (Philosophy)
- Introduction to Aboriginal Writing (Australian Literature, English)
- Languages of Australia (Linguistics)
- Looking at Drawing (Anthropology)
- Maps and Dreams: Aboriginal Historiography in the 20th Century (History)
- Old and New Debates in Aboriginal Studies (Anthropology)
- Social Inequality in Australia (Sociology)
- Aboriginal Ethnographies (Anthropology)
- Images of Identity in NE Arnhem Land (Anthropology).

iii) Student Academic Support Unit

The change of the name from Cultural and Academic Support Unit to the Student Academic Support Unit (SASU) in 1993 was thought to better reflect its primary function of service delivery and acknowledge the role that all Koori Centre staff played in cultural support. SASU was led by Maria Nugent helped by Vanessa Forrest and Lianna Taranto, who replaced Lorraine Towers when the latter took leave to complete an MEd. The regular School Visits Program around the University environs remained a feature and the Cadigal scheme continued to be a major responsibility.

In 1994 after some discontent there was a complete change of staff within SASU and Michael Chin and Katie Ayoub were left with little direction. John Hobson became coordinator in 1995 and set about reconstructing the unit and its programs. Hobson majored in linguistics with Honours in his BA from Macquarie University and held a DipEd in Adult Education from the Northern Territory University. He had ten years experience in the Northern Territory in bilingual education and Aboriginal language services. Hobson was assisted by Christine Mumbler, a descendant of the Wiradjuri people, as liaison officer and, in 1998, by Suzanne Kenney who replaced Ellis Eyre as associate lecturer (Cadigal Support) for a two-year period, and Eddie Porter. Michael Chin also worked with SASU from 1995 to 1996 as the Aboriginal Tutorial Assistance Scheme (ATAS) coordinator. As part of his duties, Chin developed a guide for use by students and tutors. In 1998, Anthony McKnight of the Kamilaroi Nation joined SASU from the Wollongong Diocese of the Catholic Education Office replacing Chin. Work in hand covered mailouts, community visits, campus tours including visits to the Orange Campus, a courses and careers camp, and data collection.

Early in 1999, Chin returned to the centre for a year as Indigenous Tutorial Assistance Scheme (ITAS) coordinator and tutor in the Indigenous Australia subject. Again, in 2004, Smith re-employed Chin to teach sociology in the Diploma 1 and 2. He recalled these varied services:

> My work at the Koori Centre was significant to me at so many levels. First, it gave me a valuable opportunity to work with Indigenous people and communities. By the time I landed in Sydney, early in 1995, my experience in the field of Indigenous education was quite limited. Second, it gave me additional impetus and incentive to continue my formal education. I now hold a Master's of Adult Education and a Graduate Diploma of TESOL and have begun to undertake doctoral studies.

Tertiary Preparation Course 1999–2005

In 1999 the Koori Centre enrolled its first intake of students for the Tertiary Preparation Course (TPC) with 22 students completing that year. Its objective was to prepare Indigenous adults for study at university level. The TPC was designed and organised by Hobson as an Away-from-Base program offered over a 12-month period, its students returning to the centre six times a year in five-day slots. Over time, many TPC students went on to join the diploma course. At the Annual Retreat at Cypress Lakes in 2005, the Koori Centre reassessed its involvement in the TPC. Numbers had fallen and costs increased at a time when the Koori Centre was seeking to stabilise its budget. Some staff argued that current resources would be better applied for degree students at Sydney. Although not all staff were convinced, a few believing that the TPC fulfilled an important equity parameter, it was decided that the TPC was no longer viable. Of the 11 students enrolled in its final year of offer in 2005 only three students completed, one of whom went on to join the diploma program. The TPC was not offered from 2006.

A Problem with Funding

In 1996 the centre lost access to the Aboriginal Tutorial Assistance Scheme (ATAS) funds in the first semester of that year brought about by the DEETYA's over-expenditure. This had severe consequences for SASU and the Indigenous students. Only three of the centre's students were able to gain ATAS tutors on the grounds of educational disability, the remainder having to be catered for by existing SASU staff drawing on $20,000 from the centre's own budget.[24]

Mooney wrote to DEETYA Indigenous Education Branch in 1997 to enquire about the possibility of being reimbursed for the money that the centre had outlaid for ATAS in the first half of 1996. Replies were in the negative. After much correspondence, Peter Buckskin, Assistant Secretary Indigenous Education Branch, replied:

> [T]he Aboriginal Tutorial Assistance Scheme (ATAS) is not an entitlement, but is available to students on a needs basis within the limit of available funds. At certain times funding limitations mean that only students most in need can access ATAS assistance. This was the situation in the first half of 1996.[25]

Bulk funding of $154,257 was granted for second semester 1996 with the requirement that it be spread across all campuses, except Cumberland and Broken Hill which fell under the auspices of Yooroang Garang which received their own funding allocation for ATAS. Difficulties still remained for the provision of ATAS support for Vocational Education and Training (VET) students. The AEAP students were deemed to be VET and not under the same conditions as undergraduate students at the University. In essence this meant that undergraduate students were allocated three hours per week of tuition while VET students received only two hours. Professor Johnstone queried this provision and Bruce Furze from DEETYA responded by saying "the weighting applied to VET student numbers under the current formula is being examined".[26]

Graduations, Special Events and Research

On 25 October 1996, another milestone was reached when Brady was awarded a PhD in education. This was a tumultuous period at Sydney with students protesting at government changes in higher education, with graduation ceremonies held at the same time. However, the celebrations were not overshadowed for Koori Centre staff and students. On the day, Brady paid tribute to the special help given her:

> I sit here as one of a handful of Indigenous Australians who have a PhD. I didn't get that by myself. It took the support of my family, my community and my colleagues for me to be able to achieve this.[27]

Brady is the first identified Indigenous Australian to be awarded a PhD in Education at the University of Sydney for the thesis "An Investigation of Indigenous Australians and non-Indigenous Australians in Education from 1788 to 1968". The following year, Marlene and Marilyn Kong, twin sisters and descendants of the Worimi people in the Port Stephens area, made history as the first Indigenous women graduates in medicine. The twins chose to come to the University of Sydney, they said, as they hoped to make a difference. As to the future: "The Aboriginal people in the Northern Territory were really keen for us to return to them. They were just so excited that we existed."[28]

Another significant academic contributor was Shino Konishi, who had tutored during her undergraduate years for the Koori Centre. She was also contracted in 1999 to produce a curriculum outline, and develop teaching notes and readings, for the Tertiary Communications Skills Unit in the TPC. After some persuasion from the director, who had headhunted her from the University of New South Wales, Konishi returned to the Koori Centre in August 2003. An Indigenous woman from Broome in Western Australia, and descendant of the Yawaru people, she had entered the University through the Cadigal Special Entry Scheme. Konishi, a History Honours student and holder of the University medal, was also the inaugural winner of the NSW Indigenous History Fellowship for research into colonial attitudes towards Aboriginal masculinity in the early colonial period.

Figure 57. Bachelor of Education (Secondary: Aboriginal Studies) and Diploma in Education (Aboriginal) graduates: Jodie Wellington, Adele Chapman-Burgess, Margaret Smith, Eileen Smith and Sharon Simms. Image courtesy of the Koori Centre.

Figure 58. Dr Wendy Brady. Image courtesy of Dr Wendy Brady.

As she explains:

> Racist stereotypes are so pervasive that we don't even recognise them for what they are. Knowing the Aboriginal community from the inside, I can recognise these stereotypes are fictions and not truths. A distressing part of my research has been the discovery that the stereotypes around today were current so long ago.[29]

Another memorable event saw five Koori Centre staff – Deirdre Dorbis, Janet Mooney, Anthony McKnight, Debbie Wray, and Katrina Thorpe – graduate with an MEd in March 1999. This day was doubly special as their graduation was shared with Doreen Alcorn, Selina Archibald, Linda Eldridge, Joy Wenner, Maureen Wenzel and Maxine Ryan, who were awarded their BEd (Secondary: Aboriginal Studies) at the same ceremony.

Research

With the closure of the Koori Centre's Curriculum Research and Development Unit, research activity diminished. However, Stack was successful in securing funding to assist individual academic staff at the Koori Centre and Yooroang Garang in research training, which Brady led at the centre and Neil Bechervaise, from the Faculty of Education, at Yooroang Garang. Stack was also appointed chair for the centre's National Priority Reserve Fund Project, "An Examination of Pedagogical Issues in Higher Education and Training Underpinning the

Development of Culturally Appropriate Module-Based Education Programs". This project was supported by a research team which included Shane Williams, Lyn Gow and Bruno Gelonesi. On Gow's resignation in July 1995, Bechervaise stepped in and completed the report. From 1996, the Koori Centre Research Committee ceased to meet and the centre's research fell back on the enthusiasm of individuals.

Moving with the Times

The Koori Centre had been slow in taking up information technology and it was not until 1993 that academic staff gained computer access. Before then, staff mostly wrote their lectures by hand and, if they wanted work typed, it was passed to an administrative staff member. Although the centre did provide a few computers for student use, their requests for greater access were not given high priority. Some arguments raised against their purchase were that they incurred substantial and recurrent maintenance costs and that only minimal use was made of existing facilities. There was also concern over duplicating resources offered by the faculties.

Realising that computer technology was increasingly important in individual learning, Hobson sought to upgrade the centre's meagre resources assisted by an Equity and Access Grant of $25,000 from the Information Technology Committee. This enabled the purchase of several computers, software, a laser printer and scanner. A purpose built internet server was obtained and the OTC was connected with the University network. Excitement over the new facility was overwhelming with the computer lab providing a thriving learning environment. Koori Centre students were provided with personal email accounts well in advance of the rest of the student population. In addition, they had online chat and Hobson also used his personal interest and expertise to construct the Koori Centre website and KooriNet, a significant internet presence, which hosted sites for over a dozen community organisations, its email lists recording over 1200 subscribers. The first Indigenous Australian search engine, BlackTracker, was introduced and was archived by the National Library of Australia's Pandora Archive from 1999 onwards. As was noted at the time, "Apart from his day job as coordinator of the centre's Student Academic Support Unit, Hobson also ran KooriNet (www.koori.usyd.edu.au), pretty much in his spare time."[30] The potential for online training for Aboriginal education was also recognised and attempts made to develop online courses began. Not everything went smoothly though – a negative assessment of one external teaching arrangement inadvertently circulated through a staff member's email saw the acting director, Michelle Blanchard, visit NAISDA to reassure its staff and students.

When IT passed to administrative staff under the Change Management Plan of 2001, momentum was lost. However, in 2008, Curtis Flood, who now had charge of the Koori Centre website, and Deborah Kirby-Parsons, received the Vice-Chancellor's Award for Support of the Student Experience for work on the Indigenous portal. Kirby-Parsons, who held a BVisArts, and GradDipVisArts had joined the centre in 2002 as executive assistant following a restructure at Sydney College of the Arts. Prior to her appointment there had been a succession of executive assistants including Indigenous personnel.[31] Kirby-Parsons resigned in 2009 and was replaced by Tatum Touma, a Euahlayi woman from north-west NSW.

Other innovative activities based on communications technology saw Koori Centre staff develop telephone and electronic communication with students in their home communities with block mode students encouraged to send staff and tutors assignments by email. This may seem normal practice in distance teaching but the centre's students were not necessarily electronically skilled from the outset and many in rural areas had no home computers. Much planning and effort went into IT teaching and ensuring access to IT equipment through local TAFE colleges, schools, community centres and libraries.

Further improvement in resource management occurred in April 1996 when Uma Ketheson, whose birthplace was Sri Lanka, was appointed part-time librarian. The online library system, Athena, was purchased, and access to other library networks such as ABN was arranged and a library security system installed. After negotiations with the Curriculum Resources Library, then housed on the third floor of the OTC, further stack space was provided along with a reading area with comfortable chairs and study tables. This extension of library facilities was important because the Curriculum Resourses Library, under the helpful Jacqui Hicks, was relocated from the first floor of the OTC to the basement of Fisher Library. Unfortunately, when the new PVC (College of Humanities and Social Sciences) Professor June Sinclair took over in 2003, she was not supportive of the centre's accommodation requirements and storage and library space within the stack area was passed to Anthropology. However, Sinclair did ensure a substantial refurbishment of the OTC building with its courtyards and interior upgraded, a major improvement in the Koori Centre's environment.

Sydney University Indigenous Students Association

In 1994, Indigenous students registered themselves with the SRC as a student association obtaining University funding. Known as Sydney University Indigenous Student Association (SUISA), the group elected Natalie Brown as their first president and funded four students to attend the inaugural National Indigenous Students Conference in Adelaide in September. The four joined over 200 young Indigenous people in passing a resolution to found a National Aboriginal and Torres Strait Student Network whose New South Wales branch was officially launched at the University of New South Wales early in 1995, with Ernie Dingo the guest speaker at a formal dinner. A camping trip at Crescent Heads for students from the Universities of Newcastle, New South Wales, and Sydney followed. However, SUISA ran into problems and was formally disbanded for financial and legal reasons a year later. After Steven Ross (né Carroll) became president he commented: "This [deregistration] was an event in itself because the continuation of the group was a major hindrance to social and political participation within the wider university community."[32]

The Indigenous student body later reformed itself as "Buncha" Aboriginal Student Association, with Steven Ross as president. In 1996, Buncha allocated $700 for Anthony Probert to attend the World Indigenous Education Conference at Albuquerque, USA; and three Buncha students, Eddie Porter, Natalie Brown and Steven Ross assisted centre staff in supervising 30 Years 11 and 12 students from across New South Wales during its inaugural Courses and Careers Camp. Also in 1996, Sydney students joined protests in Canberra over changes in Indigenous funding arrangements. "They got pretty negative press but believe me it was a chance to vent our frustration at an intransigent and draconian Coalition government."[33]

Another significant Buncha achievement was the publication of volume 1 of *Black on Black Aboriginal Studies Journal* (1998), edited by Shino Konishi, who wrote the introduction.

> The Aboriginal problem is, as it has always been, a one-sided discourse. We are often left out of it completely. We are given little chance to participate, let alone take control, in our own "protection", "assimilation", "reconciliation", and even "self-determination". No wonder some non-Aboriginal people profess to be sick of "the Aboriginal problem" – they are the only ones actively participating. We are cast in the role of accepting white ordained solutions to the "problem": Aboriginal solutions are not heard. We try to voice our own solutions, but all the soap boxes are taken. In Government we are represented by a white Minister for Aboriginal Affairs (in the wider political arena we are represented by very few endorsed and/or compromised Aboriginal spokespeople); Aboriginal women are represented by white feminists; white anthropologists and lawyers represent us in native title claims; and white academics represent us in the intellectual/discursive realm.
>
> The aim of this journal is to address these misrepresentations by non-Aborigines and to indicate to the white majority, and more importantly, the black minority, that we are perfectly capable of voicing our own opinion/solution/discourse. We want to represent ourselves, we want to be heard.[34]

Volume 2 of *Black on Black* was edited by Ross in 1999.[35] The new journal was a step up in an academic sense from earlier student publications and it was hoped that this anthology of Aboriginal writing on Aboriginal issues would become an annual event. Alas, the student body that had so involved itself graduated, and the new cohort of students had other priorities.

On 4 April 2005, a group of students met for the first time as the Klub Koori, electing Clark Webb as President, Peter Hawkins, Vice President, Ineke Wever, Treasurer, and Vivian Paul, Secretary. The association differed from previous groups in that it was not restricted to Indigenous students with membership invited from the wider student body. Out of the Klub Koori came the Australian Indigenous Mentoring Experience (AIME), the brainchild of Jack Manning-Bancroft the inaugural winner of an ANZ Scholarship and BA (Media and Communication) graduate of 2007. Jack is the son of Bronwyn Bancroft, the celebrated urban Aboriginal artist who holds an MVisArts from Sydney. In 2005, Manning-Bancroft, along with fellow students, Tom Ward, Hamish Dunn, Rashi Kalra, and Robyn Shields, initially assisted by Mooney, ran an AIME pilot program at Alexandria Park Public School. A four-year program emerged which established mentoring relationships for Indigenous high school students aiming at university entry, drawing on Indigenous and non-Indigenous volunteers from Sydney. Currently, it operates a three-stage program: the Year 9 Interactive Program, the Year 10 Leadership Program, and the Years 11 and 12 Tutoring Program. Also in 2005, AIME promoted the Indigenous Carnivale, another idea from Jack Manning-Bancroft, which brought celebrants together at an Indigenous concert and arts festival in the Manning Building on National Sorry Day. AIME is now an incorporated Indigenous not-for-profit organisation to which the University of Sydney commits funds and which is expanding to other universities.[36]

Impact of Changes

(i) Abstudy/Away-From-Base

A change of federal government policy in 1996 saw Abstudy targeted for savings, in particular, the Away-From-Base (AFB) funding. The move directly affected education students at the Koori Centre and health students at Yooroang Garang, threatening their

Figure 59. Students participate in the Reconciliation Walk across Sydney Harbour Bridge, 26 May 2000. Neville Allen and Sarah Stonestreet are holding the flag. Image courtesy of the Koori Centre.

Figure 60. Indigenous Carnivale at Manning Bar poster. Koori Centre Annual Report 2006–07.

programs. For many months, the Koori Centre and Yooroang Garang were kept in limbo about the government's policy, unable to plan for the future. Not least was confusion over its precise details with urgent meetings and email and telephone calls to DEETYA for clarification. When the director of the Koori Centre met with the other directors of centres at the NSW/ACT Aboriginal and Torres Strait Islander Higher Education Network and the National Indigenous Higher Education Network, they rejected the Commonwealth's proposition that "courses which are comprised wholly or substantially of away from base components ... will no longer be approved for Abstudy".[37] While continuing students would have their entitlements maintained, many would have to negotiate with institutions within their home state for acceptance into similar courses and for accreditation of earlier results. If implemented, the Commonwealth's proposal would have closed Sydney's certificate and diploma courses and threatened its Indigenous bachelor degree.

At that time Mooney undertook to interview the students on their reactions to the proposed changes.[38] The majority of the students' perceptions of the impact of recent changes could be categorised as "confusion" in relation to understanding how they would be affected by the proposed changes. Several students stated that they were "aware of changes", but they were "not sure" how these changes would affect them. Some students suggested that the impact of such changes had resulted in "worry and panic", and others described the impact of the proposed changes as "very unsettling". Finally, one student, concerned about the Abstudy funding cuts not only personally but for the future, stated, "could they not cut something else instead of cutting funds to educate us so that one day we will be able to educate our younger generation."

Heavy lobbying from the directors of Indigenous higher education centres led to a compromise of sorts with the government continuing to fund AFB programs but under a new formula. In late 1997, the Minister for Schools, Vocational Education and Training, Senator C. Ellison, affirmed that the new arrangements would put restrictions on hours of attendance at AFB courses. These new arrangements were implemented from 1 January 1999 requiring changes to existing curricula, an additional load on staff and students.

(ii) Loss of Aboriginal Education Assistants Program

The New South Wales state government was also reviewing public education and it determined to amalgamate school education and TAFE. Integrating the two sectors had major implications for the AEAP as the NSW DoET signalled that it would withdraw its funding (which in 1996 was already a meagre $145,039, some $20,000 lower than previous years). Under the state government plan, responsibility for the training of AEAs would pass from Sydney to the TAFE sector, mainly through regional arrangements. This decision terminated the near quarter century association of the University and the AEAs. Several in the Koori Centre felt the loss of the AEAP keenly. They feared that TAFE would not do as good a job as the University given its lack of experience and the absence of any trained teams and saw it as a retreat from equity in Aboriginal education. Other centre staff thought that the Koori Centre could well vacate what they regarded as lower level training in favour of programs related directly to Sydney's academic priorities.

From its humble beginnings, the AEAP had taken some 690 Indigenous people[39] on a significant educational journey. These graduates of the AEAP were to go on to make a considerable difference in their school and region, many becoming teachers and consultants in the NSW DoET. The final graduation in 1998 carried sadness along with recognition of student achievement, past and present.

New Degree Qualifications

In 1995–96, the centre engaged Laurie Craddock and Ray King as consultants to conduct a feasibility study for a BEd qualification for Indigenous students. Interest was considerable among AEAs and recent school leavers, and the investigators thought enrolment numbers more than sufficient. In correspondence sent to the NSW DoET in 1997, the Koori Centre proposed a BEd (Secondary: Aboriginal Studies) for 1999. "There are 60+ Diploma Graduates who constitute a pool of candidates and this is only one area of the population of suitable students for the program." However, it seems that the Koori Centre report was not considered formally by the NSW DoET for some time. When the NSW DoET did act, it wanted the University to introduce the degree almost immediately.

The Koori Centre then hired Marian Bowman, an instructional designer, to examine the time frame necessary, with Mooney writing to Trish Kelly, the Director of Personnel Programs, on receipt of Bowman's report:

> We realise that DSE are keen to begin this degree mid-1998 and understand that there are other institutions who are prepared to introduce a BEd (Sec) (Aboriginal studies) in the time frame required. For us as a Centre and because of our desire to provide the best possible degree for Aboriginal students we are unable to begin a degree in second semester 1998.[40]

The state department, however, continued on track and, in a letter dated 30 March 1998, Kelly informed the centre:

> The department is supporting twenty Aboriginal Education Assistants (AEAs) and Aboriginal Community Liaison Officers (ACLOs), to undertake a secondary teacher education program from semester 2, 1998, through a program which has been developed by the Catholic University in consultation with the department.[41]

Figure 61. Fulbright Scholarship awards 2007: Christopher Lawrence (recipient), Mrs Harriet Mayor Fulbright, Sharon Bonython-Ericson (recipient), and Sharon Galleguillos (Koori Centre lecturer), *UN*.

The NSW DoET went on to fund 20 Indigenous scholarships at the Australian Catholic University where students commenced a new Bachelor of Education Secondary degree with an Aboriginal Studies major at its Strathfield Campus in second semester, 1998.

The Koori Centre continued with planning its own bachelor's degree. Over the next 12 months, in partnership with the Faculty of Education, the Koori Centre reviewed its existing AFB programs, rewriting the DipAAEd which became the DipEd (Aboriginal), and finalising a BEd (Secondary: Aboriginal Studies). The degree was innovative in that it combined the DipEd (Aboriginal) and a four-year BEd degree. A student who entered the degree could either undertake the first two years and graduate with the DipEd (Aboriginal) or opt to complete a further two years for the Faculty of Education sponsored BEd (Secondary: Aboriginal Studies). The new degree had its first intake in 2000 when nine students enrolled.

Chancellor's Committee Scholarships

In 1997, a member of the University's Chancellor's Committee, Roger Hardy, met with the director to discuss the possibility of Indigenous students applying to the Chancellor's Committee for identified scholarships. After much discussion, it was agreed that three Undergraduate Higher Education Contribution Scheme (HECS) Bursaries, valued at $3500, would be offered annually, one of them dedicated to an AFB student. Ten smaller amounts helped pay union and book fees for first year students. From 2004, five bursaries of $500 for students other than first year were added. With the abolition of SRC fees, 15 encouragement awards of $500 were offered to Indigenous students starting from 2007.

Scholarships had also been made available through a new income line, the Indigenous Support Allocation (ISA). On the 16 August 1998, after meetings with Clapham from Yooroang Garang, Mooney from the Koori Centre, and Ross from Planning and Support, a memorandum was prepared by Professor Ken Eltis, Deputy Vice-Chancellor (Planning and Support), laying down expenditure guidelines. Funding for Indigenous support would be made available on an annual basis dependent on the load generated by Indigenous students in each college. The memorandum noted that the money should be spent in fields such as curriculum development, cultural awareness and financial support, with the PVCs to consult with the directors of the Koori Centre and Yooroang Garang. Each college was required to provide details of consultations undertaken and, eventually, how the money was expended. Scholarships became the preferred form, although different criteria applied across colleges.

Student Performance and Review

The number of Indigenous Australian EFTSU at the University increased over the period 1996–2000,[42] but unevenly, as participation, retention and success varied across the period.

Student Enrolment and Participation

1996		1997		1998		1999		2000	
Students	%	Students	%	Students	%	Students	%	Students	%
210	0.7	247	0.8	264	0.8	368	1.1	297	0.9

Retention

1997	1998	1999	2000
0.98	0.81	0.86	0.76

Success

1996	1997	1998	1999
0.89	0.81	0.91	0.78

These enrolment variations were related to the total number of students which was susceptible to shifts in course arrangements and funding. For example, the spike in enrolment in 1999 was the result of new courses coming on steam, while the fall back in 2000 related to falling diploma progression in the BEd (Secondary: Aboriginal Studies) program influenced by new opportunities opening in TAFE. There were also discrepancies in the statistics, enrolments in 2000 being short by at least 17. It was later determined that a significant decline in Indigenous numbers across the higher education sector was attributable to the changes in Abstudy allowances and the introduction of higher HECS fees. Nonetheless, the enrolment achievement at the end of the 20th century was there to see. Further, these students were supported by services, including computer resources, which had previously been unavailable. Most importantly, increasing numbers of non-Indigenous students had an opportunity to access the Koori Centre's courses and learn from Indigenous staff members.

12

Aboriginal Education into the New Millennium

> The University of Sydney is Australia's first university. It is committed to creating an environment in which the rich and diverse cultures of Indigenous Australians are known, promoted, and celebrated.
>
> Charles "Chicka" Madden, Cadigal Elder, 2006[1]

In the years up to 2000, a stable leadership emerged under Mooney as director, with Johnstone as PVC, backed by financial advice from Ross. Their combined strategies were supported by the new Board of Studies in Indigenous Studies and by networks of Indigenous people; and more Indigenous students were enrolling and visiting the centre as its support activities expanded. While the raw figures were reassuring, there was concern that the University was recruiting inadequate numbers in its regular degrees as distinct from its bridging and non-degree programs. There was also an opinion that the Koori Centre should be more closely integrated with the faculties and the administration, and that Koori Centre and Yooroang Garang relations required mending.

Under Scrutiny

The University determined to instigate a review of Aboriginal education in 1998. Although the review was welcomed initially, the relationship between the review team and Koori Centre staff soured as its particular recommendations were contested. Deputy Vice-Chancellor Professor Derek Anderson, responsible for Aboriginal education on the Camperdown Campus, chaired the review recruiting Charles Perkins as the Indigenous contact. Another nine team members joined from within the University,[2] along with Ross and Natalie Downie from administration. In 1999, the EFTSU figure for enrolments in all courses, including bridging classes, was 368. On Ross's figures (for 1989), 60 percent of the Indigenous students came from New South Wales, with 53 percent Sydney based; and they tended to be older than the average cohort, only a fifth of them being in the 18–21 age range. Almost all faculties had at least one Aboriginal student, with the greatest numbers in Health Sciences (216), Education (46), Medicine particularly Public Health (37), and Arts (32).

On 21 March 2000, Anderson passed a set of 24 recommendations to the Vice-Chancellor and Principal, Professor Gavin Brown. It urged that the University's colleges and faculties explicitly acknowledge the University's vision for Aboriginal education and promote it in their strategic plans. faculties should invite staff of the centre to include a "Welcome to Country" in their proceedings acknowledging the custodians of the land. It also wanted the Koori Centre attached to the College of Humanities and Social Sciences, although the PVC Teaching and Learning position would continue with its influence. In another level of oversight, the Koori Centre was to report to a new offshoot of the Academic Board, a Standing Committee on Indigenous Education. This move would see the Board of Studies in Indigenous Studies and the Policy Advisory Committee abolished.

Indigenous research across the University should be coordinated and respond to the needs of Indigenous communities. Targets would be set for the recruitment of postgraduate Indigenous students and more scholarships awarded. All Indigenous academic staff should be mentored. There would be three new Visiting Aboriginal Fellowships and at least one Adjunct Chair of Indigenous Education; an Oration by an internationally high-profile "race" relations leader promoted annually; and a database of Indigenous graduates compiled to track and support their professional needs. On and off campus accommodation for Indigenous students should be pursued. The review also recommended that the two Indigenous centres work closely with the central administration's Prospective Students Unit and Student Services. Finally, it asked that the University's Equity Advisory Committee take on the task of reviewing the University's Indigenous education strategy on an annual basis.

In essence, the recommendations fell into two categories. The first, which comprised the abolition of the Board of Studies in Indigenous Studies and Policy Advisory Committee, and the creation of new supervising agencies, had the effect of limiting the autonomy of the Koori Centre and reducing its access to senior Aboriginal advice. One member of the review team, Mooney, personally dissented and her reservations were backed by Koori Centre staff incensed at the proposed limitations. A Working Party established by the Board of Studies in Indigenous Studies under Blanchard, and comprising Cleverley and Mooney, with input from academic staff, forwarded a set of objections to the Vice-Chancellor.[3] The thrust of the second category, which supported scholarships, the oration, research, and the Chair, was welcomed.

The Vice-Chancellor was personally concerned about the abolition of the Board of Studies in Indigenous Studies as it had been established by Senate to supervise the Koori Centre's academic awards. He was also worried about the composition and focus of its proposed replacement, the Academic Board Standing Committee.[4] Brown queried whether it was proper for the Academic Board to have a major responsibility for Indigenous education policy and whether subsuming the Koori Centre under the College of Humanities and Social Sciences was sensible, given that the centre's responsibilities were University wide. Brown supported the recommendations in general when the review was presented to Senate, while admitting that not all issues had been resolved. Nonetheless, he did expect major

Figure 62. Vice-Chancellor, Professor Gavin Brown OA. Image courtesy of the Office of the Vice-Chancellor.

benefits to flow by 2000, subject to funding from external sources. "The Vice-Chancellor said that he trusted that the spirit of the recommendations would be implemented."[5] In the wider discussion at Senate, Jenny Beatson, a University staff representative, observed that the University at large, including Indigenous staff, had not been invited to make submissions to the review which limited its vision.

Orators and Awards

After Perkins' death on the 19 October 2000, the annual oration by a high profile race relations leader was named the Dr Charles Perkins AO Memorial Oration. Noel Pearson was the first orator on 25 October 2001, the occasion attended by the Perkins family, with Eileen Perkins awarding the Memorial Prize. Subsequent speakers were Professor Marcia Langton 2002; Associate Professor Ian Anderson 2003; Professor Lynda Tuhiwai Smith 2004; Professor Larissa Behrent and the Honourable James J. Spigelman 2005; Professor Sandra Eades 2006; Marion Scrymgour, MLA, Northern Territory Government 2007; Tom Calma, Aboriginal and Torres Strait Islander Social Justice Commissioner and Race Discrimination Commissioner 2008; and Professor Gordon Briscoe OA, academic and Indigenous activist.

Perkins was the first Indigenous person awarded an honorary doctorate at Sydney. Nominated by Professor Jeremy Webber, Dean of Law, the Doctor of Laws (honoris causa), was conferred at the Arts ceremony on 11 May 2000.[6] At the conferring, the Vice-Chancellor outlined

Figure 63. Joe Neparrnga Gumbula, family and friends celebrate the awarding of Doctor of Music (honoris causa) 2007. Image courtesy of the Koori Centre.

seminal events in Perkins' story honouring a remarkable life. The second honorary degree, the Doctor of Music (honoris causa), was awarded to Jimmy Little at the Arts ceremony on 3 June 2005.[7] Little's role as Ambassador for Literacy and Numeracy for the Department of Education, Science and Training (DEST) saw him invited by Indigenous students to speak and perform at Aboriginal and Torres Strait Islander Week celebrations, and he became a valued member of the Koori Centre's guest lecturing staff. The third honorary doctorate, the Doctor of Music (honoris causa), was conferred on Joseph Neparrnga Gumbula at the Sydney Conservatorium of Music's graduation ceremony of 4 April 2007. The same year, Gumbula became the University's first Australian Research Council Indigenous Research Fellow. Located at the Koori Centre, and working in partnership with the University of Sydney Archives, his Discovery Project with Dr Aaron Corn examined rare materials from the 1920s documenting his family's history in Arnhem Land.[8] The fourth degree of Doctor of Visual Arts (honoris causa) was conferred upon Brenda Louise Croft at the College of the Arts graduation ceremony on 6 April 2009 for her outstanding contribution to the visual arts. She is from the Gurindji people in Daguragu/Limbunya in the Northern Territory.

Change Management Plan

External reviews of the Koori Centre were less successful in initiating change in Koori Centre practice than its own internal housekeeping. The centre's evaluation of where it stood had begun around 1999 when Mooney completed the Strategic Plan for 2001–05. Mooney instigated work on a Change Management Proposal commenced under Blanchard as acting director with assistance from Cleverley. The following year with staff receiving a draft set of ideas inviting opinions and suggestions.[9] After a series of staff meetings and a restructuring retreat at Dooralong, the Change Management Proposal was passed by the University and the National Tertiary Education Union for implementation in 2002.

The three units within the centre, the AEAP, ISU and SASU, were singled out for reform. The Change Management Proposal argued that the three-unit structure put barriers in the way of the flexible use of staff and encouraged disputation over the allocation of resources. From a staff perspective, membership of a particular unit limited opportunities to work across programs; it made balanced workloads difficult to achieve; and it used academic staff in administration and technology services, limiting their academic teaching and research and reducing their opportunity for promotion. Another concern of the Change Management Proposal was the need to revitalise research as projects and publications had steeply declined. It also emphasised the need for a senior administration officer able to handle its budget in a professional way, rationalise office procedures, and lead the administration team.

After the three units were dissolved, staff members were moved into one of two streams, academic or administration. A statement of workloads for Indigenous academic staff nominated 40 percent for teaching, 30 percent research, 20 percent administration, and 10 percent Aboriginal community activities. A deputy director position was established and filled by Blanchard; Arthur Smith, who received his PhD from Ohio State and Masters from Stanford University, was appointed academic coordinator; and the office manager's position was filled by Jenny Thompson. The Research Committee was also re-established alongside an Innovations Committee covering teaching and curriculum reform. Lastly, the arrangement for Special Studies Program Leave for Indigenous staff was rediscovered and reactivated.

The movement of individuals to new tasks, which included the relocation of some offices and facilities, delayed the implementation of the plan until 2003. This period was an especially busy one as staff members with specialised knowledge were encouraged to oversee their previous areas at the same time as they undertook new duties themselves. Also, the Old Teachers College building was under renovation, a task which saw the installation of a new lift, and staff found themselves covered in dust and subject to mind-numbing noise. Issued with university-supplied earplugs, they soldiered on. Thanks to their dedication, and the patience of students, the changes were executed.

Cadigal Special Entry Program

Any redeployment of staff within the centre had to confront the issue of how best to manage the Cadigal Special Entry Program. Its academic skills teaching had fallen largely on the Cadigal lecturer whose general responsibilities covered the selection of potential students, liaison with the faculties and tutors, and oversight of the Indigenous Tutorial Assistance Scheme (ITAS). The numbers of students entering Sydney under Cadigal had fallen over a five-year period: in 2000, enrolments had dropped from 48 to 32 and, by 2003, numbers had bottomed out to less than 20.[10] It seems Abstudy and HECS had made university study less attractive and Indigenous students were also enrolling with improved UAI scores, up to three quarters of the total Indigenous degree entrants in 2003. That year, just 13 students enrolled in academic skills, five of them on reduced loads. In sum, student numbers were not increasing although those entering were better prepared. Consequently, the percentage of Cadigal students among the Indigenous students as a whole fell.

In 2004, Cleverley was invited to recommend a revised staffing plan for Cadigal, then led by Jeff Dunn, from the Wodi Wodi community of the South Coast of New South Wales. He recommended that a higher education officer handle the administrative component of the role, including the first point of contact for students, and that the associate lecturer teaching academic skills be placed under the academic coordinator. Koori Centre staff as a group should share the mentoring of students. Dunn was unhappy about the follow-through of the arrangements and he left the centre in 2005. In October, the centre employed Tanya Griffith, a descendant of the Ngiyampaa (Wongaibon) people, as its student administration officer, and Debbie Wray took over the academic side of the program.

A further review of the Cadigal program occurred in 2007 under Blanchard and Lynette Riley. The latter, a descendant of the Wiradjuri (Dubbo) and Gamilaroi (Moree) nations, was employed as academic coordinator in August 2006. Riley would take up the position of acting deputy director in 2008 while Blanchard was on study leave. Assisted by the University Learning Centre, the review of 2007 concluded that the academic skills unit failed to address the issue of students' preparedness for tertiary level study as students were not caught early enough. After consultation, a pilot project was trialed in 2008 delivering an intensive academic skills program prior to Semester 1. Now all students accepted into the University through the Cadigal Special Entry Program must either attend or else enter a one-on-one program negotiated before enrolment.

Change at the Top and in the Centre

Professor Judith Kinnear, from the Cumberland Campus, replaced Anderson as Deputy Vice-Chancellor, and Professor Paul Ramsden, appointed PVC (Teaching and Learning) in 1999, replaced Johnstone. While Kinnear passed over the day to day oversight of the Koori Centre to PVC Ramsden, she continued to involve herself directly in decision-making. After Mooney took study leave in 2000, Kinnear insisted that an Indigenous person act as director, consequently Blanchard was appointed with Cleverley as mentor, an arrangment which proved successful. In 2005, Ramsden was replaced by PVC Professor Judyth Sachs from Education, who herself would leave the University in 2007. Sachs was replaced by Professor Derrick Armstrong, Dean of the Faculty of Education and Social Work, as Acting PVC, appointed DVC (Education) in 2008.[11]

Figure 64. Koori Centre staff 2005. Top left to right: Jeff Dunn, Anthony McKnight, Peter Minter, Sharon Galleguillos. Bottom left to right: Pat Davison, Arthur Smith, Sherrie Connors, Curtis Flood, Janet Mooney, Noeleen Smith, Katrina Thorpe. Image courtesy of the Koori Centre.

An urgent need for more Indigenous staff at the University was identified in the 2003 Heads of Agreement with the tertiary education unions. A target of 25 Indigenous employees was an indicative entry level for general staff along with eight trainee cadet posts, and a minimum target (unspecified) was adopted for academic appointments. The University also committed itself to the Indigenisation of the Koori Centre and Yooroang Garang based on priority for Indigenous applications. A professorial level position would take responsibility for Indigenous employment, policy, and student and related matters. Outcomes from this agreement were addressed variously. In 2005, with the active support of Deputy Vice-Chancellor John Hearn (Academic and International), the position of professor of Indigenous studies (an identified Indigenous position) was created and advertised, with one offer made but not taken up. It was expected that the position would be re-advertised in 2007 but this did not happen.

Inside the Koori Centre there was considerable movement in staff positions. Peter Minter, an Awabakal person from the Central Coast of New South Wales, joined the centre in March 2000 as an associate lecturer (tutorial support) moving to a lectureship in 2006. In 2000, Kath French (later known as Kath Howey) joined the centre and, in 2001, the Faculty of Nursing. Dennis Foley, appointed in 2002, was awarded a PhD in 2005 before moving to a Melbourne appointment. Lisa Slater, a postgraduate student who had taught Indigenous studies, was employed in 2005; Sharon Simms, a Dharawal person and a graduate of the BEd (Secondary: Aboriginal Studies), became Schools Community Liaison Officer in 2007, taking up an associate lectureship a year later. Also in 2007, the non-Indigenous staff member, Cathie Burgess, was seconded from Tempe High School to teach Human Society and Its Environment in the BEd (Secondary: Aboriginal Studies), being appointed full time in 2009.

Among the new members of the administration staff was Sherrie Connors, a Kamilaroi woman originally from a small town, Talwood, in Queensland, who joined the centre in 2002 as ITAS coordinator. Another was Kristal Morris, the Block Programs Administrator, a descendant of the Wiradjuri and Jawoyn people, who was replaced by Carol Speechley, a Wodi Wodi woman from Wollongong. After Speechley's resignation in October 2006, Connors took her position, and John South was employed part time in 2008 to manage ITAS. In 2009, Freda Hammond, a Wiradjuri woman, was appointed from Charles Sturt University to the ITAS position full time. In 2003 after much debate at the Koori Centre Retreat the previous year, the centre re-employed a counsellor. Jenny Tebbutt, whose qualifications included BSc (Psych) UNSW, was appointed in 2003. Due to financial difficulties, the Koori Centre was unable to fund this position after 2006 and Tebbutt was employed by the UCS.

Financial Appropriation

In late 1999, there was concern about the Koori Centre budget as money due for teaching international students had not been transferred to centre accounts for several years. With the assistance of Ramsden's resourceful Executive Assistant, Virginia Burns, it was discovered that the money had been diverted to the Faculty of Education in error. After the matter was pursued in 2000, the University refused to return the $109,000 due for 2000, or for any prior years. The Koori Centre considered itself hard done by as it had undertaken the teaching and the University centre had made the mistake. A deal was finally brokered with the Dean of Education whereby the faculty would return a proportion of the money outstanding for first semester 2001, and some in-kind support – not a satisfactory outcome.

The incident over international student money was indicative of wider accounting problems. While the Koori Centre had wanted an office manager with strong financial skills appointed to handle its complex funding arrangements, this did not occur. Furthermore, the University's own accounting system was interrupted by staff changes and there was no supportive dialogue with the centre. In the early 2000s, the Koori Centre was overdrawn: not all money owed it had been paid and the centre had extra costs including redundancies. A deficit of $701,419 was estimated for 2007.[12] Recognising the seriousness of this, the Koori Centre took immediate action by transferring all funds from reserves, not filling vacancies, not replacing staff on leave without pay, and by reducing general expenditure. Patrick Snowdon, a descendant of the Boigu Island people of the Torres Strait and the Timorese, was appointed Finance and Marketing Officer. Snowdon pursued the Koori Centre's financial interests with vigour and, by the end of 2007, the deficit was substantially reduced and the income-expenditure balance of the budget was restored. Following discussion at the beginning of 2008, the Koori Centre was allocated an internal budget of $1.934 million, an increase of $317,000 over 2007, and, after a submission to the University Budget Committee in 2008, the remaining Koori Centre deficit was cleared.

The deficit situation led the University finance division to take a proactive role. As a start, it instituted a broadly conceived audit undertaken by John Mullis, from the Office of Audit, Risk Management and Assurance. Ten recommendations followed:[13]

- creation of a more supportive working relationship between Koori Centre financial staff and the Finance Officer Teaching and Learning especially in regard to the latest DEST grants
- a review of all programs based on a cost benefit analysis identifying real cost measured against income as one test of viability
- an expansion of the present proactive approach to program promotion in collaboration with the Office of Marketing and Student Recruitment
- efforts to enhance international student interest in Indigenous Australia courses
- the development of online services for local and prospective International students
- the amalgamation of the Koori Centre and Yooroang Garang
- an agreement that where the University at large gains a benefit, the Koori Centre should be reimbursed appropriately and
- that an Indigenous alumni group be formed.

Following this substantive statement, Craig Prosser, Finance Office Director, declared his confidence in the centre's financial management and promised additional advice and support. In a complementary move to strengthen the administration, Shona Smith, the faculty manager from Education and Social Work, took up a temporary part-time position as office manager. Existing functions were reviewed and redefined leading to improvements in administrative staff management. This in turn impacted positively on the centre's student support, communication between staff, and day-to-day operations.

A Return to Research

The Research Committee was re-established under the Change Management Plan and a part-time Senior Research Fellow position created through the University's Strategic Development Grants Initiative. Associate Professor Diana Day, with a background in earth and environmental sciences and in tertiary sector academic research development, was appointed with priority tasks identified in 2003.[14] An internal paper, "Research Guidelines", prepared by Day in 2004, revealed that centre research was in the low performance category with only 25–30 percent of staff active.[15] Despite the director having allowed staff/study research days, some individuals had yet to complete a postgraduate qualification over a decade, limiting the centre's capacity to supervise higher degree students. Mooney moved to reintroduce extended leave for completion of postgraduate qualification under the University's Special Study Program leave, assisting the following staff members:

- Michelle Blanchard, enrolled PhD
  University of Sydney (transferred from UTS)
  Thesis title: "The Politics of Interpretation and Representation in Indigenous Theatre and Film"

- Shino Konishi, PhD graduated 2007
  University of Sydney
  Thesis title: "Bodies in Contact: European Representations of Aboriginal Men, 1770–1803"

- Leah Lui-Chivizhe, MSc (Geography) graduated 2008
  University of Sydney
  Thesis title: "Islanders without Islands: Identity Construction and Torres Strait Islanders in Sydney"

- Peter Minter, enrolled PhD
  University of Technology
  Thesis title: "Incognita: Ecopoetics in Colonial and Postcolonial Australia"

- Janet Mooney, enrolled PhD
  University of Western Sydney.
  Thesis title: "Teaching Aboriginal Studies: A Critical Analysis of Core Aboriginal studies Subjects in Primary Teacher Education Courses"

- Lyn Riley, enrolled MEd (Hons)
  University of Western Sydney
  Thesis title: "Conditions of Success for Aboriginal Students in Schools"

- Debbie Wray, MEd (Hons) graduated 2008
  University of Western Sydney
  Thesis title: "HSC Aboriginal Studies: Strengths, Limitations, and Impact upon Aboriginal Students' Self-Concepts and Educational Outcomes".

In addition, non-degree research was undertaken by Galleguillos, Books in Homes in Australia Pilot Project, for Scholastic Australia Pty Ltd and the NSW DoET. In 2001, Melissa Burgess joined the centre as research assistant in the Cervical and Breast Screening for Aboriginal Women, a project coordinated by Juanita Sherwood in partnership with NSW Cervical Screening; and, in 2004, Clare McLisky worked with Diana Day on Black and White Science: Encouraging Indigenous Australian Students into University Science and Technology.[16] Nevertheless, research output remained problematic and Day would resign in late 2008.

Indigenous Support Money

One other research initiative was undertaken in association with the Faculty of Education and Social Work utilising Indigenous Support Fund money, $20,000 being made available for the project through the College of Humanities and Social Sciences. An audit review of the centre and faculty concentrating on teaching, learning and research into Aboriginal Studies/Perspectives was undertaken in 2002–03[17] by Cleverley, with Naomi Butcher as research assistant. The final report was based on 42 interviews with Indigenous and non-Indigenous persons, predominantly staff, and included a comprehensive curriculum mapping exercise.

Audit recommendations argued the need for curriculum revision, including covering the new mandatory requirements in public schools. More emphasis should be put on the achievement of Indigenous society and culture in the curriculum and the importance of partnership in promoting education and lessening disadvantage. It recommended that faculty and Koori Centre staff work more closely together through staff exchange and staff development and that faculty appoint Indigenous academic staff. Students in training deserved more opportunities for short-term placement in schools with high Aboriginal populations. As no research on Indigenous issues was in hand in the faculty, it proposed that the faculty and the Koori Centre together provide seed money for grant applications. The University's Research Office could also make Indigenous education a priority area. Various strategies were suggested for increasing Indigenous enrolments especially in social work, and the review wanted the Indigenous heritage of the University acknowledged through the naming of buildings and other features.

In 2008, the Koori Centre and the faculty took steps to follow up the key recommendations led by the Indigenous educator, Jane Moore, a descendant of the Palawa people. A Teaching and Learning Forum was organised by Moore on 14 February 2008, where Riley ran a kinship exercise and lectured on Indigenous education issues and Galleguillos reported on the New Zealand experience in embedding cultural knowledge. Another outcome of the review was a book chapter, "Shifting the Emphasis: Introducing Aboriginal Studies and Perspectives", written by Mooney and Moore for publication in 2010.

Postgraduate Visitors

In the early 2000s, the Koori Centre co-supervised two doctoral level students, one from Ireland, the other from Spain. Following Koori Centre sponsorship support and a submission to the Australian Consulate in Ireland by the academic coordinator, an Irish postgraduate, Fiona Murphy, won an Australian Government Postgraduate Student Research Award to investigate the concept of Reconciliation. Murphy was advised by Smith and other Koori Centre staff and met with Indigenous organisation and community members. She would forge links with the Native Title and Reconciliation (ANTaR) and was instrumental in inspiring staff to create the first Sea of Hands in the forecourt of the Quadrangle during Reconciliation Week in 2003, with a design for the installation by Deb Lennis, a tradition which is still upheld. Murphy remains very much in the hearts of the staff at the Koori Centre. She was sorely missed when she returned to Ireland and still maintains contact with staff. The other postgraduate student, Leticia Viteri Comunion, from the University of the Basque Country, was studying literature of the Basque Country at Sydney under Amaia Ibarraran, a scholar in residence, who had asked that Minter from the Koori Centre assist in 2004–05.

Another visitor to the centre in December and January 2005 was Victor Lal from Oxford University, an expert in international law pertaining to human rights and frameworks for social justice. Lal's particular interest was in Indigenous human rights in former British colonies. When Smith travelled to England he met up with Lal again.[18]

> I went to Oxford University and spent the day with him on campus, meeting various people and visiting places of particular interest. Fiona Murphy, who was back in Ireland at that stage, travelled across to Oxford for the day and joined me for part of the time I spent with Victor. I thought he was a good contact for Fiona to have in relation to her doctoral studies. They were both working in similar areas of academic interest.

Smith also recalled Lal's seminar at the Koori Centre. "I, for one, was very impressed with his work and both intellectual and ethical commitment to the ongoing struggle towards human rights and social justice, particularly for numerical minorities in the world who are oppressed and/or relatively powerless to do anything about it."

Innovation in Teaching

In the late 1990s, national research on the Indigenous studies curriculum impacted on Koori Centre teaching practices. Exciting developments in the area of teaching and learning, including the use of storytelling and oral history, were located within theories of narrative inquiry, an approach which enabled students to engage on an emotional level, non-Indigenous students especially. Other Indigenous research methodologies stressed the need for Indigenous communities to better inform teaching content and the use of symbols in Indigenous learning. In 2002, a discussion workshop, Evaluation and Indigenous Knowledges, encouraged academic staff to explore the knowledges, skills and values of their Indigenous studies courses and discuss how best to connect their epistemology with teaching and research. It was followed up by a staff poster exhibit at the 2003 Vice-Chancellor's "Showcase: Graduates for the World", and the article, "Indigenous Philosophy in Pedagogy and Research", authored by Thorpe, Minter, Lui-Chivizhe and Smith.[19]

In 2006, the Koori Centre reviewed its teaching programs introducing five new units of study in the undergraduate course:

1. Colours of Identity: Indigenous Bodies

Indigenous identity has been coupled with the colour of the body. Indigenous perspectives on identity and non-Indigenous writings are examined relating to the Indigenous body and its representation both historically and contemporarily. The imposition of identity on the Indigenous body and current theories on Indigenous identity are critiqued.

2. Indigenous Creative Expression

The concept of traditional versus contemporary is at the forefront of defining meanings for art works created by Indigenous artists. Typically, works created by Indigenous artists are delegated to either of these two categories. This unit examines the theoretical frameworks which position Indigenous artists through the study of Indigenous artistic expression. Students are given the opportunity to engage with Indigenous artists to discuss the complex issues in performance, literature, music, dance and film.

3. Issues and Rights

Aboriginal and Torres Strait Islander peoples are recovering culturally and politically from the effects of colonisation and assimilation after experiencing years of disempowerment, dislocation and social disruption. With Indigenous peoples seeking to reclaim independent social and political power, the course examines national and international developments through contemporary analyses of Indigenous rights and self-determination in the legal, political and community spheres.

4. Torres Strait History and Experiences

Torres Strait Islanders are often talked of as Australia's other Indigenous minority yet many Australians know little of the region and its people. This unit introduces students to Torres Strait societies through the themes of governance, migration and resource management. Students learn of the diversity within Torres Strait communities, Torres Strait Islander experiences of colonisation, and their responses to colonisation contrasted with those of Aboriginal people.

5. Speaking Gamilaraay 1

Gamilaraay is an Indigenous Australian language from the mid-northwest of NSW that is currently undergoing revitalisation. This unit of study will provide students with a basic competence in speaking, understanding, reading and writing Gamilaraay sufficient to recognise and construct simple utterances in the language and understand its relationships with other languages. Classes take the form of three-hour intensive oral workshops which progressively develop each student's abilities. Assessment will be by short written assignments based on lesson content and an appraisal of individual oral/aural performance together with a short essay on Gamilaraay culture or a related topic.

Scaffolding Literacy

One equity-based initiative led by David Rose was directed at literacy teaching for adults. Rose, who had a nationwide reputation as developer of the "scaffolding" approach to academic literacy, took up a Visiting Research and Teaching Fellowship after a successful joint Koori Centre – Faculty of Education and Department of Linguistics submission. While scaffolding's prime focus was on the teaching of academic reading and comprehension, the skills acquired spilled over into academic writing and course work. Koori Centre lecturers and tutors participated in the program in 2003 and new methodologies were introduced across key teaching and learning areas, particularly at TPC and diploma levels. Rose's initiatives were recognised by the University when he received the Vice-Chancellor's Award for Support of the Student Experience in October 2005. Core work undertaken in the Koori Centre's academic program appears in the *Australian Journal of Indigenous Education* paper,

"Scaffolding Academic Reading and Writing at the Koori Centre", by Rose, Lui-Chivizhe, McKnight and Smith.[20]

Garma Festival

In 2000, Blanchard and Mooney attended a working group of academics assessing the educational benefits of the Garma Festival hosted by the Yolŋu people. The Garma Indigenous Association, which included the Gumatj, Rirratjiŋu, Djapu', Galpu and Wangurri clan groups, established the Yothu Yindi Foundation in 1990. This annual festival encourages both the practice and maintenance of Yolŋu traditions in music, dance, art and ceremony, and forums which address Indigenous community issues world wide. Each year, Garma offers a different focus. Dunn, who has a music background, and Smith, were among staff who attended Garma in 2003. The two had conversations with Aaron Corn, engaged in Melbourne University's Garma experience for students. Later, Corn and Professor Alan Merritt from the Department of Music at Sydney joined with Smith and Dunn in developing two units of study: "Indigenous Australia: the Yolŋu Way", and "Indigenous Australia: Garma Fieldwork". Although the students who undertook the units reported life changing experiences, the teaching opportunities ceased after 2006 due to cost.

Indigenous Languages

The NSW Department of Aboriginal Affairs (NSW DAA) called for expressions of interest for a NSW Aboriginal Language Resource and Research Centre in 2002. After gaining support from the Department of Linguistics, and likely accommodation from the University, the Koori Centre put in an application. In early 2003, Mooney was contacted by Linda Burney, Director-General of NSW Department of Aboriginal Affairs, informing her that the University was unsuccessful, but envisaged that the Koori Centre could work in collaboration with the new Aboriginal Language Resource and Research Centre located at Tranby Aboriginal College in Glebe. Although the centre made attempts, no strong collaboration between the two places emerged.

Later that year, the possibility of an Aboriginal Languages Teaching Centre was raised by Kevin Lowe from the NSW Board of Studies and discussion began between the Koori Centre, NSW DoET and Linguistics. Collaborative activity led to an application for a Feasibility Study for a NSW Aboriginal Languages Development Institute led by Mooney and Michael Walsh, senior lecturer in linguistics, based on funding from the NSW Department of Aboriginal Affairs Major Grant Programs 2003/2004. In November 2003, Andrew Refshauge, NSW Minister of Aboriginal Affairs, wrote to the director stating:

> I had the opportunity to review many of the applications myself and am pleased to advise you I have supported a grant of $44,900.00 to assist with the costs involved with the Feasibility Study Project. This project has the potential to deliver social and economic benefits to Aboriginal people in New South Wales.[21]

The Feasibility Study Project tackled three areas: i) establishment of an institution of Aboriginal Indigenous languages at the University as a research, resource and learning centre for the revitalisation of Aboriginal languages in New South Wales and, in the long term, Australia-wide; ii) development of a conference/workshop for Aboriginal community members which could include learning one or more languages, skills for language revitalisation and opportunities to network with linguists and other interested people; and, iii) introduction of a university-level diploma course for Aboriginal people with teacher training to teach Aboriginal languages revitalisation in schools.

The project team appointed Tony Lonsdale to carry out its initial research. He produced the first of two reports in 2004 for NSW DAA, "New Ways Forward: NSW Aboriginal Languages Revitalisation Initiatives", which strongly supported the three proposals. A second report was then contracted from Susan Poetsch, "Report 2. Revitalising Aboriginal Languages in NSW: Review of Current Initiatives and Key Documents", which identified language and cultural initiatives underway around the state. Poetsch's report also summarised effective modes of support, and identified priorities for the reclamation of languages and culture. Applying tutelage from Hobson, the Koori Centre has now developed master, graduate diploma and graduate certificate qualifications in Indigenous languages education.

The NSW DoET accepts that the Master of Indigenous Languages Education provides appropriate training for qualified Aboriginal teachers seeking approval to teach an Aboriginal language. These courses are open to Indigenous Australian candidates only and are delivered in block mode. The first graduation for the Master of Indigenous Languages Education (MILE) was held in April, 2007. On their way to the graduation ceremony, students were led by Jack Manning-Bancroft and Paul Sinclair, accompanied by Indigenous graduates of the DipEd (Aboriginal) and BEd (Secondary: Aboriginal Studies). Students enjoyed a luncheon in the Naked Lady Courtyard where a Smoking and Ochre Ceremony was performed by Riley and Diane McNaboe, one of the MILE students, and a didgeridoo performance was sung by Richard Green in Dharug.

In 2007–08, the centre hosted the Ngaawa-Garay Summer School. It was a pleasure to wander the corridors of the Koori Centre hearing the Gamilaraay (north-west NSW) and Gumbaynggirr (North Coast of NSW) dialects spoken. Another Indigenous language, Wiradjuri, taught by McNaboe and Chris Kirkbright, was introduced. Hobson also took part in a review of training courses and teaching methodologies in Indigenous languages by trialling Gamilaraay as a unit of study for the New England Institute of TAFE and the Catholic Education Office, Armidale. In addition, the Indigenous Languages Institute's LingFest Conference ran for three days at the Koori Centre as part of LingFest 2008. Over 100 delegates from across New South Wales and Australia heard the plenary speaker, Chief Ron Ignace of the Skeetchestn Band, British Columbia. The Koori Centre is now a major locus in the revitalisation of Indigenous languages in the state.

Figure 65. First graduates of the Master of Indigenous Languages Education, 2006. Back: Robert Ah Wing, Amanda Stubbs, Jenni Tillett, Maureen Wenzel, Michael Jarrett, Diane McNaboe. Front: Connie Ah See, Jillean Bower and Desmond Crump. Image courtesy of the Koori Centre.

An Initiative at Orange

In 1999, the University of Sydney approached the NSW DoET to discuss a Centre for Rural Education on the University campus at Orange; the cost of the feasibility study would be met by NSW DoET, DETYA, and the University. In discussions with Stephen Crump in the Faculty of Education, two possibilities were identified:[22] a TPC, in part or in full, on the Orange Campus in 2001, and a recognised postgraduate qualification for teachers in support of Aboriginal Studies at primary and secondary levels either on-campus or through distance/flexible delivery. Talks were held with one of the centre's Diploma 1 students, Victor Wood, who worked for DETYA in Orange. A visit to Orange by Koori Centre staff,[23] and meetings with staff from the Western Institute (TAFE), Orange Campus staff, and representatives of AECG, Lands Council and other community organisations, saw a trial of two blocks of the TPC at Orange; unfortunately, due to lack of resources and the closing of the Orange campus this initiative was not realised.

In Collaboration with Nursing

In June 2002 the Dean of the Faculty of Nursing (Faculty of Nursing and Midwifery from 2005), Professor Jocalyn Lawler, wrote asking the centre to develop and teach a unit on "Indigenous Australia: History and Health" in the second year of its new degree, Bachelor of Nursing (Indigenous Australian Health).[24] The degree would also be open to non-Indigenous students. In the first instance, Kath Howey left the Koori Centre and was appointed by the Faculty of Nursing to coordinate the program, which included consultation with Yooroang Garang, the faculties of Law and Science, and local Indigenous communities. Blanchard and Thorpe wrote, coordinated and taught its Indigenous Australia: History and Health unit, both within the faculty and via video links on the Orange Campus where the block-mode course was delivered.

Lawler has provided details of the four-year qualification, which included a major in Indigenous health, history and culture, as well as specific clinical experiences in Indigenous nursing. Although the faculty was aware of a similar qualification in New Zealand, the situation in New South Wales was different. The Sydney program had access to excellent materials produced by the Congress of Aboriginal and Torres Strait Islander Nurses (CATSIN). It was also a non-exclusive degree, as Lawler explains:

> We set about developing a pattern of study for a student population that included home grown Australians, irrespective of heritage and genetic backgrounds, as well as international students who were interested in studying more broadly. The decision to make the degree open to students of all backgrounds was taken on the advice, if not at times, the insistence of the Aboriginal and Torres Strait Islander nurses who worked with us on the development team. They were adamant that there be no forms of discrimination for or against potential students on the basis of their heritage or genetic make-up.

Its Indigenous component would inform students about Indigenous history and culture and the coming of the "whitefella" and his governance and law. So past and present influences were related to current health care needs.[25] This well-constructed, exciting project was a frontrunner in curriculum design. However, shortly after the course began, to the dismay of all involved, Health Sciences announced that they would be phasing out undergraduate nursing.

On Sport

Indigenous people have a strong affinity for sportsmanship and the students at the University are no exception. From the inception of the National Indigenous Student Games (first held at Wollotuka, the University of Newcastle in 1996), the students at the University of Sydney have fielded a team. Combined winners with the University of Technology Sydney in the 2003 competition, the University of Sydney hosted the Indigenous Student Games in 2004. The games offer an opportunity to promote Aboriginal and Torres Strait Islander people and culture in a positive light and draws teams from across Australia.

Figure 66. Indigenous Women from the University team, 2006. Image courtesy of Carla McGrath.

Figure 67. University of Sydney team at the National Indigenous Tertiary Education Student Games, Brisbane, 2006. Image courtesy of Carla McGrath.

Other significant sports people over the past few years have been Paul Sinclair and Clark Webb, who played rugby league for the NSW and Australian Tertiary Side; and Ryan Bulger and Jack Manning Bancroft, who both play for the NSW Indigenous Cricket Team. Yvette Balla-Gow played for the Sydney University Women's Water Polo Club and Michelle Musselwhite, who was a member of Sydney University Flames Basketball Team, became a member of the Australian Opals in 2005 and, in the same year, National Indigenous Sportswoman. Sydney University Sports & Fitness is planning to reintroduce the Indigenous Sports Scholarship.

Internal and External Reviews

Each of the reports of the early 2000s had its own characteristics and outcomes. The Anderson Review had encouraged improvements in particular ways but was deficient in its proposed structural reforms. The Koori Centre's own Change Management Plan enhanced the internal organisational side of the Koori Centre's work, especially in regard to human resource usage, although its student support arrangements required further attention. From 2003, the Koori Centre found itself under further examination, internal and external.

i) Reviewing the Diploma and Bachelor courses

Koori Centre programs require regular updating to ensure they meet University standards. In 2003, a working party to revise the structure and content of the Diploma in Education (Aboriginal) and the Bachelor of Education (Secondary: Aboriginal Studies) was chaired by Cleverley.[26] Its tasks were to standardise course arrangements, including credit points; ensure that these standards met the teacher education requirements of the NSW DoET and the Interim NSW Institute of Teachers and to consider new subjects for inclusion/exclusion. In addition, the teaching methodology of Human Society and Its Environment was introduced in the program to widen graduates' teaching options. The revised units of study were submitted to the Board of Studies in Indigenous Studies and the Undergraduate Studies Committee (Faculty of Education and Social Work) by Smith and Thorpe in 2004, and adopted by the Academic Board.

ii) Reviews by the Academic Board and AUQA teams

Two other reviews of the Koori Centre were undertaken in line with expectations from the University and the Commonwealth government. The Academic Board reviewed the centre's operations in 2003, led by its Chairman, Professor Judyth Sachs, whose purpose was to maintain and develop high standards across the University through quality assurance and the recognition of strengths and weaknesses.[27] After interviewing staff and students within the Koori Centre, the Board team commended the Koori Centre for its successful implementation of the Change Management Plan. Its assessment observed improved coordination of the Aboriginal Studies major in Arts; ongoing research into Indigenous knowledges and pedagogy; positive feedback received from students; the recruitment of stimulating guest lecturers; outstanding resource and support facilities; and the centre's work with Indigenous communities. Main areas for improvement were also identified, including a need to formalise benchmarking arrangements with other Indigenous education centres in Australia and overseas; more staff should aim at teaching excellence awards; better use could be made of WebCT opportunities in teaching and learning; the centre should better publicise its work in literacy and pedagogy; a greater effort was needed to ensure the completion of higher degrees by staff; and student outcomes should exemplify the University's Generic Graduate Attributes. The review team also wanted the Koori Centre to seek out mentoring from staff in different faculties.

A year later, Sydney was audited by the Australian Universities Quality Agency team, with the Koori Centre supplying material for the University's Performance Portfolio.[28] AUQA's assessment was supportive of the centre's public role.

> AUQA commends the University of Sydney's Koori Centre for the strong links it has established with Indigenous communities and for the efforts it makes in recognising and promoting understanding of and respect for Indigenous Australian peoples, their knowledge and cultures.

In summary, the diploma and bachelor review updated the centre's academic housekeeping satisfactorily; and the Academic Board and AUQA statements were largely supportive of developments in hand.

In Partnership

Clearly the Koori Centre had put down strong roots, its work highly regarded by many Indigenous and non-Indigenous people on campus and outside. However, it must not stand still. It needed to forge stronger links with academic teaching and research in the faculties and with the University administration. In the early days, it was perhaps necessary to develop a strong in-house culture, however this was bought at a price and was no longer an option for the 2000s. Moving to open doors, the Koori Centre decisively welcomed staff across the University having a special interest in Indigenous education in 2006 when Sachs and Mooney established an Indigenous Education Strategic Development Working Group (IESDWG).[29] Its task was to provide advice to the Provost and Deputy Vice-Chancellor on "whole of University" initiatives, including a University action plan with outcomes monitored. In 2006, IESDWG was renamed the Indigenous Education Advisory Committee (IEAC); it now meets regularly and its operations and minutes are accessible on the University website.

At its September 2006 meeting, the IEAC agreed to investigate a single entity derived from the integration of the Koori Centre and Yooroang Garang. This new entity should provide a focus for all Indigenous activities across the University related to learning and teaching, research, student support, and community outreach.[30] After Sachs resigned, Anderson decided to pursue the idea of a new identity. During 2007 he employed Elizabeth Yashadhana who proposed a "hub and spokes" model, suggesting that the academic staff at the Koori Centre be placed in the faculties. Staff reaction was mixed. When Yashadhana left Sydney, the project stalled. After nearly 12 months of meetings and workshops uncertainty about the future began to affect staff morale. Independent rather than coordinated action was apparent in 2008 when the schools of the Faculty of Health Sciences were abolished and Yooroang Garang's academic staff moved into the Discipline of Indigenous Health Studies, with that the centre reverting to a student support role.

Still keen to proceed with a review of Indigenous education, including the idea of a single entity, Armstrong informed the IEAC meeting of 7 May 2008 that:

> I will be establishing a review panel to examine the current provision for Indigenous education and educational support services within the University. The Panel will be asked to review current policy and practice in relation to the University's specific strategies for Indigenous education.[31]

The Indigenous Education Review was held on 8–9 October, the review panel comprising Professor Michael McDaniel, Dean, Indigenous Education, University of Western Sydney; Professor Boni Robertson, Professor of Indigenous Policy, Gumurri Centre, Griffith University; and Professor Wendy Brabham, Director, The Koori Institute, Deakin University. Submissions to the review were called for faculties and interested parties throughout the University. The panel then commenced discussion with a range of senior, academic and general staff, students and community members, with a report due by the end of the year.[32] Due to the illness in the review team the review stalled but the task was completed mid-2009, and released in 2010.

Reconciliation

A highlight of the Indigenous Education Advisory Committee was the launch of the University's Reconciliation Statement on 1 June 2006 by the Vice-Chancellor Gavin Brown in the presence of Indigenous and non-Indigenous staff, students and members of the local community. The occasion was held in the Quadrangle whose central point was covered in a chalk design by Dillon Kombummerri, representative of Aboriginal and Torres Strait Islander people.

> Reconciliation Statement
>
> The University of Sydney is Australia's first university. It is committed to creating an environment in which the rich, and diverse cultures of Indigenous Australians are known, promoted, and celebrated. The University of Sydney acknowledges all of the following:
>
> *Gadigal* peoples of the *Eora* Nation; Camperdown, Darlington, Mallet Street,
>
> Newtown, Rozelle, Law School and the Conservatorium of Music;
>
> *Deerubbin* peoples Lidcombe Campus;
>
> *Tharawal* peoples Camden and Cobbitty Campuses;

Ngunnawal peoples Canberra Campus;

Wiradjuri peoples Dubbo Clinical School;

Gamilaroi peoples Moree and Narrabri Campuses;

Bundjulung peoples Lismore Campus;

Wiljali peoples Broken Hill Campus; and

Gureng Gureng peoples in the vicinity of the One Tree Island Research Station.

The first people of this land, the Australian Indigenous peoples, are the most socio-economically disadvantaged group in Australia.

The University recognises values and respects continuing Indigenous customary laws, beliefs and traditions, and the close and enduring relationship between the first peoples and their land, sea and rivers. The University is committed to the protection and support of Indigenous Australian cultural heritage, and to educating the University community about the continuing importance of this unique heritage in the lives of Australian Indigenous peoples today.

The University will actively promote reconciliation between Indigenous and non-Indigenous Australians through the following strategies and activities:

The Indigenous Education Strategy and the promotion of education for Indigenous Australian peoples at all levels in society.

The Indigenous Australians Employment Strategy.

The return of Indigenous Australians' remains held by the University to their traditional homelands.

A protocol for acknowledging traditional Indigenous custodianship of lands on which the campuses are located, as part of graduations, awards presentations and other official University ceremonies.

The incorporation of relevant Indigenous perspectives into University materials and academic programs.

Consultation and collaboration with Indigenous peoples to advance the goals of the University and Indigenous peoples.

Research with Indigenous people to promote the welfare and health of Indigenous Australians and to support and promote an understanding of Indigenous Australians' culture within the Australian community.[33]

The formal "Welcome to Country" at the launch was spoken by Charles "Chicka" Madden, a Cadigal elder. Madden applauded the University's commitment to creating an atmosphere in which the diverse cultures of Indigenous Australians are celebrated. In his formal address, Brown acknowledged past inequities and affirmed that the Reconciliation Statement marked a new beginning and an opportunity to focus on the future for Aboriginal and Torres Strait Islander peoples. He pledged the commitment of the University of Sydney to that goal.

Speaking after Brown, Phil Glendenning, Director of the Edmund Rice Centre for Social Justice and the President of Australians for Native Title and Reconciliation, emphasised the need for increased awareness and practical actions rather than lip-service to the "rhetoric of reconciliation". A passionate advocate, Glendenning shared pointed anecdotes from his world travels. His belief was that it was through the education of Australia's young people that reconciliation would occur. The proceedings concluded with a performance by the Erskineville Primary School Aboriginal Dance Group led by Terry Olsen and an invitation for all to share a lunch of Torres Strait Islander food in the MacLaurin Hall.

A positive outcome of reconciliation at Sydney University was witnessed through the launch of the Poche Centre for Indigenous Health, funded by a $10 million donation from Greg Poche. The centre will work with local and community health services to improve rural health in western NSW and the Northern Territory, conduct essential research, and educate medical and health students on Indigenous health needs. It is headed by Associate Professor Ngiare Brown, an Aboriginal doctor, and Professor Alan Cass.

Where We Stand

The Indigenous Australian population reached 517,000 in 2006, of whom 152,700, the largest number, was living in New South Wales.[34] Just over half (51 percent) of these 15- to 19-year-old Indigenous students were in school. The number holding a bachelor degree or above, six percent, was more than double the figure of ten years back. However, there is a distance to go as the ANU report, "Closing the Gaps", indicates. While the report expects the ratio of Indigenous adults with degrees or higher education to increase from 0.2 percent of adults in 2006 to 0.39 by 2041, the figure is far away from parity.[35] Also, the total number of Indigenous students studying in higher education declined in 2005, some postponing studies to take advantage of the strong labour market.

The effects of improved educational outcomes, if not spectacular, are apparent at Sydney where Indigenous students are presenting with competitive tertiary entrance results making the University an institution of choice for well prepared Indigenous people. This progress is the work of many hands. Since the late 20th century particularly, nearly 1500 identified men and women have enrolled and graduated. Our institutional achievements have mirrored the great social movements of the day. The University's first Aboriginal graduate processed in the Great Hall in the year of the Referendum of 1967. The founding of the first Aboriginal Education Centre on campus, and the decisive Mabo decision, came close together; and, around the time of the Sydney Harbour Bridge Walk, the Koori Centre took over the academic teaching of the major in Aboriginal Studies at Sydney.

Changing national attitudes towards Indigenous Reconciliation are well represented at Sydney. The Hon. Kim Santow OA, who held the position of Chancellor from 2001–07, contacted the Koori Centre on appointment asking that it provide the correct wording for Acknowledgement to Country. Thereafter all graduations at which he officiated began with an acknowledgement to the elders past and present of the Cadigal people of the Eora

Nation. The tradition has been continued by Her Excellency Professor Marie Bashir AC CVO, Governor of New South Wales, herself a strong supporter of rights for Indigenous Australians.

In 2008, the University enrolled 41 postgraduate Indigenous students and 215 undergraduates. Of the total 256, 179 were female, however female and male were equal (14 in total) in postgraduate research.[36] Another 430 non-Indigenous students were enrolled in the Koori Centre's Aboriginal Studies subjects, adding to the number of informed graduates. The total University enrolment that yeat was 47,054.

The 'green paper'[37] the University circulated in March 2010 is indicative of the influence of the Review of Indigenous Education August 2009, and of the earlier Reconciliation Statement. It affirms the seriousness with which the University now addresses Indigenous education across its campuses. The paper, a precursor to the introduction of structural reforms, argues that Indigenous understanding must penetrate University life and culture if Sydney is to be recognised, and recognise itself, as a specifically Australian university. The paper speaks eloquently of the prior rights of Indigenous students; that the University occupies Aboriginal land that was never ceded; and the fact that Indigenous people have been systematically disadvantaged and discriminated against since European settlement. Note is made of the excellent work of the Koori Centre and Indigenous and non-Indigenous academics and professional staff in supporting Indigenous students and research; and it reports that a Director of Indigenous Research Development will be appointed to build capacity in Indigenous research. The issue of the need for senior Indigenous advice to the Vice-Chancellor is accepted, as is the needs of non-Indigenous students to access Indigenous education, and the importance of a more effective engagement of local Indigenous communities. While new enrolment practices across the University are to enable a student profile more representative of the population at large. The task that the University has set itself in Indigenous education is the most comprehensive yet.

In July 2008, Dr Michael Spence, an alumnus of Sydney, returned to serve as Vice-Chancellor and Principal, with Brown stepping down from the role after 12 years. Brown's support for the Koori Centre was strong and consistent and much of Indigenous education's strength was drawn from his enthusiasm and encouragement. The centre is looking forward to its new partnership with Vice-Chancellor Spence in these challenging times. The University of Sydney is justly proud of the Indigenous people who have passed through its gates, now major contributors to an educated society from which they were once conspicuously absent. While we may celebrate how far we have travelled along the path, we recognise that there is still far to go. Here, the role of great social institutions like the University of Sydney in ensuring justice, equity, and reconciliation for Indigenous Australians represents a powerful engine for national advance.

Notes

Unless stated otherwise, all unpublished correspondence and file sources are held at the Koori Centre, The University of Sydney.

Foreword

[1] Janson 2000, pp. 4–5.

Chapter 1 – Setting the Scene

[1] Janson 2000, p. 5.

[2] L. Burney, Member for Canterbury, *Inaugural Speeches, NSW Legislative Assembly Hansard. Article 35 of 6.5.2003*, p. 39; N. Barrowclough, The Fire in Linda Burney, *Good Weekend*, 16.12.2006, p. 25; and A. Phelan, Breaking the Political Mould, *Sunday Telegraph*, 29.9.2002, p. 48.

[3] Quoted, A. Phelan, *Sunday Telegraph*, 29.9.2002, p. 48.

[4] N. Triantafillou, An Historic Victory, *Inner Western Suburbs Courier*, 24.3.2003, p. 4.

[5] Janson 2000, pp. 4–5.

[6] W. Brady, Sydney University Sacred Site, *Union Recorder*, 25.2.1998, vol. 78, no. 1, p. 9; and P. Quiddington, The Lost Tribes of Sydney, *Duran-Duran (D-D)*, May 1989, pp. 6–13.

[7] Barff 1902, p. 78.

[8] Dr D. Foley to J.F. Cleverley, Oral History, email, 14.6.2005.

[9] Turney, Byott and Chippendale 1991, p. 113.

[10] B. Luscombe, Aborigines Lay Claim to Uni, *Daily Telegraph*, 26.7.1990; and *UN*, 22/24, 31.7.90, p. 187.

[11] Statement of Claim from the Aboriginal Embassy in Ownership and Occupation of Victoria Park, flyer, City of Sydney, 2000.

[12] Cleverley 1971, p. 24.

[13] Wentworth (1979 [1919]), p.4.

[14] Wentworth (1979 [1919]), pp.115–16.

[15] Wentworth 1823, p.27.

[16] Barff 1902, p. 28.

[17] Dallen, *The University of Sydney*, p. 49.

[18] Cleverley 1971, pp. 102–03.

[19] See Brook and Kohen 1991.

[20] Board of National Education files, 1848–66, quoted in Fletcher 1989a, p. 38.

[21] Quoted, Fletcher 1989b, p. 52.

[22] Burney et al. 1982, p. 3.

[23] See J. Ramsland, The Aboriginal School at Purfleet, 1903–1965: A Case Study of the Segregation of Aboriginal Children in New South Wales, Australia, *History of Education Review*, vol. 35, no. 1, 2006, pp. 47–57.

[24] Quoted, Fletcher 1989b, p. 55.

[25] Berg 2003, p. 6.

[26] SRSCLAA, Part II, L.F. Bostock, 27.10.80, p. 657.

[27] J. Mooney to J. Cleverley, 29.12.2007.

[28] RJCLCLAA, Part II, L. Smith, 4.8.66, p. 518.

[29] Fletcher 1989a, pp. 231–32.

[30] SRSCLAA, Part I, Racism and Education, p. 175.

[31] RJCLCLAA, Part II, V.J. Truskett, 6.4.66, p. 94.

[32] RJCLCLAA, Part II, Truskett, 6.4.66, p. 93.

[33] D-D, M. Gillon, February 1972, p. 18.

[34] Janson 2000, p. 18.

[35] King and Stack 1990, p. 33.

[36] Quoted, Doukakis 2006, pp. 111–24.

[37] SRSCLAA, Part I, p. 180.

[38] RJCLCLAA, Part II, Minutes of Evidence, 13.9.67, Entry List, tabled 22.6.66, p. 405.

[39] SRSCLAA, Part I, p. 180.

[40] NISATSICF 1997, p. 36.

[41] Quoted, BBC News On Line, 9.8.07, bbc.co.uk.

[42] Smith, K. 1992, p. 148.

[43] SRSCLAA, Part II, A.T. Duncan, Aboriginal Education 1880–1980, 11.12.80, p. 812.

[44] Quoted in K. Carr, Replicate Success and Don't Dwell on Failure, *Education*, New South Wales Teachers Federation, 28.5.07, p. 31.

[45] RJCLCLAA, Part II, W.R. Geddes, 19.9.66, p. 564.

[46] Porteus 1937, p. 6.

[47] Porteus and Babcock 1926, p. 144.

[48] RJCLCLAA, Part II, Geddes, 19.9.66, p. 564.

[49] Berg 2003, p. 11.

50 SRSCLAA, Part II, Duncan, 11.12.80, p. 813.

51 RJCLCLAA, Part II, Truskett, 6.4.66, p. 99.

52 See SRSCLAA, Part II, W. Rose, 1.12.80, p. 682.

53 See Davies 2002.

54 www.usyd.edu.au/museums/collections/repatriation.shtml.

55 See Williams 1988.

56 RJCLCLAA, Part II, J.H. Buck, 5.4.66, p. 77.

57 *Record of the Jubilee Celebrations of the University of Sydney*, W. Brooks, Sydney, 1903, p. 116.

58 J. Frazer, on W.B. Spencer, *The Australian Encyclopaedia*, vol. 8, Grolier Society, Sydney, 1962, p. 231.

59 Quoted, R. Kelley, *D-D*, July/August, 1970, p. 19.

60 Branagan 2005, pp. 249, 252–53.

61 Quoted, R.A. Dart, in Elkin and Mackintosh 1974, p. 33.

62 Quoted, S. Smith, in Johnson 2000, p. 122.

63 W.F. Connell et al. 1995, p. 308.

64 Quoted, P. Turnbull, in Johnson 2000, p. 125.

65 Strange and Bashford 2008, pp. 104, 110.

66 Quoted, Strange and Bashford 2008 p. 164.

67 O.H.K. Spate, Journeyman Taylor: Some Aspects of His Work, *The Australian Geographer*, vol. 12, no. 2, 1972, pp. 115–32.

68 Quoted, Strange and Bashford 2008, p. 9.

69 Branagan 2005, p. 340.

70 A.P. Elkin, The Emergence of Psychology, Anthropology and Education, in Faculty of Arts 1952, pp. 36–40.

71 Quoted, J. Cleverley, Schooling in Papua New Guinea in Campbell and Sherington 2007, p. 210.

72 Long 1992, p. 4.

73 A.R. Radcliffe-Brown, Editorial, *Oceania*, vol. 1, no. 1, April 1930, p. 3.

74 Australia's Native Problems, *Honi Soit*, vol. 4, no. 26, 5.10.1932, p. 6.

75 Quoted, Faculty of Arts 1952, p. 38.

76 Commonwealth of Australia 1933, p. 14.

77 See Wise 1985.

78 RJCLCLAA, Part II, A.P. Elkin, 20.3.67, pp. 691, 693, 692.

79 RJCLCLAA, Part II, M. Sawtell, 31.10.66, p. 588.

80 Wise 1985, p. 221.

[81] *D-D*, Vale, D. Koller, August 1979, p. 5.

[82] Quoted, Faculty of Arts 1952, p. 30.

[83] Quoted, The Koori History Timeline, www.kooriweb.org/foley/timeline/histimeline.html.

[84] RJCLCLAA, Part II, Elkin, 20.3.67, p. 693.

[85] Quoted, Wise 1985, p. 231.

[86] Goodall 1996, pp. 196, 158–59, and footnote, and *D-D*, H. Goodall, reprinted, *SMH*, 6.8.83, November 1984, p. 12, and objection, *D-D*, G. Young, The Australian Aborigines, May 1985, p. 3.

[87] *UN*, 17/23, 20.8.85, Biography of A.P. Elkin: Man of Contradictions, SC., p. 179.

[88] Quoted, Wise, from an address, 1978, p. 246.

[89] *D-D*, Vale, D. Koller, August 1979, p. 5.

[90] Senate Minutes, 7.4.41, pp. 165–66.

[91] Senate Minutes, 5.5.41, pp. 187–88.

[92] Quoted, Kelley, *D-D*, July/August, 1970, p. 19.

Chapter 2 – Generational Change

[1] RJCLCLAA, Part II, Elkin, 20.3.67, p. 700.

[2] Quoted, L. Smith, in B. Lane, History's Lost Aborigines Emerge, *The Australian*, 5.7.2006, p. 33.

[3] SRSCLAA, Part I, Aboriginal Employment Levels and Economic Status, pp. 242, 246.

[4] E. Willmot, The Child and the System, *D-D*, February 1976, p. (i).

[5] RJCLCLAA, Part II, Elkin, 20.3.67, p. 695.

[6] RJCLCLAA, Part II, A.G. Kingsmill, 2.2.66, pp. 6, 7.

[7] Quoted, Clark 2001, p.1.

[8] *Dawn*, and *New Dawn*, August 1953, February 1957, September 1961, May 1970; Consultative Committee on Aboriginal Education and Department of Adult Education, File, 1965; and, *D-D*, February 1972, pp.17–18.

[9] SRCLAA, Part II, Duncan, 11.12.80, p. 813.

[10] *D-D*, February 1975, p. 6a.

[11] RJCLCLAA, Part II, H.C.M. King, 13.3.1967, pp. 673, 675.

[12] SRSCLAA, Part II, K.R. Campbell, 1.12.80, p. 701.

[13] SRSCLAA, Part I, Post-Secondary Education, p. 231.

[14] C. Perkins interviewed by R. Hughes 5.5.1988, Charles Perkins: Tape 1, Australian Biography, www.australianbiography.gov.au/subjects/perkins

[15] Two Aborigine Students Qualify for University in History-Making Year, *Dawn*, February 1963, p. 4.

[16] Perkins 1975, p. 29.

[17] RJCLCLAA, Part II, Perkins, 2.6.66, p. 272.

[18] Perkins 1975, p. 29.

[19] Perkins 1975, p. 29.

[20] www.usyd.edu.au/senate/committees/advisoryPerkins.shtml.

[21] Read 1990, pp. 71–72.

[22] Quoted Read, in Plater 2005, p. 9.

[23] C. Perkins, They are not going to grind me in the dirt, *New Dawn*, June 1974, vol. 5, no. 1, p. 5.

[24] Plater 2005, p. 10.

[25] Perkins, They are not going to grind me in the dirt, p. 6.

[26] RJCLCLAA, Part II, Perkins, 2.6.66, pp. 273, 280.

[27] Quoted in S. Ainger, Soccer Star to Arts Champion, *The University of Sydney Gazette*, vol. 21, no. 3, December, 1993, p. 6.

[28] Consultative Committee on Aboriginal Education and Department of Adult Education, File, 1964–1969, University of Sydney Archives.

[29] Clark 2001.

[30] Curthoys 2002, p. 39.

[31] L. Craddock, to Cleverley, 10.6.06.

[32] Quoted, *The Sunday Mirror*, 21 February 1965, in Fletcher 1989b, p. 247.

[33] Quoted, Berg 2003, pp. 8, 9.

[34] Quoted, *The Sunday Mirror*, 28.2.65, Curthoys 2002, p. 222.

[35] V.S.N., 21.2.65, quoted in Fletcher 1989b, p. 249.

[36] RJCLCLAA, Part II, Perkins, 2.6.66, p. 281.

[37] *Freedom Ride* (Curthoys 2002) Launch Details, Flyer.

[38] RJCLCLAA, Part II, Perkins, 12.7.66, pp. 426, 442.

[39] C. Perkins interviewed by R. Hughes 6.5.1988, Charles Perkins: Tape 1, Australian Biography, www.australianbiography.gov.au/subjects/perkins.

[40] C. Sant et al., Concerned Students Koori Centre to R. Martin (from *A Current Affair*, Nine Network), 1.8.96, Koori Centre.

[41] R. Martin, Note to Koori Centre, 15.8.96, Koori Centre.

[42] Plater 2005, p. 11.

[43] Quoted, (2000), Graduates, Dr Charles Nelson Perrurie Perkins OA, www.usyd.edu.au/fstudent/indigenous/exp/graduates.

[44] Janson 2000, pp. 1–2.

[45] Berg 2003, p. 8.

[46] Read 1990, p. 82.

47 RJCLCLAA, Part II, D.R. Moore, 15.8.66, pp. 530–31.

48 Quoted, G. Briscoe, in Read 1990, p. 121.

49 RJCLCLAA, Part II, Geddes, 14.11.66, p. 608.

50 RJCLCLAA, Part II, Geddes, 19.9.66, p. 563.

51 Introducing Pemulwuy College, flyer, Koori Centre.

52 Aboriginal Huntsman: Arnhem Wildlife at Risk, *UN*, vol. 8, no. 12, 14.6.76, pp. 89, 90, 93.

53 *UN*, vol. 8, no. 14, L.R. Hiatt, Letter, 28.6.76, p. 106.

54 G. Gifford, No Way for a Nice Girl to Behave, *SMH*, 14.3.1977, p. 7.

55 Aboriginal Outstations and the Davenport Report, *The National Times*, 27.6 to 2.7.77, p. 22.

56 M. Davenport, True Tales of Modern Tribalism, *The National Times*, 6.6–11.6.1977, p. 7.

57 L. Hiatt, The Outstations Controversy, *UN*, vol. 9, no. 14, 27.6.77, pp. 107, 110.

58 *D-D*, August 1977, p. 3.

59 M. Duffy, No More Empty Rhetoric Please, *SMH*, 20–21.5.2006, p. 33.

60 N. Pearson, 'Homes Built on Despair', *The Weekend Australian*, 5–6.1.2008, p. 21.

61 *Honi Soit*, vol. 4, no. 14, p. 1.

62 *D-D*, February 1973, p. 15.

63 J. Woolley in Turney, Bygott and Chippendale 1991, p. 3.

64 A. Welch, Aboriginal Education as Internal Colonialism the Schooling of an Indigenous Minority in Australia, *Comparative Education*, vol. 24, no. 2, 1988, pp. 203–15.

65 *UN*, vol. 8, no. 23, 27.9.1976, p. 186.

66 *UN*, vol. 15, no. 11, AVCC Report, 7.6.83, p. 94.

67 *UN*, vol. 16, no. 36, 18.12.84, p. 314.

68 *UN*, vol. 17, no. 19, Comment, J. Ward, 16.7.85, p. 146.

69 *UN*, vol. 17, no. 10, 23.4.85, p. 78.

70 Memo to sub-committee to consider a special admissions scheme in the Faculty of Arts for Aboriginal students, report, D.B. Smart, Acting Registrar, 21.7.87.

71 Joint Senate/Academic Board Committee on Admission Policy, Interim Report of the Working Party on Aboriginal Education, 1988.

72 R.J.R. King and R. Stack, Recommendations for Educational Equity for Aboriginal People at the University of Sydney, Aboriginal Education Centre, 1991, pp. v., *passim*, unpublished, Koori Centre.

73 M. Willsher, Report on the Accommodation Needs of Aboriginal Students at the University of Sydney, Aboriginal Education Centre, May 1991, Section 3-2, 4-2, unpublished, Koori Centre.

74 *UN*, vol. 17, no. 16, Pioneer Scheme to Aid Top Disadvantaged Students, 25.6.85, pp. 121, 127.

75 *UN*, vol. 18, no. 12, 20.5.86, p. 95.

⁷⁶ *UN*, vol. 18, no. 12, Succeed Scheme Kicks Off with 24 Students, 20.5.86, p. 95.

⁷⁷ K. Jennings to R. Winder 25.11.86, Broadway Scheme File, University of Sydney Archives.

⁷⁸ A. Jones, Media Monitors NJP L/P, 2UE, 15.6.87. Subject: Criticism of the Entrance of Disadvantaged Students to Sydney University.

⁷⁹ A. Susskind, New Quota Squeezes University Vacancies, *SMH*, 20.6.87.

⁸⁰ *SMH*, 16.6.87.

⁸¹ Gye to Ward, 1.4.1987.

⁸² Classification, Broadway Scheme, 1990, University of Sydney Archives.

⁸³ Review Committee, Broadway Scheme, Implementation, 24.5.90, Associate Professor J Mack, Acting Chair; see also *UN*, vol. 22, no. 24, 31.7.1990. pp. 186, 192, and, Vice-Chancellor's Report to Senate, Part II, 6.10.87, p. 1883.

⁸⁴ Decision of Academic Board, 14.3.2001, Broadway Special Admissions Program.

⁸⁵ *UN*, vol. 21, no. 1, 21.2.89, p. 6.

⁸⁶ Indigenous Australians Employment Strategy, Staff and Students Equal Opportunity Unit, University of Sydney, 2003, p. 10, University of Sydney Archives.

⁸⁷ Report of the Working Party of the Deputy Vice-Chancellor's Committee to Consider a Reference From the Academic Board and the Senate on Equal Opportunity in Education, 27.10.88, p. 1083, University of Sydney Archives.

⁸⁸ C. Glass, EEO Coordinator (Acting), to Associate Professor M.B. Clunies Ross 12.7.88, Attachment, Submission on the Issue of Equal Opportunity in Education at Sydney University, pp. 1–7, University of Sydney Archives.

⁸⁹ King to Clunies Ross, 21.7.88, Attachment, Equal Opportunity in Education, Submission, July 1988, University of Sydney Archives.

⁹⁰ Report of the Working Party of the Deputy-Vice-Chancellor to Consider a Reference From the Academic Board and the Senate on Equal Opportunity in Education, 27.10.88, pp. 1084, 1077–84.

⁹¹ Quoted in G. Hawks, Designed for Living, *The Gazette*, editor in chief, Susanne Ainger, vol. 21, no. 3, December, 1993, p. 6.

⁹² Ian Pedrisat to Raymond King, and email to John Cleverley, 22.1.09.

⁹³ A Brief Account of the Work of the University of Sydney in Aboriginal Education 1989, King to S.E. Dorsch, 5.9.89, Attachment.

⁹⁴ Vice-Chancellor's Report to Senate, Part II, 6.10.87, p. 1883.

Chapter 3 – Aboriginal Education and the Department of Adult Education

¹ A. Duncan, Talk to the AEC, August 1969, *AEC Newsletter*, November, 1969.

² Elkin, in Faculty of Arts 1952, p. 35.

³ *Dawn*, vol. 12, no. 1, January 1963, p. 10.

[4] RJCLCLAA, Part II, Elkin, 20.3.67, p. 700.

[5] RJCLCLAA, Part II, Elkin, 20.3.67, p. 700.

[6] RJCLCLAA, Part II, AWB Statement, 2.2.66, p. 7.

[7] Quoted, Duncan in Janson 2000, p. 6.

[8] RJCLCLAA, Part II, Duncan, 31.5.66, p. 258.

[9] Fletcher 1989a, p. 87.

[10] Quoted, Fletcher 1989b, p. 112.

[11] SRSCLAA, Part II, Duncan, 11.12.80, p. 814.

[12] RJCLCLAA, Part II, Duncan, 31.5.66, p. 258.

[13] DAEAR 1965, p. 27.

[14] Consultative Committee on Aboriginal Education News Letter, February 1969, Koori Centre.

[15] RJCLCLAA, Part II, Elkin, 20.3.67, p. 700.

[16] RJCLCLAA, Part II, Truskett, 6.4.66, p. 94.

[17] RJCLCLAA, Part II, Duncan, 31.5.66, p. 259.

[18] JOBS Project, Report of the Advisory Committee, 10.12.1970.

[19] JOBS Project, Report of the Advisory Committee, 10.12.1970.

[20] Consultative Committe on Aboriginal Education, *Submission to the Joint Committee of the Legislative Council and Legislative Assembly upon Aborigines Welfare, March 1966*, University of Sydney, 1966, p. 25.

[21] RJCLCLAA, Part II, Duncan, 31.5.66, p. 260.

[22] RJCLCLAA, Part I, Report and Minutes, 13.9.67, p. 8.

[23] RJLCLAA, Part II, C.J. Earl to G.G. Phelan, 5.12.66, p. 641.

[24] RJCLCLAA, Part II, Evidence, A. Mills, 6.4.67, p. 724.

[25] Consultative Committee on Aboriginal Education (Draft), 5.8.64, University of Sydney Archives.

[26] Berg 2003, p. 18.

[27] *New Dawn*, vol. 3, no. 10, March 1973, p. 13.

[28] Berg 2003, p. 20.

[29] Duncan Interview in Janson 2000, p. 8.

[30] Berg 2003, p. 8.

[31] The Aboriginal Story Data Base for Posterity, *D-D*, February 1987, p. 3, and *D-D*, May 1987, Vale, pp. 2–4.

[32] RJCLCLAA, Part II, A. Grey, 20.3.67, p. 679.

[33] *D-D*, c.1970.

[34] B. Ross, Aboriginal Views on the "Report on the New South Wales Bernard Van Leer

Project: Aboriginal Family Education Centres", Department of Adult Education, 1974, p. 15, unpublished, University of Sydney Archives.

[35] DAEAR, 1970, p. 31.

[36] DAEAR, 1972, p.35.

[37] A. Grey, Annual Report 1973, Department of Adult Education, p. 37, University of Sydney Archives.

[38] Grey 1974, p. 357.

[39] A. Grey, Annual Report 1973, p. 37.

[40] Grey 1974, pp. 351–68.

[41] Grey 1974, p. 395.

[42] *D-D*, February 1976, L. Johnson, Education, Education Without Disadvantage Conference, 23.11.75, pp. iv-v.

[43] More 1978, p. 4.

[44] *D-D*, July/August 1970, Quick News Flashes from Students, p. 13.

[45] *D-D*, The Weilmoringle Report and Report 1971, December 1972, pp. 8–13.

[46] *New Dawn*, Weilmoringle a Possible Model, vol.4, no. 2, July 1973, p. 13.

[47] *D-D*, The Weilmoringle Report 1971, December 1972, pp. 8 and 9–13, and P. Dargin, Innovatory Programs at Weilmoringle, in Coppell 1976, p. 83.

[48] *D-D*, December 1972, Report 1971, p. 11.

[49] Quoted, *New Dawn*, vol. 4, no. 2, July 1973, p. 33.

[50] Berg 2003, p. 21.

[51] *D-D*, February 1975, p. 3.

[52] *D-D*, April 1976, Dargin to Secretary, 3.12.75, pp. 5, 4–6.

[53] *D-D*, April 1976, Dargin to Secretary AEC, 3.12.75, pp. 6, 5.

[54] *D-D*, February 1975, Compensatory Education.

[55] *D-D*, April 1976, p. 5.

[56] Craddock, Aboriginal Education in Walgett in the 1970s, A Golden Age Stillborn, 10.5.2004, and attached comments, unpublished, courtesy of the author.

[57] Janson 2000, p. 25.

[58] Duncan, Historical Background, in S. Ball, D. Davison and S. Wale, An Evaluation of the University of Sydney Aboriginal Teacher Aide Training Program, draft, incomplete, c. October 1986.

[59] Craddock, Aboriginal Education in Walgett in the 1970s, and Janson 2000, p.25.

[60] Kirton 1989, p. 19.

[61] W. Rose, The Employment of Aboriginal Teachers Aides in N.S.W. and the Evolution of the Roles and Issues, Curriculum Document, AEAP, 1.10.87, pp. 4–5. Koori Centre.

[62] *D-D*, February 1978, p. 1.

[63] *D-D*, October 1973, Draper to Duncan, n.d., p. 22.

[64] *D-D*, March 1973, pp. 24–25, February 1972, pp.16–17, and, DAEAR 1978.

[65] *D-D*, Draper to Duncan, October 1973, pp. 21–22.

[66] Rose, AEAP, p 5, Koori Centre.

[67] *D-D*, February 1979, p. 20.

[68] More 1978, p. 19.

[69] More 1978, p. 17.

[70] E. Crawford, as told to C. Walsh, *Over My Tracks*, Penguin Books, Ringwood, 1993, pp. 254, 270, 272–73, 278.

[71] SRSCLAA, Part II, Grace Coe, 10.4.1980, p. 352.

[72] SRSCLAA, Part II, Survey of Aboriginal Staff in Departments, p. 638.

[73] W. Rose, "The Education of Aboriginal Children", at Education Without Disadvantage Conference, 23.11.75, *D-D*, February 1976, pp. i-iv.

[74] Janson 2000, p. 9.

[75] Duncan 1980.

[76] Crowley, Foreword, Aboriginal Teaching Assistants Program, Background Information and Budget Submission, 1982, Department of Adult Education.

Chapter 4 – ATA Training Underway

[1] Willmot, E., Aboriginal Teaching Aides, in Coppell 1976, p. 100.

[2] DAEAR 1972, p. 33.

[3] *D-D*, February 1975, p. 16.

[4] DAEAR 1972, p. 33.

[5] Quoted, Berg 2003, p. 23.

[6] *New Dawn*, Taking the First Step, July 1995, vol. 5, no. 3, p. 6.

[7] DAEAR 1975, p. 5.

[8] *D-D*, Some Impressions of the Aboriginal Teaching Assistants Course Extracts from and Assignment Done by Avis Ivanoff, One of the Student "Pioneers of 1975", August 1975, p. 3.

[9] *D-D*, February 1976, M. Valadian, Education for Aborigines, p. iv.

[10] *D-D*, November 1977, What Makes Me an Aboriginal, pp. 14, 17–19.

[11] Janson 2000, p. 10.

[12] More 1978, pp. 24–26.

[13] Janson 2000, p. 11.

[14] Interview in Kirton 1989, p. 97.

[15] Interview in Kirton 1989, p. 103.

[16] Aboriginal Teacher's Assistants Training Program, 1984, AEAP, p. 20, Koori Centre.

[17] Guidelines for School Visits, ATATP, March, 1979, p. 2, Koori Centre.

[18] Returns from Schools.

[19] Interview in Kirton 1989, p. 140.

[20] *D-D*, December 1975, p. 2, and February 1976, p. 7

[21] *D-D*, December 1975, p. 2.

[22] Quoted, Janson 2000, p. 9.

[23] *D-D*, November 1974, p. 14.

[24] *D-D*, February 1976, p. ii.

[25] *D-D*, February 1977, p. 2.

[26] *D-D*, April 1976, p. 2.

[27] *D-D*, February 1978, p. 3.

[28] *D-D*, February 1978, p. 4.

[29] SRSCLCAA, Part II, Post-Secondary Education, p. 233.

[30] Interview in Kirton 1989, pp. 122–23.

[31] *D-D*, Compensatory Education Committee, April 1974, p. 7.

[32] *D-D*, February 1975, p. 3.

[33] Quoted, D. Graham, *D-D*, February 1976, p. 1.

[34] SRSCLAA, Part II, Anti-Discrimination Board Submission, p. 707.

[35] *D-D*, November 1977, p. 22.

[36] Ian Viner to Sec. of Aboriginal Education Council, 30.7.76, *D-D*, October 1976, pp. 1–2.

[37] More Evaluation File, B. Kennedy, attached, and correspondence, C. Grant to Duncan, 2.11.77, and, D.H. Penny to Registrar, 5.5.78, University of Sydney Archives.

[38] *D-D*, August 1977, pp. 15, 13–14; and, see More 1978, p. 13.

[39] I.D. in King and Stack 1990, pp. 18–19.

[40] B.C. in King and Stack 1990, p. 11.

[41] Janson 2000, p. 3.

[42] Aboriginal Teacher's Assistants Training Program, 1984, AEAP, p. 17, Koori Centre.

[43] *D-D*, February, 1979, p. 3.

[44] Aboriginal Teacher's Assistants Training Program, 1984, AEAP, p. 22, Koori Centre.

[45] RSCLAA, Part II, L.J. Riley, 7.3.79, pp. 110–11.

[46] RSCLAA, Part II, S.W. Williams, 7.3.79, p. 103.

[47] SRSCLAA, Part II, O. Brown, 1.12.80, p. 696.

[48] SRSCLAA, Part II, P.J. Koenman, 1.12.80, p. 699.

[49] SRSCLAA, Part II, Submission, P. Landa, 1.12.80, p. 680.

[50] SRSCLAA, Part II, J. Lester, 1.12.80, p. 688.

[51] More 1978, p. 44.

[52] SRSCLAA, Part II, Submission, Catholic Commission Future and Peace, 25.6.79, p. 189.

[53] SRSCLAA, Part II, Aboriginal Education in New South Wales, NSW Teachers Federation, 4.12.1980, p. 735.

[54] Janson 2000, p. 26

[55] *D-D*, October 1976, J.J. Skelton, p. 1.

[56] *D-D*, June 1976, pp. 1, 5.

[57] *D-D*, August 1977, p. 4.

[58] SRSCLAA, Part I, p. 233.

[59] K. Mundine to Viner, 2.2.78, *D-D*, February 1978, p. 17.

[60] *D-D*, November 1980, p. 29.

[61] *D-D*, February 1979, pp. 1–4.

[62] Teaching Course in Jeopardy, *SMH*, October 17, 1978.

[63] Graduation Address 1979, and file, Koori Centre.

[64] Interview in Kirton 1989, p.126.

[65] BAER 1979, p. 21.

[66] Graduation Address 1979, Koori Centre.

[67] Report of Department of Adult Education to Board of Adult Education (RBAE), 6.3.81, p. 377, University of Sydney Archives.

[68] File note, M. Tierney re. John Lester, and 1980 Graduation Ceremony file, Koori Centre.

[69] 1980 Graduation Ceremony, file, Koori Centre.

[70] Awards Given to ATAs during the Years 1975 to 1983 Inclusive, Aboriginal Teaching Assistants Training Program, 1984, unpublished p. 18, Koori Centre.

[71] BAEAR 1980, p. 22, and 1981, p. 22, University of Sydney Archives.

[72] More 1978, pp. 74, 14.

[73] Duncan to S. Albert, 9.5.78.

[74] E. Oakman to Duncan, 31.5.78.

[75] *Review*, Department of Aboriginal Affairs, Research Section Newsletter, 1979, Koori Centre.

Chapter 5 – Aboriginal Engagement

[1] Report of Department of Adult Education to Board of Adult Education, 6.3.1981, p. 377, University of Sydney Archives.

[1] More 1978, p. 73.

[3] Janson 2000, p. 7.

[4] From Student to Teacher, *New Dawn*, vol. 4, no. 1, June 1973, p. 5.

[5] Messih to Duncan, 25.7.83.

[6] Interview in Kirton 1989, p. 132.

[7] B. Thorne, ATATP Course Summaries Second Session Basic Course 1982, English and Communications, distributed, 14.4.82, Koori Centre.

[8] Interview in Kirton 1989, p. 77.

[9] Interview in Kirton 1989, p. iii.

[10] Quoted, S.C., Aboriginal Teaching Assistants Graduate, *UN*, vol. 13, no. 31, 1.12.1981, p. 263.

[11] Graduation file, 1981, Koori Centre.

[12] Quoted, Broken Borders Part 1, *Message Stick*, ABC TV, 7.7.06, www.abc.net.au/tv/messagestick/stories/s1677180.htm.

[13] *D-D*, November 1982, p. 20.

[14] D. Nicholl, Speech, 2.12.81, Graduation file, 1981, Koori Centre.

[15] SRSCLAA, Part II. B.J. Murphy, 4.12.80, p. 742.

[16] RJCLCLAA, Part II, H.J. Penrith, 26.9.66, p. 583.

[17] RSCLAA, Part II, H.J. Penrith, 31.10.79, p. 278.

[18] Heiss and Minter 2008, p.124.

[19] Interview in Kirton 1989, p. 83.

[20] Craddock to Cleverley, 30.11.06.

[21] SRSCLAA, Part II, Duncan, 11.12.80, p. 818.

[22] ATATP Training Program, 1984, unpublished, pp. 8–9, Koori Centre.

[23] Janson 2000, pp. 10, 11.

[24] Interview in Kirton 1989, p. 102.

[25] Inteview in Kirton 1989, p. 111.

[26] *D-D*, May 1978, p. 23.

[27] Janson 2000, p. 9.

[28] Crowley to Swan, 18.5.81.

[29] The Results of the Training Program Enrolments: Government Schools, Non-Government Schools, Total Enrolments, Koori Centre.

[30] Department of Adult Education to Board of Adult Education, 12.6.81, Koori Centre.

[31] RBAE, 4.9.81.

[32] Swan to Duncan, 7.1.83, and, Thorne to Swan, 14.2.83.

[33] Berg 2003, p. 25.

[34] Minutes of Advisory Council [Adult Education] and Management Committee 2.3.83, 6.7.83, 9.8.83, 11.8.83, 31.9.83; Some relevant points or comments made during meeting of ATATP; Thorne to Swan, 14.2.83; Thorne to Duncan, 15.7.83; Duncan to Ramsay, 9.8.83; Thorne to Ward, 29.8.83; Ward to Swan 8.11.83; Department of Adult Education to Board of Adult Education, 22.7.83, Koori Centre.

[35] Thorne to Ward, 29.8.83, and Thorne, Ramsay and Sutton to Duncan, 15.7.83.

[36] Duncan to Ward, 21.12.83.

[37] Holding to Cavelier, 20.8.85.

[38] Thorne to Swan, 11.9.83.

[39] M. Ramsay, Evaluation Committee, 20.12.83, and, 27.1.84, Koori Centre.

[40] Duncan to Ward, 21.12.83, and 18.1.84.

[41] Ward to Duncan, 10.1.84.

[42] Swan to Ward, 7.12.83.

[43] See, BAEAR, 1982, University of Sydney Archives and Graduation file, 1982, Koori Centre.

[44] Perkins to Messih, Telegram, 11.11.83.

[45] *UN*, vol. 15, no. 32, ATAs Graduate, 6.12.83, p. 270.

[46] Graduation Address, 23.11.83, Koori Centre.

[47] See, BAEAR, 1982, University of Sydney Archives.

[48] SRSCLAA, Part II, Duncan, 11.12.80, p. 818.

[49] Janson 2000, p. 5.

[50] J.M. Ward, 25.11.81, p. 2, and, BAER, 1981, pp. 6–7, University of Sydney Archives.

[51] *D-D*, November, 1982, General Meeting, 24.8.82, p. 24.

[52] The Future of the Department of Adult Education, Associate Professor I. Jack (chair), A. Duncan, J. Simons, November 1983, p. 6, University of Sydney Archives.

[53] Duncan, Response to the Report of the Committee, c. December 1983.

[54] Duncan to Ward, 18.1.84.

[55] More to Crowley, February 1978, in More 1978.

Chapter 6 – In Partnership with Education

[1] C. Glass, EEO Coordinator (Acting), to Clunies Ross 12.7.88, Attachment, Submission on the Issue of EOE, pp. 4–5.

[2] Interview in Kirton 1989, p. 123.

[3] Interview in Kirton 1989, p. 125.

[4] Turney n.d., p. 2.

[5] Turney, Sinclair and Cairns 1980, p. 120.

[6] Turney 1996, p. 149.

[7] J.F. Cleverley, The Evolution of Aboriginal Education, *University of Sydney Gazette*, 1993, p. 4.

[8] Advisory Committee (AC), 5.8.86, Koori Centre.

[9] Duncan to Ward, 11.3.85, Enclosure, Aboriginal studies at the University of Sydney.

[10] Dunston, file note, 20.4.85, and, Ward, file note, 22.4.85, Koori Centre.

[11] Interview in Kirton 1989, p. 145.

[12] Berg 2003, p. 14.

[13] Quoted, J. Woodberry, in Kirton 1989, p. 110.

[14] Thorne to Cleverley, 24.6.85.

[15] AC, 5.7.84, attachment, Koori Centre.

[16] Thorne to Woodberry, 25.7.84.

[17] R. Morgan, Aboriginal Teaching Assistants Training Program, Administration Structure and Procedures, 1984, pp. 2–3, Koori Centre.

[18] Turney n.d., p. 3.

[19] H. Trinca, *The Australian*, 8.2.85, p. 14.

[20] Turney n.d., p. 2.

[21] Interview in Kirton 1989, p. 89.

[22] Quoted in *Pemulwuy, Newsletter of the NSW AECG Inc.*, December 2005, p. 7.

[23] AC, 24.5.85, Koori Centre.

[24] Turney n.d., p. 3.

[25] Interview in Kirton 1989, p. 76.

[26] Interview in Kirton 1989, p. 146.

[27] M. Daley, MLA, Death of "Aunty" Joyce Alice Woodberry, 18.10.2005, Private Member's Statement, Condolence, NSW Parliament, Hansard, Item 38, p. 18795.

[28] Interview in Kirton 1989, p. 128.

[29] Interview in Kirton 1989, p. 127.

[30] AC, 12.12.86, Koori Centre.

[31] AC, 1.4.87, Koori Centre.

[32] Interview in Kirton 1989, pp. 141, 96, 131.

[33] Cleverley to J. Mooney, 28.11.2007.

[34] S. Ball to Cleverley 11.9.85, and, AC, 4.4.86, Koori Centre.

[35] S.Ball, Evaluation of the University of Sydney Aboriginal Teacher Aide Training Program, incomplete, unpublished, c. October 1986, and AC, 3.3.89, Koori Centre.

[36] ibid, n.p.

[37] ibid, n.p.

[38] R. Daly, ATATP Field Trip Report of Central and Far Western NSW, 25.8.86, AEATP, 1986, Koori Centre.

[39] AC, 24.5.85, Koori Centre.

[40] AC, 24.5.85, Koori Centre.

[41] Thorne to Cleverley, 24.6.85.

[42] AC, 6.8.85, Koori Centre.

[43] Cleverley to R. Winder, 12.9.85.

[44] D-D, Aboriginal Teaching Assistants, May 1986, pp. 19–20.

[45] AEA Handbook, NSW Department of School Education, unpublished, n.p., September, 1990, Koori Centre.

[46] AC, 5.7.84, Koori Centre.

[47] Interview in Kirton 1989, p. 83.

[48] Interview in Kirton 1989, p. 102.

[49] Interview in Kirton 1989, p. 106.

[50] Interview in Kirton 1989, p. 107.

[51] Schnierer to Daly, 4.2.87.

[52] *UN*, vol. 17, no. 15, 3.12.85, p. 279.

[53] ibid.

[54] *UN*, vol. 18, no. 4, 4.3.86, p. 30, and, *D-D*, August 1986, p. 11.

[55] Interview in Kirton 1989, p. 72.

[56] AC, 12.12.86, Koori Centre.

[57] Interview in Kirton 1989, p. 91.

[58] Interview in Kirton 1989, pp. 134–35.

[59] ibid.

[60] Interview in Kirton 1989, p. 92.

[61] AC, 12.12.86, Koori Centre.

[62] AC, 7.3.87, Koori Centre.

[63] Interview in Kirton 1989, p. 107.

[64] Interview in Kirton 1989, p. 144.

[65] Report to the Advisory Committee on some Aspects of a Review of the Aboriginal Teaching Aides Training Program, 1986, unpublished, Koori Centre.

Chapter 7 – Management Restructuring and Reform

[1] *D-D*, February 1989, p. 17.

[2] King to Dorsch, 1.6.87, attached, 'The Authority and Responsibilities of the Director of the

AEAP Training Program at the University of Sydney, and King to Dorsch, 22.5.87.

[3] AC, 4.4.86, Koori Centre.

[4] *UN*, vol. 18, no. 14, 10.6.86, pp. 110, 115, and *UN*, vol. 15, no. 11, 7.6.83, p. 87.

[5] AC, 29.6.87, Koori Centre.

[6] *D-D* May 1988, p. 25, and Graduation file, 1987, Koori Centre.

[7] University of Sydney Union, Booking Function, 7.12.87, Koori Centre.

[8] AC, 27.3.84, 1.5.84, and 5.12.86, Koori Centre.

[9] Ruby to Accountant, 14.10.87, AEA Budget 1988/1989, file note, and King to Craddock 15.6.89.

[10] King to Ruby, 21.10.88.

[11] King, Proposal for 1989–90, Koori Centre.

[12] Ball, Evaluation, 1986, n.p., Koori Centre.

[13] King to Cleverley, 23.3.87, and King, Aboriginal Teachers Aides and Aboriginal Study Grants: The Fact and Fiction, Koori Centre.

[14] Cleverley to Mooney, 30.11.2007.

[15] King, Outline of Discussion and Presentation, The Aboriginal Education Assistants Program, Aboriginal Education Centre (AEC), University of Sydney, unpublished, 1991, Koori Centre.

[16] ibid.

[17] Cleverley to Mooney, 21.2.2008.

[18] Coordinator's Report, 7.9.88.

[19] King to Webster, draft, 18.7.88.

[20] Janson 2000, p. 11.

[21] *UN*, vol. 19, no. 5, 17.3.87, p. 43.

[22] AEATP Annual Report, 1988, Figure 1, unpublished, Koori Centre.

[23] Stage III Students, Causes of Adult Aboriginal Illiteracy and Some Suggested Remedies, *The NSW Adult Literacy Exchange (Special Edition)*, Sydney, 1987, and file, Koori Centre.

[24] G.H. in King and Stack 1990, pp. 17–18.

[25] AC, 30.6.88, attachment, Curriculum Document, Aims of Literacy, Koori Centre.

[26] H. Bell (1986), AEAP Principles into Practice, A Curriculum for the AEAP, unpublished, 1989, p. 15, Koori Centre.

[27] AEAP Literacy Assessment, February/March 1991, Koori Centre.

[28] Minutes, ATATP Staff Meeting, 8.5.87.

[29] Faculty of Education Working Party, Education, 3.3 Location and Accommodation, 1987.

[30] King to Ward, 4.10.88.

[31] P. Westwood to N. Downey, 10.3.89.

[32] *D-D*, February 1989, pp. 17–21.

[33] *D-D*, February 1990, p. 11.

[34] *The Gazette*, September 1989, p. 4.

[35] *UN*, vol. 19, no. 5, 17.3.87, p. 41.

[36] AC, 1.4.87, Koori Centre.

[37] J. Janson, *Black Mary and Gunjies: Two Plays*, Aboriginal Studies Press, Canberra, 1996.

[38] Janson 2000, p. 10.

[39] Certificate Course and Proposed Diploma in Aboriginal Education Assistants Education, AEAP, 1989.

[40] Aboriginal Course Unit, B.Ed. (Primary), Year 3, September 1989, pp. 1–3.

[41] A Core Course in Aboriginal Education: The First Year of the Program – An Evaluation, unpublished, 1989, Koori Centre.

[42] King to Cleverley, 21.10.88.

[43] King to D. Wansbrough, 21.10.88.

[44] Application 1990, Higher Education Equity Program, 1989, Koori Centre.

[45] Janson 2000, p. 27.

[46] A Proposal for Upgrading from the Certificate to the Diploma in the AEAP, R. King, University Fellow, T. Goring Goring, Director, Aboriginal Education, 1990, Koori Centre.

[47] Ward, Senate, 6.10.87, p. 1883.

[48] Ward to King, 16.3.88.

[49] Annual Report AEC, 1989, p. 3, Koori Centre.

[50] V-C Report to Senate, Part IIA, 3.4.89, 1989, University of Sydney Archives.

[51] AEAP Annual Report, 1988, Koori Centre.

[52] Memorandum, G. Findlay, to V. Arbon, W. Adams, and E. Eagan, 8.7.93, Attachment D.

Chapter 8 – Creating a Centre

[1] *Philosophy, Aims and Policy Guidelines for ATSIS Education*, National Aboriginal Education Committee, Australian Government Publishing Service, 1985, p. 22.

[2] Aboriginal Newsheet, Aboriginal Education Units, 1988, Koori Centre.

[3] *Monash Reporter*, vol. 5, no. 88, 6.7.88, and, *D-D*, August 1988, p. 11.

[4] University of New South Wales Aboriginal Support Program, 1988, Koori Centre.

[5] Ball, Evaluation, Koori Centre..

[6] Notes, Working Party of the Faculty of Education, held 26.8.1987.

[7] Equal Opportunity in Education Report, 27.10.1988, University of Sydney Archives.

[8] King to Dorsch, Application, 23.2.87.

[9] Abstudy Special Support Structures/Course Funding Application, 1987.

[10] King to Sutton, Application, 9.6.87.

[11] Turney to Ward, 28.8.87.

[12] A Proposal for the Establishment of an Aboriginal Education Centre Located in the Faculty of Education to Serve Aboriginal Students Across the University of Sydney, 1987. Higher Education Equity Project for Aboriginals/Abstudy Special Courses Application.

[13] D.B. Smart to members of the sub-committee appointed to consider a special admissions scheme in the Faculty of Arts for Aboriginal students, 21.7.87.

[14] King to Dorsch, 12.9.88.

[15] King to Preston, 10.4.89.

[16] Notes, Faculty Working Party on Aboriginal Education Centre, 3.8.87, 12.8.87.

[17] Report of the Working Party on Aboriginal Education, Faculty of Education, 1987.

[18] V-C Report to Senate, 6.10.87.

[19] Notes from a meeting, 16.6.88.

[20] Interim Report of the Working Party on Aboriginal Education, Joint Senate, Academic Board Committee on Admission Policy, 1988.

[21] Notes from a meeting, 16.6.88.

[22] Report of the Vice-Chancellor's Working Party on Aboriginal Education in the University, 1988.

[23] Notes from a meeting, 16.8.88.

[24] Report of the Vice-Chancellor's Working Party on Aboriginal Education in the University, 1988.

[25] Melbourne University, Aboriginal Employment and Training Strategy Proposal, 1988.

[26] Report of the Vice-Chancellor's Working Party on Aboriginal Education in the University, 1988.

[27] ibid.

[28] ibid.

[29] Academic Board, vol. 5, 1989, Reports of the Admissions Committee, 19.6.89, 12.5.89, p. 307.

[30] Koder 1989, pp. 154–57.

[31] The Allocation of Funds Under the Aboriginal Participations Initiatives Scheme, 1988/1989.

[32] Quoted, A. Sarzin, Long Road to Harvard, *The Gazette*, no. 3, December 1993, p. 7.

[33] *UN*, vol. 25, no. 13, 8.6.93, p. 102.

[34] Joel Gibson, Blazing a Trail to Harvard, *SMH*, 4.4.2009, p. 17.

[35] Draft of the Education Profile for the AEU, 1991–1993, Cumberland College of Health Sciences, Koori Centre.

[36] *UN*, vol. 22, no. 2, 20.2.90, pp. 9, 13.

[37] University of Sydney, Aboriginal Education Centre, Annual Report, 1989, p. 4.

38 King to K. Satour, 29.8.89.

39 *UN*, vol. 22, no. 2, 20.2.90, p. 9.

Chapter 9 – Aboriginal Education Centre – Early Years

1 S. Ainger, Charles Perkins Speaks on Aboriginal Education, *UN*, vol. 23, no. 29, 15.10.91, p. 238.

2 *UN*, File, AEC Media, 1.10.91, and see, *UN*, vol. 23, no. 29, pp. 231, 238, and AEC Annual Report, 1991, pp. 12–14.

3 AEC Media File, 1.10.91.

4 *UN*, vol. 23, no. 17, Pioneer heads Aboriginal Centre, S.A., 18.6.91, p. 133.

5 AEC Annual Report, 1991, p. 9.

6 Annual Report, Koori Centre/Aboriginal Education Unit, 1993, p. 8.

7 AEC Annual Report, 1991, p.3.

8 Curriculum Advisory Committee Position Paper, 1990, p. 2.

9 "A.F.", in King, and Stack, *Researching Community*, 1991, pp. 5, 29, Koori Centre.

10 R. Delaney and L. Towers, Community Liaison and Outreach, AEC, 1991, Koori Centre.

11 AEC Annual Report, 1991, p. 20.

12 King, A Rural Centre for AEA Training, 8.6.89, Koori Centre.

13 AEC, Operational Plan, 1993–1995, Triennium, p. 13.

14 T. Riley-Gibson, AEAP, Stage 1 Dubbo Rural Centre, Pilot Program, 1990, p. 16.

15 R. Carney, Paper, Academic Futures (Training, Accreditation, Careers), Regional Workshop, Wesley College, 12–14.12.1990.

16 Janson 2000, p. 16.

17 Aboriginal Education Unit Operational Plan 1993–1995, NSW Department of School Education, AEAP Certificate Course and Regional Workshop.

18 Correspondence, MAC, AEC, file, Koori Centre.

19 Notes of meeting with AEAs, 8.5.90, RCIADIC, L. Casson, (Chair), at AEC, Mackie.

20 *D-D*, Aboriginal Higher Education Students by Institution and State, 1989, p. 11.

21 Cleverley to H. Ross 8.6.90, draft.

22 Aboriginal Enrolments in Tertiary Institutions in NSW, 1989, 30.4.90.

23 King to Satour, 29.8.89.

24 Aboriginal Participation in Higher Education, 1991–1993 Triennium, Institutional Planning and Development of Aboriginal Education Strategies, 1990, p. 4.

25 Aboriginal Participation in Higher Education, 1991–1993 Triennium, Institutional Planning and Development of Aboriginal Education Strategies, University of Sydney, p. 20.

26 ATSI Participation in Higher Education, 1993–1995, draft, p. 8.

[27] G. Findlay to Arbon, Adam, Webster and Westwood, 7.9.92, and Ross to Koder, 21.7.92.

[28] University of Sydney Profile Submission, 1993–1995, Draft, ATSI Education Strategies, E.

[29] ATSI Education Strategy, 1994–1996, Ross, 20.5.1993.

[30] MAC, 21.5.93, Draft ATSI Education Strategy Plan, 1994–1996.

[31] State, National and Provider Performance against Access and Participation Rates for Indigenous Higher Education, 1999–2004, Koori Centre.

[32] ATSI Students Commencing at the University of Sydney (Excluding Cumberland in 1991), Re-enrolment, Discontinuation and Graduation in 1991–May 1993.

[33] Cleverley to Mooney, 3.12.07.

[34] Dorsch, file note, MAC, 4.5.92.

[35] *D-D*, February 1977, p. 2.

[36] S. Ainger, First Aboriginal Social Work Graduate Contributes to Novel Pilot Project, *The Gazette*, September 1990, p. 9.

[37] Annual Report Koori Centre, 1996, p. 17.

[38] AEC Annual Report, 1991, p. 6.

[39] AEC Annual Report, 1991, p. 6.

[40] Westwood to Downey, 10.3.89.

[41] Westwood to Stack, 14.2.92.

[42] Stack to Millington, 29.1.92.

[43] Westwood to Stack, 14.2.92.

[44] MAC, 13.4.92, Koori Centre.

[45] Turney to Cleverley, 24.4.92.

[46] Westwood to Turney, 29.4.92.

[47] Cleverley to Mooney, 1.2.08, and see Westwood to Turney, 22.5.92.

[48] Turney to Dorsch, 4.5.92.

[49] M. Willsher, Report on the Accommodation Needs of Aboriginal Students at the University of Sydney, 1991, Recommendation 2.2.

[50] Stack to J. Black, 14.3.90.

[51] Cleverley to Mooney, 3.12.07.

[52] King to Cleverley, 17.7.06.

[53] *D-D*, February 1991, 11.12.90, pp. 12–14, and, Annual Report AEC 1991, p. 11.

Chapter 10 – Independence

[1] Senate Minutes, 2.11.92, Report of the Vice-Chancellor, Pt. I.

[2] Criteria for Director, MAC, 15.4.92.

[3] Director, Aboriginal Centre, c. March 1991, University of Sydney Archives.

[4] King, Some Issues for 1990 and After, p. 7, Koori Centre.

[5] Arbon to McNicol, 2.9.92; AEC, Koori Centre Name Change, and file note 11.9.92.

[6] See also, ARKC/AEU Annual Report (Koori Centre/Aboriginal Education Unit), 1992, pp. 13–14, and, ARKC/AEU, 1993, p. 6.

[7] See, AEC Annual Reports, Koori Centre/AEU 1990–1993.

[8] M. Nugent and V. Arbon, More than an Accessory: A Critical Approach to Aboriginal Access Programs, Koori Centre, unpublished, 1993, pp. 2, 7–9, Koori Centre.

[9] ARKC/AEU Annual Report, 1993, p. 17.

[10] Minutes of a meeting with Professor B. Thom, Chair of the University Research Committee, 31.10.91, AEC.

[11] R. King and L. Craddock, A Review of the University of Sydney Cadigal Access and Support Program, Appendix B, pp. 38–39, 51, unpublished, Koori Centre.

[12] The Cadigal 1994 Program Report, Commencing Cadigal Students, Koori Centre, n.d.

[13] King and Craddock, A Review of the University of Sydney Cadigal, p. 32, Koori Centre.

[14] J. Mullis et al., Koori Centre Audit: Administrative and Financial, 2007, p. 10.

[15] Proposal to Reconstitute the AEC Research Committee, I. Stewart, 25.3.92, and Stewart, Working Proposal, 30.3.92.

[16] Arbon to L. Cram, Chair, University Policy Advisory Committee, Academic Board, 27.4.93.

[17] Arbon to J. Mack 23.8.93.

[18] Arbon to M. Kennedy, Evaluation Unit, DSE, 6.5.92.

[19] ARKC/AEU Annual Report, 1992, p. 3.

[20] Stewart, Craddock, Williams, Walton Smith to Arbon 17.3.93, and, Arbon to Stewart 9.3.93.

[21] Notes from a Discussion at NSW DoSE, 17.6.93, L. Craddock, p.4.

[22] Notes, 18.6.93.

[23] Craddock to Cleverley, c. August 1996.

[24] P. Nean to Arbon, 31.8.92.

[25] Notes from a Discussion at NSW DoSE, 17.6.93, L. Craddock, pp. 1–2.

[26] K. Boston to Arbon, 18.8.93.

[27] Boston to Cleverley, 5.3.93.

[28] Notes from a Discussion at NSW DoSE, 17.6.93, L. Craddock, p. 1.

[29] L. Craddock to Cleverley, 15.10.08.

[30] *UN*, vol. 25, no. 25, 21.9.93, p. 193.

[31] AEA Handbook, September 1990.

[32] *UN*, vol. 25, no. 25, 21.9.93, p.193.

[33] *UN*, vol. 25, no. 29, 2.11.93, p. 229.

[34] ARKC/AEU Annual Report, 1993, p. 6.

[35] ARKC/AEU Annual Report, 1993, p.8.

[36] King, Some Issues for 1990 and After, p. 7, Koori Centre.

[37] P. Crittenden, Memorandum to Professor John Mack, Academic Board, to Academic Board, 18.12.93, Academic Group D, Item 14, pp. 6–7.

[38] Academic Board Minutes 9.12.93, Report from Chair, Item 14, p. 6.

Chapter 11 – The Koori Centre

[1] Personal email correspondence, 2008.

[2] AEU Annual Report, 1994, p. 8. The University of Sydney. Koori Centre – Broadway Campus, Aboriginal Education Unit – Cumberland Campus.

[3] AEU Annual Report, 1994, p. 11. The University of Sydney. Koori Centre – Broadway Campus, Aboriginal Education Unit – Cumberland Campus.

[4] The University of Sydney: Aboriginal and Torres Strait Islander Education Strategic Plan – 1998 – 2000 Triennium.

[5] *UN*, vol. 26, no. 7, 29.3.94, p. 3.

[6] P.J. Crittenden, Memorandum to Veronica Arbon. Management Advisory Committee, Board of Studies, etc. Internal Correspondence, University of Sydney, 1993.

[7] AEU Annual Report, 1996, p. 2. The University of Sydney: Koori Centre – Broadway Campus; Aboriginal Education Unit – Cumberland Campus.

[8] Board membership: – external appointees: Professor Bettina Cass, Dean, Faculty of Arts; Sheila Van Holst, Faculty of Nursing; Ian Hughes, Faculty of Health Sciences; and D.J. Ah Kee, the AECG. The internal centre appointees were: Janet Mooney, Acting Coordinator AEAP; Dierdre Dorbis and Phillip Veness Lecturers in the AEAP; Wendy Brady, Head of ASU, and Ann Flood, lecturer; and John Hobson, Head of SASU. The student representative was Bobby Lakshman and Noeleen Smith was Secretary to the Board. Apologies were presented from Professor Geoffrey Sherington, Dean of the Faculty of Education.

[9] Minutes of the Meeting of Board of Studies in Indigenous Studies, 5.10.1995.

[10] Minutes of the Policy Advisory Committee Meeting. Item 4 (i) and (ii) 18.08.1998.

[11] Minutes of the Policy Advisory Group for Indigenous Education. 5 September 2002.

[12] Aboriginal Education Assistants Program Field Trip, 1995.

[13] AEU Annual Report, 1994, p. 8. The University of Sydney: Koori Centre – Broadway Campus; Aboriginal Education Unit – Cumberland Campus.

[14] Part-time AEAP staff included Robert Veel and Rhonda Toole, with assistance from guest lecturers including Ed Lukaszewski of the University Counselling Service and Dulcie Flower from the Aboriginal Medical Centre in Redfern.

[15] Nitin Indurkhya, *Mitigar*, Koori Centre, 1995, p.15.

[16] Karen Brown, A Lesson in History, *Mitigar*, p. 14.

[17] Kerry Skinner, *Mitigar*, p. 5.

[18] Roger Holten, *Mitigar*, p. 26.

[19] Cheryl Sant, *Mitigar*, pp. 8–9.

[20] Darren Ah-See, *Mitigar*, p. 39.

[21] Directors Report. Policy Advisory Committee Meeting. Tuesday 18 November 1997.

[22] Aboriginal Studies Major, 25/09/98, Koori Centre.

[23] Personal email correspondence, 2008.

[24] AEU Annual Report, 1994, p. 8. The University of Sydney: Koori Centre – Broadway Campus; Aboriginal Education Unit – Cumberland Campus.

[25] DEETYA correspondence, Peter Buckskin Assistant Secretary Indigenous Education Branch, 8.09.1997 and DEETYA correspondence, Peter Buckskin Assistant Secretary Indigenous Education Branch, 6.11.1997.

[26] DEETYA correspondence, Bruce Furze, Director Indigenous Education Assistance Section, 10.11.1997.

[27] *UN*, vol. 28, no. 30, 31/10/96, p. 5.

[28] *UN*, vol. 29, no. 8, 1.5.97, p. 1.

[29] *UN*, vol. 30, no. 27, 5.11.98, p. 5.

[30] KooriNet Review Report to Committee, p. 15.

[31] Other Executive Assistants positions were held by Kirstin Thorpe, Michelle Mathews, Worrell Blow, Tanya Koenamen, and Katheryne Miller, and non-Indigenous staff members Gaye Wolnizer, Lucinda Halbert, Ruth Rinot and Noeleen Smith.

[32] AEU Annual Report, 1996, p. 20. The University of Sydney: Koori Centre – Broadway Campus; Aboriginal Education Unit – Cumberland Campus.

[33] AEU Annual Report, 1996, p. 20. The University of Sydney: Koori Centre – Broadway Campus; Aboriginal Education Unit – Cumberland Campus.

[34] *Black on Black: The University of Sydney Aboriginal Students' Aboriginal Studies Journal*, vol. 1, 1998, Paper Tiger Printing, Sydney, p. 5.

[35] *Black on Black: The University of Sydney Aboriginal Students' Aboriginal Studies Journal*, vol. 2, 1999, Paper Tiger Printing, Sydney.

[36] www.aimementoring.com.

[37] 1997–98 Budget, Government changes to ABSTUDY briefing paper. May 1997.

[38] J. Mooney, Crisis in Indigenous Australian Higher Education: A Critical Analysis of the Impact of Recent Government Policies, Master of Education Long Essay, 1998, unpublished, University of Western Sydney.

[39] Koori Centre. AEAP database.

[40] Correspondence between Janet Mooney, Director of the Koori Centre, and Trish Kelly, Director of Personnel NSW Department of School Education, March 1998.

[41] DSE. Correspondence of Trish Kelly, Director of Personnel NSW Department of School Education. 30.03.1998.

[42] University of Sydney, Aboriginal and Torres Strait Islander Participation in Higher Education 2001–2003 Triennium.

Chapter 12 – Aboriginal Education into the New Millennium

[1] Review of Aboriginal Education in the University of Sydney 1998.

[2] Other members were: Professor Diane Austin-Broos (Postgraduate Co-ordinator, Anthropology), Kathleen Clapham (Head of Yooroang Garang), Charles Davison (President of the AECG), Margaret Edmonds (Director, Students Services), Professor Hal Kendig (Dean, Faculty of Health Sciences), Janet Mooney (Director, Koori Centre), Professor Don Nutbeam (Public Health and Community Medicine), Professor Geoff Sherington (Dean, Faculty of Education), and Professor Jeremy Webber (Dean, Faculty of Law). See also Report of the Committee Established by the Vice-Chancellor to Review Aboriginal Education in the University of Sydney, Koori Centre.

[3] Board of Studies in Indigenous Studies, 2000. Response from the Board of Studies in Indigenous Studies Working Party, chaired by Michelle Blanchard, to consider the Anderson Review, 12.04.2000.

[4] Vice-Chancellor's Preliminary Response to the Report of the Committee Established to Review Aboriginal Education in the University of Sydney.

[5] Senate Minutes, 5.6.2000, Report of the Vice-Chancellor and Principal, p. 994.

[6] www.usyd.edu.au/senate/committees/advisoryPerkins.shtml.

[7] www.usyd.edu.au/senate/committees/LittleJ.shtml.

[8] www.usyd.edu.au/senate/Gumbula.shtml.

[9] Change Management Proposal, 16.1. 2002, Koori Centre 2006.

[10] J. Cleverley, Comments and Recommendations on Staffing for the Cadigal and Aboriginal Tutorial Scheme Arrangements Following the Implementation of the Change Management Proposal, Koori Centre, April 2004, and, Director's Assistant to Cleverley, email, 6.2.2004, and Koori Centre Self Evaluation Report, 2003.

[11] www.foh.usyd.edu.au/conf07/about/index.php.

[12] Budget, Administration, 2007, Koori Centre.

[13] C. Prosser, Director, to D. Armstrong, Deputy Provost, (Learning and Teaching), Draft Report, Koori Centre Audit Administrative and Financial. p. 2.

[14] Research Priorities Koori Centre, 2003.

[15] Draft, Research Guidelines, Internal Document, Koori Centre, 29.4.2004.

[16] McLisky and Day 2004.

[17] Cleverley, comments, pp. 21–28.

[18] Arthur Smith to Janet Mooney, email, 07.11.08.

[19] *Synergy*, no. 18, 2003.

[20] *The Australian Journal of Indigenous Education*, vol. 32, 2003, pp. 41–49.

[21] Correspondence, Andrew Refshauge, NSW Minister of Aboriginal Affairs to Mooney. November 2003.

[22] Briefing Paper Orange Campus, Arthur Smith, 2000, Koori Centre.

[23] Arthur Smith Head IEU, John Hobson Head, SASU, Kath French, Acting Head, ISU, Liaison Officer Pat Davison, and academic staff Debbie Wray, Leah Lui, and Sharon Galleguillos.

[24] Correspondence, Professor Jocalyn Lawler to Janet Mooney. 6 June 2002.

[25] Lawler to Mooney, email, 18 November 2008.

[26] Other members were John Hughes, Mike Horsley and Carmel Young from the Faculty of Education and Social Work; Arthur Smith, Debbie Wray and Noeleen Smith from the Koori Centre; Maureen Wenzel, a graduate of the BEd (Secondary: Aboriginal Studies) teaching in Western Sydney. Sharon Galleguillos and Deborah Kirby-Parsons from the Koori Centre, and Leslie Scanlon from the faculty, also participated.

[27] Other members: Professors Michael Jackson and Rif Ebeid, and Rachel Symons, Quality Assurance Officer (Learning and Teaching), and Academic Board Review Guidelines.

[28] Australian Universities Quality Agency, *Report of an Audit of The University of Sydney December 2004*. Australian Universities Quality Agency, Audit Report Number 28, p. 5.

[29] www.usyd.edu.au/learning/governance/indig_strategy.shtml#tor.

[30] www.usyd.edu.au/learning/governance/indigenous_docs/iesd_meeting_10_minutes.pdf.

[31] Minutes of the Indigenous Education Advisory Committee meeting, 7 May 2008.

[32] www.usyd.edu.au – Indigenous Education Advisory Committee 2006+ Learning & Teaching.

[33] www.usyd.edu.au/learning/governance/indigenous_docs/reconciliation_statement.pdf

[34] ABS website 2006, Paragraph 39.

[35] J.C. Altman, N. Biddle and B.H. Hunter, How Realistic Are the Prospects for 'Closing the Gaps' in Socioeconomic Outcomes for Indigenous Australians?, CAEPR Discussion Paper No. 287/2008, ANU College of Arts and Social Sciences, p. 9, www.anu.edu.au/caepr/Publications/DP/2008DP287.php.

[36] Statistics 2008, Sttistics Snapshot, Students as at 31 March 2008, Table 1.11: Aboriginal/Torres Strait Islander Enrolments by Faculty of Course Registrations, Course Level and Gender, University of Sydney, 2009.

[37] Chapter 5.6, Developing a Coordinated Approach to Indigenous Education, The University of Sydney 2011–2015 Green Paper, The University of Sydney, March 2010, pp. 74–75.

Abbreviations

AC (Adult Education)	Advisory Committee (1981–83, ATATP)
AC (AEATP/AEC)	Advisory Committee (1984–90, AEATP/AEC)
AEA	Aboriginal Education Assistant
AEAP	Aboriginal Education Assistants Program (1990–98)
AEATP	Aboriginal Education Assistants Training Program (1984–89)
AEC	Aboriginal Education Centre (1989–92, thereafter Koori Centre)
AEC (NSW)	Aboriginal Education Council (NSW)
AEU	Aboriginal Education Unit (Cumberland College of Health Sciences, later Yooroang Garang)
AFB	Away From Base
AFEC	Aboriginal Family Education Centre
AHSSP	Aboriginal Health Science Support Scheme
APB	Aboriginal Protection Board
ASU	Aboriginal Studies Unit
ATA	Aboriginal Teachers Aide
ATATP	Aboriginal Teaching Assistants Training Program (from 1984 Aboriginal Education Assistants Training Program)
AWB	Aboriginal Welfare Board
BAEAR	Board of Adult Education Annual Report
CAS	Centre for Aboriginal Studies (Sydney College of Advanced Education)
CRDU	Curriculum Research and Development Unit
D-D	*Duran-Duran, (Messenger)*, Newsletter of the Aboriginal Education Council (NSW)
DAA	Department of Aboriginal Affairs
DAEAR	Department of Adult Education Annual Report
EFTSU	Effective Full Time Student Unit
FCAATSI	Federal Council for the Advancement of Aboriginal and Torres Strait Islanders
IEU	Indigenous Education Unit
ISU	Indigenous Support Unit

ITAS	Indigenous Tutorial Assistance Scheme
ITATE	Institute of Technical and Adult Teacher Education
MAC	Management Advisory Committee (1990–94, AEC/Koori Centre)
MC	Management Committee (1983–84, ATATP)
NAIDOC	National Aboriginal and Islander Observance Committee
NAISDA	National Aboriginal and Islander Skills Development Association
NESA	National Employment Strategy for Aboriginals
NSW AECG	NSW Aboriginal Education Consultative Group
NSW DoET	NSW Department of Education and Training (since 1997)
NSW DoSE	NSW Department of School Education (1989–97)
NSW DoE	NSW Department of Education (1915–89), prior to 1915 it was know as NSW Department of Public Instruction (1880–1915)
RACLO	Regional Aboriginal Community Liaison Officer
RJCLCLAA	*Report from the Joint Committee of the Legislative Council and Legislative Assembly upon Aborigines Welfare*
SASU	Student Academic Support Unit
SMH	*The Sydney Morning Herald*
SRSCLAA	*Second Report from the Select Committee of the Legislative Assembly upon Aborigines*
TPC	Tertiary Preparation Course
UCS	University Coounselling Service
UN	*The University of Sydney News*

Selected Bibliography

Barff, H.E. (1902). *A Short Historical Account of the University of Sydney, in Connection with the Jubilee Celebrations 1852–1902*, Angus & Robertson, Sydney.

Berg, S. (2003). *The Aboriginal Education Council (NSW): Celebrating 40 Years, 1963–2003*, The Aboriginal Education Council (NSW), Artarmon.

Branagan, D.F. (2005). *T.W. Edgeworth David: A Life*, National Library of Australia, Canberra.

Brook, J. and Kohen, J.L. (1991). *The Parramatta Native Institution and the Black Town: A History*, University of New South Wales Press, Sydney.

Burney, L., Lester, J. and Riley, L. within the Directorate of Special Programs (1982). *Strategy for Teaching Aboriginal Children*, Support Document No. 5, New South Wales Department of Education, Sydney.

Campbell, C. and Sherington, G. (2007). *Going to School in Oceania*, Greenwood Press, Westport, Conn.

Clark, J. (2001). Abschol More than a Scholarship Scheme, *NLA News*, October 2001, vol. XI, no. 1, www.nla.gov.au/pub/nlanews/2001/oct01/story-3.pdf

Cleverley, J.F. (1971). *The First Generation: School and Society in Early Australia*, Sydney University Press.

Cleverley, J.F. (2004). *Audit of Aboriginal Studies/Perspectives and Related Issues in the Professional Activities of the Faculty of Education and Social Work in Association with the Koori Centre*, Koori Centre, University of Sydney.

Commonwealth of Australia (1933). *Territory of Papua: Annual Report 1933–1934*, Government Printer, Canberra.

Connell, W.F., Sherington, G.E., Fletcher, B.H., Turney, C. and Bygott, U. (1995). *Australia's First: A History of The University of Sydney Volume 2 1940–1990*, The University of Sydney in association with Hale & Iremonger, Sydney.

Coppell W.G. (ed.) (1976). *The Walgett Papers on Aboriginal Education in NSW*, Centre for the Advancement of Teaching Education Monograph, no. 10, Centre for Advancement of Teaching, Macquarie University.

Curthoys, A. (2002). *Freedom Ride: A Freedom Rider Remembers*, Allen & Unwin, Crows Nest, N.S.W.

Davies, S.M. (2002). Collected: *150 Years of Aboriginal Art and Artefacts at the Macleay Museum*, Macleay Museum, University of Sydney.

Doukakis, A. (2006). *The Aboriginal People, Parliament and "Protection" in New South Wales, 1856–1916*, The Federation Press, Annandale.

Duncan, A. (1980). *Building Bridges: The Home-School Coordinator Project of the Aboriginal Education Council – An Evaluation*, Department of Adult Education, University of Sydney.

Elkin, A.P. and Mackintosh, N.W.G. (eds.) (1974). *Grafton Elliot Smith: The Man and His Works*, Sydney University Press, Sydney.

Faculty of Arts, University of Sydney (1952). *One Hundred Years of the Faculty of Arts: A Series of Commemorative Lectures Given in the Great Hall, University of Sydney, During April and May 1952*, Angus & Robertson, Sydney.

Fletcher, J.J. (1989a). *Clean, Clad and Courteous: A History of Aboriginal Education in New South Wales*, J.J. Fletcher, Sydney.

Fletcher, J.J. (1989b) *Documents in the History of Aboriginal Education in New South Wales*, J.J. Fletcher, Sydney.

Goodall, H. (1996). *Invasion to Embassy Land in Aboriginal Politics in New South Wales, 1770–1972*, Allen & Unwin in association with Black Books, St Leonards, N.S.W.

Grey, A. (1974). *Aboriginal Family Education Centres A.F.E.C.: A Final Report to the Bernard Van Leer Foundation, 1969–1973*, Department of Adult Education, University of Sydney.

Heiss, A. and Minter, P. (eds) (2008). *Macquarie Pen Anthology of Aboriginal Literature*, Allen & Unwin, Crows Nest, N.S.W.

Janson, J. (2000). Interview, Koori Centre History, The University of Sydney, Research and Interviews, 1.12. 2000, unpublished, Koori Centre.

Johnson, M. (2000). 'Cranial connections': Queensland's 'Talgai Skull' Debate of 1918 and Custodianship of the Past. *Aboriginal History*, vol. 24, pp. 117–31.

King, R.J.R. and Stack, R. (1990). Researching Community: Aboriginal Perspectives, Aboriginal Education Centre, unpublished report, Koori Centre.

Kirton, J. (1989). A Co-ordinator's View of the Aboriginal Education Assistants Program 1975–1988: From a Non-Aboriginal Perspective, (Draft), M.A. (Education) Project, School of Education, Macquarie University.

Koder L.M. (ed.) (1989). *In Transit: Sydney CAE, 1982–1989*, Sydney College of Advanced Education, Sydney.

Long, J. (1992). *The Go-Betweens: Patrol Officers in Aboriginal Affairs Administration in the Northern Territory 1936–74*, North Australia Research Unit, Australian National University, Casuarina, N.T.

McLisky, C. and Day, D. (2004). Black and White Science: Encouraging Indigenous Australian Students into University Science and Technology, University of Sydney.

More, A.J. (1978). *A Solid Link in the Chain: The Aboriginal Teaching Assistants' Training Programme – An Evaluation*, Department of Adult Education, University of Sydney.

NISATSICF (1997). National Inquiry into the Separation of Aboriginal and Torres Strait Islander Children from their Families (Australia). *Bringing Them Home: Report of the National Inquiry into the Separation of Aboriginal and Torres Strait Islander Children from their Families*, Human Rights and Equal Opportunities Commission, Commonwealth of Australia, Sydney.

Perkins, C. (1975). *A Bastard Like Me*, Ure Smith, Sydney.

Plater, D. (2005). An Enduring Legacy, *The University of Sydney Gazette*, November, pp. 9–11.

Porteus, S.D. (1937). *Primitive Intelligence and Environment*, Macmillan, New York.

Porteus, S.D. and Babcock, M.E. (1926) *Temperament and Race*, R.G. Badger, Boston.

Read, P. (1990). *Charles Perkins: A Biography*, Viking, Ringwood, Vic.

RJCLCLAA Part II (1967). New South Wales. Parliament Joint Committee on Aborigines Welfare. *Report from the Joint Committee of the Legislative Council and Legislative Assembly upon Aborigines Welfare*, Part II, Minutes of Evidence, Government Printer, Sydney.

Smith, K., (1992). King Bungaree: A Sydney Aborigine Meets the Great South Pacific Explorers, 1799–1830, Kangaroo Press, Kenthurst, NSW.

SRSCLAA Part I (1981). New South Wales. Parliament. Legislative Assembly. Select Committee upon Aborigines. *Second Report from the Select Committee of the Legislative Assembly upon Aborigines*, Part I, Report and Minutes of Proceedings, Government Printer, Sydney.

SRSCLAA Part II (1981). New South Wales. Parliament. Legislative Assembly. Select Committee upon Aborigines. *Second Report from the Select Committee of the Legislative Assembly upon Aborigines*, Part II, Minutes of Evidence, Government Printer, Sydney.

Strange, C. and Bashford, A. (2008). *Griffith Taylor: Visionary Environmentalist Explorer*, National Library of Australia, Canberra.

Turney, C. (n.d.) Aboriginal Education, typescript, Koori Centre.

Turney, C. (1996). *Tales Out of School, College and University: Memoirs of an Educator, 1931–95*, Sydmac Academic Press, St Ives, N.S.W.

Turney, C., Byott, U. and P. Chippendale (1991). *Australia's First: A History of the University of Sydney Volume 1 1850–1939*, The University of Sydney in association with Hale & Iremonger, Sydney.

Turney, C., Sinclair, K.E. and L.G. Cairns (1980). *Isolated Schools: Teaching, Learning and Transition to Work*, Sydney University Press, Sydney.

Wentworth, W.C. (1979 [1819]). *Statistical, Historical, and Political Description of the Colony of New South Wales and Its Dependent Settlements in Van Diemens Land …* , Facsimile Edition, Doubleday, Lane Cove.

Wentworth, W.C. (1823). *Australasia*, G. & W.B. Whittacker, London.

Williams, R. (1988). *The Settlement: A History of the University of Sydney Settlement Neighbourhood Centre, 1891–1986*, Sydney University Monographs Number Four, University of Sydney.

Wise, T. (1985). *The Self-Made Anthropologist: A Life of A.P. Elkin*, Allen & Unwin, Sydney.

Index

A

Aarons, Audrey 114
Aboriginal Adult Education 36, 50, 66, 108
  Diploma 100
Aboriginal and Islander Dance Company 93
Aboriginal and Islander Dance Theatre 37
Aboriginal and Torres Strait Islander Commission (ATSIC) 173
Aboriginal and Torres Strait Islander Strategic Plan 1994–96 193
Aboriginal Community Liaison Officers (ACLOs) 218
Aboriginal Education
  Vice-Chancellor's Working Party 152, 153
Aboriginal Education Assistants (AEAs) 33, 41, 63, 88, 118, 123, 124–26, 128, 132–33, 135–37, 139–40, 145, 168, 170–74, 176, 200, 217–18
  duties 123
  practice teaching 136
Aboriginal Education Assistants Program (AEAP) 102, 111, 125, 162, 166–67, 169–70, 172, 174, 176, 186, 197–98, 200–01, 203, 209, 217, 225. *See also* Indigenous Education Unit (IEU)
Mitigar 202
Aboriginal Education Assistants Training Program (AEATP) 45, 57, 59, 63, 123, 125–26, 128–29, 131–32, 135–36, 138–39, 142–43, 145, 147, 149, 151, 153–54, 156–59, 217. *See also* Aboriginal Teaching Assistants Training Program (ATATP)
  1988 Report 145
  Advisory Committee (AC) 131–33, 143 149
  budget 133–34
  curriculum 125, 140, 142
  Curriculum Advisory Committee 142
Diploma of Aboriginal Assistants Education (DipAAEd) 142–44
Pukuda Multhi Puthala: Dreamtime All the Time 140
Wiimpatjai Bulka Pipinja: Black Fellas' Messages 132, 140
Aboriginal Education Centre (AEC) x, 132, 147–52, 154–55, 158–59, 161–62, 165–67, 172, 175, 177–79, 181, 183–85, 195. *See also* Koori Centre
  establishment 154, 157
  funding 149–50, 159
  Interim Management Committee 149
  Management Advisory Committee 172–73, 179
  official opening 161–63
  Orientation Scheme 154–55
  Outreach Program 154–55
  Special Studies Program 176
  Working Party 150–54
Aboriginal Education Council (NSW) 36, 38, 52, 54–55, 57, 59, 61, 69, 78–79, 85, 94, 113, 133, 169–70
  Berg, Shirley 114
Aboriginal Education Resource Centre 98
Aboriginal Education Social Club 178
Aboriginal Education Strategic Initiatives Program (AESIP) 159
Aboriginal Embassy 5
Aboriginal Family Education Centres (AFECs) 53, 56–57
Aboriginal Higher Education Network 170
Aboriginal Home-School Coordinators Scheme (AHSCS) 65
Aboriginal Housing Cooperative 36
Aboriginal Language Resource and Research Centre 234
Aboriginal Languages Teaching Centre 234
Aboriginal Legal Centre 37

Aboriginal Medical Service 37
Aboriginal Participation Initiatives (API) 159
Aboriginal Protection Board (APB) 8, 11
Aboriginal Secondary Grants Scheme (AB-SEG) 28
Aboriginal Studies major 206
Aboriginal Studies Unit (ASU) 169, 186, 197, 205. *See also* Indigenous Studies Unit (ISU)
Aboriginal Study Grants Scheme (Abstudy). *See* Abstudy
Aboriginal Teachers Aides (ATAs) 1, 10, 13, 56–59, 61–62
Aboriginal Teachers Aides Training Program x, 2, 23–24
Aboriginal Teaching Assistants (ATAs) 62–76, 79–89, 95–96, 98, 100, 102, 104–05, 107, 112–14, 117, 120–22. *See also* Aboriginal Education Assistants (AEAs)
  duties 121–23
  Duty Statement 63
Aboriginal Teaching Assistants Training Program (ATATP) 63, 66–68, 71, 73–75, 78–79, 84–85, 87, 89, 91–92, 98–100, 102–04, 107–08, 111–23, 128, 156, 177, 195, 201. *See also* Centre for Continuing Education; *See also* Aboriginal Education Assistants Training Program (AEATP)
  Advisory Committee 99–101, 114–16, 122, 128–29
  certificate 73, 75, 82, 88
  curriculum 72, 96–97, 104, 124–25, 128
  Curriculum Advisory Committee 124, 126, 135
  Curriculum Development Committee 124
  funding 84–88
  library and resources centre 126
  Management Committee 101–04, 114
  reform 103
  syllabus 96
Aboriginal Tutorial Assistance Scheme (ATAS) 208–09. *See also* Indigenous Tutorial Assistance Scheme (ITAS)
Aboriginal Welfare Board (AWB) 8, 23, 27, 29, 35, 50, 53–54, 66

  1961 report 13
  scholarships 28
  welfare officers 20
Aborigines Protection Act of 1909 11
Abschol 28, 30, 31, 32, 34
Abstudy 40, 175, 186, 215–17, 226
  Away-From-Base (AFB) funding 215, 217, 219
Acklin, Fay 165
Adams, Bill 178
Adams, Chris 76, 85, 87, 92, 98, 173
Adjunct Chair of Indigenous Education 222
Adult Education. *See also* Centre for Continuing Education
  Advisory Committee (AC) 100–01
  Management Committee (MC) 101–04
Ahmat, Cynthia 202
Ah See, Connie 236
Ah Wing, Robert 236
Albert, Stephen 85
Alcorn, Doreen 211
Alexander, Christian 47
Alexandria Park Public School 215
Allan, Ronald 87
Allen, Heather 61, 67, 76, 86
Allport, Tom 60
Allsop, Joan 112
Altman, Sam 142
Anderson, Derek 194, 221–22, 226, 240
Anderson, Ian 223
Anderson, Kay 135, 142, 168, 171
Anderson Review 239
Anu, Christine 162
Aquilina, John 93
Arbon, Veronica x, 5, 162–63, 167, 173, 175–76, 179, 183–86, 193, 195, 197–98, 200
Archibald, Helen 180
Archibald, Selina 211
Armidale College of Advanced Education 95
Armstrong, Derrick 226, 241
A Solid Link in the Chain 88–89
ATA Times 98
Austin-Broos, Diana 206
Australian-Aboriginal Fellowship (AAF) 52
Australian Catholic University 219
Australian Council of Churches 38
Australian Indigenous Mentoring Experience (AIME) 214–15

Australian Institute of Aboriginal and Torres Strait Islander Studies (AIATSIS) 136, 167–68, 186
Australian Journal of Indigenous Education 233
Australian Museum 142
Australian Research Council Indigenous Research Fellow 224
Australians for Native Title and Reconciliation (ANTaR) 231, 243
Australian Universities Quality Agency (AUQA) 240
Away-From-Base (AFB) funding 215, 217, 219
Ayoub, Katie 208

B

Bachelor of Education (Secondary: Aboriginal Studies) 217–18, 220, 239
Baldwin Spencer, Walter 16, 19–20
Balla-Gow, Yvette 239
Ball, Sam 42–43, 79, 120, 125, 133, 152, 164
Bancroft, Bronwyn 214
Bandler, Faith 24
Bashir, Marie 244
Beardsley, Grace 86
Beatson, Jenny 223
Bechervaise, Neil 211
Beck, Peter 138
Bedford, Eric 86
Behrent, Larissa 223
Bell, Helen 138
Belvoir St Theatre 142
Bennett, Elaine 136, 171, 201
Berg, Shirley 55, 114
Berndt, Ronald and Catherine 21
Beuzeville, Peter 144, 166, 171, 173
Black, Lady Joyce 47, 104, 180–81
Black Native Institute 7
Black on Black Aboriginal Studies Journal 214
Black, Robert H. 35
Black, Sir Hermann 49, 74, 180–81
Blair, Nerida 159
Blair, Roslyn 91
Blanchard, Michelle 205, 212, 222, 225–26, 229, 234, 237
   Change Management Proposal 225

Boardman, Graham 156
Board of National Education 7
Board of the National Aboriginal and Islander Skills Development Association (NAISDA) 37
Bolton, Yvonne 76, 98
Bombaderry Children's Home 11, 95
Bonner, Senator Neville 36, 84
Bonython-Ericson, Sharon 218
Bostock, Lester 8
Bostock, Rita 76
Bostock, Terry 36
Bower, Jillean 236
Bowman, Marian 218
Brabham, Wendy 241
Brady, Wendy 169, 176, 185–86, 200, 204, 209, 211
Brand, Angela 138
Breckenridge, Judith 170
Brewarrina Central 98
Bridger, Pearl 142
Brindle, Ken 55
   Ken Brindle Memorial Scholarships 56
Bringing Them Home 11
Briscoe, Gordon 33, 223
Broadway Scheme 43, 153
Brockman, Penelope 138
Brown, Gavin 222–23, 241, 243–44
Brown, Ken 192
Brown, Natalie 138, 165, 168, 201, 213
Brown, Ngiare 243
Brown, Olive 63–64, 83, 88
Brown, Sharon 138
Brown, Ursula 202
Buck, Mary-Lou 38
Buckskin, Peter 209
Buddy, J.R. 93
Buggie, Jack 60, 62, 68
Bulger, Ryan 239
Buncha (Aboriginal Student Association) 214
   Black on Black Aboriginal Studies Journal 214
Bungaree, Chief 12
Bungaree, John 12
Burgess, Cathie 227
Burgess, Melissa 230

Burnam Burnam (Henry Penrith) 95
Burney, Linda 1, 100, 107, 117, 131, 150, 152, 162, 173, 234
Burns, Virginia 228
Butcher, Naomi 230
Butler, Kevin 201
Butt, John 138, 168
Button, Mary 65
Button, Pauline 38
Byno, Vera 57–58, 67

C

Cable, Ken 43
Cadigal 2–3
Cadigal Special Admissions Scheme 186–87, 197, 207, 210, 225–26
Calma, Tom 223
Campbell, Margret 38, 150, 156
Carmichael, Auntie Beryl 186
Carney, Rachel 172
Carrick, John 84
Carroll, Steven. *See* Ross, Steven
Cass, Alan 243
Cass, Bettina 199, 206
Casson, Louise 173–74
Cavelier, Rodney 127, 149
Centre for Aboriginal Education 139
Centre for Aboriginal Studies 113
Centre for Continuing and Adult Education 107
Centre for Continuing Education 108
Centre for Rural Education 236
Chaney, Senator Fred 88
Chapman-Burgess, Adele 210
Chapman, John 177
Chapman, Victor 12
Chin, Michael 197, 208
Clague, Liesa 44
Clapham, Dr Kathleen 200–01, 219
Cleveland Street High 38
Cleverley, John 112, 114–15, 117–19, 122, 125, 129, 133, 135, 139, 143, 147–48, 156, 162, 164, 172–74, 176, 178–81, 193–94, 201, 222, 225–26, 230, 239
Clunies Ross, Margaret 44, 152
Coe, Grace 64
Coe, June 138
Cohen, Marie 136, 142
Collarenebri Central 99
Collis, Kelli 168–69
Colombo Plan 25
Conference of Commonwealth and State Aboriginal Authorities, (1937) 8
Congress of Aboriginal and Torres Strait Islander Nurses (CATSIN) 237
Connors, Sherrie 227
Conroy, Rhonda 92, 98
Conservatorium of Music 194
Cook, Kevin 164
Cook, Trevor 98
Coombs, H.C. ("Nugget") 33, 89
Cootamundra 11
Corn, Aaron 224, 234
Council of Education 8
Cowlishaw, Gillian 206
Craddock, Laurie 32, 60, 79, 84, 103–04, 143–44, 169, 217
Crawford, Auntie Ev 63–65, 98
Crawford, Laurie 80
Crittenden, Paul 192, 195, 198–99
Croft, Brenda Louise 224
Crombie, Lillian 141
Crossley, Grace 127
Crowley, Des 66–67, 93, 99–100, 107, 112
Crump, Desmond 236
Crump, Stephen 236
Cultural and Academic Support Unit (CASU) 169, 186, 191, 207. *See also* Student Academic Support Unit (SASU)
Cumberland College of Health Sciences (CCHS) 155, 157, 159
  Aboriginal Education Unit (AEU) 155, 157–59, 163, 165, 175, 185, 193–94
  Aboriginal Health Science Support Program (AHSSP) 157, 185–86. *See also* Yooroang Garang
Curraey, Leslee 76, 85, 87
Curriculum Research and Development Unit (CRDU) 169–70, 184–85

D

Daley, Michael 118
Dallen, Robert 7
Daly, Rick 121, 128, 135, 138
Daniels-Woodberry, Narelle 118
Dargin, Pat 58

Dargin, Peter 57–59
Davenport, Michael. *See* Gifford, Graham
Davies, Anna 192
Davies, Joss 76
Davison, Delma 79, 120, 136
Davison, Norma 134
Davison, Pat 200, 227
Davison, Veronica 141, 180
Dawson, A. Madge 76
Day, Diana 229–30
Day, George 71
Day of Mourning and Protest 24
Deakin University 241
Delaney, Raylene 163, 169, 171
Delaney, Shannon 137, 161, 163
Department of Aboriginal Affairs (DAA) 35, 99–100, 114–15, 124, 132–33, 159, 234–35
  Major Grant Programs 234
Department of Adult Education x, 35–36, 66–67
  Aboriginal Adult Education 23
Department of Education, Science and Training (DEST) 224
  Little, Jimmy 224
Department of Education, Training and Youth Affairs (DETYA) 199, 236
Department of Employment, Education and Training (DEET) 133, 143, 149–50, 159, 173, 175
  Multicultural and Cross Cultural Supplementation Program 142
Department of Employment, Education, Training and Youth Affairs (DEETYA) 195, 199, 209, 216
  Bruce Furze 209
  Indigenous Education Branch 209
  Peter Buckskin 209
Department of Public Instruction 8
Department of Technical Education 28
De Serve, Willie 3
Dingo, Ernie 213
Diploma of Aboriginal Assistants Education (DipAAEd) 142–44, 158, 167, 174–75, 180–81, 186, 195, 197, 199, 219
Dixon, Chicka 32

Donaldson, Robert 11
Donovan, Raymond (Wirrungah Dungirr) 141, 174
Dorbis, Deirdre 200–01, 211
Dorsch, Susan 127, 131–32, 143, 145, 149, 164, 173, 176–77, 179, 194, 198
Douglas, Darryl 112
Douglas, Jane 92
Downie, Natalie 221
Doyle, Julie 167, 170, 182
Draper, Eric 61
Duncan, Alan 35, 49, 51–55, 60, 65, 67, 73–74, 77, 79, 83, 85–87, 89, 91–93, 96, 98, 100, 102–04, 107–08, 109, 111–14, 116, 119, 126
Dunlop, J. 51
Dunn, Hamish 214
Dunn, Jeff 226–27, 234
Dunston, John 113, 116–17, 122, 131–32
Duran-Duran 39, 69, 80

E

Eades, Sandra 223
Eagleson, Robert 47, 79
Edgeworth David, T.W. 16–20, 23
Edmonds, Margaret 199
Edmund Rice Centre for Social Justice 243
Effective Full Time Student Unit (EFTSU) 143, 159, 165, 174–75, 197, 219, 221
Eggleston, John 36
Eldridge, Linda 211
Elkin, Adolphus Peter (A.P) 21–24, 27, 32, 35, 49–50, 53, 113
Elliot Smith, Grafton 20–21, 23
Ellison, C. 217
Ellwood, Bill 5
Eltis, Ken 194, 199, 219
Emery, John 156
Eora 2, 6
Eora Centre 37
Equal Employment Opportunity (EEO) 44
Equal Opportunity in Education Committee (EOE) 147, 153
Ernabella 135
Erskineville Primary School Aboriginal Dance Group 243
Eyre, Ellis 208

F

Federated Council for the Advancement of Aboriginal and Torres Strait Islanders (FCAATSI) 52
Field, Jackie 76, 88
Field, Roslyn 173
Firth, Raymond W. 20
Flood, Ann 52, 56, 141, 161, 180, 186, 204
Flood, Curtis 200, 212, 227
Foley, Dennis 3, 227
Foley, Ruby 3
Forrest, Vanessa 169, 207
Forrest, Victor 103
Foundation for Aboriginal Affairs 15, 33, 35, 56
Freedom Ride 32, 94
Freeman, Cathy 33
Freire, Paulo 57
French, Charles 50
French, Kath 227
Fulbright Scholarship 218
Fulford, Wayne 165
Furze, Bruce 209

G

Gagen, T.M. 155
Galleguillos, Sharon 201–02, 218, 227, 230–31
Garma Festival 234
Gaskell, Ed 60
Gaynor, Lee 55
Geddes, William Robert 12–13, 35, 56
　Foundation for Aboriginal Affairs 35
Gelonesi, Bruno 197, 212
Gifford, Graham: Michael Davenport (pseud) 39
Glass, Catherine 45, 111
Glendenning, Phil 243
Golding, Ali 142
Gordon, Lila 170
Goreng-Goreng, Tjanara 204
Gow, Lyn 212
Graham, Cassandra 169
Grassby, Al 93
Gray, Lavina 142
Gray, Paul 34
Green, David 76, 86
Green, Richard 7, 235

Green, Sue 191, 204
Grey, Alexander (Lex) 56–57
Griffith, Tanya 226
Griffith University 241
Grose Farm 4
Grose, Francis 4
Groundwater-Smith, Susan 142
Groves, Bert 55
Guiness, Catherine 52
Gulargambone Central School 10
Guth, Steven 53
Gye, Richard 43

H

Hammond, Freda 228
Hansen, Beth 32
Hardy, Roger 219
Harris, Dorothy 138
Harrison, Jack 185
Harrison, Stephen 139
Hart, Charles 21
Hasluck, Paul 30
Hawkins, Peter 214
Hayman, Norma 69, 71, 76
Hearn, John 227
Hewson, John 31
Hiatt, Les 38–39, 143, 150, 152
Hickling, Gwen 180
Hicks, Jacqui 213
Higher Education Contribution Scheme (HECS) 219–20, 226
　bursaries 219
Hobson, John 208, 212, 235
Holding, Clyde 103
Hollings Cohen, Phyllis 86
Holten, Rachel 170
Hooper, Wayne 76
Hoskins, Larry 34
Howey, Kath 237. *See also* French, Kath
Hudson, Hugh 41
Hughes Report (1988) 159
Hunt, Geoffrey 76

I

Ibarraran, Amaia 231
Ignace, Chief Ron 235
Indigenous Carnivale 215–16
Indigenous Counselling Unit (ICU) 178

Indigenous Education Advisory Committee (IEAC) 240–41
Indigenous Education Strategic Development Working Group (IESDWG) 240
Indigenous Education Unit (IEU) 201
Indigenous Sports Scholarship 239
Indigenous Studies Unit (ISU) 204–06, 225. *See also* Aboriginal Studies major
Indigenous Support Allocation (ISA) 219
Indigenous Tutorial Assistance Scheme (ITAS) 208, 226, 228
Indurkhya, Nitin 202
Ingram, Norma 150, 156
Institute of Nursing Studies (INS) 156
Ivanoff, Avis 23, 65, 68

J

Jack, Ian 108
   Jack Committee 108
Jackson, Lisa 178, 204
James, Colin 36
James Meehan High School 140
Janson, Julie 71–73, 92, 97–98, 106, 135–36, 138, 171–72, 201
   Black Mary 140
   Gunjies 140–41
Jarrett, Michael 236
Job Opportunities through Better Skills (JOBS) 53
Jobson, Suzanne 44, 145
Johnson, Iris 180
Johnson, Les 69, 79
Johnstone, Richard 198–201, 206, 209, 221, 226
Joint Committee on Aboriginal Welfare (1966) 13, 24, 27, 31, 33, 54
Jones, Alan 43
Jones, Ken 41

K

Kaberry, Phyllis 22
Kalra, Rashi 214
Keane, Maurice 13
Keeley, Barbara 140, 180
Keipert, Ray 150
Kelley, Reubin 16
Kelly, Denise 70
Kelly, Pam 100
Kelly, Trish 218
Kennedy, Barbara 76, 79, 88
Kennedy, David 141
Kenney, Suzanne 208
Ketheson, Uma 213
Kinchela Boys Home 11, 95
King, H.C.M. 28
King, Ray 45, 120, 128–29, 131–33, 135, 139, 143–45, 149–53, 155–59, 162, 168, 170, 177–78, 184, 194, 217
Kinnear, Judith 226
Kirby, James 31
Kirby-Parsons, Deborah 212
Kirinari Hostel 100
Kirkbright, Chris 235
Kirton, Jane 111, 113
Kitchener, Kevin 173–74
Klub Koori 214
   Australian Indigenous Mentoring Experience (AIME) 214
Knight, Ken 107
Kociumbas, Jan 201
Koder, Michael 155
Koeneman, Pam 83, 142
Koller, Deirdre 24, 76
Kombummerri, Dillon 241
Kong, Marilyn 210
Kong, Marlene 192, 210
Konishi, Shino 210, 214, 230
Koori Centre 1–3, 5, 7, 14, 21, 32, 34, 36, 50, 52, 82–83, 112, 132, 145, 156, 163, 165, 171, 175, 179, 181, 184–85, 191. *See also* Aboriginal Education Centre (AEC)
   Academic Board Standing Committee 222
   Board of Studies in Indigenous Studies 198–99, 221–22
   budget deficit 228
   Change Management Plan 205, 229, 239
   Change Management Proposal 225
   computer lab 212–13
   Curriculum Research and Development Unit 211
   external review 224
   Innovations Committee 225
   KooriNet 212
   Management Advisory Committee (MAC) 191, 194–95, 200

Master of Indigenous Languages Education 235
  Ngaawa-Garay Summer School 235
  Policy Advisory Committee (PAC) 195, 199, 222
  Research Committee 225, 229
  restructure 193–94
  Special Studies Program Leave 225
  Strategic Plan (2001–05) 225
  teaching programs 232
  Tertiary Preparation Course (TPC) 208
Kramer, Leonie 140, 181

L

Lal, Victor 232
Langley, Phillip 162
Langton, Marcia 39, 223
La Perouse Public School 106, 114, 116–17
La Perouse Study Centre 36
Lawler, Jocalyn 237
Lawrence, Christopher 218
Legge, Melinda 202
Lennis, Deb 231
Lester, John 88, 98, 181
Lewis, John 51
Liddle, Alan 92
Little, Jimmy 141, 224
Lock, Maria 7
Lonsdale, Tony 235
Lougher, Clarice 3
Lovell, Robert 128
Lowe, Kevin 201, 234
Lui-Chivizhe, Leah 205, 230, 232, 234
Lukaszewski, Ed 150

M

Mackie, Alexander 23
Mackintosh, Neil (Mac) 17–18, 23
Mack, John 152, 195
Macleay Museum 3, 14, 21
Macleay, William John 13
Macquarie, Governor Lachlan 7
Madden, Charles "Chicka" 221, 242
Manning-Bancroft, Jack 214–15, 235, 239
Manton, Beverley 86
Marett, Alan 143
Marsden, Rev. Samuel 7
Martin Committee 107

Martin, Monica 138
Martin, Ray 33
Martin Report, 1964 vi
Maskell, John 138, 168
Master of Indigenous Languages Education (MILE) 235–36
Matraville High School 122
McCarthy, Edith 86
McDaniel, Michael 241
McDonald, Denis 46
McIntosh, Steven 177
McKnight, Anthony 208, 211, 227, 234
McLeod, Kerry 68, 76
McLisky, Clare 230
McMillan, John 23
McNab, Julie 114, 116, 121
McNaboe, Diane 235–36
McNicol, Don 140, 161–62, 183–84, 193
Mehi Crescent 10
Mercer, Milton 142
Merritt, Alan 234
Messel, Harry 38–39
Messih, Nadia 92, 98, 106, 114, 116, 127–28, 138
Metherell, Dr Terry 139, 164–65
Metropolitan Local Aboriginal Land Council 42
Miller, Ashlee 202
Miller, Lydia 142
Minter, Peter 227, 230–32
Mitchell, Dundi 170
Mitigar 202
Modini, Denise 100
Monash Orientation Scheme for Aborigines (MOSA) 147, 153
Mondini, Denise 92–93, 96–98, 101
Moonahcullah Aboriginal Station 51
Mooney, Graham 173
Mooney, Janet 136–37, 166–67, 170–71, 176, 198–201, 209, 211, 214–15, 218–19, 221–22, 225–27, 229–31, 234, 240
Moore, Jane 231
More, Arthur 65, 79, 88, 109
  A Solid Link in the Chain 88–89
Moree High School 98
Morgan, Pastor Abel 61
Morgan, Robert (Bob) 55, 94, 116–18, 132, 138, 149

Morris, Kristal 228
Mort, Neil 132
Mosely, Lillian 81
Mullis, John 228
Mulock, Hon. Ron J. 104
Mumbler, Christine 44, 208
Mundine, Kay 55, 65, 84–85
Murawina 37–38
Murphy, Fiona 231–32
Musselwhite, Michelle 239

N

Naden, Neville 180
NAIDOC Week 145
National Aboriginal and Torres Strait Student Network 213
National Aboriginal Education Committee (NAEC) 79, 85, 93, 101, 103, 105, 114, 147, 149
National Indigenous Higher Education Network 216
National Indigenous Student Games 237
National Indigenous Students Conference 213
National Referendum of 1967 ix, 27
National Sorry Day 215
National Tertiary Education Union 225
Native Police 12
Nean, Phil 55, 173
Neparrnga Gumbula, Joe 224
Newcastle University 204
Newman, Jennifer 162, 165
New South Wales Aboriginal Educational Consultative Group (NSW AECG) 38, 98–103, 114, 117, 122, 127, 148, 170, 195, 199, 236
New South Wales Aboriginal Languages Development Institute
  feasibility study 234–35
New South Wales Board of Studies 234
  Aboriginal Curriculum Unit 201
New South Wales Department of Education and Training (NSW DoET) 198, 217, 219, 234–36, 239
  Aboriginal Programs Unit 201
New South Wales Department of Education (NSW DoE) 8–11, 13, 63, 65, 67, 75, 78, 83, 94–95, 97, 100, 104–06, 112, 114, 116, 121–24, 128, 133, 135, 138–39, 147, 159
  Aboriginal Education Unit 98, 125
  Aboriginal Studies Syllabus 125
New South Wales Department of School Education (NSW DoSE) 166, 170–73, 186, 195, 201
  Aboriginal Education Unit 166
New South Wales Teachers Federation 126
Ngaawa-Garay Summer School 235
Nicholls, David 94, 100
Nicholls, Pastor Doug 54
Nicholson, Charles 6
Nightingale, Florence 7
Noffs, Rev. Ted 29
Noonuccal, Oodgeroo (Kath Walker) 36, 54, 76
Normal Institution 12
Norman, Heidi 191
Nugent, Maria 169, 185–86, 207
Nura Gili Aboriginal Research and Resource Centre 204

O

Office of Aboriginal Affairs 33
Old Teachers College (OTC) 198, 212–13
Olsen, Denella 170
Olsen, Terry 243
Orana Education Centre 170–71, 201
Orange Campus 208, 237
  Centre for Rural Education 236
Orcher, Phyllis 170
O'Rourke, Terese 142
Orr, Helene 186
O'Shane, Lorna 150
O'Shane, Pat 87, 127, 136, 152
Over My Tracks 63
Oxford University 232

P

Pan-Pacific Science Congress (1923) 20
Patch, David 40
Patterson, Lee 170
Pauling, Sue 55
Paul, Vivian 214
Pearson, Noel 39, 45–46, 223
Pemulwuy College 38
Penrith, Henry. *See* Burnam Burnam

Percival, Bob 171
Perdrisat, Ian 47, 138, 150
Perkins, Charles vi, ix, 28–34, 104, 162, 183, 221, 223
   Dr Charles Perkins AO Memorial Oration and Prize 34, 223
   Foundation for Aboriginal Affairs 33
   Freedom Ride 32, 94
   Office of Aboriginal Affairs 33
Perkins, Eileen 223
Perkins, Neville 34, 55
Perry, Belinda 200–01
Peters-Little, Frances 138
Phelan, Gwendoline 54
Phillip, Governor Arthur 4, 6
Pitjantjatjara people 135
Pittman, Marylyn 205
Poche, Greg 243
Poetsch, Susan 235
Porter, Christine 200
Porter, Eddie 208, 214
Porteus, Stanley D. 12
Portway, Sarah 134
Preston, Hugh 149
Probert, Anthony 214
Prosser, Craig 229
Prosser, David 156
Public Instruction Act of 1880 8
Public Service Association Union 123, 126
Pukuda Multhi Puthala: Dreamtime All the Time 140

R

Radcliffe-Brown, Alfred R. 20–21
Radio Redfern 127
Radio Skid Row 48
Ralph, Alice 118
Ralph, Ken 114, 173
Ralph, Laurel 100
Ramsay, Margaret 101
Ramsden, Paul 200, 226, 228
Ramstead, Florence 114
Rata, Matiu 52
Rawlings, Steve 139
Read, Peter 73
Reay, Marie 21
Reconciliation Walk 215, 243
Reddy, Stella 198

Refshauge, Andrew 234
Regional Aboriginal Community Liaison Officers (RACLOs) 65
Reynolds, Henry 73
Richards, Keith 191
Richardson, Gary 57
Ridgeway, Aden 34
Ridgeway, Jay 193
Ridgeway, Liam 193
Riley-Gibson, Terrill 171, 177–78
Riley, Lynette 205, 226, 230–31, 235
Riley, Lynette June 82
Rivers, Alex 156
Rivers, John 92
Roberts, Lyn 177
Robertson, Boni 241
Roberts, Stephen Henry 30
Robinson, Debbie 87
Robinson, Marie 142
Robinson, Victoria 192
Roper, Tom 48
Rose, David 233
Rose, Deborah 47
Rose, William (Bill) 60–61, 64, 69, 100, 103
Ross, Helen 199, 219, 221
Ross, Steven (né Carroll) 213–14
Rowland, Sir James 180–81
Royal Commission into Aboriginal Deaths in Custody 132, 173
Ruby, Alan 131, 139–40
Ryan, Maxine 211
Ryan, Senator Susan 103
Ryan, Vilma 38, 156

S

Sachs, Judyth 226, 239–40
Salisbury, Stephen 176
Santow, Kim 243
Saunders, Justine 141
Sawtell, Michael 23
Schnierer, Peter 106–07, 118–19, 122, 124–25, 128, 150, 152
scholarships 40
   Indigenous Support Allocation (ISA) 219
Scott, Lewis 140
   Saving the Children 140
Scott, Sylvia 163
Scrymgour, Marion 223

Sea of Hands 231
Selby, Barbara 88
Selby, Justice David 88
Select Committee of the Legislative Assembly upon Aborigines 1979-81 82, 83
Select Committee on Aboriginal Welfare (1980) 95
Sharpe, Fenton 171
Shelley, Rev. William 7
Sherwood, Juanita 205, 230
Shields, Robyn 214
Simms, Sharon 210, 227
Simpson, Christine 165
Sinclair, June 213
Sinclair, Paul 235, 239
Skelton, John 53, 74, 76, 177
Slater, Lisa 227
Slim, Sir William 9
Smith, Arthur 201-02, 225, 227, 231-32, 234, 239
Smith, Christine 201
Smith, Eileen 210
Smith, Julie 201
Smith, Margaret 210
Smith, Noeleen 163, 227
Smith, Robert 170
Smith, Shona 229
Smith, Terry 47
Snodgrass, John 156
Snowdon, Patrick 228
South, John 228
Speechley, Carol 228
Spence, Michael 244
Spigelman, James 31-32, 223
Stack, Joshua 161, 163
Stack, Rosemary 107, 125, 132, 134-36, 150, 158, 163, 167-68, 171, 173, 176, 186, 198-201, 211
St Andrews College 3
Stanley, Vickie 70
Stanner, William 21
Stapleton, Tom 36
Stewart, Diane 100
Stewart, Ian 170, 185
Stewart, Lyn 199
Stolen Generation 11, 98
Street, Val 43

Strokowsky, Mike 132
Stroobant, Ray 112
Stubbs, Amanda 236
Student Academic Support Unit (SASU) 197-98, 207-09, 225
Student Representative Council 5
Students for Action for Aboriginal Affairs 32
SUCCEED scheme 43, 120, 153-54
Sutton, Evan 101, 143, 149-50, 159, 173
Swain, Tony 47
Swan, Doug 10, 99-100, 103, 117
Sydney College of Advanced Education (SCAE) 38, 155-56, 175
    Centre for Aboriginal Studies (CAS) 155-56, 158, 178-79
    Institute of Nursing Studies (INS) 156
    Koder, Michael 155-56
    Sydney Institute of Education (SIE) 156-75
Sydney College of the Arts 169, 186, 194, 212, 224
Sydney Conservatorium of Music 224
Sydney University. *See* University of Sydney
Sydney University Aboriginal Education Centre (SUAEC). *See* Aboriginal Education Centre
Sydney University Indigenous Student Association (SUISA) 213
Sykes, Roberta 103
Synott, John 36

T

Talbot, Cedric 162
Talgai skull 17-18
Tamisari, Franca 206
Taranto, Lianna 207
Taylor, Thomas Griffith (Griff) 18-20
Teachers' Handbook 11
Tebbutt, Jenny 228
Tertiary Preparation Course (TPC) 208, 233, 236
The Settlement Neighbourhood Centre 15, 132, 170
Thom, Bruce 185
Thompson, Christian 34
Thompson, Jenny 225
Thorne, Barry 74, 91-93, 96-98, 100-06, 111, 114, 122, 124-25, 173

Thorne, Darrell 98
Thorpe, Katrina 204, 206, 211, 227, 232, 237, 239
Tierney, Moira 87, 91–92
Tillett, Jenni 202, 236
Timbery, Dawn 170
Tingha Primary School 104
Toomey, Bill 177
Toomey, Les 99
Touma, Tatum 213
Towers, Lorraine 126, 169, 171, 207
Townsend, Clare 170
Tranby Aboriginal College 37, 50, 52, 132, 138, 142, 234
  Aboriginal Language Resource and Research Centre 234
Trevorrow, Bruce 11
Trindall, A. 165
Truskett, Vernon 13, 53
Tuhiwai Smith, Lynda 223
Turney, Cliff 108, 111–17, 119, 124, 143, 150, 164, 173, 179, 194
Tyrrell, Davina 79, 104, 114, 164, 169
Tyson, Chris 59

U

Unaipon, David 193
University Counselling Service (UCS) 177
  Indigenous Counselling Unit (ICU) 178
University of Newcastle 237
University of New South Wales (UNSW) 147, 153
  Nura Gili Aboriginal Research and Resource Centre 204
University of Sydney
  Aboriginal Education Social Club 178
  Aboriginal Studies Unit (ASU) 169, 191
  Centre for Aboriginal Studies 113
  Chancellor's Committee 219
  College of Humanities and Social Sciences 222, 230
  Cultural and Academic Support Unit (CASU) 169, 191
  Department of Adult Education 100–02, 107–09
  Department of Anthropology 197, 205
  Department of Education 108–09, 111–13, 115, 118–19
  Department of History 201
  Department of Linguistics 234
  Department of Music 234
  Department of Public Health 204, 221
  Equity Advisory Committee 222
  Faculty of Arts 149, 153, 186, 194, 199, 205, 221
  Faculty of Dentistry 153
  Faculty of Economics 176
  Faculty of Education 131, 135, 142–43, 145, 149–56, 169, 178, 186, 193–95, 197–98, 202, 211, 219, 221, 228, 236
  Faculty of Education and Social Work 226, 229–30, 239
  Faculty of Health Sciences 186, 221, 241
  Faculty of Medicine 153, 221
  Faculty of Nursing 197, 199, 204, 237
  Flames Basketball Team 239
  Indigenous Education Advisory Committee (IEAC) 240
  Indigenous Education Strategic Development Working Group (IESDWG) 240
  Orange campus 208, 236–37
  Reconciliation Statement 241–42
  School of Public Health and Tropical Medicine 21
  Special Study Leave program 200, 209
  University of Sydney News (UN) 93, 125, 178
University of Technology Sydney (UTS) 153, 237
University of Western Sydney 241

V

Valadian, Margaret 69
Veel, Robert 164, 166
Veness, Phil 201
Veness, Phillip 186
Victoria Park 5
Vincent, Margaret 181
Viner, Robert Ian 79, 84–85
Visiting Aboriginal Fellowships 222
Viteri Comunion, Leticia 231
Vocational Education and Training (VET) 209

W

Wakool Kungarah (One Blood) 191

Wale, Stephen 92, 120
Walgett High School 60
Walgett Public School 60
Walhallow Public School 61
Walker, Auntie Emily 10, 141
Walker, Kath (Oodgeroo Noonuccal) 36, 54, 76
Walsh, Michael 234
Walton-Smith, Jennifer 170
Wansbrough, David 140
Ward, John 41, 48, 103–04, 107, 113–14, 145, 152–55, 162, 181
  Ward Report 153, 155
Ward, Tom 214
Ware, Helen 137–38, 168
Waterview Group 29
Watson, Eunice 3
Watson, Ken 204
Watt, Gwen 53
Watts, Betty 103
Webb, Clark 214, 239
Webber, Jeremy 223
Weilmoringle Public School 57–59
Weisbrot, David 206
Wellington, Jodie 210
Wenner, Joy 211
Wentworth, William Charles 6
Wenzel, Maureen 211, 236
Wever, Ineke 214
White Australia policy 19, 25
White, Patrick 55
Whitlam, Gough 84
Widders, Terry 169
Wiimpatjai Bulka Pipinja: Black Fellas' Messages 132, 140
Willenski, Peter 31
Williams, Clive 55
Williams, Joy 142
Williams, Laurel 114, 119
Williams, Margaret 28
Williams, Maureen 42
Williams, Norma 100
Williams, Peter ix, 28–30, 32
Williams, Robyn 126–28, 132
Williams, Shane 170, 212
Williams, Sheilagh 77, 82–83, 98
Williams, Sir Bruce x, 107
Williams, Tom 36
Williams, Wayne Wunun 162
Willis, Robyn 59
Willmot, Eric 67, 69, 75, 86, 91, 103
Willsher, Michele 179
Wilmot, Eric 76
Wilson, Carol 76
Wilson, J. (Jimmy) 17–18
Wilson, J.L.J. (Lascelles) 50–51
Winder, Robert 122
Windradyne Aboriginal Education Resource Centre 107, 132
Wiradjuri 1
Wollotuka Aboriginal and Torres Strait Islander Education Centre (Newcastle University) 204
Women's College 43
Woodberry, Joyce 106–07, 114–18
Woodenbong Aboriginal School 52
Wood, Victor 236
Woolley, John 3
Wran, Jill 94
Wran, Neville 94
Wray, Debbie 201, 211, 226, 230
Wylie, Joyce 112

Y

Yarramundi 7
Yashadhana, Elizabeth 240
Yooroang Garang x, 157, 197–98, 200–01, 209, 211, 215, 219, 221, 227, 229, 237, 240–41
Yothu Yindi Foundation 234
Young, Carmel 142, 150

Z

Zaremba, Barbara 158

www.ingramcontent.com/pod-product-compliance
Lightning Source LLC
Chambersburg PA
CBHW061139230426
43662CB00026B/2470